CRIMINAL OFFENSES AND DEFENSES IN ALABAMA

by
John J. Chiarkas
Nicholas L. Chiarkas, Jr.
and
Keith W. Veigas, Jr.

with
Richard L. Owens
Mary Anne Coley
Rhonda Nunn
Peyton Hyslop
Sam O. Ray
(research team)

THE HARRISON COMPANY, PUBLISHERS
3110 Crossing Park • Norcross, Georgia 30071

This book is dedicated
to the
Fall 1981
Criminal Law Class
of
Dr. Nicholas Chiarkas

PREFACE

This book is a compilation of the substantive criminal law of Alabama as of January, 1982. Crimes and defenses are outlined and relevant case law interpreting them is presented.

This is the first book to bring together this body of law in Alabama. This book is intended to be used as a quick "desk reference" for the practicing attorney and judges and should not replace diligent research.

The primary focus of this book is the Criminal Code, Title 13A of the Alabama Code. In addition, substantial attention has been given to Title 4 (aviation), Title 12 (juveniles), Title 15 (procedure), Title 20 (drugs), Title 32 (motor vehicles), and Title 36 (ethics) of the Alabama Code.

The book is arranged by topics in alphabetical order. The crime(s) and corresponding section(s) of the Alabama Code are presented first, followed by the specific statutory provision(s). The classification of the crime(s) and critical comment follow. Common defenses and, in many cases, a query are then presented. Finally, cross references and footnotes complete the section.[2]

In writing this book it became clear that any project which seeks to incorporate, summarize, and analyze not only the criminal statutes, but the thousands of cases interpreting those statutes, would fall short of perfection. However, I sought and still seek such a goal. To that end we invite any comments, suggestions, or questions by our colleagues of the Alabama Bench and Bar and by our colleagues in the education field. Please address them to Dr. Nicholas L. Chiarkas, Jr., Cumberland School of Law, 800 Lakeshore Drive, Birmingham, Alabama 35229.

Dr. Nicholas L. Chiarkas, Jr.
Birmingham, Alabama
September, 1982

1. This book will be supplemented periodically to maintain its integrity and timeliness.

2. This scheme is modified where appropriate.

ACKNOWLEDGMENT

Any book of this scope and magnitude requires much more effort than just that of its authors. The year and a half that we worked on this project was greatly aided by, among others, a dedicated group of law students. Their work in finding and helping to organize the case and statutory materials dating back, in some cases, to the mid-1800's was invaluable and sincerely appreciated. They also helped in proofreading and cite checking the preliminary drafts of the book. Their abilities augur well for the future of the Alabama Bar. In alphabetical order they are: Wendy Brooks (class of 1983), Mary Anne Coley (class of 1983 — also mentioned below), Faye Easter (class of 1982), David Glicken (class of 1982), Cindy Harris (class of 1982, Tulane Law School), Peyton B. Hyslop (class of 1983, who, along with Sam Ray, did more than his share of research and organizing), Eileen R. Malcom (class of 1983), Stephen L. Mangan (class of 1982), Tobias M. Mendelson (class of 1983), Colleen Mitchell (class of 1984), Allison Newell (class of 1984), Rhonda Nunn (class of 1983 — also mentioned below), Richard Owens (class of 1982 — also mentioned below), Robert S. Pierce (class of 1982), Sam O. Ray (class of 1983), Michelle Rowe (class of 1984), and Sherry Scott (class of 1984).

Three students have not only contributed so specially and significantly but stayed with this project right to the end (notwithstanding the onslaught of final examinations). They deserve separate mention. We view their assistance to be that of colleagues, rather than research assistants. Without their support and efforts, this book would have been impossible. They are Mary Anne Coley (class of 1983), Rhonda Nunn (class of 1983), and Richard Owens (class of 1982). In addition, as Richard has done on several other books, he assisted in the organization and final proofreading of the manuscript.

We would also like to thank several of our colleagues for their support and assistance. They are Professor Charles Gamble for his encouragement and advice, Professor Jack Hood for his assistance with proofreading and suggested comments, and Professor Frank House for his assistance in the form of many thought-provoking queries and analytical discussions.

A special thanks to United States Attorney Robert Joe McLean; to Thomas Kenney (former police partner); to Paul M. Kurtz (author of *Criminal Offenses in Georgia,* The Harrison Company); to Judge Charles Nice for all his support and advice; to Attorney Russ Tarver, (Tarver and Veigas, Birmingham, Alabama) for the use of his staff and offices, as well as for his support and assistance; and to the Alabama Criminal Defense Lawyers Association.

Thanks to Dr. Bruce Newell (Ole Miss quarterback #10, class of 1968) and Russell Cochran for their thoughts and thoughtfulness.

In addition, we would like to express our appreciation to the staff and members of the Cumberland Law Review and the American Journal of Trial Advocacy.

We thank Steven Levine (President of BAR/BRI Review, a subsidiary of Harcourt Brace Jovanovich) for his support and assistance with information, research, and resources to complete this project. And thank you, Martha Morgan, Irene Morissette, and Patty Hammac, for the typing, retyping, and proofreading within an impossible schedule.

And, although they would be the first to say this is not necessary, we must thank our parents, Linda, Betsy, Erica (who challenges our thoughts and perspectives), Nicky (who teaches us patience and kindness), Christopher (for his courage and acceptance), and Adrienne (for her energy and lift).

Finally, and perhaps most importantly, Professor John P. H. Dethman, Jr., for the long hours of proofreading, editing, and discussions triggering many substantive modifications. His work and efforts were so awesome that he was asked to be represented as a co-author on this book. However, his ability and contributions are equalled only by his modesty and integrity; and, therefore, even this insufficient thank you will come as an utter surprise to him . . . Thank you, John.

INTRODUCTION

It must be noted at the outset that every attorney should be aware of the intention of the drafters in codifying the controlling criminal laws of the state. Not only is this important in understanding the significance of the Code in total, but it points the way for creative defense work.

Section 13A-1-3 of the Alabama Code sets forth the general purposes of the drafters in codifying the Criminal Code by means of six short statements. They are as follows:

"(1) To proscribe conduct that unjustifiably and inexcusably causes or threatens substantial harm to individual and/or public interests;

"(2) To give fair warning of the nature of the conduct proscribed and of the punishment authorized upon conviction;

"(3) To define the act or omission and the accompanying mental state that constitute each offense;

"(4) To differentiate on reasonable grounds between serious and minor offenses and to prescribe proportionate penalties for each;

"(5) To insure the public safety by preventing the commission of offenses through the deterrent influence of the sentences authorized, the rehabilitation of those convicted and their confinement when required in the interests of public protection; and

"(6) To prevent arbitrary or oppressive treatment of persons accused or convicted of offenses."

In a "defense analysis" of the above purposes one might argue that a particular offense under the Code is unconstitutionally vague if it does not meet the "fair warning" requirement of section 13A-1-3(2) of the Alabama Code.

CITE THIS WORK

Chiarkas, Chiarkas, and Veigas, Criminal Offenses and Defenses in Alabama

QUICK INDEX*

*Bold-face entries standing alone refer to self-contained corresponding coverage within the volume. "See" entries refer to the catchword under which the bold-face topic is treated.

TABLE OF CODE SECTIONS

Code of Ala. 1975 §§	Criminal Offenses in Alabama
4-2-6 through 4-2-11	Aviation
12-15-1, 12-15-9, 12-15-13, 12-15-15	Juvenile proceedings
13A-1-3	Introduction
13A-1-8, 13A-1-9	Multiple convictions
13A-2-3	Strict liability
13A-2-6	Mistake
13A-2-7	Consent
13A-2-20 through 13A-2-26	Liability
13A-3-1	Insanity
13A-3-2	Intoxication
13A-3-3	Immaturity
13A-3-22	Public duty
13A-3-23	Force in defense of a person
13A-3-24	Force by person with parental, custodial, or special responsibilities
13A-3-25	Force in defense of premises
13A-3-26	Force in defense of property (other than premises)
13A-3-27	Force in making an arrest or preventing an escape
13A-3-28	Force in resisting arrest (prohibited)
13A-3-30	Duress
13A-3-31	Entrapment
13A-4-1	Solicitation
13A-4-2	Attempt
13A-4-3	Conspiracy
13A-5-6, 13A-5-7, 13A-5-11, 13A-5-12	Sentencing
13A-5-9, 13A-5-10	Habitual felony offender
13A-5-39 through 13A-5-59	Death penalty
13A-6-2	Murder
13A-6-3	Manslaughter
13A-6-4	Homicide, criminally negligent
13A-6-20 through 13A-6-22	Assault
13A-6-23	Menacing
13A-6-24	Reckless endangerment
13A-6-25	Coercion
13A-6-41, 13A-6-42	Unlawful imprisonment
13A-6-43, 13A-6-44	Kidnapping
13A-6-45	Custody, interference with
13A-6-61, 13A-6-62	Rape
13A-6-63, 13A-6-64	Sodomy
13A-6-65	Sexual misconduct
13A-6-66, 13A-6-67	Sexual abuse
13A-6-68	Indecent exposure
13A-6-69	Child, enticing for immoral purposes
13A-6-70	Consent
13A-7-2 through 13A-7-4	Trespass, criminal

Code of Ala. 1975 §§	Criminal Offenses in Alabama
13A-7-5 through 13A-7-7	Burglary
13A-7-8	Burglar's tools, possession of
13A-7-21 through 13A-7-23	Mischief, criminal
13A-7-23.1	Desecration of tombstones
13A-7-25, 13A-7-26	Tampering
13A-7-27, 13A-7-28	Noxious substance, use or possession of
13A-7-29	Littering
13A-7-41 through 13A-7-43	Arson
13A-7-44	Explosives, possession of
13A-7-60	Real estate, taking or retaking possession of
13A-7-61	Stock at large under common fence
13A-8-2 through 13A-8-5, 13A-8-12	Theft of property
13A-8-6 through 13A-8-9, 13A-8-12	Theft of lost property
13A-8-10 through 13A-8-10.3, 13A-8-12	Theft of services
13A-8-11, 13A-8-12	Unauthorized use of vehicle/Unlawful breaking and entering a vehicle
13A-8-13 through 13A-8-15	Extortion
13A-8-16 through 13A-8-19	Receiving stolen property
13A-8-20, 13A-8-21	Bringing stolen property or property obtained by false pretense elsewhere into this state
13A-8-22	Obscuring identity of vehicle
13A-8-40 through 13A-8-44	Robbery
13A-8-61 through 13A-8-64	Shopping carts, abandonment or removal
13A-8-80 through 13A-8-86	Copying, sale, or possession of record[ing] device
13A-9-2 through 13A-9-4	Forgery
13A-9-5 through 13A-9-8	Forged instrument, criminal possession of
13A-9-9	Forgery device, criminal possession of
13A-9-10	Simulation, criminal
13A-9-11	Signature obtained by deception
13A-9-12	False instrument offered for recording
13A-9-13.1 through 13A-9-13.3	Negotiable instrument, negotiating a worthless
13A-9-14, 13A-9-15	Credit card or debit card, illegal possession of or fraudulent use
13A-9-17	Slugs, unlawfully using
13A-9-18	Impersonation, criminal
13A-9-19, 13A-9-20	Change bills
13A-9-41	Business practices, deceptive
13A-9-42, 13A-9-44	Advertising, false
13A-9-43, 13A-9-44	Advertising, bait
13A-9-45	Business records, falsifying
13A-9-46, 13A-9-47	Defrauding secured and judgment creditors
13A-9-48	Fraud in insolvency
13A-9-49	Financial statement, issuing false
13A-9-50	Financial institutions, failing, receiving deposits in
13A-9-51	Misapplication of property
13A-9-52	Coal (sale and delivery of) mixed with other substances or materials or with different quality of coal

Code of Ala. 1975 §§	Criminal Offenses in Alabama
13A-10-2	Obstructing governmental operations
13A-10-3	Inspection, refusal to permit
13A-10-4	Report, required, failing to file
13A-10-5, 13A-10-6	Peace officer, refusing to aid
13A-10-7	Compounding
13A-10-8, 13A-10-9	False alarm/False reporting to law enforcement authorities
13A-10-10, 13A-10-11	Impersonating public servant
13A-10-12	Governmental records, tampering with
13A-10-31 through 13A-10-33	Escape
13A-10-34, 13A-10-35	Escape, permitting or facilitating
13A-10-36 through 13A-10-38	Prison contraband, promoting
13A-10-39, 13A-10-40	Bail jumping
13A-10-41	Resisting arrest
13A-10-42 through 13A-10-45	Hindering prosecution/Hindering apprehension of escapee
13A-10-61	Bribery of public servants
13A-10-62	Conflict of interest, failure to disclose
13A-10-63	Trading in public office
13A-10-82	Confidential information, misuse of
13A-10-101 through 13A-10-108	Perjury
13A-10-109	Unsworn falsification to authorities
13A-10-121	Bribing a witness
13A-10-122	Bribe receiving by a witness
13A-10-123	Intimidating a witness
13A-10-124	Witnesses, tampering with
13A-10-125	Bribing a juror
13A-10-126	Bribe receiving by a juror
13A-10-127	Intimidating a juror
13A-10-128	Jury tampering
13A-10-129	Physical evidence, tampering with
13A-10-130	Judicial proceedings, interference with
13A-10-131	Legal process, simulating
13A-11-2	Treason
13A-11-3	Riot
13A-11-4	Riot, inciting to
13A-11-5	Unlawful assembly
13A-11-6	Disorderly persons, failure to disperse
13A-11-7	Disorderly conduct
13A-11-8	Harassment or harassing communications
13A-11-9	Loitering
13A-11-10	Intoxication, public
13A-11-11	Falsely reporting an incident
13A-11-12	Desecration of venerated objects
13A-11-13	Corpse, abuse
13A-11-14	Animals, cruelty to
13A-11-31, 13A-11-36	Eavesdropping
13A-11-32, 13A-11-36, 13A-11-37	Surveillance
13A-11-33, 13A-11-34, 13A-11-37	Eavesdropping device, possession of

Code of Ala. 1975 §§	Criminal Offenses in Alabama
13A-11-35	Divulging illegally obtained information
13A-11-50 through 13A-11-53	Weapons, carrying concealed
13A-11-54	Rifle, shotgun walking cane, carrying
13A-11-56	Firearms, use while fighting in public place
13A-11-57	Pistol, bowie knife, selling to minors
13A-11-59	Firearms, possession by persons participating in, attending, etc., demonstrations at public places
13A-11-72, 13A-11-76	Pistols, possession and delivery
13A-11-73 through 13A-11-84	Pistols, license to carry
13A-11-120	Bribery, commercial
13A-11-121	Bribe, receipt of commercial
13A-11-122	Business, conspiracy, combination, or agreement to interfere with or hinder
13A-11-123	Blacklist, maintaining
13A-11-141 through 13A-11-143	Sports, offenses relating to
13A-11-160 through 13A-11-164	Libel and defamation
13A-11-180 through 13A-11-186	Felons, registration of
13A-11-200 through 13A-11-203	Sex offenders, registration of
13A-11-220	Hazard, creating
13A-11-221	Commodities, transportation of
13A-11-222, 13A-11-223	Party lines
13A-11-224	Gunpowder, storing
13A-12-1	Sunday, certain acts prohibited
13A-12-2	Sunday, holding public markets and trading
13A-12-3	Cigarettes, selling to minor
13A-12-4	Cockfighting or keeping a cockpit
13A-12-21, 13A-12-22	Gambling
13A-12-23	Gambling, conspiracy to promote
13A-12-24 through 13A-12-26, 13A-12-28, 13A-12-30	Gambling, possession of records
13A-12-27, 13A-12-28	Gambling, possession of device
13A-12-31	Gambling, legalized pari-mutuel betting not affected
13A-12-50 through 13A-12-58	Gambling places
13A-12-70 through 13A-12-75	Lottery paraphernalia, transportation of
13A-12-90 through 13A-12-92	Gambling, possession, etc., of stamp prima facie evidence of violation of gambling laws
13A-12-110 through 13A-12-113	Prostitution
13A-12-130	Lewdness, public
13A-12-150 through 13A-12-159	Obscene matter, importation, display, distribution, etc.
13A-12-171 through 13A-12-179	Obscene materials, sale, exhibition, etc., to minors
13A-12-191 through 13A-12-198	Obscene materials displaying or depicting children
13A-13-1	Bigamy
13A-13-2	Adultery
13A-13-3	Incest
13A-13-4	Nonsupport

Code of Ala. 1975 §§	Criminal Offenses in Alabama
13A-13-5	Child, abandonment of
13A-13-6	Child welfare, endangering
13A-13-7	Abortion
13A-14-1	Maiming one's self to escape duty or obtain alms
13A-14-2	Closed meetings
13A-14-3	Marathon contests
13A-14-4	Clergyman, fraudulently pretending to be
13A-14-5	Advertisements for state or federal peace officer magazines or journals, solicitation of
15-3-1 through 15-3-8	Statute of limitations
20-2-1 through 20-2-93	Controlled substances
32-1-1 through 32-18-8	Motor vehicle crimes
36-25-5 through 36-25-14	Ethics violations

ABANDONMENT OF SHOPPING CARTS. See SHOPPING CARTS, ABANDONMENT OR REMOVAL.

ABDUCTION. See CUSTODY, INTERFERENCE WITH; JUVENILE PROCEEDINGS; KIDNAPPING; UNLAWFUL IMPRISONMENT.

ABORTION. Code of Ala. 1975, § 13A-13-7.

Charged as: Inducing or attempting to induce abortion, miscarriage or premature delivery of woman.

A person commits abortion when he "willfully administers to any pregnant woman any drug or substance . . . [or by other means induces] an abortion . . . or aids [or] abets [in so doing]."

Classification.

Statutory penalty: fined not less than $100.00 nor more than $1,000.00 and may be imprisoned in the county jail or sentenced to hard labor for the county for not more than 12 months.[1]

Defenses.

(1) It is a defense to § 13A-13-7 if the action was "necessary to preserve [the] life or health [of the woman] and [was] done for that purpose."

1. *See Code of Ala. 1975, § 13A-13-7 and Acts 1951, No. 956, p. 1630.*

ACCESSORIES. See HINDERING PROSECUTION/HINDERING APPREHENSION OF ESCAPEE.

ACCIDENT, TRAFFIC. See MOTOR VEHICLE CRIMES.

ACCOMPLICES. See HINDERING PROSECUTION/HINDERING APPREHENSION OF ESCAPEE.

ADULTERY. Code of Ala. 1975, § 13A-13-2.

"A person[1] commits adultery when he[2] engages in sexual intercourse[3] with another person who is not his spouse **and** lives in cohabitation[4] with **that** other person when he **or** that other person is married."[5]

Classification.

Class B misdemeanor.

ADULTERY.—Cont'd.

Comments.

At common law adultery was only a private wrong for which the injured husband had a right of action in damages.[6] The breadth of these proscriptions leads one to question their constitutionality, as they regulate the intimate details of the individual's private life. In fact, the dearth of appellate cases, as well as the drafters' comments, suggests that the proscriptions of adultery are not taken seriously by either law enforcement officials or the public at large.[7]

Defenses.

It is a defense to adultery if either party to the crime reasonably believed that both he and his partner were both unmarried.[8] It is not clear whether the "reasonable belief" has to be continuous throughout the relationship and at what point there is a concurrence between knowledge (mens rea) and sexual intercourse and living in cohabitation. For example, Paul and Susan have been engaging in sexual intercourse on a regular basis for a period of six months. One day Susan discovers that Paul is married to another woman. They have sexual intercourse one last time and never see each other again. Has Susan engaged in adultery according to § 13A-13-2 of the Alabama Code? Probably not. Is "living in cohabitation" satisfied if Paul spends one night a week with various women? That is, if he spends one night a week with Susan while he is married to Jane, he falls within the meaning of § 13A-13-2 of the Alabama Code; but what if, while married to Jane, he spent one night with Susan, another with Barbara, and so on, never spending more than one night with any particular person, but engaging in these "extramarital sexual relationships" on a regular basis, would he still fall within the meaning (and intent) of § 13A-13-2 of the Alabama Code? Again, probably not. Additionally, there is strong support for an "intention of the drafters" defense. Some of the most difficult problems faced by the criminal courts are those cases that fall under the letter of a law but seem to be inconsistent with its spirit.

ADULTERY.—Cont'd.

All such cases, according to Pascal,[9] indicate an unavoidable defect in rules of law. To remedy this defect, Aristotle[10] tells us, the intention of the lawmaker should be consulted. Such handling of the difficult case is what Aristotle means by the term "equitable." The law that equity is called upon to correct may be a just rule, but that does not prevent its being unjustly applied. Equity prevents the injustice of misapplication by dispensing justice in the particular case according to the spirit, not the letter, of the law.

Query.

To the extent that we justify plea bargaining as a means to lighten an already overburdened court docket, we suffer from goal displacement by codifying laws for the mere purpose of plea bargaining (see the drafters' comments to § 13A-13-2 of the Alabama Code, fourth paragraph, last sentence).

Cross references.

See BIGAMY.

---

1. *A person is defined as "a human being, and where appropriate, a public or private corporation . . ." Code of Ala. 1975, § 13A-1-2(6). See Code of Ala. 1975, § 13A-11-70(3), § 13A-12-150(7), and § 13A-12-170(9). "Male" or "female" is not defined, with one exception at Code of Ala. 1975, § 13A-6-60(4), where a female is defined as "[a]ny female person who is not married to the actor."*
2. *"He" as used here would indicate male or female.*
3. *Sexual intercourse is defined at Code of Ala. 1975, § 13A-6-60(1) and asserts that sexual intercourse "has its ordinary meaning and occurs upon* **any** *penetration, however slight; emission is not required." If by "ordinary meaning" the drafters meant the one in Black's Law Dictionary, we would submit that it is restricted to the "carnal copulation of a male and a female." However, it must be noted that in at least three other sections, Code of Ala. 1975, § 13A-12-150(5), § 13A-12-170(6), and § 13A-12-190(7), sexual intercourse is defined as "intercourse, whether genital-genital, oral-genital, anal-genital or oral-anal, and whether between persons of the same or opposite sex . . ." In addition, the comments to Code of Ala. 1975, § 13A-12-113 speak of "heterosexual intercourse," which would lead one to believe that if the drafters meant only heterosexual intercourse here, they would have so specified. On the other hand, following the definition of sexual intercourse at Code of Ala. 1975, § 13A-6-60(1), § 13A-6-60(2), "deviate sexual intercourse" is "any act of sexual gratification between persons not married to each other, involving the sex organs of one person and the mouth or anus of another," which would again tend to lead us back to Black's.*
4. *According to the drafters "lives in cohabitation" is the equivalent of "living in adultery," which in turn "has been interpreted by the courts to mean that the conduct must be open and notorious, Quartemas v. State, 48 Ala. 269 (1872),* **and** *the meetings must be continuous* **or** *there must be an agreement to have regular meetings. Burgett v. State, 37 Ala. App. 469, 70 So. 2d 429 (1954)." See comments to Code of Ala. 1975, § 13A-13-2.*
5. *"Marriage" will have its ordinary meaning; however, there might be some question as to "persons living together in cohabitation." See Code of Ala. 1975, § 13A-6-60(4), although (to date) this interpretation (in Alabama) has been limited to the crime of rape.*
6. *2 Am. Jur. 2d., Adultery and Fornication, § 2 (1962).*
7. *See Bryan v. Bryan, 126 So. 2d 484, 271 Ala. 625 (1961). See also, State of Iowa v. Ronek, 176 N. W. 2d 153 (Supreme Court of Iowa, April 7, 1970); Dale v. State of Oklahoma, 449 P. 2d 921 (Court of Criminal Appeals of Oklahoma, January 15, 1969).*
8. *See Code of Ala. 1975, § 13A-13-2(b).*
9. *See particularly Pascal's Provincial Letters and Pensees.*
10. *See particularly Aristotle's Ethics Book V and Politics Book III.*

ADVERTISEMENTS FOR STATE OR FEDERAL PEACE OFFICER MAGAZINES OR JOURNALS, SOLICITATION OF. Code of Ala. 1975, § 13A-14-5.

Charged as: Solicitation of advertisements for state or federal peace officer magazines or journals.

"It shall be unlawful for any person, firm or corporation to solicit advertisement in this state to appear in any state or federal peace officers magazine or journal without such person, firm or corporation first having qualified[1] with the attorney general of the state of Alabama to solicit such

ADVERTISEMENTS FOR STATE OR FEDERAL PEACE OFFICER MAGAZINES OR JOURNALS, SOLICITATION OF.—Cont'd.

advertisement as hereinafter provided in this section."

Classification.

Misdemeanor and upon conviction shall be fined not less than $1,000.00 and imprisoned in the county jail not more than one year.

Comments.

The intent of the section seems clear. Any specific criteria, however, for "qualification," beyond being published quarterly, is not stated.[2] The drafters have not commented on the rationale or the particular wording of the statute. It would appear the discretion in the hands of the attorney general was intended. This could raise interesting constitutional questions.

Defenses.

(1) First amendment challenges would seem the most reasonable.

---

1. *"Any person, firm or corporation who holds himself out to be affiliated with any state or federal peace officers association who publishes a peace officers magazine or journal may qualify with the attorney general and receive a certificate of qualification from him by furnishing proof to the attorney general that he does in truth and in fact represent a legitimate federal or a state peace officers association and that the publication which he purports to represent is published at least quarterly." Code of Ala. 1975, § 13A-14-5.*
2. *Code of Ala. 1975, § 13A-14-5.*

ADVERTISING. See ADVERTISING, BAIT; ADVERTISING, FALSE; BUSINESS PRACTICES, DECEPTIVE.

ADVERTISING, BAIT. Code of Ala. 1975, § 13A-9-43.

Charged as: Bait advertising.

"A person commits the crime of bait advertising if in any manner, including advertising or other means of communication[1] to the public or to a substantial number of persons, he offers to sell property[2] or services[3] with the intent, plan or purpose not to sell or provide the advertised property or services:

"(1) At the price at which he offered them; or

"(2) In a quantity sufficient to meet the reasonably expected public demand, unless the advertisement discloses a limitation of quantity; or

"(3) At all."

Classification.

Class A misdemeanor.

Comments.

If an advertisement is false or misleading, and knowingly or recklessly made, it would fall within the section on false advertising.[4] This section, however, prohibits bait advertising only as it applies to the advertising of a product with an intent either to sell on different terms or to sell other merchandise. The drafters of the Code created this separate offense because if a purchaser buys merchandise other than that advertised, there is no theft by deception.[5] The customer has not been deceived by the advertising into actually purchasing the product.

Special limitation is provided for broadcasters and publishers in § 13A-9-44 of the Alabama Code.[6]

Defenses.

(1) Lack of intent, plan, or purpose not to sell the item or items in a manner other than as advertised.

(2) Advertisement did not promote property or services.

(3) Advertisement is not addressed to the public or a substantial number of persons.

Cross references.

See Limitation on criminal liability for false advertising and bait advertising by broadcasters, publishers, etc., § 13A-9-44 of the Alabama Code; Theft by deception defined, § 13A-80-1(1) of the Alabama Code. See ADVERTISING, FALSE.

---

1. *"Falsely make" as defined in Code of Ala. 1975, § 13A-9-1(4).*
2. *"Any money, tangible or intangible personal property, property (whether real or personal) the location of which can be changed (including things growing on, affixed to or found in land and documents, although the rights represented hereby have no physical location), contract right,*

ADVERTISING, BAIT.—Cont'd.

chose-in-action, interest in or claim to wealth, credit or any other article or thing of value of any kind.

"Commodities of a public utility nature, such as gas, electricity, steam and water, constitute property, but the supplying of such a commodity to premises from an outside source by means of wires, pipes, conduits or other equipment shall be deemed a rendition of a service rather than a sale or delivery of property." Code of Ala. 1975, § 13A-8-1(10). See Code of Ala. 1975, § 13A-8-10, Theft of services.

3. *"'Services' includes, but is not necessarily limited to, labor, professional services, transportation, telephone or other public services, accommodation in motels, hotels, restaurants or elsewhere, admission to exhibitions, computer services and the supplying of equipment for use." Code of Ala. 1975, § 13A-8-10(b).*
4. *Code of Ala. 1975, § 13A-9-42.*
5. *Code of Ala. 1975, § 13A-8-1(1).*
6. *Limitation on criminal liability for false advertising and bait advertising by broadcasters, publishers, etc.*

"A television or radio broadcasting station, or a publisher or printer of a newspaper, magazine or other form of printed advertising, which broadcasts, publishes or prints a false advertisement or a bait advertisement of another person or a telephone company which furnishes service to a subscriber, without knowledge of the advertiser's or subscriber's intent, plan or purpose, does not commit a crime under sections 13A-9-42 and 13A-9-43." Code of Ala. 1975, § 13A-9-44.

ADVERTISING, FALSE. Code of Ala. 1975, § 13A-9-42.

Charged as: False advertising.

"A person commits the crime of false advertising if, in connection with the promotion of a sale, transfer, consumption or use of property[1] or services,[2] he makes or causes to be made[3] a false or misleading statement in any advertisement addressed to the public or to a substantial number of persons."

Classification.

Class B misdemeanor.

Comments.

While specific types of false advertising are prohibited throughout the Code, this section encompasses most of these variant statutes. The false advertising must be made in connection either with the promotion of a sale of property or services or with the promotion of an increase in the consumption of property or services. Requiring that the advertisement be addressed to the public or a substantial number of persons apparently excludes individualized, face-to-face representation. Strict liability is not applied to false advertising.

Special limitation is provided for broadcasters and publishers in § 13A-9-44 of the Alabama Code.[4]

Defenses.

(1) Section 13A-9-42(b) of the Alabama Code provides that "[i]t is a defense to a prosecution under this section if the actor acts neither knowingly nor recklessly in making the false or misleading statement or in causing it to be made. The burden of injecting the issue is on the defendant, but this does not shift the burden of proof."

(2) Advertisement did not promote property or services.

Cross references.

See Theft by deception defined, § 13A-8-1(1) of the Alabama Code; Obtaining property by deception, § 13A-8-1 of the Alabama Code. See ADVERTISING, BAIT.

---

1. *Code of Ala. 1975, § 13A-8-1(10).*
2. *Code of Ala. 1975, § 13A-8-10(b).*
3. *"Falsely make" as defined in Code of Ala. 1975, § 13A-9-1(4).*
4. *Limitation on criminal liability for false advertising and bait advertising by broadcasters, publishers, etc.*

"A television or radio broadcasting station, or a publisher or printer of a newspaper, magazine or other form of printed advertising, which broadcasts, publishes or prints a false advertisement or a bait advertisement of another person or a telephone company which furnishes service to a subscriber, without knowledge of the advertiser's or subscriber's intent, plan or purpose, does not commit a crime under sections 13A-9-42 and 13A-9-43." Code of Ala. 1975, § 13A-9-44.

AIDING AND ABETTING. See HINDERING PROSECUTION/HINDERING APPREHENSION OF ESCAPEE.

AIRCRAFT. See AVIATION.

AIRPLANE. See AVIATION.

AIRPORT. See AVIATION.

ALARM. See FALSE ALARM/FALSE REPORTING TO LAW ENFORCEMENT AUTHORITIES.

ANIMALS. See COCKFIGHTING OR KEEPING A COCKPIT; GAMBLING, LEGALIZED PARI-MUTUEL BETTING NOT AFFECTED; STOCK AT LARGE UNDER COMMON FENCE.

ANIMALS, CRUELTY TO. Code of Ala. 1975, § 13A-11-14.

Charged as: Cruelty to animals.

"A person commits the crime of cruelty to animals if, except as otherwise authorized by law, he intentionally[1] or recklessly:[2]

"(1) Subjects any animal to cruel mistreatment; or

"(2) Subjects any animal in his custody to cruel neglect;[3] or

"(3) Kills or injures without good cause[4] any animal belonging to another."

Classification.

Class B misdemeanor.

Comments.

The purpose of this statute is not to address the criminality of injuring or killing an animal; rather, it is aimed at unlawful "cruelty" to animals. Cruel treatment, cruel killing, or injury of an animal is the scope of this statute. Note that the phrase "without good cause" is included to cover situations that justify killing or injuring an animal (e.g., marauding dogs) belonging to another.

Defenses.

(1) Justification.

(2) Accident.

---

1. *"A person acts intentionally with respect to a result or to conduct described by a statute defining an offense, when his purpose is to cause that result or to engage in that conduct." Code of Ala. 1975, § 13A-2-2(1).*
2. *"A person acts recklessly with respect to a result or to a circumstance described by a statute defining an offense when he is aware of and consciously disregards a substantial and unjustifiable risk that the result will occur or that the circumstance exists. The risk must be of such nature and degree that disregard thereof constitutes a gross deviation from the standard of conduct that a reasonable person would observe in the situation. A person who creates a risk but is unaware thereof solely by reason of voluntary intoxication, as defined in subdivision (e)(2) of section 13A-3-3, acts recklessly with respect thereto." Code of Ala. 1975, § 13A-2-2(3).*
3. *"A person acts with criminal negligence with respect to a result or to a circumstance which is defined by statute as an offense when he fails to perceive a substantial and unjustifiable risk that the result will occur or that the circumstance exists. The risk must be of such nature and degree that the failure to perceive it constitutes a gross deviation from the standard of care that a reasonable person would observe in the situation. A court or jury may consider statutes or ordinances regulating the defendant's conduct as bearing upon the question of criminal negligence." Code of Ala. 1975, § 13A-2-2(4).*
4. *"Good cause" is not a term defined by the statute or anywhere else in this title, but would encompass those justifications provided by statutes under this title relating to use of force against other persons. See, generally, Code of Ala. 1975, §§ 13A-3-20 through 13A-3-31.*

ARREST. See RESISTING ARREST; UNLAWFUL IMPRISONMENT.

ARSON. Code of Ala. 1975, §§ 13A-7-41 through 13A-7-43.

"A person commits the crime of arson in the first degree if he intentionally[1] damages a building[2] by starting or maintaining[3] a fire or causing an explosion,[4] and when:

"(1) Another person is present in such building at the time, and

"(2) The actor knows that fact, or the circumstances are such as to render the presence of a person therein a reasonable possibility."[5] § 13A-7-41 of the Alabama Code.

"A person commits the crime of arson in the second degree if he intentionally damages a building by starting or maintaining a fire or causing an explosion." § 13A-7-42 of the Alabama Code.

"A person commits the crime of arson in the third degree if he recklessly[6] damages a

ARSON.—Cont'd.

building by a fire or an explosion." § 13A-7-43 of the Alabama Code.

Classification.

Class A felony, arson in the first degree.

Class B felony, arson in the second degree.

Class C felony, arson in the third degree.

Comments.

There are two basic changes in the new law: (1) it expands the scope of structures covered from "dwellings" to all "buildings",[7] and (2) it includes explosion as a means of causing the damage. The elements of the new crime in the first degree are: (1) the intentional damaging of a building by fire or explosion; (2) presence of another person in the building and (3) knowledge of such person's presence or circumstances which create a reasonable possibility of another's presence. The damage to the building must diminish its value or impair its utility, but need not be substantial. Additionally, it is not necessary that the person present sustain injury. Both first and second degree arson require an intent to damage the building. Determination of intent is accomplished by use of objective criteria. It is assumed that "a person intends the foreseeable, natural and probable consequences of his 'voluntary' act." the fundamental distinction between first and second degree arson is that in second degree arson there is no requirement that another person be in the building. Second and third degree arson may be distinguished on the basis of the element of intent. Third degree arson requires only that the damage be accomplished recklessly, not intentionally. The offender need realize only that there exists "a substantial and unjustifiable risk" by starting or maintaining a fire or causing an explosion.

Cross references.

See MISCHIEF, CRIMINAL.

---

1. *For a burning to constitute arson in any degree under existing law, the burning must be willful and malicious. Code of Ala. 1975, §§ 13-2-20, 13-2-21 and 13-2-22 require the burning to be "wilfully" done. In Morris v. State, 124 Ala. 44, 27 So. 336 (1899), the court held that the burning*

ARSON.—Cont'd.

must be willful and malicious. A burning that occurs as a result of simple negligence is not sufficient. Burning by accidental or natural causes must be satisfactorily excluded to constitute proof of the crime. Colvin v. State, 32 Ala. App. 142, 22 So. 2d 544 (1945). The Criminal Code formulation is adopted primarily from Michigan Revised Criminal Code §§ 2801—2807, which were derived from Article 150, New York Revised Penal Law.

2. *Building, as used in Code of Ala. 1975, §§ 13A-7-41 through 13A-7-43, was intended to mean any "structure which may be entered and utilized by persons for business, public use, lodging or the storage of goods, and includes any vehicle, railway car, aircraft or watercraft used for the lodging of persons or for carrying on business therein. Where a building consists of two or more units separately secured or occupied, each unit shall not be deemed a separate building." Code of Ala. 1975, § 13A-7-40(1).*
3. *While the Michigan and New York Codes use the terminology, "by starting a fire or causing an explosion," the federal formulation is "starts or maintains a fire or causes an explosion." §§ 1701, 1702, Proposed New Federal Criminal Code, seem preferable to cover situations where the defendant technically did not start the original fire, or, if he did, at that time it was nonhazardous and without any mens rea. There may be cases where defendant adds fuel to an existing fire or otherwise causes it to get out of control. Thus, the proposal speaks in the alternative, "by starting or maintaining a fire." Cf. Commonwealth v. Cali, 141 N. E. 510 (Mass. 1923) (original accidental fire; defendant purposely refrained from any attempt to extinguish it in order to collect insurance; held: arson).*
4. *Explosion, as used in Code of Ala. 1975, §§ 13A-7-41 through 13A-7-43, was intended to mean "[a] rapid, sudden and violent expansion of air or relinquishment of energy with resultant pressures that are capable of producing destructive effects on contiguous objects or of destroying life or limb. 'Explosion' includes, but is not limited to, a sudden and rapid combustion, causing violent expansion of the air, or the sudden bursting or breaking up or in pieces from an internal or other force. 'Explosion' is not limited to cases caused by combustion or fire, but it may result from decomposition or chemical action." Code of Ala. 1975, § 13A-7-40.*
5. *The seriousness of the penalty for first degree*

ARSON.—Cont'd.

arson under Code of Ala. 1975, § 13A-7-41 is based on the danger to human life inherent in burning or causing an explosion in a building where people are present. It should be noted that Code of Ala. 1975, § 13A-7-41 requires only that a person be inside the building at the time of the offense, not that he suffer injury or loss of life as a result of the burning or explosion. Arson in the second degree, Code of Ala. 1975, § 13A-7-42, differs from first degree arson in that no person is present in the building at the time of the offense, or, if a person is present in the building, the circumstances would not have led a man of ordinary intelligence and reason to believe a person was present therein.

6. *The distinguishing criterion between second degree arson, Code of Ala. 1975, § 13A-7-42, and third degree arson, Code of Ala. 1975, § 13A-7-43, is the accompanying mental element. Arson in the third degree is "recklessly" damaging a building by fire or explosion. Under this section, the defendant must realize that there is "a substantial and unjustifiable risk" that damage will result when he starts or maintains the fire or when he causes an explosion. Code of Ala. 1975, § 13A-2-2(3) defines "recklessly" by stating that "[a] person acts recklessly with respect to a result or to a circumstance described by a statute defining an offense when he is aware of and consciously disregards a substantial and unjustifiable risk that the result will occur or that the circumstance exists. The risk must be of such nature and degree that disregard thereof constitutes a gross deviation from the standard of conduct that a reasonable person would observe in the situation. A person who creates a risk but is unaware thereof solely by reason of voluntary intoxication, as defined in subdivision (e)(2) of section 13A-3-3, acts recklessly with respect thereto." On the other hand, mere criminal negligence as defined in Code of Ala. 1975, § 13A-2-2(4) ("[a] person acts with criminal negligence with respect to a result or to a circumstance which is defined by statute as an offense when he fails to perceive a substantial and unjustifiable risk that the result will occur or that the circumstance exists. The risk must be of such nature and degree that the failure to perceive it constitutes a gross deviation from the standard of care that a reasonable person would observe in the situation. A court or jury may consider statutes or ordinances regulating the defendant's conduct as bearing upon the question of criminal negligence") does not suffice for liability under Code of Ala. 1975, § 13A-7-43.*

7. *See note 2, supra.*

ASSAULT. Code of Ala. 1975, §§ 13A-6-20 through 13A-6-22.

"A person commits the crime of assault in the first degree if:

"(1) With intent[1] to cause serious physical injury[2] to another person, he causes serious physical injury to any person by means of a deadly weapon[3] or a dangerous instrument;[4] or

"(2) With intent to disfigure another person seriously and permanently, or to destroy, amputate or disable permanently a member or organ of his body, he causes such an injury to any person; or

"(3) Under circumstances manifesting extreme indifference to the value of human life, he recklessly[5] engages in conduct which creates a grave risk of death[6] to another person, and thereby causes serious physical injury to any person; or

"(4) In the course of and in furtherance of the commission or attempted commission of arson in the first degree, burglary in the first or second degree, escape in the first degree, kidnapping in the first degree, rape in the first degree, robbery in any degree, sodomy in the first degree or any other felony clearly dangerous to human life, or of immediate flight therefrom, he causes a serious physical injury to another person." § 13A-6-20 of the Alabama Code.

"A person commits the crime of assault in the second degree if:

"(1) With intent to cause serious injury to another person, he causes serious physical injury to any person; or

"(2) With intent to cause physical injury[7] to another person, he causes physical injury to any person by means of a deadly weapon or a dangerous instrument; or

"(3) He recklessly causes serious physical injury to another person by means of a deadly weapon or a dangerous instrument; or

"(4) For a purpose other than lawful medical or therapeutic treatment, he intentionally causes stupor, unconsciousness or other

ASSAULT.—Cont'd.

physical or mental impairment or injury to another person by administering to him, without his consent, a drug, substance or preparation capable of producing the intended harm." § 13A-6-21 of the Alabama Code.

"A person commits the crime of assault in the third degree if:

"(1) With intent to cause physical injury to another person, he causes physical injury to any person; or

"(2) He recklessly causes physical injury to another person; or

"(3) With criminal negligence[8] he causes physical injury to another person by means of a deadly weapon or a dangerous instrument; or

"(4) With intent to prevent a peace officer from performing a lawful duty, he causes physical injury to any person." § 13A-6-22 of the Alabama Code.

Classification.

Class B felony, assault in the first degree.

Class C felony, assault in the second degree.

Class A misdemeanor, assault in the third degree.

Comments.

Title 13A of the Alabama Code provides four significant changes from existing law:

(1) Assault is limited to the actual infliction of some physical injury;

(2) "Assault with intent" crimes are eliminated and are now treated as attempts under § 13A-4-2 of the Alabama Code;

(3) It is now proper to charge "attempted assault" where there is an unsuccessful effort to inflict physical injury;

(4) In certain instances, the Criminal Code provides punishment for assault caused by reckless behavior.

Assault in the first degree now covers four situations:

(1) Intentional infliction of serious physical injury by means of a deadly weapon;

(2) Intentionally disfiguring, destroying, or disabling another (which is the same crime as mayhem under the old Criminal Code § 13-1-7);

(3) Recklessly causing serious physical injury to another by manifesting extreme indifference to human life (thus, shooting into a crowd wantonly, but without any specific homicidal intent, would be first degree assault if the result were a serious nonfatal injury);

(4) Causing serious injury to another during the commission of certain life-endangering felonies (thus creating a "felony-assault" doctrine which is new to Alabama law).

Assault in the second degree now covers:

(1) Seriously injuring another person either intentionally without a deadly weapon, or unintentionally by recklessly using a deadly weapon or dangerous instrument;

(2) Nonserious injury to another person intentionally caused by means of a deadly weapon or dangerous instrument; and

(3) Intentionally causing unconsciousness, stupor, or other injury to another person by administering drugs or other substances without the victim's consent.

Assault in the third degree now covers:

(1) Intentionally or recklessly causing any injury to another person;

(2) Criminal negligence causing any injury by means of a deadly weapon or dangerous instrument; and

(3) The physical injury of any person while acting with intent to prevent a peace officer from performing his duties. It changes the existing law significantly by providing liability for criminally negligent conduct.

Defenses.

Under assault in the first degree, except for situations involving the "felony-assault" doctrine:

(1) Lack of intent to injure, or failure to prove under the circumstances extreme indifference to the value of human life.

(2) Lack of serious physical and/or permanent physical injury.

(3) Where required, failure to prove that the instrument used was either dangerous or a deadly weapon.

(4) Consent.

(5) Justification for the use of force.

Under situations involving the "felony-assault" doctrine:

(1) Failure to prove commission or attempted commission of one of the listed

ASSAULT.—Cont'd.

felonies charged.

(2) Failure to prove that the serious physical injury to another person was committed in the course of **or** in the furtherance of committing or attempting to commit one of the listed felonies.

The same defenses apply to assault in the second degree and assault in the third degree. Additionally, physical injury to any person that results from intending to prevent a peace officer from performing an unlawful act does not fall within the crime of assault in the third degree.

Cross references.

See Felony-murder, § 13A-6-2(a)(2) of the Alabama Code; Justification and excuse for use of force, §§ 13A-3-20 through 13A-3-31 of the Alabama Code; Robbery in the first degree, § 13A-8-41(a)(2). See ATTEMPT; MURDER; ROBBERY.

---

1. *According to Code of Ala. 1975, § 13A-2-2(1):*
   "A person acts intentionally with respect to a result or to conduct described by a statute defining an offense, when his purpose is to cause that result or to engage in that conduct."
2. *"Serious physical injury" according to Code of Ala. 1975, § 13A-1-2(9) is defined as:*
   "Physical injury which creates a substantial risk of death, or which causes serious and protracted disfigurement, protracted impairment of health or protracted loss or impairment of the function of any bodily organ."
3. *"Deadly weapon" according to Code of Ala. 1975, § 13A-1-2(11) is defined as:*
   "A firearm or anything manifestly designed, made or adapted for the purposes of inflicting death or serious physical injury, . . ."
   This code section also contains a noncomprehensive list of specific deadly weapons. An instrument may or may not be a deadly weapon, according to the manner of its use and the subject upon which it is used. Williams v. State, 251 Ala. 397, 39 So. 2d 37 (1948).
4. *"Dangerous instrument" according to Code of Ala. 1975, § 13A-1-2(12) is defined as:*
   "Any instrument, article or substance which, under the circumstances in which it is used, attempted to be used or threatened to be used, is highly capable of causing death or serious physical injury, and such term includes a 'vehicle,' . . ."
   "Vehicle" according to Code of Ala. 1975, § 13A-1-2(13) is defined as:

ASSAULT.—Cont'd.

   "Any 'propelled vehicle,' as defined in subdivision (9) of section 13A-8-1, and such term includes any propelled device by which any person or property is transported on land, water or in the air, and includes motor vehicles, motorcycles, motorboats, and aircraft, and any vessel, whether propelled by machinery or not."
5. *According to Code of Ala. 1975, § 13A-2-2(3):*
   "A person acts recklessly with respect to a result or to a circumstance described by a statute defining an offense when he is aware of and consciously disregards a substantial and unjustifiable risk that the result will occur or that the circumstance exists. The risk must be of such nature and degree that disregard thereof constitutes a gross deviation from the standard of conduct that a reasonable person would observe in the situation. A person who creates a risk but is unaware thereof solely by reason of voluntary intoxication, as defined in subdivision (e)(2) of section 13A-3-3, acts recklessly with respect thereto."
6. *No specific definition of the term "grave risk of death" is given, but an example cited in commentary following Code of Ala. 1975, §§ 13A-6-20 through 13A-6-22 demonstrates what the codifiers probably had in mind. If defendant shoots into a crowd, wantonly but with no specific homicidal intent, this would be first degree assault if the resulting injury was serious but not fatal.*
7. *"Physical injury," according to Code of Ala. 1975, § 13A-1-2(8) is defined as:*
   "Impairment of physical condition or substantial pain."
8. *According to Code of Ala. 1975, § 13A-2-2(4):*
   "A person acts with criminal negligence with respect to a result or to a circumstance which is defined by statute as an offense when he fails to perceive a substantial and unjustifiable risk that the result will occur or that the circumstance exists. The risk must be of such nature and degree that the failure to perceive it constitutes a gross deviation from the standard of care that a reasonable person would observe in the situation. A court or jury may consider statutes or ordinances regulating the defendant's conduct as bearing upon the question of criminal negligence."

ASSEMBLY. See RIOT; UNLAWFUL ASSEMBLY.

ATTEMPT. Code of Ala. 1975, § 13A-4-2.

"A person is guilty of an attempt to commit a crime if, with the intent to commit a specific offense, he does any overt act towards the commission of such offense."[1]

Comments.

Generally, although there is evidence that the ancients punished attempted crimes as well as the substantive crimes themselves,[2] early English law did not punish any conduct short of the substantive crime.[3] Beginning in the fourteenth century, attempted felonies were sometimes punished under the doctrine of voluntas reputatur pro facto — the intent is to be regarded as the act.[4] From these isolated cases of attempted serious felonies, the doctrine grew through development in the Court of Star Chamber until in 1801 a British court could flatly state that "all offenses of a public nature, that is, all such acts or attempts as tend to the prejudice of the community, are indictable."[5]

Today the primary rationale for "attempt" as an inchoate crime, is that it permits state intervention early in the criminal process, thus shielding the public from greater danger. To this end, criminal attempt is similar to criminal conspiracy.

Not only does the punishment of attempt protect the public from more serious criminal acts, but it also helps to identify anti-social individuals who are in need of the sanctions of the criminal law. As the Model Penal Code drafters wrote, an attempt "yields an indication that the actor is disposed toward such activity, not alone on this occasion but on others."[6] Thus, the same restraint and rehabilitative purposes served by the general criminal law are served by punishing those who attempt to commit crimes. The Model Penal Code drafters point out that failure to punish those who fortuitously fail to reach their goal "would involve inequality of treatment that would shock the common sense of justice."[7] It should be pointed out, however, that deterrence of the general populace is not served by punishing attempts. The threat of being punished for an attempt is

ATTEMPT.—Cont'd.

unlikely to deter those who have already demonstrated that the punishment of the substantive offense is not a deterrence to them.[8]

Attempt is a specific intent crime. It requires a showing that the person intended to commit the substantive offense. Commission of acts that would tend toward a particular offense would not be enough for liability, although the presence of such acts would be very helpful in proving the existence of mens rea. For example, if a defendant were apprehended immediately after throwing a lighted match into a barn, this act alone would not be attempted arson because the prosecution additionally would have to convince the jury of an intent to burn the barn. The act, of course, would be a fact to be weighed in the determination of the actor's intent.

The above hypothetical may be used to explore the precise meaning of the deceptively simple "intent to commit a crime" mens rea for attempt. For example, does the prosecution have to prove that the defendant knew that arson was a crime? Because the state punishes most substantive crimes without requiring such proof, no such proof ought to be required as an element of the proof in attempt.

Ignorance of the existance or content of the law is no more a defense to an attempted crime than it is to the substantive crime itself.[9] In the arson attempt case, the prosectuion would have to prove an intent to burn the barn. Since attempt law is designed, at least in part, to interrupt the criminal process and prevent the substantive offense, its mens rea ought to be defined to identify those, and only those, who intend that the ultimate offense be committed. Only those who intend to burn intend that the crime of arson be committed.

Classification.

According to § 13A-4-2(d) of the Alabama Code, "[a]n attempt is a:

"(1) Class A felony if the offense attempted is murder.

"(2) Class B felony if the offense attempted is

ATTEMPT.—Cont'd.

a Class A felony.

"(3) Class C felony if the offense attempted is a Class B felony.

"(4) Class A misdemeanor if the offense attempted is a Class C felony.

"(5) Class B misdemeanor if the offense attempted is a Class A misdemeanor.

"(6) Class C misdemeanor if the offense attempted is a Class B misdemeanor.

"(7) Violation if the offense attempted is a Class C misdemeanor."

Defenses.

Generally, "[a]n attempt to commit a crime consists of three elements: First, the intent to commit the crime; second, the performance of some overt act towards the committing of the crime; and, third, the failure to consummate the crime."[10]

Section 13A-4-2(c) of the Alabama Code states that "[a] person is not liable under this section if, under circumstances manifesting a voluntary and complete renunciation of his criminal intent, he avoided the commission of the offense attempted by abandoning his criminal effort and, if mere abandonment is insufficient to accomplish such avoidance, by taking further and affirmative steps which prevented the commission thereof. The burden of injecting this issue is on the defendant, but this does not shift the burden of proof."

On the issue of impossibility, more effort has been devoted to unraveling the mysteries of impossibility as a defense to attempt than perhaps any other single issue in the substantive criminal law.[11] It is often said that factual impossibility is no defense to attempt liability. If the pickpocket tries to pick an empty pocket, this will be an attempt at theft;[12] if the defendant tries to kill with an unloaded[13] or defective[14] gun, it is still attempted homicide, etc.[15] The rationale of these cases apparently is that the defendant ought not to be acquitted merely because facts, unknown to him, made the success of his criminal venture impossible.

On the other hand, some courts have held that a legal impossibility would excuse a

ATTEMPT.—Cont'd.

defendant from attempt liability. The most famous case in this group is People v. Jaffe,[16] where the defendant received goods he mistakenly thought were stolen and was prosecuted for attempted receipt of stolen goods. The appellate court reversed the conviction on the grounds that since the defendant had done everything he intended to do and it still was not the substantive offense of receiving stolen goods, there could be no attempt liability. It is suggested that Jaffe and cases following it[17] are simply wrong both in result and in the description of the cause of the impossibility. The reason the Jaffe defendant could not commit the substantive crime of receipt is not because of any legal impossibility but because the goods he received were not stolen. He should be viewed identically to the pickpocket reaching into the empty pocket and not be afforded a defense.

The drafters apparently attempted to avoid all such problems as deciding which are legal and which are factual impossibility situations by providing in § 13A-4-2(b) of the Alabama Code that "[i]t is no defense under this section that the offense charged to have been attempted was, under the attendant circumstances, factually or legally impossible of commission, if such offense could have been committed had the attendant circumstances been as the defendant believed them to be." Although this is an admirable effort at correcting wrongly decided cases like Jaffe, it still leaves up in the air what might be described as "true legal impossibility" cases.

The classic case of true legal impossibility is Wilson v. State,[18] an early Mississippi attempt case. Here the defendant altered the numbers on a check and was charged with attempted forgery. The substantive crime of forgery was defined as the alteration of a material part of the document, and the commercial law of the state provided that in case of a conflict on a check between the amount as written and the numerals that the words would control. The numbers on a check are not a material part of the check, and forgery had not been

ATTEMPT.—Cont'd.

committed.

But had attempted forgery been committed? The Mississippi Supreme Court said no. A similar hypothetical has been suggested in which a defendant thinks that it is against the law to smuggle lace into the country without paying a duty on it; but, unbeknownst to the defendant, the law has been repealed the day before he brings the lace into the country without paying the duty. Given that the defendant has not committed smuggling, has there been an attempted smuggling? The drafters of the hypothetical say no attempt has taken place.[19]

Abandonment, or renunciation, is the other important defense in an attempt case in Alabama. This defense, found in the law of many states,[20] exonerates those defendants who, after having committed the actus reus of attempt, voluntarily renounce their criminal activity. Permitting renunciation after the commission of the actus reus of a crime to serve as a defense is very unusual. The return of stolen goods to a theft victim is not any more a defense than an apology to an assault victim.

The reason for the providing of such a defense in attempt stems from the status of the crime as an inchoate offense. The actus reus of the crime in itself is not the ultimate harm. The Model Penal Code suggests that there are two related considerations militating toward the allowance of a renunciation defense. First, "renunciation of criminal purposes tends to negative dangerousness."[21] The individual who renounces his criminal activity is not really very dangerous after all. Second, provision of this defense "encourage[s] actors to desist from pressing forward with their criminal designs."[22] The existence of this defense can be seen to further the twin purposes of the crime: identification of dangerous individuals and the prevention of the underlying substantive offense.

Cross references.

See CONSPIRACY; SOLICITATION.

---

1. *Code of Ala. 1975, § 13A-4-2(a).*
2. *For a complete history of the law of attempt, see*

ATTEMPT.—Cont'd.

Hall, General Principles of Criminal Law 558-74 (2d ed. 1960).

3. *2 Pollack & Maitland, History of English Law 508 (2d ed. 1923).*
4. *Ballentine's Law Dictionary 1352 (3rd ed. 1969).*
5. *Rex v. Higgins, 2 East 5 (1801).*
6. *M. P. C. § 5.01, Comment at 25 (Tent. Draft No. 10, 1960).*
7. *M. P. C. § 5.01, Comment at 25 (Tent. Draft No. 10, 1960).*
8. *It has been said that there is a slight deterrent effect here on the individual who has planned the kind of crime in which detection is highly unlikely unless the plan "miscarries in some way." LaFave & Scott, Criminal Law § 59 at 427 (1972).*
9. *LaFave & Scott, Criminal Law § 59 at 428 (1972).*
10. *Ard v. State, 358 So. 2d 792, certiorari denied, Ex parte Ard, 358 So. 2d 794 (Ala. Cr. App. 1978); Reed v. State, 372 So. 2d 872, reversed, 372 So. 2d 876 (Ala. Cr. App. 1978); Whiddon v. State, 53 Ala. App. 280, 299 So. 2d 326 (1973) ("The 'preparation' for commission of an offense [within the rule that preparation alone is not sufficient to constitute an attempt to commit a specific crime] consists in devising or arranging the means or measures necessary for commission of the crime, while an 'attempt' or 'overt act' is a direct movement toward the commission, after the preparations are made").*
11. *For a partial listing of the voluminous literature on the subject, consult LaFave & Scott, Criminal Law § 60 at 438, n. 1 (1972).*
12. *People v. Fiegelman, 33 Cal. App. 2d 100, 91 P. 2d 156 (1939).*
13. *State v. Damms, 9 Wis. 2d 183, 100 N. W. 2d 592 (1960).*
14. *People v. Van Buskirk, 113 Cal. App. 2d 789, 249 P. 2d 49 (1952).*
15. *See, generally, LaFave & Scott, Criminal Law § 60 at 440-41 (1972).*
16. *People v. Jaffe, 185 N. Y. 497, 78 N. E. 169 (1906).*
17. *See LaFave & Scott, Criminal Law § 60 at 443 (1972).*
18. *Wilson v. State, 85 Miss. 687, 38 So. 46 (1905).*
19. *The creators of the hypothetical mentioned in the text are Deans Sanford Kadish and Monrad Paulsen, Kadish & Paulsen, Criminal Law and Its Processes 365 (3rd ed. 1975). The hypothetical is a spinoff of the original Lady Eldon hypothetical suggested in I Wharton's Criminal Law 223, n. 2 (9th ed. 1885).*
20. *In 1960, the Model Penal Code draftsmen claimed that most jurisdictions provided for a*

ATTEMPT.—Cont'd.

renunciation defense in attempt cases. Model Penal Code § 5.01, Commentary at 70 (Tent. Draft No. 10, 1960).

21. Model Penal Code § 5.01, Commentary at 71 (Tent. Draft No. 10, 1960).

22. Model Penal Code § 5.01, Commentary at 72 (Tent. Draft No. 10, 1960).

AUTO THEFT. See MOTOR VEHICLE CRIMES; THEFT OF PROPERTY; UNAUTHORIZED USE OF VEHICLE/UNLAWFUL BREAKING AND ENTERING A VEHICLE.

AUTOMOBILES. See MOTOR VEHICLE CRIMES; OBSCURING IDENTITY OF VEHICLE; UNAUTHORIZED USE OF VEHICLE/UNLAWFUL BREAKING AND ENTERING A VEHICLE.

AVIATION. Code of Ala. 1975, §§ 4-2-6 through 4-2-11.

Activities involving or associated with aviation in the state are regulated by the provisions set forth in Title 4 of the Alabama Code. Chapter 2 of that title creates five criminal offenses, which are listed below. Unauthorized use or possession of an aircraft is the only offense classified as a felony. For punishment of that offense, § 4-2-11 provides for imprisonment not to exceed 5 years. There is no provision for a fine. All other offenses under this title are classified as misdemeanors with specific provisions for punishment[1] by imprisonment for not more than one month and/or a fine of not more than $100.00.

Section 4-2-6 of the Alabama Code. Domestic animals or fowl on airports, landing fields or other aeronautical facilities.

"It shall be [a misdemeanor] for any owner or keeper of any domestic animal or fowl to allow such domestic animal or fowl to run at large and enter or be upon any premises constituting an airport, restricted landing area or other aeronautical facility."

Section 4-2-7 of the Alabama Code. Trespass and operation of vehicles on airports, landing fields or other aeronautical facilities.

"It shall be [a misdemeanor] for any person

AVIATION.—Cont'd.

or or persons to trespass upon the area within the boundaries of any airport or to operate any vehicles upon or drive across any licensed airport, landing field or other aeronautical facility, unless such are used for administrative and maintenance purposes and are operated by the airport authorities or state and municipal law-enforcement officers having jurisdiction."

Section 4-2-9 of the Alabama Code. Use of aircraft for hunting, etc., prohibited.

"It shall be [a misdemeanor] for any person to hunt, pursue, worry or kill any wild waterfowl or other birds or animals by any means whatever during such time as said person is upon any kind of aircraft."

Section 4-2-10 of the Alabama Code. Reckless operation of aircraft.

"[It shall be a misdemeanor for any person to] operate any aircraft within the airspace over, above or upon the lands and waters of the state of Alabama, carelessly and heedlessly in wilful or wanton disregard of the rights or safety of others or without due caution and circumspection or in a manner so as to endanger or be likely to endanger any person or property . . ."

Section 4-2-11 of the Alabama Code. Unauthorized use, possession, etc., of aircraft.

"[It shall be a felony for any person to] wilfully and without authority take possession of or use an airplane or unlawfully remove or take any component parts of an airplane and [for] any person to assist in, or be a party to, such taking, illegal possession of or use of an airplane or component parts belonging to another . . ."

Comments.

These sections create special protections to aviation interests by the creation of these miscellaneous criminal offenses.

Related provisions of Title 13A of the Alabama Code may sanction these actions. Defense attorneys, however, should keep these offenses in mind as lesser offenses to which a defendant could plead. For the prosecuting attorney, their value may be in plea bargaining. In some instances these

AVIATION.—Cont'd.

provisions may be broader in coverage and require a lesser burden of proof than an offense under Title 13A of the Alabama Code.

Cross references.

See MISCHIEF, CRIMINAL; THEFT OF LOST PROPERTY; THEFT OF PROPERTY; THEFT OF SERVICES; TRESPASS AND OPERATION OF VEHICLES ON AIRPORTS, LANDING FIELDS, OR OTHER AERONAUTICAL FACILITIES.

---

1. Code of Ala. 1975, § 4-2-12.

BAIL JUMPING. Code of Ala. 1975, §§ 13A-10-39 and 13A-10-40.

"A person commits the crime of bail jumping in the first degree if, having been lawfully released from custody,[1] with or without bail, upon condition that he will subsequently appear at a specified time and place in connection with a charge of his having committed murder or any Class A or B felony, he fails to appear at the time and place." § 13A-10-39(a) of the Alabama Code.

"A person commits the crime of bail jumping in the second degree if, having been lawfully released from custody, with or without bail, upon condition that he will subsequently appear at a specified time and place in connection with a charge of his having committed any misdemeanor or Class C felony, he fails to appear at that time and place." § 13A-10-40(a) of the Alabama Code.

Classification.

Class C felony, first degree.

Class A misdemeanor, second degree.

Comments.

These sections apply equally to persons released on bail or on their own recognizance. Only an intentional failure to appear is made criminal. If the defense of an unintentional failure to appear is used, it is for the trier of fact to evaluate defendant's excuse. The defendant has the burden of proof of explaining his nonappearance. The difference between the sections is based upon the classification of the offense

BAIL JUMPING.—Cont'd.

charged. A special exception is made for persons charged with misdemeanor traffic violations. In this area, forfeiture of bail is often treated as a substitute for payment of a fine.

Defenses.

(1) The defendant's failure to appear was unintentional or was unavoidable and due to circumstances beyond his control.[2]

(2) This section does not apply to a person released from custody on condition that he will appear in connection with a charge of having committed a misdemeanor in violation of Title 32 of the Alabama Code.

---

1. "A restraint or detention by a public servant pursuant to a lawful arrest, conviction or order of court, but does not include mere supervision of probation or parole, or constraint incidental to release on bail". Code of Ala. 1975, § 13A-10-30(b)(1).

2. The burden of injecting the defense of an unintentional failure to appear, or unavoidability and circumstances beyond his control, is on the defendant.

BAIT ADVERTISING. See ADVERTISING, BAIT.

BANKRUPTCY AND INSOLVENCY. See FINANCIAL INSTITUTIONS, FAILING, RECEIVING DEPOSITS IN; FRAUD IN INSOLVENCY.

BANKS AND FINANCIAL INSTITUTIONS. See FINANCIAL INSTITUTIONS, FAILING, RECEIVING DEPOSITS IN; FRAUD IN INSOLVENCY.

BATTERY. See ASSAULT.

BEGGARS. See LOITERING; MAIMING ONE'S SELF TO ESCAPE DUTY OR OBTAIN ALMS.

BIGAMY. Code of Ala. 1975, § 13A-13-1.

"A person commits bigamy when he[1] intentionally contracts or purports[2] to contract a marriage[3] with another person when he[4] has a living spouse. A person who contracts a marriage outside this state, which would be bigamous if contracted in

BIGAMY.—Cont'd.

this state, commits bigamy by cohabiting in the state with the other party to such a marriage."

Classification.

Class C felony.

Comments.

To some extent, one ought to argue in defense of a charge of bigamy the nonapplicability of the basic policies[5] justifying penal sanctions, as set forth by the drafters, to the particular circumstances surrounding his case.

Defenses.

Defenses against a charge of bigamy include, according to § 13A-13-1(b) of the Alabama Code, reasonable belief "that his previous marriage is void or was dissolved by death, divorce or annulment; or [he] and the prior spouse have been living apart for five consecutive years next prior to the subsequent marriage, during which time the prior spouse was not known by him to be alive."[6] In addition, the comments following § 13A-13-1 of the Alabama Code provide for two other "good faith" situations that may provide a defense for one charged with bigamy. "One is where a married person engages an attorney to obtain a divorce, signs the papers to be filed, pays money to initiate the proceedings, but without taking further legal action, and a divorce not being ultimately obtained, remarries. The other involves remarrying without waiting 60 days after the divorce decree or during the pendency of an appeal. § 30-2-10. Remarriage within the proscribed time has been held bigamous. State v. Brand, 242 Ala. 15, 6 So. 2d 446 (1941), the divorce being deemed inoperative. But cf. Fitts v. Fitts, 284 Ala. 109, 222 So. 2d 696 (1969) which, while not a bigamy case, held divorce decrees are final, not interlocutory, and distinguished *Brand* because there the trial court that issued the decree and which retained jurisdiction set it aside for good cause within 30 days. Such procedural rules relating to divorce are beyond the scope of the Criminal Code."

Cross references.

See ADULTERY; INCEST.

BIGAMY.—Cont'd.

---

1. *"He," as used in the Alabama Code, indicates male or female.*
2. *According to the comments following Code of Ala. 1975, § 13A-13-1, "[t]he language 'purports to contract' is used to cover the situation where, for example, the partner of the second marriage is, by reason of youth or mental defect, legally incapable of contracting marriage. The fact that the second marriage could not be legally contracted would not provide a technical defense to prosecution."*
3. *This is intended, according to the comments following Code of Ala. 1975, § 13A-13-1, to apply "not only to marriages which are officially contracted, but also where either the prior or subsequent marriage, or both, is a common law marriage, which type of marriage is presently recognized in Alabama. Including common law marriages under this section continues present Alabama law. Hampton v. State, 37 Ala. App. 427, 69 So. 2d 727 (1953); Martin v. State, 31 Ala. App. 86, 13 So. 2d 203 (1943). The burden, of course, is on the state to prove both marriages beyond a reasonable doubt. Edwards v. State, 34 Ala. App. 373, 40 So. 2d 103 (1949); Fuquay v. State, 217 Ala. 4, 114 So. 898 (1927)."*
4. *Although the committee rejected a proposal to expressly include an unmarried person as a principal to the offense, where "an unmarried party knowingly enters into a bigamous marriage, he may be liable as an aider and abettor of the married partner in committing bigamy."*
5. *According to the comment following Code of Ala. 1975, § 13A-13-1, "[t]he basic policies justifying penal sanctions for this conduct include the public affront at the flouting of social obligations, the provocation to retaliation by the first spouse and the harm imposed on an innocent person fraudulently mislead into a void marriage by one who knows that he is ineligible because of a previous marriage."*
6. *According to Code of Ala. 1975, § 13A-13-1(b)(3), "[t]he burden of injecting the issues [incorporated in the stated defenses] . . . is on the defendant, but this does not shift the burden of proof."*

BLACKLIST, MAINTAINING. Code of Ala. 1975, § 13A-11-123.

Charged as: Maintaining a blacklist.

"Any person, firm, corporation or association of persons who maintains what is commonly called a blacklist[1] or notifies any

BLACKLIST, MAINTAINING.
—Cont'd.

other person, firm, corporation or association that any person has been blacklisted by such person, firm, corporation or association or who uses any other similar means to prevent any person from receiving employment from whomsoever he desires to be employed by shall be guilty of a misdemeanor."

Classification.

Misdemeanor.

Comments.

The statute prohibits the maintenance as well as the publication of information concerning an individual for the purpose of preventing such individual from securing gainful employment. Because the concepts embodied in this statute are similar to contract and tort liability, an aggrieved party could also bring a civil action against a person who violates this statute.[2] Though the statute is broadly written, similar statutes have withstood attacks that they were unconstitutional or void for vagueness.[3] The accused need not actually have prevented an individual from securing his desired employment to be culpable under this statute.[4] The intent of the accused is, however, crucial to determination of criminal liability.[5]

Defenses.

(1) Failure to prove defendant published or maintained negative information intended to prevent another from securing employment.

(2) Negative information elicited by prospective employer.

(3) Information maintained or published for another purpose.

(4) Defendant had no reason to believe information he possessed or published would prevent individual from gaining employment.

Cross references.

See LIBEL AND DEFAMATION.

---

1. *"A list of persons marked out for special avoidance, antagonism, or enmity on the part of those who prepare the list or those among whom it is intended to circulate." Black's Law Dictionary (4th ed.) This definition was cited and*

BLACKLIST, MAINTAINING.
—Cont'd.

relied upon in Dick v. Northern Pac. Ry. Co., 86 Wash. 211, 150 P. 8 (1915) and Johnson v. Oregon Stevedoring Co., 270 P. 772 (1928).

2. *See Johnson v. Oregon Stevedoring Co., 270 P. 772 (1928), in which case the court considered criminal liability as well as assessment of damages for tortious conduct.*
3. *In State v. Dabney, 141 P. 2d 303 (1943), the court quoted Black's (see note 1, supra) and cited a Supreme Court decision: "It is the well settled rule of construction that language used in a statute which has a settled meaning, sanctioned by judicial decision, is presumed to be used in that sense by the legislative body." Kepner v. United States, 195 U. S. 100, 24 S. Ct. 797, 802, 49 L. Ed. 114 (1904). A Minnesota statute similar to the Alabama statute was held constitutional in Scheffer v. Justus, 85 Minn. 279, 88 N. W. 759 (1902). See also Johnson v. Oregon Stevedoring Co., 270 P. 777 (1928).*
4. *"All that is required under the statute here under consideration is that the former employer blacklisted a former employee with the intent and for the purpose of preventing such former employee from thereafter obtaining work." State v. Dabney, 141 P. 2d 303, 309 (1943). The statute referred to stated, in pertinent part, "No firm, corporation or individual shall blacklist or require a letter of relinquishment, or publish, or cause to be published or blacklisted any employee . . . with intent and for the purpose of preventing such employee . . . from engaging in securing similar or other employment . . ." 40 O. S. 1941 §§ 172 and 173.*
5. *"An intent to injure by preventing future employment is the essence of the offense of blacklisting." State v. Dabney, 141 P. 2d 303, 308 (1943).*

BLACKMAIL. See EXTORTION.

BOARDS AND COMMISSIONS. See CLOSED MEETINGS.

BOOKMAKING. See GAMBLING.

BREAKING AND ENTERING. See BURGLARY.

BRIBE, RECEIPT OF COMMERCIAL.

Code of Ala. 1975, § 13A-11-121.

Charged as: Receiving commercial bribe.

"A person commits the crime of receiving a commercial bribe if:

BRIBE, RECEIPT OF COMMERCIAL. —Cont'd.

"(1) As an employee or agent, and without the consent of his employer or principal, he solicits, accepts or agrees to accept any benefit from another person upon an agreement or understanding that the benefit will improperly influence his conduct in relation to his employer's or principal's affairs; or

"(2) As a hiring agent or an official or employee in charge of employment, he solicits, accepts or agrees to accept any benefit from another person upon an agreement or understanding that someone shall be hired, retained in employment or discharged or suspended from employment; or

"(3) As a fiduciary, and without the consent of his beneficiary, he solicits, accepts or agrees to accept any benefit from another person upon an agreement or understanding that the benefit will improperly influence his conduct in his fiduciary capacity."

Classification.

Class A misdemeanor.

Comments.

This statute is intended to cover the solicitation, acceptance, or agreement by an employee or agent to accept a benefit, without the consent of his principal, employer, or beneficiary, "upon an agreement or understanding" that the benefit will improperly influence his conduct in his employment relation. Consent of the person bribed is a prerequisite to commission of the crime, and criminal intent may be implied as an element of the offense.

Defenses.

(1) Failure to prove consent.

(2) Failure to prove acceptance was coupled with an intent to improperly influence his conduct.

(3) Section 13A-11-121(a)(2) of the Alabama Code does not apply to any person conducting a private employment agency licensed and operating under the laws of Alabama.

Query.

Can failure to deny an offer of a bribe

BRIBE, RECEIPT OF COMMERCIAL. —Cont'd.

constitute commission of the offense by implication under a "tacit admission" theory?

Cross references.

See Bribery and Corrupt Influence, chapter 10, article 3 of Title 13A of the Alabama Code. See BRIBERY, COMMERCIAL.

BRIBE RECEIVING BY A JUROR.

Code of Ala. 1975, § 13A-10-126.

"A person commits the crime of bribe receiving by a juror[1] if he solicits, accepts or agrees to accept any pecuniary benefit[2] upon an agreement or understanding that his vote, opinion, decision or other action as a juror will thereby be corruptly influenced."

Classification.

Class C felony.

Comments.

Bribe Receiving by a Juror, as in Bribe Receiving by a Witness, § 13A-10-122 of the Alabama Code, requires more than proof of intent; it requires proof of an understanding or agreement that the juror's vote, opinion, decision, or other action would be corruptly influenced. The thing received by the juror has been limited in this section to any pecuniary benefit.

Defenses.

(1) No agreement and understanding, even if there was proof of intent.

(2) The defense of entrapment might be of particular interest in this context; see ENTRAPMENT.

(3) Juror had not been summoned or his name drawn at the time the benefit was agreed upon.

(4) The "thing" received has no pecuniary benefit.

Cross references.

See ATTEMPTS; BRIBERY OF PUBLIC SERVANTS; SOLICITATION.

---

1. *"Any person who is a member of any jury, including a grand jury, impaneled by any court of this state or by any public servant authorized by law to impanel a jury. The term juror also includes any person who has been summoned or*

BRIBE RECEIVING BY A JUROR. —Cont'd.

whose name has been drawn to attend as a prospective juror." Code of Ala. 1975, § 13A-10-120.

2. *"Benefit in the form of money, property, commercial interests or anything else the primary significance of which is economic gain." Code of Ala. 1975, § 13A-10-60(b)(2).*

BRIBE RECEIVING BY A WITNESS. Code of Ala. 1975, § 13A-10-122.

"A witness or a person believing he will be called as a witness in any official proceeding[1] commits the crime of bribe receiving by a witness if he solicits, accepts or agrees to accept any thing of value[2] upon an agreement or understanding that:

"(1) His testimony will thereby be corruptly influenced;

"(2) He will attempt to avoid legal process summoning him to testify; or

"(3) He will attempt to absent himself from an official proceeding to which he has been legally summoned."

Classification.

Class C felony.

Comments.

This section does not require that the person actually be called as a witness, but only that he believes he might be called as a witness. Unlike § 13A-10-121 of the Alabama Code (Bribing a witness), this section requires more than intent on the part of the witness, but rather requires that an "understanding" be reached before the crime can be committed.

This section does not apply to the payment of additional compensation to an expert witness over and above the amount otherwise prescribed by law to be paid a witness. Ordinary compensation plus pay for any special preparation, research, or exam is not a bribe.[3] However, if an expert witness solicits or accepts a bribe to testify falsely, then the expert would be committing the offense of bribe receiving.[4]

Defenses.

(1) A thing of value was not accepted or agreed to.

(2) A gratuitous gift was accepted.

(3) No intent on part of witness or no understanding or agreement existed between the parties.

(4) The witness is an expert witness and entitled to such compensation.

Cross references.

See ATTEMPT; BRIBERY OF PUBLIC SERVANTS; BRIBING A WITNESS; SOLICITATION.

---

1. *Official proceeding, as defined in Code of Ala. 1975, § 13A-10-100(b)(5), includes those witnesses heard "before any legislative, judicial, administrative, or other government agency or official authorized to hear evidence under oath."*
2. *The 1979 Amendment substituted "thing of value" for pecuniary benefit. Originally the Code did not define bribery. However, the courts held that a corrupt offer of "any gift, gratuity, or thing of value" to a juror was sufficient to constitute a bribe. Caruthers v. State, 74 Ala. 406 (1883).*
3. *Code of Ala. 1975, § 13A-10-122(b).*
4. *Code of Ala. 1975, § 12-21-181; Hartley v. Ala. National Bank of Montgomery, 247 Ala. 651, 25 So. 2d 680 (1946).*

BRIBERY, COMMERCIAL. Code of Ala. 1975, § 13A-11-120.

Charged as: Commercial bribery.

A person commits the crime of commercial bribery if he:

"(1) Confers, or agrees or offers to confer, any benefit upon any employee or agent without the consent of the latter's employer or principal, with intent to improperly influence his conduct in relation to his employer's or principal's affairs; or

"(2) Confers, or agrees or offers to confer, any benefit upon any fiduciary without the consent of the latter's beneficiary, with intent to improperly influence him to act or conduct himself contrary to his fiduciary obligation."

Classification.

Class A misdemeanor.

Comments.

This statute prohibits bribery that extends into the world of private business. It is directed toward the actor who tenders the bribe and requires as an element of the offense that he act with the intent to improperly influence the conduct of

BRIBERY, COMMERCIAL.—Cont'd.
another person on a matter that concerns the other person's employment obligation. It provides that the same protections against improper influences toward public servants should extend to private employers. However, without the consent of the person bribed, the bribery itself results in no property loss to the victim. Thus, for commission of this crime, all that is necessary is to have the requisite intent and to commit some objectively discernible act in furtherance thereof. Consent is no defense.

Defenses.

(1) Lack of requisite intent.

(2) Some acts to influence the conduct of another are not improper.

(3) Failure to prove that the conduct to be influenced would affect the employment obligation or a fiduciary obligation.

Query.

Would lack of "knowledge" that the action is "improper" provide a defense? Would the scope of this statute include the hiring process where one is already employed? If so, would the offer of future employment without first gaining the consent of the present employer subject one to prosecution?

Cross references.

See Bribery and Corrupt Influence, chapter 10, article 3 of Title 13A of the Alabama Code. See ATTEMPT; BRIBE, RECEIPT OF COMMERCIAL; COERCION; DURESS; ENTRAPMENT; EXTORTION; SOLICITATION.

BRIBERY OF PUBLIC SERVANTS.

Code of Ala. 1975, § 13A-10-61.

"(a) A person commits the crime of bribery if:

"(1) He offers, confers or agrees to confer thing of value[1] upon a public servant[2] with the intent that the public servant's vote, opinion, judgment, exercise of discretion or other action in his official capacity will thereby be corruptly influenced; or

"(2) While a public servant, he solicits, accepts or agrees to accept any pecuniary benefit[3] upon an agreement or understanding that his vote, opinion, judgment, exercise of discretion or other action as a public servant will thereby be corruptly influenced.

"(b) It is not a defense to a prosecution under this section that the person sought to be influenced was not qualified to act in the desired way, whether because he had not yet assumed office, lacked jurisdiction or for any other reason."

Classification.

Class C felony.

Comments.

Under this section both the giving and receiving of a benefit[4] are combined. By including the term "corruptly influenced," the intent of defendant to have the public official act improperly is required. Using the term "thing of value" in subsection (1), as opposed to "pecuniary benefit" in subsection (2), means that a person bribing a public official with anything of value would be chargeable, while the public official would be chargeable only if he received a pecuniary benefit. Impossibility is not a defense.

Defenses.

(1) Lack of intent.

Cross references.

See ATTEMPT; COERCION; DURESS; ENTRAPMENT; EXTORTION; SOLICITATION.

---

1. *The term "thing of value" is not defined in the Alabama Code. See Caruthers v. State, 74 Ala. 406 (1883), for discussion of "gift, gratuity or thing of value."*
2. *"Any officer or employee of government, including legislators and judges and any person or agency participating as an adviser, consultant or otherwise in performing a governmental function" (Code of Ala. 1975, § 13A-10-1(7).) or any persons who "have been elected, appointed or designated to become a public servant although not yet occupying that position." Code of Ala. 1975, § 13A-10-60(3).*
3. *Pecuniary benefit is a "[b]enefit in the form of money, property, commercial interests or anything else the primary significance of which is economic gain. Expenses associated with social occasions afforded public servants and party officers shall not be deemed a pecuniary benefit*

BRIBERY OF PUBLIC SERVANTS.—Cont'd.

within the meaning of this article." Code of Ala. 1975, § 13A-10-60(b)(2).

4. *A benefit is "[a]ny gain or advantage to the beneficiary, including any gain or advantage to a third person pursuant to the desire or consent of the beneficiary." Code of Ala. 1975, § 13A-10-60(b)(1).*

BRIBING A JUROR. Code of Ala. 1975, § 13A-10-125.

"A person commits the crime of bribing a juror[1] if he offers, confers or agrees to confer any pecuniary benefit[2] upon a juror with the intent that the juror's vote, opinion, decision, or other action as a juror will thereby be corruptly influenced."

Classification.

Class C felony.

Comments.

This section, the counterpart of § 13A-10-121 of the Alabama Code, Bribing a witness, requires only an intent on the part of the briber, and not an understanding or agreement between the briber and the juror.

The bribes in this section are limited to those consisting of pecuniary benefits.

Defenses.

(1) No show or intent to bribe.

(2) No belief that the person approached was going to be a juror.

(3) The thing conferred was of no pecuniary benefit (economic gain).

(4) The defense of entrapment might be of particular interest in this context; see ENTRAPMENT.

Cross references.

See ATTEMPT; BRIBERY OF PUBLIC SERVANT; SOLICITATION.

---

1. *"JUROR. Any person who is a member of any jury, including a grand jury, impaneled by any court of this state or by any public servant authorized by law to impanel a jury. The term juror also includes any person who has been summoned or whose name has been drawn to attend as a prospective juror." Code of Ala. 1975, § 13A-10-120.*

2. *"PECUNIARY BENEFIT. Benefit in the form of money, property, commercial interests or anything else the primary significance of which is economic gain." Code of Ala. 1975, § 13A-10-60(b)(2).*

BRIBING A WITNESS. Code of Ala. 1975, § 13A-10-121.

"A person commits the crime of bribing a witness if he offers, confers or agrees to confer any thing of value[1] upon a witness or a person he believes will be called as a witness in any official proceeding[2] with intent to:

"(1) Corruptly influence the testimony of that person;

"(2) Induce that person to avoid legal process summoning him to testify; or

"(3) Induce that person to absent himself from an official proceeding to which he has been legally summoned."

Classification.

Class C felony.

Comments.

Section 13A-10-121 of the Alabama Code does not require that the person approached and offered a bribe actually be called as a witness. It requires only that the offeror believe that the person sought to be bribed is about to be called as a witness. The Code does not require an understanding or agreement that the testimony of a witness be influenced. It only requires that the offeror have an intent that the witness testify corruptly.

Theoretically, payment to an expert witness is to compensate him fairly, not to influence his testimony. "This section does not apply to the payment of additional compensation to an expert witness over and above the amount otherwise prescribed by law to be paid to a witness."[3] The amount paid is to be for ordinary compensation and not extra pay.[4] This rule has been found inapplicable where special preparation, research, or examination is required.[5] An expert can, however, be the object of an attempted bribe if the bribe was meant to cause him to testify falsely.

Defenses.

(1) No "value."

(2) No intent existed on the part of the offeror.

BRIBING A WITNESS.—Cont'd.

Cross references.

See ATTEMPT; BRIBE RECEIVING BY A WITNESS; BRIBERY OF PUBLIC SERVANTS; SOLICITATION.

---

1. *The 1979 amendment substituted "thing of value" for pecuniary benefit. Originally, the Alabama Code did not define bribery. The courts, however, held that a corrupt offer of "any gift, gratuity, or thing of value" to a juror was sufficient to constitute a bribe. Caruthers v. State, 74 Ala. 406 (1883).*
2. *Witness in any official proceeding, as defined in Code of Ala. 1975, § 13A-10-100(b)(5) includes those witnesses "before any legislative, judicial, administrative or other government agency or official authorized to hear evidence under oath," as well as depositions and evidence viva voce.*
3. *Code of Ala. 1975, § 13A-10-121(b).*
4. *Code of Ala. 1975, § 12-21-181.*
5. *Harvey v. Alabama National Bank of Montgomery, 247 Ala. 651, 25 So. 2d 680 (1946).*

BRINGING STOLEN PROPERTY OR PROPERTY OBTAINED BY FALSE PRETENSE ELSEWHERE INTO THIS STATE. Code of Ala. 1975, §§ 13A-8-20 and 13A-8-21.

"Any person who fraudulenty brings into this state any personal property which he knew was stolen[1] elsewhere shall, on conviction, be punished as if he had stolen it in this state." § 13A-8-20 of the Alabama Code.

"Any person who brings or causes to be brought into this state any money or other personal property obtained from another by any false pretense, with intent to defraud, shall, on conviction, be punished as if he had stolen the same." § 13A-8-21 of the Alabama Code.

Classification.

The classifications for these sections depend upon the classification of theft to which each relates.

Defenses.

(1) Claim of right.[2]

(2) Lack of intent to deprive.

(3) Lack of knowledge that property was stolen.

Cross references.

See THEFT OF LOST PROPERTY; THEFT OF PROPERTY.

---

1. *"STOLEN. Obtained by theft, theft by*

BRINGING STOLEN PROPERTY OR PROPERTY OBTAINED BY FALSE PRETENSE ELSEWHERE INTO THIS STATE.—Cont'd.

appropriating lost property, robbery or extortion." Code of Ala. 1975, § 13A-8-1(12).

2. *"(a) It is a defense to a prosecution under [§§ 13A-8-2 through 13A-8-11 of the Alabama Code] (theft of lost property, theft of property, theft of services and unauthorized use of vehicle) that the actor . . . [h]onestly believed that he had a claim to the property or services involved which he was entitled to assert in the manner which forms the basis for the charge against him.*
   "(b) The burden of injecting the issue of claim of right is on the defendant, but this does not shift the burden of proof." Code of Ala. 1975, § 13A-8-12.

BURGLAR'S TOOLS, POSSESSION OF. Code of Ala. 1975, § 13A-7-8.

Charged as: Possession of burglar's tools.

A person commits the crime of possession of burglar's tools if he:

"Possesses any explosive, tool, instrument or other article adapted, designed or commonly used for committing or facilitating the commission of an offense involving forcible entry into the premises or theft by a physical taking; and . . . [i]ntends to use the thing possessed in the commission of [an offense involving forcible entry into the premises or theft by a physical taking]."

Classification.

Class C felony.

Comments.

This crime consists of two basic elements: (1) possession of the "tools" which are used to commit an offense involving forcible entry or theft by physical taking, concurrent with (2) an intent to use such "tools" to commit such an offense. With regard to the latter element, the commentary states: "evidence that accused had just committed a burglary and was found in possession of the spoils, or that the articles found in accused's possession were identical to those used in recent burglaries has been held admissible to show the felonious intent of the accused in having the tools in his possession." Murray v State, 43 Ala. App. 5, 178 So. 2d

BURGLAR'S TOOLS, POSSESSION OF.—Cont'd.

233 (1965). The above conclusion drawn by the commentators was from the dictum in that case. Additionally, it should be noted that such dictum was not supported by Alabama law. Instead, the court cited State v. Heflin, 388 Mo. 236, 89 S. W. 2d 939 (1935) and Fuqua v. State, 246 Miss. 191, 145 So. 2d 152 (1962). Perhaps more useful is the case of Davis v. State, 87 Ala. 10, 6 So. 266 (1888), which indicates that "[t]he purpose of the statute is the security of property and the prevention of crime, by declaring the possession of implements or instruments which are capable of aiding the commission of burglary or larceny, with design and intent to use them, a criminal offense." This indicates the requisite intent is a present intent. Therefore, evidence of recent burglaries, or even possession of the spoils, is no more relevant than previous convictions for burglary (except in the case where the offender is stopped enroute from the scene of the crime). Once intent is established and it is concluded that the "tools" are "designed or commonly used" in such offenses, it is of no importance that the "tools" had a legal use (i.e., tire iron, screwdriver, prybar, and flashlight in a mechanic's car).

Defenses.

(1) Lack of requisite intent.

(2) Lack of concurrent intent and possession.

(3) Did not possess an instrument, etc., used for facilitating forcible entry.

BURGLARY Code of Ala. 1975, §§ 13A-7-5 through 13A-7-7.

"A person commits the crime of burglary in the first degree if he knowingly[1] and unlawfully enters or remains unlawfully[2] in a dwelling[3] with intent[4] to commit a crime[5] therein, and, if, in effecting entry or while in dwelling or in immediate flight therefrom, he or another participant in the crime: (1) Is armed with explosives[6] or a deadly weapon;[7] or (2) Causes physical injury[8] to any person who is not a participant in the crime; or (3) Uses or threatens the immediate use of a dangerous instrument."[9] § 13A-7-5 of the Alabama Code.

"(a) A person commits the crime of burglary in the second degree if he knowingly enters or remains unlawfully in a building with intent to commit theft[10] or a felony[11] therein and, if in effecting entry or while in the building or in immediate flight therefrom, he or another participant in the crime: (1) Is armed with explosives or a deadly weapon; or (2) Causes physical injury to any person who is not a participant in the crime; or (3) Uses or threatens the immediate use of a dangerous instrument.

"(b) In the alternative . . . a person commits the crime of burglary in the second degree if he unlawfully enters a lawfully occupied dwellinghouse[12] with intent to commit a theft or a felony therein." § 13A-7-6 of the Alabama Code.

"A person commits the crime of burglary in the third degree if he knowingly enters or remains unlawfully in a building with intent to commit a crime therein." § 13A-7-7 of the Alabama Code.

Classification.

Class A felony, burglary in the first degree.
Class B felony, burglary in the second degree.
Class C felony, burglary in the third degree.

Comments.

Burglary is, in essence, criminal trespass[13] (entering or remaining unlawfully in a building) with the intent to commit a crime therein. Such conduct without any other aggravating factors is culpable as burglary in the third degree. If the intruder: (1) is armed with explosives or a deadly weapon; or (2) causes physical injury to a person who is not a participant in the crime; or (3) uses or threatens the immediate use of a dangerous instrument, these aggravating factors raise the level of culpability to first or second degree burglary.

One can be guilty of second degree burglary if one of the aggravating factors is present and the intruder knowingly and unlawfully enters or remains in a building with intent to commit theft or a felony therein. In the alternative, if the intruder enters an occupied dwelling with the intent to commit a theft or felony therein, second

BURGLARY—Cont'd.

degree burglary has been committed though none of the aggravating factors mentioned above is present.

First degree burglary is accomplished whenever one knowingly and unlawfully enters or remains in a dwelling (occupied or not) with the intent to commit any crime therein, coupled with any of the aggravating factors.

To sustain a burglary conviction the State must establish: (1) the intruder "entered or remained unlawfully"; (2) the intruder "knowingly entered or remained"; (3) the invaded premises constitute a building; (4) the intruder intended to commit a crime (theft or a felony if second degree burglary is charged).

There is no requirement that a technical "breaking" be established. The use of force may be relevant on the issue of license or privilege.[14] Because the state must also prove "knowledge," the fact that the intruder was not aware that he had no license or privilege would cause the state's case to fail.

The time of day that the unlawful intrusion occurred is irrelevant. If the building is a dwelling, occupancy at the time of intrusion is only relevant for conviction of second degree burglary when no aggravating factors are present. Note: Nighttime burglary of an occupied dwelling when any of the occupants is intentionally killed by the defendant is one of the aggravated offenses for which the death penalty may be imposed.[15]

According to the commentary, it is unlcear whether dwellinghouse as used in § 13A-7-6(b) of the Alabama Code means "dwelling" as defined in § 13A-7-1(3) of the Alabama Code or only "house" in the traditional sense.

The commentary also suggests that it is not clear whether conviction under § 13A-7-6(b) of the Alabama Code can be included as a lesser included offense of first degree burglary.

Cross references.

See TAKING OR RETAKING POSSESSION OF REAL ESTATE; TRESPASS, CRIMINAL.

BURGLARY—Cont'd.

---

1. *"KNOWINGLY. A person acts knowingly with respect to conduct or to a circumstance described by a statute defining an offense when he is aware that his conduct is of that nature or that the circumstance exists." Code of Ala. 1975, § 13A-2-2(2).*
2. *"ENTER OR REMAIN UNLAWFULLY. A person 'enters or remains unlawfully' in or upon premises when he is not licensed, invited or privileged to do so. A person who, regardless of his intent, enters or remains in or upon premises which are at the time open to the public does so with license and privilege unless he defies a lawful order not to enter or remain, personally communicated to him by the owner of such premises or other authorized person. A license or privilege to enter or remain in a building which is partly open to the public is not a license or privilege to enter or remain in that part of the building which is not open to the public. A person who enters or remains upon unimproved and apparently unused land, which is neither fenced nor otherwise enclosed in a manner designed to exclude intruders, does so with license and privileges unless notice against trespass is personally communicated to him by the owner of such land or other authorized person, or unless such notice is given by posting in a conspicuous manner." Code of Ala. 1975, § 13-7-1(4).*
3. *"DWELLING. A building which is used or normally used by a person for sleeping, living or lodging therein." Code of Ala. 1975, § 13A-7-1(3).*
4. *"INTENTIONALLY. A person acts intentionally with respect to a result or to conduct described by a statute defining an offense, when his purpose is to cause that result or to engage in that conduct." Code of Ala. 1975, § 13A-2-2(1).*

   Though the State must prove intent to commit a crime, the crime need not actually be consummated. Wicks v. State, 44 Ala. 398 (1870), although commission of the crime is conclusive of criminal intent.
5. *"CRIME. A misdemeanor or a felony." Code of Ala. 1975, § 13A-1-2(5).*
6. *"EXPLOSIVES. Any chemical compound or mechanical mixture that is commonly used or intended for the purpose of producing an explosion and which contains any oxidizing and combustive units or other ingredients in such proportions, quantities or packing that an ignition by fire, by friction, by concussion, by detonator or by chemical action of any part of the*

BURGLARY—Cont'd.

compound or mixture may cause a sudden generation of highly heated gases that the resultant gaseous pressures are capable of producing destructive effects on contiguous objects or of destroying life or limb." Code of Ala. 1975, § 13A-7-40(2).

7. *"DEADLY WEAPON. A firearm or anything manifestly designed, made or adapted for the purposes or inflicting death or serious physical injury, and such term includes, but is not limited to, a pistol, rifle or shotgun; or a switch-blade knife, gravity knife, stiletto, sword or dagger; or any billy, blackjack, bludgeon or metal knuckles." Code of Ala. 1975, § 13A-1-2(11).*
8. *"PHYSICAL INJURY. Impairment of physical condition or substantial pain." Code of Ala. 1975, § 13A-1-2(8).*
9. *"DANGEROUS INSTRUMENT. Any instrument, article or substance which, under the circumstances in which it is used, attempted to be used or threatened to be used, is highly capable of causing death or serious physical injury, and such term includes a 'vehicle,'. . ." Code of Ala. 1975, § 13A-1-2(12). And note that Code of Ala. 1975, § 13A-1-2(13) defines vehicle as any "propelled vehicle," including "any propelled device by which any person or property is transported on land, water or in the air, and includes motor vehicles, motorcycles, motorboats and aircraft, and any vessel, whether propelled by machinery or not."*
10. *Theft — "A person commits the crime of theft of property if he:*

    "(1) Knowingly obtains or exerts unauthorized control over the property of another, with intent to deprive the owner of his property; or

    "(2) Knowingly obtains by deception control over the property of another, with intent to deprive the owner of his property." Code of Ala. 1975, § 13A-8-2.
11. *"FELONY. An offense for which a sentence to a term of imprisonment in excess of one year is authorized by this title." Code of Ala. 1975, § 13A-1-2(4).*
12. *"DWELLING. A building which is used or normally used by a person for sleeping, living or lodging therein." Code of Ala. 1975, § 13A-7-1(3). And Code of Ala. 1975, § 13A-7-1(2) defines building as "[a]ny structure which may be entered and utilized by persons for business, public use, lodging or the storage of goods, and such term includes any vehicle, aircraft or watercraft used for the lodging of persons or carrying on business therein. Where a building consists of two or more units separately occupied or secured, each shall be deemed both a separate building and a part of the main building."*
13. *See TRESPASS, CRIMINAL.*
14. *License or privilege — The attorney should consider a more in-depth review of Restatement of Torts 2d, Ch. 8.*
15. *See Code of Ala. 1975, § 13A-5-31(4).*

BUSINESS, CONSPIRACY, COMBINATION, OR AGREEMENT TO INTERFERE WITH OR HINDER. Code of Ala. 1975, § 13A-11-122.

Charged as: Conspiracy, combination, or agreement to interfere with or hinder business.

"Two or more persons who, without a just cause or legal excuse for so doing, enter into any combination, conspiracy, agreement, arrangement or understanding for the purpose of hindering, delaying or preventing any other persons, firms, corporation or association of persons from carrying on any lawful business shall be guilty of a misdemeanor."

Classification.

Misdemeanor.

Comments.

The application of this statute could have far-reaching results. Acts which may not be criminal when committed by individuals can become criminal when committed by two or more.

Defenses.

(1) Failure to prove two or more persons acted in concert toward the same end.

(2) Just cause or legal excuse.

(3) Failure to prove requisite criminal intent.

(4) The business hindered was not "lawful."

Query.

Is the prohibition against price-fixing the exclusive intent of this statute? Does "person" include application to business entities?

Cross references.

See ATTEMPTS; BRIBE, RECEIPT OF COMMERCIAL; BRIBERY, COMMERCIAL; COERCION; DURESS; SOLICITATION.

BUSINESS PRACTICES, DECEPTIVE. Code of Ala. 1975, § 13A-9-41.

Charged as: Deceptive business practices.

"A person commits the crime of deceptive business practices if in the course of engaging in a business, occupation, or profession, he:

"(1) Uses or possesses for use a false weight or measure,[1] or any other device for falsely determining or recording any quality or quantity; or

"(2) Sells, offers or exposes for sale, or delivers, less than the represented quantity of any commodity or service; or

"(3) Takes or attempts to take more than the represented quantity of any commodity or service when as buyer he furnishes the weight or measure; or

"(4) Sells, offers or exposes for sale adulterated[2] commodities; or

"(5) Sells, offers or exposes for sale mislabeled[3] commodities."

Classification.

Class B misdemeanor.

Comments.

Subdivision (1) deals with false weights. Subdivision (3) extends the prohibition against the use or possession of false weights or measures to those who purchase commodities. Subdivision (2) deals with short weights. Injunctive relief, civil suits for damages, and revocation of licenses of the offending person or company may also be used to control improper sales.

Defenses.

"It shall be a defense to a prosecution under this section if the actor acts neither knowingly nor recklessly. The burden of injecting the issue is on the defendant, but this does not shift the burden of proof." Mental culpability must be shown, and strict liability is specifically rejected. § 13A-9-41(b) of the Alabama Code.

Cross references.

See, generally, §§ 2-12-2, 2-12-11, 2-3-12, 2-13-13, 2-13-20, 2-17-10, 2-19-1, 2-19-3, 2-22-3, 2-22-4, 2-22-7, 2-25-42, 2-26-13, 2-27-14, 2-27-16, 2-29-9, 8-16-91, 8-16-95, 8-16-96, 8-16-98, 8-16-104, 8-16-105, 8-17-24, 8-17-61, 8-17-83, 8-17-93, 8-17-111, 8-17-134, 8-17-139, 8-17-174, 20-1-5,

BUSINESS PRACTICES, DECEPTIVE.—Cont'd.

20-1-27, 20-1-28, 20-1-50 through 20-1-52, and 20-1-92 of the Alabama Code; Power of municipalities to provide public scales and inspection of weights and measures, § 11-47-17 of the Alabama Code; theft by deception defined, § 13A-8-1(1) of the Alabama Code.

---

1. *"Weight or measure is defined as any scale or mechanical measuring device." Code of Ala. 1975, § 8-16-1.*
2. *" 'Adulterated' means varying from the standard of composition or quality prescribed by statute or lawfully promulgated administrative regulation, or if none, as set by established commercial usage." Code of Ala. 1975, § 13A-9-41(c).*
3. *" 'Mislabeled' means:*

"(1) Varying from the standard of truth or disclosure in labeling prescribed by statute or lawfully promulgated administrative regulation, or if none, as set by established commercial usage; or

"(2) Represented as being another person's product, though otherwise labeled accurately as to quality and quantity." Code of Ala. 1975, § 13A-9-41(d). The provision also applies to all misbranding.

BUSINESS RECORDS, FALSIFYING. Code of Ala. 1975, § 13A-9-45.

Charged as: Falsifying business records.

"A person commits the crime of falsifying business records if, with intent to defraud,[1] he:

"(1) Makes or causes a false entry in the business records[2] of an enterprise;[3] or

"(2) Alters, erases, obliterates, deletes, removes or destroys a true entry in the business records of an enterprise when he knows the retention or preservation of a true entry is required by law independent of this section; or

"(3) Omits to make a true entry in the business records of an enterprise in violation of a duty to do so which he knows to be imposed upon him by law; or

"(4) Prevents the making of a true entry or causes the omission thereof in the business records of an enterprise when he knows a true entry is required by law independent of this section."

BUSINESS RECORDS, FALSIFYING. —Cont'd.

Classification.

Class B misdemeanor.

Comments.

An entity engaged in practically any activity except a governmental one[4] qualifies for the protection of its records under this section. This section requires proof of an intent to defraud. Protection is not for the records themselves. It is aimed at the prevention of contemplated frauds committed through the use of the falsified business records.

Defenses.

(1) Lack of intent.

(2) Lack of knowledge that the law requires such entry.

Cross references.

See FORGERY; GOVERNMENTAL RECORDS, TAMPERING WITH.

---

1. "A purpose to use deception, as defined in section 13A-8-1(1), or to injure another person's interest which has value, as defined in section 13A-8-1(14)." Code of Ala. 1975, § 13A-9-1(8).

2. " 'Business record' means any writing or article kept or maintained by an enterprise for the purpose of evidencing or reflecting its condition or activity." Code of Ala. 1975, § 13A-9-45(c).

3. " 'Enterprise' means any entity of one or more persons, corporate or otherwise, engaged in business, commercial, professional, industrial, eleemosynary, political or social activity." Code of Ala. 1975, § 13A-9-45(b).

4. See Code of Ala. 1975, § 13A-10-12.

CAPITAL PUNISHMENT. See DEATH PENALTY.

CARRYING CONCEALED WEAPONS. See WEAPONS, CARRYING CONCEALED.

CHANGE BILLS. Code of Ala. 1975, §§ 13A-9-19 and 13A-9-20.

"Any officer or agent of any private corporation or association or any other person who makes, emits, signs or countersigns, or causes or procures to be made, emitted, signed or countersigned, without authority of law, any paper to answer the purpose of money, or for general circulation, shall, on conviction, be fined not more than $500.00 and may also be imprisoned in the county jail or sentenced to hard labor for the county for not more than one year." § 13A-9-19 of the Alabama Code.

"Any person who passes or circulates in this state any paper issued without authority of law to answer the purpose of money shall, on conviction, be fined not less than $20.00 nor more than $100.00." § 13A-9-20 of the Alabama Code.

Classification.

Penalties provided in the statute (see above).

Comments.

These statutes make it a crime to produce or circulate any paper that serves the purpose of money. While no comment to the section exists, this section may outlaw scrip used earlier in this century in company towns and at company stores.

Query.

You might want to consider a plea to counterfeiting as an option.

CHILD, ABANDONMENT OF. Code of Ala. 1975, § 13A-13-5.

Charged as: Abandonment of child.

"A man or woman[1] commits the crime of abandonment of a child when, being a parent, guardian or other person legally charged with the care or custody of a child less than 18 years old, he or she deserts such child in any place with intent wholly to abandon it."

Classification.

Class A misdemeanor.

Comments.

Patterned after New York Revised Penal Law § 260.00, this Alabama law creates a separate offense, distinct from nonsupport (the elements of the later continuing offense need no longer be proved to sustain a conviction for abandonment as previously required by Crossley v. State, 25 Ala. App. 384, 145 So. 170 (1932)). The new law requires "intent to wholly abandon." The commentary suggests that abandonment by one parent, or by another party in loco parentis, is insufficient if another, in the same relationship to the child, remains.

CHILD, ABANDONMENT OF.—Cont'd.
Similarly, there must be an intent to "wholly abandon" at the time, that is, not to return.

Defenses.

(1) Lack of required relationship to the object child, or existence of legally related party whose presence indicates that the child is not abandoned.

(2) Child's legal disability removed. Cragford Bank v. Cummings, 113 So. 243, 216 Ala. 377 (1927); Donegan v. Davis, 66 Ala. 362 (1880).

(3) Lack of intent to abandon, or affirmatively, intent to return.

Cross references.

See CHILD WELFARE, ENDANGERING; JUVENILE PROCEEDINGS; NONSUPPORT.

---

1. So stated to indicate mother or other person may abandon.

CHILD, ENTICING FOR IMMORAL PURPOSES. Code of Ala. 1975, § 13A-6-69.

Charged as: Enticing child to enter vehicle, house, etc., for immoral purposes.

"It shall be unlawful for any person[1] with lascivious intent to entice, allure, persuade or invite, or attempt[2] to entice, allure, persuade or invite, any child under 16 years of age to enter any vehicle, room, house, office or other place for the purpose of proposing to such child the performance of an act of sexual intercourse or an act which constitutes the offense of sodomy or for the purpose of proposing the fondling or feeling of the sexual or genital parts of such child or the breast of such child, or for the purpose of committing an aggravated assault on such child, or for the purpose of proposing that such child fondle or feel the sexual or genital parts of such person."

Classification.

First conviction — Fine up to $5,000 and/or imprisonment up to 5 years.

Second conviction — Imprisonment from 2—10 years and not eligible for probation.

Comments.

There is some question as to the age of the person being charged and whether or not that could have some effect on the constitutionality of the statute. This is one of the very few crimes that includes, within its own description, the attempt to commit the crime.

Defenses.

(1) Did not have "lascivious" intent.

(2) It is not clear whether one can base a defense on the age of the actor (see query).

(3) Did not have purpose described in the statute.

Query.

Marcie, 15 years old, attempts to entice John, 15 1/4 years old, for any of the stated purposes. Would this fall under § 13A-6-69 of the Alabama Code? This could present a vagueness problem. Are persons married to each other excluded?

Cross references.

See INDECENT EXPOSURE; LEWDNESS, PUBLIC; SEXUAL ABUSE.

---

1. Although we can assume any sex, can we also assume any age?

2. This is one of the few crimes that includes its own attempt within its description.

CHILD SUPPORT, TREATMENT, ETC., FAILURE TO PAY. See CHILD, ABANDONMENT OF; CHILD WELFARE, ENDANGERING; JUVENILE PROCEEDINGS; NONSUPPORT.

CHILD WELFARE, ENDANGERING. Code of Ala. 1975, § 13A-13-6.

"A man or woman commits the crime of endangering the welfare of a child when:

"(1) He or she knowingly directs or authorizes a child less than 16 years of age to engage in an occupation involving a substantial risk of danger to his life or health; or

"(2) He or she, as a parent, guardian or other person legally charged with the care or custody of a child less than 18 years of age, fails to exercise reasonable diligence in the control of such child to prevent him or her from becoming a 'dependent child'[1] or a 'delinquent child' . . ."[2]

CHILD WELFARE, ENDANGERING.
—Cont'd.

Classification.

Class A misdemeanor.

Comments.

The statute prohibits a "person" from using child labor in an occupation involving a "substantial risk of danger" to the life or health of such a child. The use of the words "directs" and "authorizes" indicates that the class of person potentially culpable is not limited to parents or employers, but includes "any person" so empowered or situated. Secondly, this section is intended to make criminal the failure of parents **or** persons in loco parentis to discharge their legal duty of care and custody of the child. Culpability is based upon a person's failure to exercise "reasonable deligence" in fulfilling his duties in order to prevent the child from becoming a "dependent" or a "delinquent" child. The apparent intent of this section is to protect not only the child, but also the community and state.

The terms "remedial treatment," "spiritual means," "accredited practitioner," and "a recognized church" (see § 13A-13-6(b) of the Alabama Code) are undefined and await judicial interpretation.

Defenses.

(1) Lack of required relationship to the child or the existence of legally related party whose presence relieves the actor of the standard of care owing.

(2) Person charged did not knowingly direct or authorize the child to engage in such dangerous act.

(3) Age of the child does not meet statutory minimums.

(4) Occupation not normally considered dangerous.

(5) Parent exercised reasonable diligence.

(6) Parent is incapable of supervising due to alcoholism, mental state, etc.

(7) The child is under 19, and person charged has provided remedial treatment by spiritual means alone in accordance with the tenets and practices of a recognized church or religious denomination by a duly accredited practitioner in lieu of medical treatment.

CHILD WELFARE, ENDANGERING.
—Cont'd.

(8) There may be serious First Amendment questions concerning the individual rights of the child-citizens as against the sectarian privileges and traditions of the area.[3]

Query.

It is a defense to criminal culpability under this section (see § 13A-13-6(b) of the Alabama Code) if the "endangering" of the "welfare of the child" was under the auspices of a "religious accredited practitioner." Would this include a person having a child handle a poisonous snake to purge the child's sins or heal a particular ailment?

Cross references.

See CHILD, ABANDONMENT OF; JUVENILE PROCEEDINGS; NONSUPPORT.

---

1. "Dependent child. A child:

"a. Who, for any reason is destitute, homeless or dependent on the public for support; or

"b. Who is without a parent or guardian able to provide for his support, training or education; or

"c. Whose custody is the subject of controversy; or

"d. Whose home, by reason of neglect, cruelty or depravity on the part of his parent, parents, guardian or other person in whose care he may be, is an unfit and improper place for him; or

"e. Whose parent, parents, guardian or other custodian neglects or refuses, when able to do so or when such service is offered without charge, to provide or allow medical, surgical or other care necessary for such child's health or well-being; or

"f. Who is in such condition or surroundings or is under such improper or insufficient guardianship or control as to endanger his morals, health or general welfare; or

"g. Who has no proper parental care or guardianship; or

"h. Whose parent, parents, guardian or custodian fail, refuse or neglect to send such child to school in accordance with the terms of the compulsory school attendance laws of this state; or

"i. Who has been abandoned by his parents, guardian or other custodian; or

"j. Who is physically, mentally or emotionally abused by his parents, guardian or other custodian or who is without proper parental care and control necessary for his well-being because of the faults or habits of his parents, guardian or other custodian or their neglect or refusal, when

CHILD WELFARE, ENDANGERING. —Cont'd.

able to do so, to provide them; or

"k. Whose parents, guardian or other custodian are unable to discharge their responsibilities to and for the child; or

"l. Who has been placed for care or adoption in violation of the law; or

"m. Who for any other cause is in need of the care and protection of the state; and

"n. In any of the foregoing, is in need of care or supervision." Code of Ala. 1975, § 12-15-1(10).

2. "DELINQUENT CHILD. A child who has committed a delinquent act and is in need of care or rehabilitation." Code of Ala. 1975, § 12-15-1(9).

3. "A person does not commit an offense under section 13A-13-4 or section 13A-13-6 for the sole reason he provides a child under the age of 19 years or a dependent spouse with remedial treatment by spiritual means alone in accordance with the tenets and practices of a recognized church or religious denomination by a duly accredited practitioner thereof in lieu of medical treatment." Code of Ala. 1975, § 13A-13-6(b).

CHILDREN. See CHILD, ABANDONMENT; CHILD WELFARE, ENDANGERING; CIGARETTES, SELLING TO MINOR; JUVENILE PROCEEDINGS; NONSUPPORT; OBSCENE MATERIALS DISPLAYING OR DEPICTING CHILDREN; OBSCENE MATERIALS, SALE, EXHIBITION, ETC., TO MINORS; PISTOL, BOWIE KNIFE, SELLING TO MINORS.

CIGARETTES, SELLING TO MINOR. Code of Ala. 1975, § 13A-12-3.

Charged as: Selling cigarettes to minors.

It is a crime to sell, barter, exchange, or give to any minor any cigarettes, cigarette tobacco, or cigarette paper, or any substitute for either of them.

Classification.

A violation.[1]

Comments.

While there is no commentary to this statute, its apparent purpose is to keep minors from smoking until they reach the age of majority. In view of the number of cigarette machines in use and the inability to prevent their use by minors, this statute may have little practical effect.

Defenses.

(1) The recipient of the tobacco product was not a minor.

(2) The material acquired by the minor was not of the kind proscribed by the statute.

Query.

(1) Is marijuana a substitute for tobacco?

(2) Would the sale, barter, exchange, or gift of pipe tobacco and/or a pipe fall within the scope of the statute?

Cross references.

See Punishment and sentences generally, § 13A-5-1 of the Alabama Code; Punishment of offenses, § 13A-1-7 of the Alabama Code. See JUVENILE PROCEEDINGS.

---

1. On conviction, the defendant shall be fined not less than $10 nor more than $50 and/or imprisoned in the county jail or sentenced to hard labor for the county for not more than 30 days.

CLASSES OF CRIMES. See SENTENCING.

CLERGYMAN, FRAUDULENTLY PRETENDING TO BE. Code of Ala. 1975, § 13A-14-4.

Charged as: Fraudulently pretending to be clergyman.

It is a crime for any person, being in a public place, to fraudulently pretend by garb or outward array to be a minister of any religion, or nun, priest, rabbi or other member of the clergy.

Classification.

Unclassified misdemeanor with specific punishment of a fine not exceeding $500.00 and/or confinement in the county jail not to exceed one year.

Comments.

This law protects the integrity of the clergy. It may also be meant to discourage the use of such pretense within a confidence scheme. In this regard, the law is preemptive in character in that law enforcement officials can act prior to the completed act to arrest and punish the wrongdoer. On the other hand, the fact that

CLERGYMAN, FRAUDULENTLY PRETENDING TO BE.—Cont'd.

the statute is originally the product of the 1965 Executive Session may, when viewed in historical perspective, raise some question as to the purpose behind the statute and why it has been reenacted.[1]

Defenses.

(1) Not in a public place.

(2) Actually a member of the clergy.

Query.

What test is applicable to determine whether one is in fact a member of the clergy?

Cross references.

See IMPERSONATION, CRIMINAL.

---

*1. Code of Ala. 1975, § 13A-11-3, Commentary on Riot, states that "[i]n Cox v. Louisiana, 379 U.S. 559, 574 (1965), the United States Supreme Court declared: 'Nothing we have said here . . . is to be interpreted as sanctioning riotous conduct in any form or demonstrations, however peaceful their conduct or commendable their motives, which conflict with properly drawn statutes and ordinances designed to promote law and order, protect the community against disorder, regulate traffic, safeguard legitimate interests in private and public property, or protect the administration of justice and other essential governmental functions.' " However, the 60's revealed that many statutes were not properly drawn, nor were they designed to promote law and order, **but** were in fact utilized to violate civil rights.*

CLOSED MEETINGS. Code of Ala. 1975, § 13A-14-2.

Charged as: Executive or secret sessions of certain boards.

"No executive or secret session shall be held by any of the following named boards, commissions or courts of Alabama, namely: Alabama public service commission; school commissions of Alabama; board of adjustment; state or county tax commissions; any county commission, any city commission or municipal council; or any other body, board or commission in the state charged with the duty of disbursing any funds belonging to the state, county or municipality, or board, body or commission to which is delegated any legislative or judicial function; except, that executive or secret sessions may be held by any of the above named boards or commissions when the character or good name of a woman or man is involved."

Classification.

Misdemeanor and fined not less than $10.00 nor more than $500.00. Any person who remains in attendance upon any meeting of any of the above-named boards or bodies which is being held in secret or executive session shall be deemed guilty of violating the provisions of § 13A-14-2 of the Alabama Code.

Comments.

Although not inclusive, the state proscribes a specific list of entities that must comply with the requirements of this law. These are:

1. Alabama public service commission
2. School commissions of Alabama
3. Board of adjustment
4. State and county tax commissions
5. County commissions
6. City commissions or councils

A specific exception to the statute provides that it shall not be applicable in instances where the good name or character of an individual is involved.

Defenses.

(1) The character or good name of an individual was involved.

(2) Meeting was open.

(3) Defendant did not remain in attendance after learning about the nature of the meeting.

COAL (SALE AND DELIVERY OF) MIXED WITH OTHER SUBSTANCES OR MATERIALS OR WITH DIFFERENT QUALITY OF COAL. Code of Ala. 1975, § 13A-9-52.

"Any person who knowingly sells and delivers[1] any coal which has been mixed or loaded in the delivery container together with any substance or material other than coal or together with coal of a different quality with intent to defraud[2] the purchaser of such coal or with the intent to obtain a higher price for such coal by

COAL (SALE AND DELIVERY OF) MIXED WITH OTHER SUBSTANCES OR MATERIALS OR WITH DIFFERENT QUALITY OF COAL.—Cont'd.

inducing the purchaser to believe that such coal is of a higher quality or different quality than is actually delivered shall be guilty . . ."

Classification.

Class A misdemeanor, and shall, upon conviction, be fined not less than $100.00 nor more than $2,000.00 for each offense, and may also be imprisoned in the county jail for not more than one year for each offense.

Comments.

Only the special historical and economic significance of coal to Alabama provides a basis for this section since any action covered would also be covered by § 13A-9-41 of the Alabama Code (Deceptive business practices). It is interesting to note that an adulterated coal delivery carries a Class A misdemeanor penalty, while adulteration of other commodities carries a Class B misdemeanor penalty.

Defenses.

(1) Lack of intent.

(2) Lack of knowledge of incorrect mixture in delivery.

(3) Constitutional question of different penalty for one commodity in relation with all others.

Cross references.

See BUSINESS PRACTICES, DECEPTIVE.

---

1. *"For the purposes of this section, the sale and delivery of each delivery container shall constitute a separate offense. A delivery container is a truck, railroad car, barge or any other means or device by which coal is delivered to the purchaser. Sale and delivery is consummated when the container is accepted by the purchaser." Code of Ala. 1975, § 13A-9-52(b).*
2. *"A purpose to use deception, as defined in section 13A-8-1(1), or to injure another person's interest which has value, as defined in section 13A-8-1(14)." Code of Ala. 1975, § 13A-9-1(8).*

COCAINE. See CONTROLLED SUBSTANCES.

COCKFIGHTING OR KEEPING A COCKPIT. Code of Ala. 1975, § 13A-12-4.

Charged as: Keeping cockpit; cockfighting.

It is a crime for any person to keep a cockpit or who, in any public place, fights cocks.

Classification.

A violation.[1]

Comments.

Maintenance of a public or private cockpit under this statute is sufficient for conviction, whether or not the proscribed activity takes place therein. The statute is concerned only with the person who fights cocks, and the person who owns the cockpit. Those who gamble, encourage, or by indirect means perpetuate cockfighting are not within the scope of the statute. It is not a violation under this statute to own or possess a cock.

Defenses.

(1) The defendant does not own or keep a cockpit.

(2) The animals were not cocks within the meaning of this statute.

(3) The defendant was not engaged in fighting a cock.

Query.

(1) It would appear that one who fights cocks in a private place is outside the scope of this section.

(2) Is it possible for an area to have a dual purpose (e.g., barn stall used as a cockpit)?

Cross references.

See Punishment and sentences generally, § 13A-5-1 of the Alabama Code; Punishment of offenses, § 13A-1-7 of the Alabama Code. See SENTENCING.

---

1. *On conviction, the defendant shall be fined not less than $20 nor more than $50.*

COERCION. Code of Ala. 1975, § 13A-6-25.

Charged as: Criminal coercion.

"A person commits the crime of criminal coercion if, without legal authority, he threatens to confine, restrain or to cause physical injury to the threatened person or another, or to damage the property or reputation of the threatened person or another with intent thereby to induce the

COERCION.—Cont'd.

threatened person or another against his will to do an unlawful act or refrain from doing a lawful act."

Classification.

Class A misdemeanor.

Comments.

The conduct proscribed by this statute is intimidation designed to interfere with another's freedom of action. The extortion of money or property and the coercion of official behavior are treated as criminal in other provisions of this title. Note that successful intimidation is not required before the offense can be committed. It is not essential that the victim actually act or refrain from acting. Threat of harm to another is not limited to a threat of present harm, but includes a threat of imminent or future use of force.

Defenses.

(1) Person acts with legal authority.

(2) Listed acts committed, but without use of a threat.

(3) Lack of intent to induce the threatened person or another against his will to do an unlawful act or refrain from doing a lawful act.

(4) Even though there is a threat made with the intent to induce the threatened person to commit an act against his will, if the act sought to be committed is a lawful act, then the statute does not apply.

Query.

Where there is a threat to charge another with a crime with the honest belief that the threatened charge is true and the defendant's sole purpose is to induce reasonable action to correct the believed wrong, would the defendant fall within the scope of the statute?

Cross references.

See Theft and related offenses, extortion, §§ 13A-8-13 through 13A-8-15 of the Alabama Code; Threat, definition, § 13A-8-1(13)a. of the Alabama Code. See CONSPIRACY; EXTORTION; INTIMIDATING A JUROR; INTIMIDATING A WITNESS; ROBBERY.

COMMODITIES, TRANSPORTATION OF. Code of Ala. 1975, § 13A-11-221.

Charged as: Hindering transportation of commodities.

"A person commits the crime of hindering transportation of commodities if, intentionally and without lawful authority, he forcibly stops or hinders the operation of any vehicle transporting farm or commercial products within the state for the purpose of delaying the transportation or interfering with the loading or unloading of farm or commercial products."

Classification.

Class B misdemeanor.

Comments.

This section was introduced into the Alabama criminal law in 1977. Adopted from the Michigan Revised Criminal Code, most of its interpretation has been in that state. Violation of this statute would not preclude charges of violating other Alabama statutes regulating vehicles.[1] This statute supplements the interstate prohibitions and, theoretically, could be a separately punishable offense within one continuous criminal activity.

Defenses.

(1) Lack of intent.

(2) Lawful authority.[2]

(3) No use of force in stopping or hindering the operation of vehicle.

(4) Vehicle not transporting commodities described in the statute.

Cross references.

See MOTOR VEHICLE CRIMES.

---

1. *See Code of Ala. 1975, § 32-8-23 (unauthorized damaging or tampering with vehicles), making it a misdemeanor if anyone, willfully and without right to do so, damages or tampers with a vehicle or any of its parts or components; Code of Ala. 1975, § 13A-8-11 (unauthorized use of vehicles), in which one who intends to deprive the owner of his vehicle temporarily is guilty of a Class A misdemeanor.*

2. *Code of Ala. 1975, § 32-5A-4 provides that a police officer has authority to direct traffic and instruct vehicles to stop. See also Code of Ala. 1975, § 32-5A-193, making it a crime for the driver of a vehicle to flee or attempt to escape the police after the officer has signaled the driver to stop.*

COMPOUNDING. Code of Ala. 1975, § 13A-10-7.

"A person commits the crime of compounding if he gives or offers to give, or accepts or agrees to accept, any pecuniary benefit or other thing of value in consideration for:

"(1) Refraining from seeking prosecution of a crime; or

"(2) Refraining from reporting to law enforcement authorities the commission or suspected commission of any crime or information relating to the crime."

Classification.

Class A misdemeanor.

Comments.

This section forbids the acceptance of anything of value in return for a failure to seek prosecution or for a failure to report an actual or suspected crime. Crime is defined in § 13A-1-2(5) of the Alabama Code to include both felonies and misdemeanors. Apparently the person could be prosecuted for giving or accepting consideration even though the commentary states this section is limited to the person receiving the benefit.

Defenses.

(1) Benefit was restitution or indemnification.

(2) Victim reimbursement.

(3) It is a defense to a prosecution under this section that the pecuniary benefit did not exceed an amount which the actor reasonably believed to be due as restitution or indemnification for harm caused by the offense. But note the burden of injecting this defense is on the defendant.

Cross references.

BRIBERY OF PUBLIC SERVANTS; BRIBING A WITNESS; OBSTRUCTING GOVERNMENTAL OPERATIONS.

CONCEALED WEAPON. See WEAPONS, CARRYING CONCEALED.

CONFIDENTIAL INFORMATION, MISUSE OF. Code of Ala. 1975, § 13A-10-82.

Charged as: Misuse of confidential information.

CONFIDENTIAL INFORMATION, MISUSE OF.—Cont'd.

"A public servant[1] commits the crime of misuse of confidential information if in contemplation of official action by himself or by a governmental unit with which he is associated, or in reliance on information to which he has access in his official capacity and which has not been made public, he:

"(1) Acquires a pecuniary interest[2] in any property, transaction or enterprise which may be affected by such information or official action;

"(2) Speculates or wagers on the basis of such information or action; or

"(3) Aids another to do any of the foregoing."

Classification.

Class B misdemeanor.

Comments.

Misuse of confidential information for private gain is prohibited. This section addresses only the **acquisition** of private investments, and does not make illegal the **disposal** of private investments that are about to be affected by information not yet publicized. Administrative rules and regulations are considered more appropriate than the Criminal Code as a means of controlling public servants' investments that may become subject to an action of their governmental unit.

Defenses.

(1) Proof that information was actually known to the public.

(2) The interest acquired was not pecuniary.

(3) The defendant was not associated with the specific governmental unit that held confidential information.

Cross references.

See Dealing in state securities, § 40-1-25 of the Alabama Code.

---

1. *"Any officer or employee of government, including legislators and judges and any person or agency participating as an adviser, consultant or otherwise in performing a governmental function." Code of Ala. 1975, § 13A-10-1(7).*

2. *Pecuniary benefit is defined in Code of Ala. 1975, § 13A-10-60(b)(2) as a "[b]enefit in the form of money, property, commercial interests or anything else the primary significance of which is*

CONFIDENTIAL INFORMATION, MISUSE OF.—Cont'd.

economic gain. Expenses associated with social occasions afforded public servants and party officers shall not be deemed a pecuniary benefit within the meaning of this article."

CONFIDENTIAL INFORMATION, USE OR DISCLOSURE OF FOR PRIVATE FINANCIAL GAIN. Code of Ala. 1975, § 36-25-8.

"No public official or employee shall use or disclose confidential information gained in the course of or by reason of his position or employment in any way that could result in financial gain other than his regular salary as such state officer for himself, his family or for any other person."

Comments.

It should be noted that actual financial gain is not required. Thus, it would seem that we are looking for six elements:

(1) public official or employee
(2) uses or discloses
(3) confidential information
(4) gained through his employment
(5) that could result in a financial gain
(6) for him, his family, or any other person.

Defenses.

(1) The information was not confidential.
(2) That no financial gain could result.
(3) Not a public official or employee.
(4) Public official or employee did not use or disclose the information in question.
(5) Did not gain the information in question by reason of his position or employment.
(6) There was no gain for himself, his family, or any other person.

Query.

Since no actual gain is required, could the official or employee be found guilty of this offense where disclosure is a result of negligence?

Cross references.

See CONFIDENTIAL INFORMATION, MISUSE OF; CONFLICT OF INTEREST, FAILURE TO DISCLOSE; TRADING IN PUBLIC OFFICE.

CONFLICT OF INTEREST, FAILURE TO DISCLOSE. Code of Ala. 1975, § 13A-10-62.

CONFLICT OF INTEREST, FAILURE TO DISCLOSE.—Cont'd.

Charged as: Failure to disclose conflict of interest.

"A public servant[1] commits the crime of failing to disclose a conflict of interest if he exercises any substantial discretionary function in connection with a government[2] contract, purchase, payment or other pecuniary transaction without advance public disclosure[3] of a known potential conflicting interest[4] in the transaction."

Classification.

Class A misdemeanor.

Comments.

If a public servant is in a position to exercise "any substantial discretionary function," a disclosure of any potential conflicting interest should be made public. The official commentary notes that the general rule is that such situations are complicated and are best handled by civil and administrative remedies. Normally, these noncriminal sanctions should be entirely satisfactory.

(1) Failure of official to exercise any substantial discretionary function.
(2) Lack of knowledge.
(3) Conflict of interest present but not in connection with a **government** contract, purchase, payment, or other pecuniary transaction.

---

1. *Public servant "includes persons who presently occupy the position of a public servant, as defined in section 13A-10-7(7), or have been elected, appointed or designated to become a public servant although not yet occupying that position." Code of Ala. 1975, § 13A-10-60(b)(3).*
2. *"The state, county, municipality or other political subdivision thereof." Code of Ala. 1975, § 13A-10-1(2).*
3. *"Public disclosure include public announcement or notification to a superior officer or the attorney general." Code of Ala. 1975, § 13A-10-62(c).*
4. *"A 'potential conflicting interest' exists, but is not limited to, when the public servant is a director, president, general manager or similar executive officer, or owns directly or indirectly a substantial portion of any nongovernmental entity participating in the transaction." Code of Ala. 1975, § 13A-10-62(b).*

CONSENT. Code of Ala. 1975, § 13A-2-7.

Generally, "[t]he consent of the victim to conduct charged to constitute an offense or to the result thereof is a defense if such consent negatives a required element of the offense or precludes the infliction of the harm or evil sought to be prevented by the law defining the offense."

More specifically, § 13A-2-7(b) of the Alabama Code states that:

"When conduct is charged to constitute an offense because it causes or threatens bodily harm, consent to such conduct or to the infliction of such harm is a defense only if:

"(1) The bodily harm consented to or threatened by the conduct consented to is not serious; or

"(2) The conduct and the harm are reasonably foreseeable hazards of joint participation in a lawful athletic contest or competitive sport; or

"(3) The consent establishes a justification for the conduct under article 2 of chapter 3 of [Title 13A of the Alabama Code]."

On the other hand: "assent does not[1] constitute consent if:

"(1) It is given by a person who is legally incompetent to authorize the conduct; or

"(2) It is given by a person who by reason of immaturity, mental disease or defect, or intoxication is manifestly unable and known by the actor to be unable to make a reasonable judgment as to the nature or harmfulness of the conduct; or

"(3) It is given by a person whose consent is sought to be prevented by the law defining the offense; or

"(4) It is induced by force, duress or deception."[2] § 13A-2-7(c) of the Alabama Code.

Drafters note that courts have traditionally accepted consent as a defense to criminal liability in cases of insignificant injury where there is no public policy to the contrary. Participation in "acceptable" athletic events with established rules will not support a simple assault and battery charge although minor bodily harm is foreseeable. "Acceptable" sports do not include a private fist fight or any activity where the threatened bodily harm is serious.

Section 13-2-7(c)(3) of the Alabama Code applies to certain types of sexual misconduct where, as the offense is defined by statute, the victim's consent or lack thereof is irrelevant to the crime charged.

Cross references.

See Justification and excuse, §§ 13A-3-20 through 13-3-31 of the Alabama Code; Lack of consent, § 13A-6-70 of the Alabama Code; Responsibility, §§ 13A-3-1 through 13A-3-3 of the Alabama Code; Sexual offenses, §§ 13A-6-60 through 13A-6-70 of the Alabama Code. See ASSAULT; CHILD, ENTICING FOR IMMORAL PURPOSES; COERCION; ENTRAPMENT; FORCE BY PERSON WITH PARENTAL, CUSTODIAL, OR SPECIAL RESPONSIBILITIES; FORCE IN DEFENSE OF A PERSON; FORCE IN DEFENSE OF PREMISES; FORCE IN DEFENSE OF PROPERTY (OTHER THAN PREMISES); FORCE IN MAKING AN ARREST OR PREVENTING AN ESCAPE; FORCE IN RESISTING ARREST (PROHIBITED); IMMATURITY; INDECENT EXPOSURE; INSANITY; INTOXICATION; MENACING; PUBLIC DUTY; RAPE; RECKLESS ENDANGERMENT; SEXUAL ABUSE; SEXUAL MISCONDUCT; SODOMY.

---

1. *Unless otherwise provided by the Alabama Criminal Code or by the law defining the offense itself.*
2. *Bayett v. State, 42 Ala. App. 220, 159 So. 2d 628 (1964).*

CONSPIRACY. Code of Ala. 1975, § 13A-4-3.

"(a) A person is guilty of criminal conspiracy if, with the intent that conduct constituting an offense[1] be performed, he agrees with one or more persons to engage in or cause the performance of such conduct,[2] and any one or more of such persons does an overt act to effect an objective of the agreement.[3]

"(b) If a person knows or should know that

CONSPIRACY.—Cont'd.

one with whom he agrees has in turn agreed or will agree with another to effect the same criminal objective, he shall be deemed to have agreed[4] with such other person, whether or not he knows[5] the other's identity."

Classification.

According to § 13A-4-3(g) of the Alabama Code, "[c]riminal conspiracy is a:

"(1) Class A felony if an object of the conspiracy is murder.

"(2) Class B felony if an object of the conspiracy is a Class A felony.

"(3) Class C felony if an object of the conspiracy is a Class B felony.

"(4) Class A misdemeanor if an object of the conspiracy is a Class C felony.

"(5) Class B misdemeanor if an object of the conspiracy is a Class A misdemeanor.

"(6) Class C misdemeanor if an object of the conspiracy is a Class B misdemeanor.

"(7) Violation if an object of the conspiracy is a Class C misdemeanor."

Note: "Accomplice liability for offenses committed in furtherance of a conspiracy is to be determined as provided in section 13A-2-23." § 13A-4-3(f) of the Alabama Code.

Comments.

The crime of conspiracy, as it is generally known today, began its development in the seventeenth century.[6] Prior to that, combinations to procure false indictments were punishable, but only if the person falsely accused was actually indicted and acquitted.[7] By the 1600's, however, the law had begun to focus on the agreement itself, making it subject to punishment regardless of whether its purpose was achieved.[8]

Two primary objectives are said to be promoted by punishing a conspiracy. First, as an inchoate crime-like attempt, punishment of conspiracy enables law enforcement officials to halt criminal activity before a substantive crime is committed, thus protecting society from the greater harm of the substantive crime; second, it is argued that there is special danger inherent in group criminal activity. Group activity facilitates more complex kinds of crime, increases the likelihood of success, and multiplies the opportunities for other criminal activities.[9] In order to serve both state interests, the crime of conspiracy ordinarily is defined as including the actus reus of agreement between two or more people with a mens rea of an intent either to do an unlawful act or to do a lawful act by unlawful means. Judge Learned Hand dubbed conspiracy "the darling of the modern prosecutor's nursery"[10] because of the opportunities for abuse in the hands of an aggressive district attorney. The characterization is apt, given the often elusive nature of the agreement and the relaxed evidentiary rules associated with conspiracy. The crime also lends itself to joint trials at which one defendant is encouraged and facilitated in any attempts to convict co-conspirators.

Conspiracy in Alabama finds its importance as a theory connecting an individual as a party to a particular substantive offense. Under this theory, which has survived the new code,[11] a conspirator is a party to substantive offenses carried out by co-conspirators during the course of the conspiracy. This conspiracy/complicity rule is very common in the United States,[12] and its current validity under the Alabama Criminal Code is supported by the official comments following it.

In every conspiracy there is an agreement and an object offense or offenses toward which the conspiracy is directed. Despite the earlier common law rule to the contrary,[13] most states today declare that the conspiracy and the object offenses are separate and that there is no merger between a conspiracy and the completed substantive offense.[14] The rationale for this rule is that the dangers of group crime are separate from the dangers of the object offense; and, thus, in its conspiracy statute, the state is vindicating state interests separate from those that are protected by the object offense. Under the no-merger rule, acquittal of the object offense will not bar conviction for conspiracy and vice versa.[15] The most important result of the

CONSPIRACY.—Cont'd.

no-merger rule is that a defendant can be convicted and sentenced for both the conspiracy and the object offense even if the conspiracy was successfully carried out.[16]

While the commission of an overt act in furtherance of the conspiracy is not required in all jurisdictions,[17] this section does require the state to prove an overt act "to effect the object" of the conspiracy. Two aspects of the overt act requirement can be troublesome: first, does the evidence prove the existence of an overt act? second, how is the overt act requirement distinguishable from the required act of agreement?

Recent Alabama decisions,[18] while undoubtedly correct, lack a conceptual framework within which to analyze the question of whether there is a sufficient overt act. More difficult cases can be hypothesized. While cutting the telephone wires into a house in contemplation of a rape of the occupant is sufficient, would the act of purchasing wire cutters be sufficient? Would the telephoning of the hardware store to inquire of the availability of wire cutters be sufficient? No test has been offered by the courts that could be utilized to decide these more difficult cases. It is submitted that such a test is necessary if the overt act requirement is to serve its ostensible function of separating shared bad ideas from criminal conspiracies.[19]

It would appear that two alternative approaches could be taken in defining the standard for a finding of the presence of an overt act. The issue, of course, will arise when a conspiracy is detected at a very early stage and there has been immediate intervention. Courts in some states have required that such an act must be the beginning of the consummation of the object crime or satisfy an element of the offense, but the better reasoned view is that the act must merely be consistent with the criminal objective and intended to further that objective.[20]

It must be pointed out that a person may not only be found guilty of conspiracy with some person unknown to the police, but

CONSPIRACY.—Cont'd.

may in fact be guilty of conspiracy with someone unknown to himself.[21] While the notion that a person can enter into an agreement with a person he does not know may seem illogical, upon closer scrutiny the logic of the rule is apparent. In large criminal conspiracies, one person quite likely does not know all the other parties to the enterprise; nonetheless, an agreement impliedly exists between all such parties. In order for such an inference to be acceptable, however, the defendant actually must know either that he is participating in a large criminal enterprise or that the enterprise was of the sort which necessarily involves a large number of people. In this way it is inferred that a person who sells illicit drugs to the public knows that his supplier must either import or manufacture the drugs or be involved with someone who does. That knowledge on the part of the dealer is sufficient to include the dealer and the importer in a single conspiracy.[22]

Defenses.

Section 13A-4-3(c) of the Alabama Code provides that "[a] person is not liable under this section if, under circumstances manifesting a voluntary and complete renunciation of his criminal purpose, he gave a timely and adequate warning to law enforcement authorities or made a substantial effort to prevent the enforcement of the criminal conduct contemplated by the conspiracy. Renunciation by one conspirator, however, does not affect the liability of another conspirator who does not join in the abandonment of the conspiratorial objective. The burden of injecting the issue of renunciation is on the defendant, but this does not shift the burden of proof."

Section 13A-3-4(e) points out that "[a] conspirator is not liable under this section if, had the criminal conduct contemplated by the conspiracy actually been performed, he would be immune from liability under the law defining the offense or as an accomplice under section 13A-2-24."

However, of special interest are provisions (1), (2), and (3) set out in § 13A-4-3(d) of the

CONSPIRACY.—Cont'd.

Alabama Code, which state that "[i]t is no defense to a prosecution for criminal conspiracy that:

"(1) The person, or persons, with whom defendant is alleged to have conspired has been acquitted, has not been prosecuted or convicted, has been convicted of a different offense or is immune from prosecution, or

"(2) The person, or persons, with whom defendant conspired could not be guilty of the conspiracy or the object crime because of lack of mental responsibility or culpability, or other legal incapacity or defense, or

"(3) The defendant belongs to a class of persons who by definition are legally incapable in an individual capacity of committing the offense that is the object of the conspiracy."

It is also "no defense to a prosecution for criminal solicitation, . . . attempt, . . . or . . . criminal conspiracy, . . . that the offense . . . conspired was actually committed."[23] However, "[a] person may not be convicted on the basis of the same course of conduct of both the actual commission of an offense and:

"(1) An attempt to commit the offense; or

"(2) Criminal solicitation of the offense; or

"(3) Criminal conspiracy of the offense."[24]

And "[a] person may not be convicted of more than one of the offenses defined in sections 13A-4-1, 13A-4-2 and 13A-4-3 for a single course of conduct designed to commit or to cause the commission of the same crime."[25]

Finally, it should be noted that "[a] conspiracy formed in [Alabama] to do and act beyond [this] state, which, if done in this state, would be a criminal offense, is indictable and punishable in this state in all respects as if such conspiracy had been to do such act in this state."[26]

Cross references.

See ATTEMPT; GAMBLING, CONSPIRACY TO PROMOTE; SOLICITATION.

---

1. *U. S. v. Meacham, 626 F. 2d 503 (5th Cir. 1980) ("In order to successfully prosecute a conspiracy, the government must be able to point to two*

CONSPIRACY.—Cont'd.

separate provisions: one making act of conspiring a crime and one making the object of the conspiring a crime"); Pinkerton v. U. S., 145 F. 2d 252 (5th Cir. 1944) ("A conspiracy is . . . a combination of two or more persons, by concerted action, to accomplish a criminal or unlawful purpose, or some purpose not in itself criminal or unlawful, by criminal or unlawful means").

2. *U. S. v. Berry, 644 F. 2d 1034, (5th Cir. 1981) ("Although an agreement between the conspirators and the defendant is an essential element of the conspiracy conviction, the agreement may be inferred from the concert of action"); Mabry v. State, 110 So. 2d 250, 40 Ala. App. 129 (1959), certiorari dismissed, 268 Ala. 660, 110 So. 2d 260 (1959) ("In general a conspiracy comes into being 'when two or more persons enter upon an unlawful enterprise with a common purpose to aid, assist, advise, or encourage each other in whatever may grow out of the enterprise upon which they enter, each is responsible civilly and criminally for everything which may consequently and proximately result from such unlawful purpose, whether specifically contemplated or not, and whether actually perpetrated by all or less than all of the conspirators' ").*

3. *Kendrick v. State, 377 So. 2d 1112 (Ala. Cr. App. 1979), writ denied Ex parte Kendrick, 377 So. 2d 1114 (Ala. 1979) ("a common enterprise or adventure may be entered into on the spur of the moment without prearrangement and with no particular acts necessary"), Smith v. State, 368 So. 2d 298 (Ala. Cr. App. 1978), writ quashed Ex parte Smith, 368 So. 2d 305 (Ala. 1978) ("While a conspiracy involves a community of purpose, it may be formed in a flash or an instant without prearrangement. . . . The conspiratorial agreement may arise on the spur of the moment"); Hollingsworth v. State, 366 So. 2d 326 (Ala. Cr. App. 1978), certiorari denied 366 So. 2d 333 (Ala. 1979), quoting Howell v. State, 339 So. 2d 138 (Ala. Cr. App. 1976) ("A conspiracy necessary to fix guilt on all participants must be one in which all have a meeting of the minds, (though only for an instant) to commit the crime charged").*

4. *Williams v. State, 383 So. 2d 547 (Ala. Cr. App. 1979), affirmed Ex parte Williams, 383 So. 2d 564 (Ala. 1980), certiorari denied 449 U. S. 995, 101 S. Ct. 534, 66 L. Ed. 2d 293 (1980) ("Any word or act contributing to the commission of felony, intended to incite or encourage its accomplishment, makes one a coconspirator");*

CONSPIRACY.—Cont'd.

Neal v. State, 372 So. 2d 1331 (Ala. Cr. App. 1979), appeal after remand 372 So. 2d 1348 (Ala. Cr. App. 1979), writ denied Ex parte Neal, 372 So. 2d 1348 (Ala. 1979) ("It is well established that when, by prearrangement or on the spur of the moment, two or more persons enter upon a common enterprise or adventure and a criminal offense is contemplated, then each is a conspirator, and if the purpose is carried out, each is guilty of the offense committed, whether he did any overt act or not"); Casher v. State, 368 So. 2d 565 (Ala. Cr. App. 1979), writ denied Ex parte Casher, 368 So. 2d 567 (Ala. 1979) ("If the contemplated criminal purpose is carried out, each conspirator is guilty of the crime committed, whether or not he did any overt act in the active commission of the crime"); U. S. v. Bobo, 586 F. 2d 355 (5th Cir. 1978), certiorari denied Rowan v. U. S., 440 U. S. 976, 99 S. Ct. 1546, 59 L. Ed. 2d 795 (1979), rehearing denied 441 U. S. 957, 99 S. Ct. 2188, 60 L. Ed. 2d 1062 (1979) ("[P]resence alone is insufficient to establish participation in a conspiracy"; . . . "[O]nce having joined the conspiracy and not having withdrawn [the conspirator] cannot insulate himself from the actions of his coconspirators").

5. *U. S. v. DeLucca, 630 F. 2d 294 (5th Cir. 1980) ("In order to connect a defendant to a conspiracy, the prosecution must demonstrate that the defendant entered into an agreement with others knowingly and for the purpose of achieving an illegal objective"); U. S. v. Jordan, 627 F. 2d 683 (5th Cir. 1980) ("In order to be convicted of a conspiracy one must have knowledge of such conspiracy and must intend to join or associate himself with the objective of the conspiracy. . . . [The defendants] must be aware of the essential nature and scope of the enterprise and intend to participate"); U. S. v. Bobo, 586 F. 2d 355 (5th Cir. 1978), certiorari denied Rowan v. U. S., 440 U. S. 976, 99 S. Ct. 1546, 59 L. Ed. 2d 795 (1979), rehearing denied 441 U. S. 957, 99 S. Ct. 2188, 60 L. Ed. 2d 1062 (1979) ("[A] member of a conspiracy need not know of every transaction in the illegal scheme, so long as he knows of its general scope").*
6. *For an excellent overview of conspiracy, see LaFave and Scott, Criminal Law §§ 61-2 (1972) [hereinafter LaFave & Scott].*
7. *See Sayre, Criminal Conspiracy, 35 Harv. L. Rev. 393, 393—403 (1922).*
8. *Pulterers' Case, 77 Eng. Rep. 813 (1611).*
9. *See, generally, Callanan v. United States, 364 U. S. 587, 81 S. Ct. 321, 5 L. Ed. 2d 312 (1961).*

CONSPIRACY.—Cont'd.

10. *Harrison v. United States, 7 F. 2d 259, 263 (2d Cir. 1925).*
11. *Code of Ala. 1975, § 13A-4-3.*
12. *See Perkins, Criminal Law 684 (2d Ed. 1969).*
13. *At common law, the conspiracy was said to merge into the completed offense and could not be prosecuted. See People v. Tavormina, 257 N. Y. 84, 89-90, 177 N. E. 317, 318 (1931).*
14. *LaFave & Scott, § 62 at 494; Bassiouni, Substantive Criminal Law, Inchoate Crimes, § 3.6 at 222 (1978).*
15. *LaFave & Scott, § 62 at 494.*
16. *LaFave & Scott, § 62 at 494.*
17. *See LaFave & Scott, § 62 at 476.*
18. *See comments following Code of Ala. 1975, § 13A-4-3: "[W]hile Alabama presently does not require proof of an overt act as an element of conspiracy, such requirement has been added here. Its significance is to require proof beyond the bare agreement and, perhaps, to give more chance to defendant for renunciation, or abandonment, of his criminal intent." It would, thus, appear that this section is intended to side-step the strict requirements of Burk v. U. S., 134 F. 2d 879 (5th Cir. 1943) and Connelly v. State, 30 Ala. App. 91, 1 So. 2d 606 (1941), certiorari denied 241 Ala. 132, 1 So. 2d 608 (1941).*
19. *LaFave & Scott, § 62 at 477.*
20. *LaFave & Scott, § 62 at 477.*
21. *Notwithstanding the fact that "[p]ersons cannot conspire when they are not aware of one another's existence. United States v. Falcone, 311 U. S. 205 (1940)" (comments following this section), ". . . an agreement is possible although the parties are unaware of each other's particular identity. Blumenthal v. United States, 332 U. S. 539 (1947). When one joins an ongoing criminal enterprise he runs the risk of having an unknown number of associates. United States v. Andolscheck, 142 F. 2d 503 (2d Cir. 1944) (Judge Hand, 'He takes his chances.' ")*
22. *United States v. Bruno, 105 F. 2d 921 (2d Cir. 1939), rev'd on other grounds, 308 U. S. 287, 84 L. Ed. 257 (1939). See also State v. Clark, 14 Del. 536, 33 A. 310 (1891); James v. Monson, 137 Wis. 478, 119 N. W. 179 (1909) (civil conspiracy).*
23. *See Code of Ala. 1975, § 13A-4-5(a).*
24. *See Code of Ala. 1975, § 13A-4-5(b).*
25. *See Code of Ala. 1975, § 13A-4-5(c).*
26. *See Code of Ala. 1975, § 13A-4-4 ("conspiracy formed in this state to commit crime elsewhere indictable here").*

CONTEMPT. See JUDICIAL PROCEEDINGS, INTERFERENCE WITH.

CONTRABAND. See CONTROLLED SUBSTANCES; PRISON CONTRABAND, PROMOTING.

CONTRACTS BETWEEN STATE AGENCIES AND PUBLIC OFFICIALS OR EMPLOYEES PROHIBITED. Code of Ala. 1975, § 36-25-11.

Charged as: Entering into contracts with state agencies.

"Unless exempted under Alabama competitive bid laws or otherwise permitted to do so under law, no public official or employee, or a member of his family, and no business with which any of them is associated shall enter into any contract to provide goods or services which is to be paid in whole or in part out of state, county or municipal funds unless the contract has been awarded through a process of public notice and competitive bidding and a copy of such contract is filed with the commission."

Comments.

This section further provides that any contract to be allowed must not be the result of post bid negotiations.

Defenses.

(1) Exempted under Alabama competitive bid laws.

(2) The contract has been awarded through a process of public notice and competitive bidding, and a copy of such contract is filed with the commission.

(3) Permitted under law (the attorney should spend time reviewing the numerous exceptions possible under this charge).

(4) Not a public official or employee or family member of a public official or employee or in business with any public official or employee.

(5) Agreement did not constitute a contract.

(6) The contract was not to provide goods or services.

(7) No state, county, or municipal funds were to be used.

Cross references.

See CONFIDENTIAL INFORMATION, MISUSE OF; CONFLICT OF INTEREST, FAILURE TO DISCLOSE; ETHICS VIOLATIONS; TRADING IN PUBLIC OFFICE.

CONTRIBUTING TO THE DELINQUENCY OF A MINOR. See CHILD, ABANDONMENT OF; CHILD WELFARE, ENDANGERING; CIGARETTES, SELLING TO MINOR; JUVENILE PROCEEDINGS; NONSUPPORT; OBSCENE MATERIALS, SALE, EXHIBITION, ETC., TO MINORS; OBSCENE MATERIALS DISPLAYING OR DEPICTING CHILDREN; PISTOL, BOWIE KNIFE, SELLING TO MINORS.

CONTROLLED SUBSTANCES. Code of Ala. 1975, §§ 20-2-1 through 20-2-93.

Charged as: Prohibited acts A, § 20-2-70 of the Alabama Code.

"Except as authorized by [Chapter 2, Title 20 of the Alabama Code] any person who possesses, sells, furnishes, gives away, obtains or attempts to obtain by fraud, deceit, misrepresentation or subterfuge or by the forgery or alteration of a prescription or written order or by the concealment of material fact or by use of false name or giving a false address controlled substances enumerated in schedules I,[1] II,[2] III,[3] IV[4] and V[5] is guilty of a felony . . ."

Classification.

Felony and, upon conviction, for the first offense may be imprisoned for not less than two nor more than 15 years and, in addition, may be fined not more than $25,000.00, provided that any person who possesses any marijuana for his personal use only is guilty of a misdemeanor and, upon conviction for the offense, shall be imprisoned in the county jail for not more than one year, and in addition, shall be fined not more than

CONTROLLED SUBSTANCES.
—Cont'd.

$1,000.00 [for the first offense]. In addition, any person who violates this section with respect to a counterfeit substance enumerated in schedules I through V is guilty of a felony and, upon conviction, for the first offense may be imprisoned for not less than two nor more than 15 years and may be fined not more than $25,000.00.

Charged as: Prohibited acts B, § 20-2-71 of the Alabama Code.

"It is unlawful for any person:

"(1) Who is subject to [§§ 20-2-50 through 20-2-58 of the Alabama Code] to distribute or dispense a controlled substance in violation of section 20-2-58;

"(2) Who is a registrant to manufacture a controlled substance not authorized by his registration or to distribute or dispense a controlled substance not authorized by his registration to another registrant or other authorized person;

"(3) To refuse or fail to make, keep or furnish any record, notification, order form, statement, invoice or information required under this chapter; provided, however, that upon the first conviction of a violator under this provision said violator shall be guilty of a misdemeanor and shall be assessed a penalty of $1,000.00. Subsequent convictions shall subject the violator to the penalty provision set forth [under 'Classification' below];

"(4) To refuse an entry into any premises for any inspection authorized by this chapter; or

"(5) Knowingly to keep or maintain any store, shop, warehouse, dwelling, building, vehicle, boat, aircraft or other structure or place which is resorted to by persons using controlled substances in violation of this chapter for the purpose of using these substances or which is used for keeping or selling them in violation of [§§ 20-2-1 through 20-2-93 of the Alabama Code]."

Classification.

Felony and, upon conviction, may be imprisoned for not less than two nor more than 15 years and, in addition, may be fined not more than $25,000.00.

CONTROLLED SUBSTANCES.
—Cont'd.

Charged as: Prohibited acts C, § 20-2-72 of the Alabama Code.

"It is unlawful for any person:

"(1) To distribute as a registrant a controlled substance classified in schedules I[6] or II,[7] except pursuant to an order form as required by section 20-2-57;[8]

"(2) To use in the course of the manufacture or distribution of a controlled substance a registration number which is fictitious, revoked, suspended or issued to another person;

"(3) To acquire or obtain possession of a controlled substance by misrepresentation, fraud, forgery, deception or subterfuge;

"(4) To furnish false or fraudulent material information in or omit any material information from any application, report or other document required to be kept or filed under this chapter or any record required to be kept by this chapter; or

"(5) To make, distribute or possess any punch, die, plate, stone or other thing designed to print, imprint or reproduce the trademark, trade name or other identifying mark, imprint or device of another or any likeness of any of the foregoing upon any drug or container or labeling thereof so as to render the drug a counterfeit substance."

Classification.

A felony and, upon conviction, may be imprisoned for not less than two nor more than 15 years and, in addition, may be fined not more than $25,000.00.

Comments.

The fact that the person charged is a doctor, pharmacist, etc., is **not** a defense under this section.[9]

Possession of marijuana for personal use is not determined by the quantity involved.[10] (The smaller the quantity of marijuana possessed, of course, the more consistent it would be with personal use.)[11] In an appropriate case, possession for personal use only may constitute a lesser included offense.[12]

The defense attorney should be aware that in

CONTROLLED SUBSTANCES.
—Cont'd.

a narcotics prosecution possession of a controlled substance by an ultimate user or person in possession of a controlled substance pursuant to a lawful order of a practitioner does not constitute a violation of the Controlled Substances Act.[13] He should also be aware that in a prosecution for illegal possession of marijuana, there is a presumption that the possession is for other than personal use. The showing of possession for personal use is a defense, and the burden of proof is on the defendant.[14]

Defenses.

(1) Lack of knowledge by the accused of the presence of the controlled substance. This is an essential element and prerequisite to conviction for the offense of illegal possession of a controlled substance under the Alabama Controlled Substances Act,[15] and the mere presence of a defendant in an automobile is not sufficient to establish the requisite knowledge of the presence of the drug.[16]

(2) Lack of one of the three essential elements necessary for the proof of possession of controlled substances. Those elements are: (1) actual or potential physical control, (2) intention to exercise dominion, and (3) external manifestation of intent and control.[17]

(3) Where a person is in possession, but not exclusive possession of premises, it may not be inferred that he knew of the presence of any controlled substance found there unless there are other circumstances tending to buttress this inference.[18]

(4) While nonexclusive possession may raise the suspicion that all occupants had knowledge of the contraband found, a mere suspicion is not enough; what is required is some evidence that connects the defendant with the contraband that is found.[19]

Cross references.

For D.W.I./D.U.I. see MOTOR VEHICLE CRIMES; PRISON CONTRABAND, PROMOTING.

---

1. *"The state board of health shall place a substance in schedule I if it finds that the substance:*
"(1) Has high potential for abuse; and

CONTROLLED SUBSTANCES.
—Cont'd.

"(2) Has no accepted medical use in treatment in the United States or lacks accepted safety for use in treatment under medical supervision." Code of Ala. 1975, § 20-2-22.

Code of Ala. 1975, § 20-2-23 presents a listing of schedule I controlled substances:

"(1) Any of the following opiates, including their isomers, esters, ethers, salts, and salts of isomers, esters and ethers, unless specifically excepted, whenever the existence of these isomers, esters, ethers and salts is possible within the specific chemical designation:

a. Acetylmethadol;
b. Allylprodine;
c. Alphacetylmethadol;
d. Alphameprodine;
e. Alphamethadol;
f. Benzethidine;
g. Betacetylmethadol;
h. Betameprodine;
i. Betamethadol;
j. Betaprodine;
k. Clonitazene;
l. Dextromoramide;
m. Dextrorphan;
n. Diampromide;
o. Diethylthiambutene;
p. Dimenoxadol;
q. Dimepheptanol;
r. Dimethylthiambutene;
s. Dioxaphetyl butyrate;
t. Dipipanone;
u. Ethylmethylthiambutene;
v. Etonitazene;
w. Etoxeridine;
x. Furethidine;
y. Hydroxpethidine;
z. Ketobemidone;
aa. Levomoramide;
bb. Levophenacylmorphan;
cc. Morpheridine;
dd. Noracymethadol;
ee. Norlevorphanol;
ff. Normethadone;
gg. Norpipanone;
hh. Phenadoxone;
ii. Phenampromide;
jj. Phenomorphan;
kk. Phenoperidine;
ll. Piritramide;
mm. Proheptazine;
nn. Properidine;
oo. Racemoramide;
pp. Trimeperidine.

CONTROLLED SUBSTANCES.
—Cont'd.

"(2) Any of the following opium derivatives, their salts, isomers and salts of isomers, unless specifically excepted, whenever the existence of these salts, isomers and salts of isomers is possible within the specific chemical designation:

a. Acetorphine;
b. Acetyldihydrocodeine;
c. Benzylmorphine;
d. Codeine methylbromide;
e. Codeine-N-Oxide;
f. Cyprenorphine;
g. Desomorphine;
h. Dihydromorphine;
i. Etorphine;
j. Heroin;
k. Hydromorphinol;
l. Methyldesorphine;
m. Methyldihydromorphine;
n. Morphine methylbromide;
o. Morphine methylsulfonate;
p. Morphine-N-Oxide;
q. Myrophine;
r. Nicocodeine;
s. Nicomorphine;
t. Normorphine;
u. Pholcodine;
v. Thebacon.

"(3) Any material, compound, mixture or preparation which contains any quantity of the following hallucinogenic substances, their salts, isomers and salts of isomers, unless specifically excepted, whenever the existence of these salts, isomers and salts of isomers is possible within the specific chemical designation:

a. 3,4-methylenedioxy amphetamine;
b. 5-methoxy-3,4-methylenedioxy amphetamine;
c. 3,4,5-trimethoxy amphetamine;
d. Bufotenine;
e. Diethyltryptamine;
f. Dimethyltryptamine;
g. 4-methyl-2,5-dimethoxyamphetamine;
h. Ibogaine;
i. Lysergic acid diethylamide;
j. Marihuana;
k. Mescaline;
l. Peyote;
m. N-ethyl-3-piperidyl benzilate;
n. N-methyl-3-piperidyl benzilate;
o. Psilocybin;
p. Psilocyn;
q. Tetrahydrocannabinols."

2. "The state board of health shall place a substance in schedule II if it finds that:

CONTROLLED SUBSTANCES.
—Cont'd.

"(1) The substance has high potential for abuse;
"(2) The substance has currently accepted medical use in treatment in the United States or currently accepted medical use with severe restrictions; and
"(3) The abuse of the substance may lead to severe psychic or physical dependence." Code of Ala. 1975, § 20-2-24.

Code of Ala. 1975, § 20-2-25 presents a listing of schedule II controlled substances as follows:

"(1) Any of the following substances, except those narcotic drugs listed in other schedules, whether produced directly or indirectly by extraction from substances of vegetable origin or independently by means of chemical synthesis or by combination of extraction and chemical synthesis:

"a. Opium and opiate and any salt, compound, derivative or preparation of opium or opiate.
"b. Any salt, compound, isomer, derivative or preparation thereof which is chemically equivalent or identical with any of the substances referred to in paragraph a, but not including the isoquinoline alkaloids of opium.
"c. Opium poppy and poppy straw.
"d. Coca leaves and any salt, compound, derivative or preparation of coca leaves and any salt, compound, derivative or preparation thereof which is chemically equivalent or identical with any of these substances, but not including decocainized coca leaves or extractions which do not contain cocaine or ecgonine.

"(2) Any of the following opiates, including their isomers, esters, ethers, salts and salts of isomers, whenever the existence of these isomers, esters, ethers and salts is possible within the specific chemical designation:

a. Alphaprodine;
b. Anileridine;
c. Bezitramide;
d. Dihydrocodeine;
e. Diphenoxylate;
f. Fentanyl;
g. Isomethadone;
h. Levomethorphan;
i. Levorphanol;
j. Metazocine;
k. Methadone;
l. Methadone—Intermediate, 4-cyano-2-dimethylamino-4, 4-diphenylbutane;
m. Moramide—Intermediate, 2-methyl-3-morpholino-1, 1-diphenyl-propane-carboxylic acid;
n. Pethidine;

CONTROLLED SUBSTANCES.
—Cont'd.

o. Pethidine—Intermediate-A, 4-cyano-1-methyl-4-phenylpiperidine;
p. Pethidine—Intermediate-B, ethyl-4-phenylpiperidine-4-carboxylate;
q. Pethidine—Intermediate-C, 1-methyl-4-phenylpiperidine-4-carboxylic acid;
r. Phenazocine;
s. Piminodine;
t. Racemethorphan;
u. Racemorphan."

3. "The state board of health shall place a substance in schedule III if it finds that:
"(1) The substance has a potential for abuse less than the substances listed in schedules I and II;
"(2) The substance has currently accepted medical use in treatment in the United States; and
"(3) Abuse of the substance may lead to moderate or low physical dependence or high psychological dependence." Code of Ala. 1975, § 20-2-26.
Code of Ala. 1975, § 20-2-27 presents a listing of schedule III controlled substances as follows:
"(1) Any material, compound, mixture or preparation which contains any quantity of the following substances having a potential for abuse associated with a stimulant effect on the central nervous system:
a. Amphetamine, its salts, optical isomers and salts of its optical isomers;
b. Phenmetrazine and its salts;
c. Any substance which contains any quantity of methamphetamine, including its salts, isomers and salts of isomers;
d. Methylphenidate.
"(2) Unless listed in another schedule, any material, compound, mixture or preparation which contains any quantity of the following substances having a potential for abuse associated with a depressant effect on the central nervous system:
a. Any substance which contains any quantity of a derivative of barbituric acid, or any salt of a derivative of barbituric acid, except those substances which are specifically listed in other schedules;
b. Chlorhexadol;
c. Glutethimide;
d. Lysergic acid;
e. Lysergic acid amide;
f. Methyprylon;
g. Phencyclidine;
h. Sulfondiethylmethane;
i. Sulfonethylmethane;
j. Sulfonmethane.

CONTROLLED SUBSTANCES.
—Cont'd.

"(3) Nalorphine.
"(4) Any material, compound, mixture or preparation containing limited quantities of any of the following narcotic drugs or any salts thereof:
"a. Not more than 1.8 grams of codeine or any of its salts, per 100 milliliters or not more than 90 milligrams per dosage unit, with an equal or greater quantity of an isoquinoline alkaloid of opium;
"b. Not more than 1.8 grams of codeine or any of its salts per 100 milliliters or not more than 90 milligrams per dosage unit, with one or more active, nonnarcotic ingredients in recognized therapeutic amounts;
"c. Not more than 300 milligrams of dihydrocodeinone or any of its salts per 100 milliliters or not more than 15 milligrams per dosage unit, with a fourfold or greater quantity of an isoquinoline alkaloid of opium;
"d. Not more than 300 milligrams of dihydrocodeinone or any of its salts per 100 milliliters or not more than 15 milligrams per dosage unit, with one or more active, nonnarcotic ingredients in recognized therapeutic amounts;
"e. Not more than 1.8 grams of dihydrocodeine or any of its salts per 100 milliliters or not more than 90 milligrams per dosage unit, with one or more active, nonnarcotic ingredients in recognized therapeutic amounts;
"f. Not more than 300 milligrams of ethylmorphine or any of its salts per 100 milliliters or not more than 15 milligrams per dosage unit, with one or more ingredients in recognized therapeutic amounts;
"g. Not more than 500 milligrams of opium per 100 milliliters or per 100 grams or not more than 25 milligrams per dosage unit, with one or more active, nonnarcotic ingredients in recognized therapeutic amounts;
"h. Not more than 50 milligrams of morphine or any of its salts per 100 milliliters or per 100 grams with one or more active, nonnarcotic ingredients in recognized therapeutic amounts." However, it should be pointed out that "[t]he state board of health may except by rule any compound, mixture or preparation containing any stimulant or depressant substance listed in [Code of Ala. 1975, §§ 20-2-27(a)(1) and (2)] from the application of all or any part of this chapter if the compound, mixture or preparation contains one or more active medicinal ingredients not having a stimulant or depressant effect on the central nervous system and if the admixtures are

CONTROLLED SUBSTANCES.
—Cont'd.

included therein in combinations, quantity, proportion or concentration that vitiate the potential for abuse of the substances which have a stimulant or depressant effect on the central nervous system." See Code of Ala. 1975, § 20-2-27(b).

4. *"The state board of health shall place a substance in schedule IV if it finds that:*
"(1) The substance has a low potential for abuse relative to substances in schedule III [see note 3, supra];
"(2) The substance has currently accepted medical use in treatment in the United States; and
"(3) Abuse of the substance may lead to limited physical dependence or psychological dependence relative to the substances in schedule III [see note 3, supra]." Code of Ala. 1975, § 20-2-28.
Code of Ala. 1975, § 20-2-29 presents a listing of schedule IV controlled substances, as follows:
"Any material, compound, mixture or preparation which contains any quantity of the following substances having a potential for abuse associated with a depressant effect on the central nervous system:
a. Barbital;
b. Chloral betaine;
c. Chloral hydrate;
d. Ethchlorvynol;
e. Ethinamate;
f. Methodhexital;
g. Meprobamate;
h. Methylphenobarbital;
i. Paraldehyde;
j. Petrichloral;
k. Phenobarbital."
However, Code of Ala. 1975, § 20-2-29(b) points out that "[t]he state board of health may except by rule any compound, mixture or preparation containing any depressant substance listed in subsection (a) from the application of all or any part of this chapter if the compound, mixture or preparation contains one or more active medicinal ingredients not having a depressant effect on the central nervous system and if the admixtures are included therein in combinations, quantity, proportion or concentration that vitiate the potential for abuse of the substances which have a depressant effect on the central nervous system."

5. *"The state board of health shall place a substance in schedule V if it finds that:*
"(1) The substance has low potential for abuse relative to the controlled substances listed in schedule IV [see note 4, supra];
"(2) The substance has currently accepted medical use in treatment in the United States; and
"(3) The substance has limited physical dependence or psychological dependence liability relative to the controlled substances listed in schedule IV [see note 4, supra]." Code of Ala. 1975, § 20-2-30.
Code of Ala. 1975, § 20-2-31 presents a listing of schedule V controlled substances as follows:
"Any compound, mixture or preparation containing limited quantities of any of the following narcotic drugs, which also contains one or more nonnarcotic active medicinal ingredients in sufficient proportion to confer upon the compound, mixture or preparation valuable medicinal qualities other than those possessed by the narcotic drug alone:
"a. Not more than 200 milligrams of codeine or any of its salts per 100 milliliters or per 100 grams;
"b. Not more than 100 milligrams of dihydrocodeine or any of its salts per 100 milliliters or per 100 grams;
"c. Not more than 100 milligrams of ethylmorphine or any of its salts per 100 milliliters or per 100 grams;
"d. Not more than 2.5 milligrams of dephenozylate and not less than 25 micrograms of atropine sulfate per dosage unit;
"e. Not more than 100 milligrams of opium per 100 milliliters or per 100 grams."

6. *See note 1, supra.*
7. *See note 2, supra.*
8. *"Controlled substances in schedules I [see note 1, supra] and II [see note 2, supra] shall be distributed by a registrant to another registrant only pursuant to an order form. Compliance with the provisions of federal law respecting order forms shall be deemed compliance with this section."*
9. *Chesteen v. State, 365 So. 2d 102 (Ala. Crim. App. 1978), cert. denied, 365 So. 2d 108 (Ala. 1978).*
10. *See Butts v. State, 346 So. 2d 497 (Ala. App. 1977), cert. denied, 346 So. 2d 500 (Ala. 1977); Lee v. State, 350 So. 2d 743 (Ala. Crim. App. 1977); Roberts v. State, 349 So. 2d 89 (Ala. Crim. App. 1977), cert. denied, 349 So. 2d 94 (Ala. 1977); Lee v. State, 350 So. 2d 743 (Ala. Crim. App. 1977); Coleman v. State, 344 So. 2d 1249 (Ala. Crim. App. 1977); Law v. State, 342 So. 2d 412 (Ala. Crim. App. 1976), cert. denied, 342 So.*

CONTROLLED SUBSTANCES.
—Cont'd.

2d 413 (Ala.), cert. denied, 434 U. S. 919, 98 S. Ct. 392, 54 L. Ed. 2d 276 (1977).

11. *Roberts v. State, 349 So. 2d 89 (Ala. Crim. App. 1977), cert. denied, 349 So. 2d 94 (Ala. 1977).*
12. *Brisbon v. State, 378 So. 2d 743 (Ala. Crim. App. 1979).*
13. *Walker v. State, 358 So. 2d 800 (Ala. Crim. App. 1978); Temple v. State, 366 So. 2d 740 (Ala. Crim. App. 1978); Roberts v. State, 349 So. 2d 89 (Ala. Crim. App. 1977), cert. denied, 349 So. 94 (Ala. 1977).*
14. *Barnett v. State, 373 So. 2d 1226 (Ala. Crim. App. 1979); Lee v. State, 350 So. 2d 743 (Ala. Crim. App. 1977); Roberts v. State, 349 So. 2d 89 (Ala. Crim. App. 1977), cert. denied, 349 So. 2d 94 (Ala. 1977).*
15. *Temple v. State, 366 So. 2d 740 (Ala. Crim. App. 1978).*
16. *Roberts v. State, 349 So. 2d 89 (Ala. Crim. App. 1977), cert. denied, 349 So. 2d 94 (Ala. 1977). It should be noted that defendant's presence in an automobile in which drugs were found, where coupled with the evidence of his ownership, dominion, and complete control over the vehicle, his state of intoxication without the odor of alcoholic beverages, his known past involvement with drugs, and the location of the drugs in the rear engine compartment of the appellant's vehicle constituted circumstantial evidence of the appellant's knowledge and possession of the drugs; where there is not evidence that someone other than defendant had recent access to the rear compartment where the drugs were found, trial court properly submitted the issue to the jury. Reed v. State, 368 So. 2d 326 (Ala. Crim. App. 1979).*
17. *Lee v. State, 350 So. 2d 743 (Ala. Crim. App. 1977).*
18. *Temple v. State, 366 So. 2d 740 (Ala. Crim. App. 1978).*
19. *Temple v. State, 366 So. 2d 740 (Ala. Crim. App. 1978).*

CONTROLLED SUBSTANCES — DRUG PARAPHERNALIA; SALE, DISTRIBUTION, ADVERTISEMENT, ETC. Code of Ala. 1975, § 20-2-75.

It shall be unlawful for any person or corporation, knowing[1] the drug related nature of the object, to:

(1) sell, lend, rent, lease, give, exchange, or otherwise distribute to any person any drug related object,[2] or

(2) to display for sale, or possess with the intent to distribute, any drug related object,[3] or

(3) to distribute or disseminate in any manner to any person any advertisement of any kind or notice of any kind which gives information, directly or indirectly, on where, or how, or from whom, or by what means any drug related object[4] may be obtained or made. See § 20-2-75(b) of the Alabama Code.

Classification.

Class A misdemeanor, first offense.

Class C felony, second offense.

Comments.

"All instruments, devices, and objects which are distributed or possessed in violation of this section are hereby declared to be contraband and subject to forfeiture as provided for in section 20-2-93." § 20-2-75(f) of the Alabama Code.

Defenses.

(1) Recipient of drug related object has a prescription from a licensed medical practitioner or psychiatrist for the controlled substance for which the object is primarily intended to be used.

(2) Hypodermic syringe or needle was:

(a) dispensed by a licensed pharmacist or practitioner licensed to dispense legal drugs, or

(b) was marketed for a legitimate medical purpose.

(3) Drug related object was designed or marketed as useful primarily for veterinary or agricultural purposes.

---

1. *"'Knowing' . . . means either actual or constructive knowledge of the drug related nature of the object, and a person or corporation has constructive knowledge of the drug related nature of the object if he or it has knowledge of facts which would put a reasonable and prudent person on notice of the drug related nature of the object." Code of Ala. 1975, § 20-2-75(b).*

CONTROLLED SUBSTANCES — DRUG PARAPHERNALIA; SALE, DISTRIBUTION, ADVERTISEMENT, ETC.—Cont'd.

2. *" 'Drug related object' means any instrument, device, or object which is designed, produced or marketed as useful primarily for one or more of the following purposes:*
"(1) To inject, ingest, inhale, or otherwise introduce into the human body marijuana or a controlled substance;
"(2) To enhance the effect on the human body of marijuana or a controlled substance;
"(3) To test the strength, effectiveness, or purity of marijuana or a controlled substance;
"(4) To process or prepare for introduction into the human body marijuana or a controlled substance;
"(5) To conceal any quantity of marijuana or a controlled substance;
"(6) To contain or hold marijuana or a controlled substance while it is being introduced into the human body." Code of Ala. 1975, § 20-2-75(a).
3. *See note 2, supra.*
4. *See note 2, supra.*

CONTROLLED SUBSTANCES — FORFEITURES AND SEIZURES.
Code of Ala. 1975, § 20-2-93.

As a final note, the defense attorney should be aware of the fact that in addition to other penalties,

"(a) The following are subject to forfeiture:

"(1) All controlled substances which have been manufactured, distributed, dispensed or acquired in violation of [the Controlled Substances Act];

"(2) All raw materials, products and equipment of any kind which are used or intended for use in manufacturing, compounding, processing, delivering, importing or exporting any controlled substance in violation of [the Controlled Substances Act];

"(3) All property which is used or intended for use as a container for property described in subdivisions (1) or (2) of this subsection;

* * *

"(5) All conveyances, including aircraft, vehicles or vessels, which are used or intended for use to transport in any manner to facilitate the transportation for the

CONTROLLED SUBSTANCES — FORFEITURES AND SEIZURES.—Cont'd.

purpose of sale or receipt of property described in subdivisions (1) or (2) of this subsection; provided, however that:

"a. No conveyance used by any person as a common carrier in the transaction of business as a common carrier is subject to forfeiture under this section unless it appears that the owner or other person in charge of the conveyance is a consenting party or privy to a violation of [the Controlled Substances Act];

"b. No conveyance is subject to forfeiture under this section by reason of any act or omission established by the owner thereof to have been committed or omitted without his knowledge or consent; and

"c. A forfeiture of a conveyance encumbered by a bona fide security interest is subject to the interest of the secured party if he neither had knowledge of nor consented to the act or omission;

"(6) All books, records and research products and materials, including formulas, microfilm, tapes and data, which are used or intended for use in violation of [the Controlled Substances Act].

"(b) Property subject to forfeiture under this chapter may be seized by state, county or municipal law enforcement agencies upon process issued by any court having jurisdiction over the property. Seizure without process may be made if:

"(1) The seizure is incident to an arrest or a search under a search warrant or an inspection under an administrative inspection warrant;

"(2) The property subject to seizure has been the subject of a prior judgment in favor of the state in a criminal injunction or forfeiture proceeding based upon [the Controlled Substances Act];

"(3) The state, county or municipal law enforcement agency has probable cause to believe that the property is directly or indirectly dangerous to health or safety; or

"(4) The state, county or municipal law enforcement agency has probable cause to

CONTROLLED SUBSTANCES — FORFEITURES AND SEIZURES.—Cont'd.

believe that the property was used or is intended to be used in violation of [the Controlled Substances Act].

* * *

"(d) Property taken or detained under this section shall not be subject to replevin but is deemed to be in the custody of the state, county or municipal law enforcement agency subject only to the orders and judgment of the court having jurisdiction over the forfeiture proceedings. When property is seized under [the Controlled Substances Act], the state, county or municipal law enforcement agency may:

"(1) Place the property under seal;

"(2) Remove the property to a place designated by it;

"(3) Require the state, county or municipal law enforcement agency to take custody of the property and remove it to an appropriate location for disposition in accordance with law.

"(e) When property is forfeited under this chapter the state, county or municipal law enforcement agency may:

"(1) Retain it for official use; . . .

"(2) Sell that which is not required to be destroyed by law and which is not harmful to the public. The proceeds from the sale authorized by this subsection shall be used, first, for payment of all proper expenses of the proceedings for forfeiture and sale, including expenses of seizure, maintenance of or custody, advertising and court costs; and the remaining proceeds from such sale shall be awarded and distributed by the court to the municipal, and/or county, and/or state general fund whose law enforcement agencies or departments are determined by the court to have been a participant in the investigation resulting in the seizure, and such award and distribution shall be made on the basis of the percentage as determined by the court, which the respective agency or department contributed to the police work resulting in

CONTROLLED SUBSTANCES — FORFEITURES AND SEIZURES.—Cont'd.

the seizure;

"(3) Require the state, county or municipal law enforcement agency to take custody of the property and remove it for disposition in accordance with law.

"(f) Controlled substance listed in schedule I[1] that are possessed, transferred, sold or offered for sale in violation of this chapter are contraband and shall be seized and summarily forfeited to the state. Controlled substances listed in schedule I which are seized or come into the possession of the state, the owners of which are unknown, are contraband and shall be summarily forfeited to the state.

"(g) Species of plants from which controlled substances in schedules I[2] and II[3] may be derived which have been planted or cultivated in violation of this chapter or of which the owners or cultivators are unknown or which are wild growths may be seized and summarily forfeited to the state."

Finally, as a possible general defense the attorney should be aware that under § 20-2-114 of the Alabama Code (unless excepted) ". . . the controlled substances therapeutic research program[4] shall be [applicable, although] limited to cancer chemotherapy patients and glaucoma patients, who are certified to the review committee by an authorized practitioner as being in such medical condition necessary for the treatment of glaucoma, or the side effects of chemotherapy in cancer patients; such authorization shall be upon such terms and conditions as may be consistent with the public health and safety. To the extent of the applicable authorization, persons are exempt from prosecution in Alabama for possession, production, manufacture or delivery of cannabis."

---

1. *For a list of schedule I controlled substances, see note 1 under CONTROLLED SUBSTANCES, supra.*

CONTROLLED SUBSTANCES — FORFEITURES AND SEIZURES.—Cont'd.

2. *For a list of schedule I controlled substances, see note 1 under CONTROLLED SUBSTANCES, supra.*
3. *For a list of schedule II controlled substances, see note 2 under CONTROLLED SUBSTANCES, supra.*
4. *Code of Ala. 1975, § 20-2-113 establishes "... by the state board of medical examiners the controlled substances therapeutic research program. The board shall administer the program by a review committee. The board shall promulgate such rules and regulations as are necessary for the proper administration and implementation of the program. Such promulgations shall be formulated to consider those pertinent rules and regulations promulgated by the federal drug enforcement agency, food and drug administration and the national institute on drug abuse."*

CONTROLLED SUBSTANCES — USE BY VETERINARIANS AND DENTISTS. Code of Ala. 1975, § 20-2-74.

"It shall be unlawful for any practitioner of dentistry to prescribe, administer or dispense any controlled substance enumerated in schedules I through V[1] for any person not under his treatment in his regular practice of his profession or for any practitioner of veterinary medicine to prescribe, administer or dispense any controlled substance enumerated in schedules I through V for the use of human beings; provided, however, that the provisions of this section shall be construed not to prevent any lawfully authorized practitioner of medicine from furnishing or prescribing in good faith for the use of any habitual user of substances enumerated in schedules I through V who is under his professional care such substances as he may deem necessary for their treatment, when such prescriptions are not given or substances furnished for the purpose of maintaining addiction or abuse."

Classification.

Any person who violates this section shall be guilty of a felony and shall, on conviction thereof, be subject to imprisonment for not less than two nor more than 15 years.

Comments.

Section 20-2-74 of the Alabama Code makes it unlawful for a dentist to prescribe certain drugs to a person not his patient or for a veterinarian to prescribe certain drugs for humans. However, it is important to note that, as against licensed physicians this statute has been found unconstitutional;[2] and this is true, "regardless of whether or not [he acts] in good faith."[3]

Defenses.

(1) Licensed physician.

(2) Person was under treatment in a dentist's regular practice of his profession.

(3) Substance does not fall within schedules I through V.

---

1. *For lists of controlled substances, see notes 1 through 5 under CONTROLLED SUBSTANCES, supra.*
2. *State v. Bradford, 368 So. 2d 317 (Ala. Crim. App. 1979).*
3. *"In its simplest form, the statute states that it shall be unlawful for (1)* ***a practitioner of dentistry*** *to prescribe certain drugs to a person not his patient, or (2)* ***a practitioner of veterinary medicine*** *to prescribe certain drugs for human use. Nowhere in § 505 does the legislature state that it shall be unlawful for a* ***practitioner of medicine*** *to do anything. A limitation or rule of construction is added to § 505 stating that the section '****shall be construed*** *not to prevent any lawfully authorized practitioner of medicine from furnishing or prescribing in good faith for the use of any habitual user of substances enumerated ... who is under his professional care such substances as he may deem necessary for their treatment' when the drugs are not to maintain addiction. (Emphasis supplied.)*

"Whatever the purpose of the quoted rule of construction, the act could not be construed as applying to physicians, regardless of whether or not they act in good faith, simply because the only prohibitions in the statute specifically apply only to dentists and veterinarians." State v. Bradford, 368 So. 2d 317 (Ala. Crim. App. 1979).

CONTROLLED SUBSTANCES — TRAFFICKING IN CANNABIS, COCAINE, ETC.; MANDATORY MINIMUM TERMS OF IMPRISONMENT. Code of Ala. 1975, § 20-2-80.

Any person who knowingly sells, manufactures, delivers, or brings into this state, or who is knowingly in actual or constructive possession of, in excess of one kilo or 2.2 pounds of cannabis, 28 grams or more of cocaine[1] or of any mixture containing cocaine, 4 grams or more of any

CONTROLLED SUBSTANCES — TRAFFICKING IN CANNABIS, COCAINE, ETC.; MANDATORY MINIMUM TERMS OF IMPRISONMENT.—Cont'd.

morphine, opium, or any salt, isomer, or salt of an isomer thereof, including heroin,[2] is guilty of a felony.

Classification.

Unclassified with the following schedule of minimum mandatory imprisonment and fines based upon the type of controlled substance and its quantity:

CONTROLLED SUBSTANCE	QUANTITY	SENTENCE	FINE
Cannabis	more than 2.2 lbs. but less than 2,000 lbs.	3 years	$ 25,000
Cannabis	more than 2,000 lbs. but less than 10,000 lbs.	5 years	50,000
Cannabis	10,000 lbs. or more	15 years	200,000
Cocaine	at least 28 grams but less than 200 grams	3 years	50,000
Cocaine	at least 200 grams but less than 400 grams	5 years	100,000
Cocaine	400 grams or more	15 years	250,000
Morphine, opium, salts, isomers (heroin)	at least 4 grams but less than 14 grams	3 years	50,000
Morphine, opium salts, isomers (heroin)	at least 14 grams but less than 28 grams	10 years	100,000
Morphine, opium, salts, isomers (heroin)	28 grams or more	25 years	500,000

Comments.

The above schedule of fines and imprisonments reflects minimum and mandatory sentences. Section 20-2-81 of the Alabama Code specifically provides that there is to be no suspension, reduction, probation, or parole of such sentences. The one exception to this provision occurs if offenders provide substantial assistance in the identification, arrest, or conviction of accomplices, accessories, co-conspirators, or principals. It is within the discretion of the judge, upon adequate showing of such assistance, to reduce or suspend the sentence.

Defenses.

(1) The term marijuana does not include the mature stalks of the plant, fiber produced from the stalks, oil or cake made from the seeds of the plant, any other compound, manufacture, salt, derivative, mixture, or preparation of the mature stalks, fiber, oil, or cake or the sterilized seed of the plant which is incapable of germination.[3]

(2) Lack of knowledge of controlled substance.

(3) See Title 20, chapter 12 of the Alabama Code.

---

1. *See Code of Ala. 1975, § 20-2-25(1).*
2. *See Code of Ala. 1975, §§ 20-2-23(2) and 20-2-25(1)(a).*
3. *Code of Ala. 1975, § 20-2-2(15).*

COPYING, SALE, OR POSSESSION OF RECORD[ING] DEVICE. Code of Ala. 1975, §§ 13A-8-80 through 13A-8-86.

It is a crime to:

"(1) Knowingly transfer or cause to be transferred, directly or indirectly, by any means, any sounds recorded on a phonograph record, disc, wire, tape, film or other article on which sounds are recorded, with the intent to sell or cause to be sold, or to be used for profit through public performance, such article on which sounds are so transferred, without consent of the owner;[1] or

"(2) Manufacture, distribute or wholesale any article with the knowledge that the sounds are so transferred without consent of the owner." § 13A-8-81 of the Alabama Code.

". . . knowingly retail or possess for the purpose of retailing any record[ing] device that has been produced, manufactured, distributed or acquired at wholesale in violation of any provision of this [statute]." § 13A-8-82 of the Alabama Code.

Classification.

Transfer, manufacture, distribution, and wholesale are classified as a felony with specific provisions in the statute for the following punishment:

1st offense — 1—3 years' imprisonment and/or up to $25,000 fine.

2nd offense — 3—10 years' imprisonment and/or up to $100,000 fine.

Possession or retail is an unclassified misdemeanor and is, therefore, punishable as a Class C misdemeanor.[2]

Comments.

The statute provides that it is a felony to reproduce recorded sounds with intent to sell or use for public performance for profit without the consent of the owner of the recording. It is also a felony to manufacture, distribute, or wholesale where in that process the sounds are transferred without the consent of the owner. Possession for retail or retailing are simply misdemeanors. The interest sought to be protected is clear, but the characteristic or target offender is not as readily ascertainable. It appears that

COPYING, SALE, OR POSSESSION OF RECORD[ING] DEVICE. —Cont'd.

copying for individual use, or even for giving away copies, is permissible so long as the act does not constitute manufacturing. It is the copying for sale or profit that is prohibited. Only minor penalties have been established for the retailer. The focus would be on the pirateer and his accomplice manufacturer or bulk wholesaler. There is a specific exemption for application of the law to radio and television broadcasters acting in their trade.[3] Although there is no criminal penalty attached, this law requires the name of the manufacturer of the recorded material be displayed on all packaging of the recording.[4] There is further provision for summary confiscation of a recording that is illegal under this statute, or any other unauthorized recording and associated duplicating equipment.[5] The application of such a provision without a prior judicial proceeding would certainly seem to fly in the face of constitutional due process protection.

Defenses.

(1) Consent of owner.

Query.

Would claim of right constitute a viable offense where appropriate?

---

1. *"[T]he term 'owner,' . . . shall mean the person who owns the master phonograph record, master disc, master tape, master film or other device used for reproducing recorded sounds on phonograph records, discs, tapes, films or other articles on which sound is recorded and from which the transferred sounds are directly or indirectly derived." Code of Ala. 1975, § 13A-8-80.*
2. *Code of Ala. 1975, § 13A-5-4.*
3. *Code of Ala. 1975, § 13A-8-81(3).*
4. *Code of Ala. 1975, § 13A-8-83.*
5. *Code of Ala. 1975, § 13A-8-84.*

CORPSE, ABUSE. Code of Ala. 1975, § 13A-11-13.

Charged as: Abuse of a corpse.

CORPSE, ABUSE.—Cont'd.

"A person commits the crime of abuse of a corpse if, except as otherwise authorized by law, he knowingly treats a human corpse in a way that would outrage ordinary family sensibilities."

Classification.

Class A misdemeanor.

Comments.

Broadly written, this statute punishes conduct covered by other code provisions[1] as well as any other type of conduct regarding a corpse that would "outrage ordinary family sensibilities."[2] The culpable party must knowingly[3] perform such acts with a human corpse and know that these acts would outrage the ordinary family sensibilities.[4] The statute neither defines "corpse" nor explicity sets out what conduct is authorized by law, except to the extent that it incorporates previous code provisions. The failure to expressly define, or make reference to, what is lawful or unlawful conduct leaves the statute vulnerable to attack based on its lack of notice.

Defenses.

(1) Conduct authorized by law.
(2) Object not a human corpse.
(3) Lack of knowledge that object is a human corpse.
(4) Conduct would not outrage ordinary family sensibilities.
(5) Lack of knowledge that conduct would outrage ordinary family sensibilities.
(6) Family not outraged.[5]

Cross references.

See Buying dead bodies, § 13-6-82 of the Alabama Code; Defacing tombstone, trees, shrubbery, etc., § 13-6-85 of the Alabama Code; Removing dead body from grave, § 13-6-80; Violating grave with intent to steal or remove dead body, § 13-6-83. See DESECRATION OF TOMBSTONES; DESECRATION OF VENERATED OBJECTS.

---

1. *Previous punitive sections in the Alabama Code on the subject are: § 13-6-80 (Removing dead body from grave); § 13-6-82 (Buying dead bodies); § 13-6-83 (Violating grave with intent to steal or remove dead body, etc.); § 13-6-84*

CORPSE, ABUSE.—Cont'd.

(Mutilating dead bodies); § 13-6-85 (Defacing tombstones, trees, shrubbery, etc.).

2. *Sensibilities of family must be based on contemporary local community standards.*
3. *"A person acts knowingly with respect to conduct or to a circumstance described by a statute defining an offense when he is aware that his conduct is of that nature or that the circumstance exists." Code of Ala. 1975, § 13A-2-2(2).*
4. *"When a statute defining an offense prescribes as an element thereof a specified culpable mental state, such mental state is presumed to apply to every element of the offense unless the context thereof indicates to the contrary." Code of Ala. 1975, § 13A-2-4(a).*
5. *Though the official commentary makes this statement, the statute itself does not state that actual outrage of the family is a prerequisite to criminal liability.*

CREATING A HAZARD. See HAZARD, CREATING.

CREDIT CARD OR DEBIT CARD, ILLEGAL POSSESSION OF OR FRAUDULENT USE OF. Code of Ala. 1975, § 13A-9-14.

Charged as: Illegal possession of or fradulent use of credit card or debit card.

"(a) A person commits the crime of illegal possession of a credit[1] or debit[2] card if, knowing that he does not have the consent of owner, he takes, exercises control over or otherwise uses such card.

"(b) A person commits the crime of fraudulent use of a credit card or debit card if he uses, attempts to use or allows to be used, a credit card or debit card for the purpose of obtaining property,[3] services[4] or anything else of value with knowledge that:

"(1) The card is stolen;[5] or

"(2) The card has been revoked or cancelled; or

"(3) For any other reason his use of the card is unauthorized by either the issuer or the person to whom the credit card or debit card is issued.

"The mere use by the original issuee of a credit card or debit card which has expired is not within [these provisions]."

CREDIT CARD OR DEBIT CARD, ILLEGAL POSSESSION OF OR FRAUDULENT USE OF.—Cont'd.

Classification.

Class C felony.

Comments.

Two crimes are covered in this section. First is the illegal possession of a credit or debit card, and second is the fraudulent use of a credit or debit card. Most, if not all, credit and debit cards are owned at all times by the issuer. The person who was issued the card, therefore, may be prosecuted under this section, as well as a person who takes the card from the person in legitimate possession of such card. It is not necessary to actually obtain anything; using the card for such a purpose is sufficient.

Defenses.

(1) Lack of knowledge that the card is stolen, revoked, or cancelled.

(2) Belief that possession or use is authorized.

Cross references.

See BUSINESS RECORDS, FALSIFYING; RECEIVING STOLEN PROPERTY; THEFT OF PROPERTY; THEFT OF SERVICES.

---

1. *" 'Credit card' means any instrument, writing or other evidence, whether known as a credit card, credit plate, charge plate or by any other name, which purports to evidence an undertaking to pay for property or services delivered or rendered to or upon the order of a designated person or bearer." Code of Ala. 1975, § 13A-9-14(c).*
2. *" 'Debit card' means any instrument or writing or other evidence known by any name issued with or without fee by an issuer for the use of a depositor in obtaining money, goods, services or anything else of value, payment of which is made against funds previously deposited in an account with the issuer." Code of Ala. 1975, § 13A-9-14(d).*
3. *"Any money, tangible or intangible personal property, property (whether real or personal) the location of which can be changed (including things growing on, affixed to or found in land and documents, although the rights represented hereby have no physical location), contract right, chose-in-action, interest in or claim to wealth, credit or any other article or thing of value of any kind.*

   "Commodities of a public utility nature, such as gas, electricity, steam and water, constitute property, but the supplying of such a commodity to premises from an outside source by means of wires, pipes, conduits or other equipment shall be deemed a rendition of a service rather than a sale or delivery of property." Code of Ala. 1975, § 13A-8-1(10). See § 13A-8-10, Theft of services.
4. *" 'Services' includes, but is not necessarily limited to, labor, professional services, transportation, telephone or other public services, accommodation in motels, hotels, restaurants or elsewhere, admission to exhibitions, computer services and the supplying of equipment for use." Code of Ala. 1975, § 13A-8-10(b).*
5. *Reporting of credit card lost, stolen or mislaid.*

   "(a) Any person who reports or attempts to report a credit card as being lost, stolen or mislaid knowing the report to be false violates this subsection and shall be fined not more than $1,000.00 or imprisoned not more than one year, or both.

   "(b) Any cardholder who, with intent to defraud, uses a credit card which has previously been reported lost, stolen or mislaid violates this subsection and shall be fined not more than $1,000.00 or imprisoned not more than one year, or both." Code of Ala. 1975, § 13A-9-15.

CREDITOR. See CREDIT CARD OR DEBIT CARD, ILLEGAL POSSESSION OF OR FRAUDULENT USE OF; DEFRAUDING SECURED AND JUDGMENT CREDITORS.

CRIMINALLY NEGLIGENT HOMICIDE. See HOMICIDE, CRIMINALLY NEGLIGENT.

CRUELTY TO ANIMALS. See ANIMALS, CRUELTY TO.

CULPABILITY. See LIABILITY; STRICT LIABILITY.

CUSTODY. See CUSTODY, INTERFERENCE WITH; JUVENILE PROCEEDINGS.

CUSTODY, INTERFERENCE WITH.
Code of Ala. 1975, § 13A-6-45.

Charged as: Interference with custody.

"A person commits the crime of interference with custody if he knowingly takes or entices:

"(1) Any child under the age of 18 from the lawful custody of its parent, guardian or other lawful custodian, or

"(2) Any committed person[1] from the lawful custody of its parent, guardian or other lawful custodian."

Comments.

The principal purpose of the statute is to protect parental custody against unlawful interruption. However, to the extent that interference with custody was intended to be a lesser included offense of kidnapping (§§ 13A-6-43 and 13A-6-44 of the Alabama Code), the objective of the two provisions are not consistent. Kidnapping statutes are designed to protect persons from physical danger, while this interference with custody statute is designed to protect the parental custody. The focus of the state in the former is the person abducted; in the latter, it is the parent(s) of the person abducted (assuming the abductee was under the age of 18). Just as a defendant can be charged with two murders if in a single shotgun blast two people are killed, it appears that an abductor could be convicted under both the kidnapping and the interference with custody statutes. However, the defense attorney should not hesitate to bring a constitutional attack against such prosecution. This analogy also applies in a comparison of the unlawful imprisonment statutes. §§ 13A-6-41 and 13A-6-42 of the Alabama Code.

The offense is complete when the person "knowingly takes or entices" the victim away from the lawful custody of another. There need not be an abduction[2] (as is necessary for a kidnapping) nor restraint[3] (as is necessary for unlawful imprisonment). Also, the "taking" need not have been successful; the crime is complete when the person only "entices"[4] the victim.

CUSTODY, INTERFERENCE WITH.
—Cont'd.

Subsection (b) of the statute provides a defense:

"A person does not commit a crime under this section if:

"(1) The actor is a relative of the child, and

"(2) The actor's sole purpose is to assume lawful control of the child."

To avail himself of this defense, the defendant has the burden of injecting this issue, but this does not shift the burden of proof. The purpose of this provision is to prevent abuse in certain custody battles between estranged parents.[5]

It appears that acquiescence or consent by the legal custodian from whose possession the child was taken will be a complete defense. The acquiescence or consent by the child is irrelevant since the "victim" is the legal custodian.

Defenses.

(1) The person is a relative of the child, and the actor's sole purpose is to assume lawful control of the child.

(2) Consent of the legal custodian from whom the child was taken.

(3) The person did not "knowingly" take or entice.

(4) The "child" was not under 18 years old and was not a "committed person."

Query.

1. If two 17-year-olds elope without the consent of the legal custodian of either, would both be charged with interference with custody?
2. If the person is a relative of the child and does not have the right to assume lawful control of the child at the time of the taking, but does obtain lawful control shortly after the taking, could he qualify for the defense provided for in the statute?

Cross references.

See Unauthorizedly bringing child into state for adoption, §§ 38-7-15 and 38-7-16 of the Alabama Code. See JUVENILE PROCEEDINGS; KIDNAPPING; UNLAWFUL IMPRISONMENT.

---

1. A committed person is "in addition to anyone committed under judicial warrant, any neglected, dependent or delinquent child,

CUSTODY, INTERFERENCE WITH. —Cont'd.

mentally defective or insane person or any other incompetent person entrusted to another's custody by authority of law." Code of Ala. 1975, § 13A-6-45(a)(2).

2. *To abduct is "[t]o restrain a person with intent to prevent his liberation by either:*
   "(a) Secreting or holding him in a place where he is not likely to be found, or
   "(b) Using or threatening to use deadly physical force." Code of Ala. 1975, § 13A-6-40(2).
3. *To restrain is "[t]o intentionally or knowingly restrict a person's movements unlawfully and without consent, so as to interfere substantially with his liberty by moving him from one place to another, or by confining him either in the place where the restriction commences or in a place to which he has been moved. Restraint is 'without consent' if it is accomplished by:*
   "(a) Physical force, intimidation or deception, or
   "(b) Any means, including acquiescence of the victim, if he is a child less than 16 years old or an incompetent person and the parent, guardian or other person or institution having lawful control or custody of him has not acquiesced in the movement or confinement." Code of Ala. 1975, § 13A-6-40(1).
4. *To entice is to wrongfully solicit, allure, tempt or coax. "Enticement of a child is inviting, persuading or attempting to persuade a child to enter any vehicle, building, room or secluded place with intent to commit an unlawful sexual act upon or with the person of said child." Black's Law Dictionary 477 (1979).*
5. *Code of Ala. 1975, § 12-15-15 provides for the punishment of those persons who remove or conceal any delinquent, dependent child or child in need of supervision; thus, for those persons who fall within this defense it is not a protection against a charge under Code of Ala. 1975, § 12-15-15, Removal, concealment, etc., of delinquent or dependent child or child in need of supervision, etc.; interference with performance of duties by probation officer, etc. See also Code of Ala. 1975, § 12-15-14, Disregarding, etc., of lawful order of court or interference with custody of child under jurisdiction of court.*

DEATH PENALTY.[1] Code of Ala. 1975, §§ 13A-5-39 through 13A-5-59.

In 1980, the United States Supreme Court, in Beck v. Alabama,[2] struck down Alabama's death penalty statute.[3] The new capital punishment act[4] enumerates specific crimes to which the death penalty may apply.[5] If at any time the act is declared unconstitutional, those defendants previously sentenced to death shall have their sentences commuted to life imprisonment without parole. From that time forward the enumerated offenses shall be punishable by life without parole.

The proceedings shall be conducted in a bifurcated trial: first, a trial to determine guilt and, second, a sentencing hearing. Even if the defendant decides to plead guilty,[6] the State must still prove to the jury the defendant's guilt beyond a reasonable doubt. The defendant can waive his right to trial by jury; however, it must also be waived by the State and consented to by the court. If there is a jury trial, the jury has the option to return a guilty verdict on a lesser included offense.[7]

After the jury returns a guilty verdict, the sentence hearing begins to determine whether to recommend to the judge life without parole or death. Unless it is impossible or impractical, the same jury is used in both phases. The sentence hearing is conducted in the same procedure as the first trial, with opening and closing statements and the presentation of evidence. Any evidence that has probative value is admissible, except for that evidence obtained in violation of any constitutional rights of the defendant. Even hearsay is admissible, provided the defendant is accorded a fair opportunity for rebuttal.

At the sentence hearing, the state must prove beyond a reasonable doubt an aggravating circumstance.[8] If the State fails to so prove the existence of at least one such circumstance, then the sentence shall be life without parole. The defendant has the opportunity to interject any mitigating circumstances.[9] If a mitigating circumstance is raised, the state has the burden to disprove it by a preponderance of the evidence. After hearing all the evidence, the jury must deliberate and return a written advisory verdict, taking into account the weight of any aggravating and mitigating circumstances.[10] The verdict must also specify their vote: a simple

DEATH PENALTY.—Cont'd.

majority recommending life without parole, or at least ten jurors in support of the death penalty. If the jurors are deadlocked, a mistrial will be ordered. That order has no effect upon the earlier guilty verdict.

Before the judge imposes sentence, he must review a presentence report. The report is also available to both parties who may respond to it. The report and any responses to it will become a part of the record. This permits aggravating and mitigating circumstances to be argued again. The judge shall enter into the record a written fact summary, specifically relating the defendant's participation, and his written findings as to the weight of each aggravating and mitigating circumstance.[11]

In those cases where the judge imposes the death penalty, there is automatic review by the Alabama Court of Criminal Appeals. They shall review the entire record, particularly the sentence hearing and the trial judge's written findings. If any error is found that adversely affects the defendant's rights, the sentence shall be remanded with appropriate instructions. If they find no such error, the court shall explicitly address the issue of whether or not the death penalty is the proper sentence.[12] The court has three options: (1) affirm the sentence of death; (2) set aside the death sentence and remand to the trial court for correction of any errors; or (3) if they determine the sentence to be inappropriate, set aside the death sentence and remand, ordering life without parole.

One procedural safeguard that is carried forward from the old statute is the requirement that any appointed defense counsel must have no less than five years' prior experience in the active practice of criminal law.[13]

Cross references.

See N. Chiarkas, Alabama Criminal Trial Practice, § 26-9 (Capital punishment). See SENTENCING.

---

1. *See Justice Maddox's excellent opinion in Beck v. State, 396 So. 2d 645, 648-53 (Ala. 1981), on remand from the United States Supreme Court; and for an in-depth treatment comparing Act No.*

DEATH PENALTY.—Cont'd.

81-178 to the old death penalty statute, see E. Carnes, Alabama's 1981 Capital Punishment Statute, 42 The Alabama Lawyer 456 (1981).

2. *Beck v. Alabama, 447 U. S. 625, 100 S. Ct. 2382, 65 L. Ed. 2d 392 (1980).*
3. *Code of Ala. 1975, §§ 13A-5-30 through 13A-5-38.*
4. *Act No. 81-178, Alabama Legislature, Regular Session, 1981, effective July 1, 1981, as codified in Code of Ala. 1975, §§ 13A-5-39 through 13A-5-59.*
5. *Code of Ala. 1975, § 13A-5-40. "The following are capital offenses:*

"(1) Murder by the defendant during a kidnapping in the first degree or an attempt thereof committed by the defendant;

"(2) Murder by the defendant during a robbery in the first degree or an attempt thereof committed by the defendant;

"(3) Murder by the defendant during a rape in the first or second degree or an attempt thereof committed by the defendant; or murder by the defendant during sodomy in the first or second degree or an attempt thereof committed by the defendant;

"(4) Murder by the defendant during a burglary in the first or second degree or an attempt thereof committed by the defendant;

"(5) Murder of any police, sheriff, deputy, state trooper, federal law enforcement officer, or any other state or federal peace officer of any kind, or prison or jail guard, while such officer or guard is on duty or because of some official or job-related act or performance of such officer or guard;

"(6) Murder committed while the defendant is under sentence of life imprisonment;

"(7) Murder done for a pecuniary or other valuable consideration or pursuant to a contract or for hire;

"(8) Murder by the defendant during sexual abuse in the first or second degree or an attempt thereof committed by the defendant;

"(9) Murder by the defendant during arson in the first or second degree committed by the defendant; or murder by the defendant by means of explosives or explosions;

"(10) Murder wherein two or more persons are murdered by the defendant by one act or pursuant to one scheme or course of conduct;

"(11) Murder by the defendant when the victim is a state or federal public official or former public official and the murder stems from or is caused by or is related to his official position, act, or capacity;

"(12) Murder by the defendant during the act of unlawfully assuming control of any aircraft by

DEATH PENALTY.—Cont'd.

use of threats or force with intent to obtain any valuable consideration for the release of said aircraft or any passenger or crewman thereon or to direct the route or movement of said aircraft, or otherwise exert control over said aircraft;

"(13) Murder by a defendant who has been convicted of any other murder in the 20 years preceding the crime; provided that the murder which constitutes the capital crime shall be murder as defined in subsection (b) of this section [capital offenses means murder as defined in Code of Ala. 1975, § 13A-6-2(a)(1), but not as defined in Code of Ala. 1975, § 13A-6-2(a)(2) and (3)]; and provided further that the prior murder conviction referred to shall include murder in any degree as defined at the time and place of the prior conviction; and

"(14) Murder when the victim is subpoenaed, or has been subpoenaed, to testify, or the victim had testified, in any preliminary hearing, grand jury proceeding, criminal trial or criminal trial or criminal proceeding of whatever nature, or civil trial or civil proceeding of whatever nature, in any municipal, state, or federal court, when the murder stems from, is caused by, or is related to the capacity or role of the victim as a witness."

6. *The state is still allowed to enter into plea bargaining agreements.*

7. *The inability of a jury to do so under the prior death penalty statute was a major issue in the Beck v. Alabama decision. See note 2, supra.*

8. *See Code of Ala. 1975, § 13A-5-45(e).*

Code of Ala. 1975, § 13A-5-49 defines aggravating circumstances as follows:

"(1) The capital offense was committed by a person under sentence of imprisonment;

"(2) The defendant was previously convicted of another capital felony or a felony involving the use or threat of violence to the person;

"(3) The defendant knowingly created a great risk of death to many persons;

"(4) The capital offense was committed while the defendant was engaged or was an accomplice in the commission of, or an attempt to commit, or flight after committing, or attempting to commit, rape, robbery, burglary or kidnapping;

"(5) The capital offense was committed for the purpose of avoiding or preventing a lawful arrest or effecting an escape from custody;

"(6) The capital offense was committed for pecuniary gain;

"(7) The capital offense was committed to disrupt or hinder the lawful exercise of any governmental function or the enforcement of laws; or

"(8) The capital offense was especially heinous, atrocious or cruel compared to other capital offenses."

9. *Code of Ala. 1975, § 13A-5-45(g) "mitigating circumstances shall include, but not be limited to, the following:*

"(1) The defendant has no significant history of prior criminal activity;

"(2) The capital offense was committed while the defendant was under the influence of extreme mental or emotional disturbance;

"(3) The victim was a participant in the defendant's conduct or consented to it;

"(4) The defendant was an accomplice in the capital offense committed by another person and his participation was relatively minor;

"(5) The defendant acted under extreme duress or under the substantial domination of another person;

"(6) The capacity of the defendant to appreciate the criminality of his conduct or to conform his conduct to the requirements of law was substantially impaired; and

"(7) The age of the defendant at the time of the crime." Code of Ala. 1975, § 13A-5-51.

And, according to Code of Ala. 1975, § 13A-5-52 "[i]n addition to the mitigating circumstances specified in section 13A-5-51, mitigating circumstances shall include any aspect of the defendant's character or record and any of the circumstances of the offense that the defendant offers as a basis for a sentence of life imprisonment without parole instead of death, and any other relevant mitigating circumstance that the defendant offers as a basis for a sentence of life imprisonment without parole instead of death."

10. *Code of Ala. 1975, § 13A-5-46(e) provides that "[a]fter deliberation, the jury shall return an advisory verdict as follows:*

"(1) If the jury determines that no aggravating circumstances as defined in section 13A-5-49 exist, it shall return an advisory verdict recommending to the trial court that the penalty be life imprisonment without parole;

"(2) If the jury determines that one or more aggravating circumstances as defined in section 13A-5-49 exist but do not outweigh the mitigating circumstances, it shall return an advisory verdict recommending to the trial court that the penalty be life imprisonment without parole;

"(3) If the jury determines that one or more aggravating circumstances as defined in section 13A-5-49 exist and that they outweigh the mitigating circumstances, if any, it

DEATH PENALTY.—Cont'd.

shall return an advisory verdict recommending to the trial court that the penalty be death."

11. Code of Ala. 1975, § 13A-5-48 provides that the process "of weighing the aggravating and mitigating circumstances to determine the sentence shall not be defined to mean a mere tallying of aggravating and mitigating circumstances for the purpose of numerical comparison."

12. Code of Ala. 1975, § 13A-5-53(b) provides that "[i]n determining whether death was the proper sentence in the case the Alabama court of criminal appeals, subject to review by the Alabama supreme court, shall determine:

"(1) Whether the sentence of death was imposed under influence of passion, prejudice, or any other arbitrary factor;

"(2) Whether an independent weighing of the aggravating and mitigating circumstances at the appellate level indicates that death was the proper sentence; and

"(3) Whether the sentence of death is excessive or disproportionate to the penalty imposed in similar cases, considering both the crime and the defendant."

13. Code of Ala. 1975, § 13A-5-54 was adopted intact from Code of Ala. 1975, § 13A-5-37.

DECEPTION. See SIGNATURE OBTAINED BY DECEPTION.

DECEPTIVE BUSINESS PRACTICES. See BUSINESS PRACTICES, DECEPTIVE.

DEFAMATION. See LIBEL AND DEFAMATION.

DEFENSES. See under specific defense (e.g., ENTRAPMENT, INSANITY, etc.).

DEFRAUDING SECURED AND JUDGMENT CREDITORS. Code of Ala. 1975, §§ 13A-9-46 and 13A-9-47.

"A person commits the crime of defrauding secured creditors if he destroys, removes, conceals, encumbers, transfers or otherwise deals with property[1] subject to a security interest[2] with intent to hinder enforcement of that interest." § 13A-9-46 of the Alabama Code.

"A person commits the crime of defrauding judgment creditors if he:

"(1) With fraudulent intent[3] removes property subject to execution from a county to prevent it being levied upon by an execution; or

"(2) Secretes, assigns, conveys or otherwise disposes of property with intent to defraud[4] a judgment creditor." § 13A-9-47 of the Alabama Code.

Classification.

Class A misdemeanor.

Comments.

The statutes extend protection to any security interest in personal property.[5] Section 13A-9-46 of the Alabama Code deals specifically with fraud upon secured creditors. This section imposes criminal sanctions on debtors who act with an intent to hinder the enforcement of their creditor's security interest. Because rights represented by a judgment are not secured transactions as defined by the Uniform Commercial Code, § 13A-9-47 of the Alabama Code extends similar protection to judgment creditors.

Defenses.

(1) Lack of intent.

(2) Belief that property conveyed was not subject to the actions of either a secured or judgment creditor.

Cross references.

See Secured transactions, §§ 7-9-101 through 7-9-507 of the Alabama Code, particularly "security interest" and secured transactions as defined in §§ 7-1-201(37) and 7-9-104(h) of the Alabama Code; Theft and related offenses, §§ 13A-8-1 through 13A-8-22 of the Alabama Code. See BUSINESS RECORDS, FALSIFYING; MISAPPLICATION OF PROPERTY.

---

1. "Any money, tangible or intangible personal property, property (whether real or personal) the location of which can be changed (including things growing on, affixed to or found in land and documents, although the rights represented hereby have no physical location), contract right, chose-in-action, interest in or claim to wealth, credit or any other article or thing of value of any kind.

"Commodities of a public utility nature, such as gas, electricity, steam and water, constitute

DEFRAUDING SECURED AND JUDGMENT CREDITORS.—Cont'd.

property, but the supplying of such a commodity to premises from an outside source by means of wires, pipes, conduits or other equipment shall be deemed a rendition of a service rather than a sale or delivery of property." Code of Ala. 1975, § 13A-8-1(10). See Code of Ala. 1975, § 13A-8-10, Theft of services.

2. *Code of Ala. 1975, § 13A-9-46(b) defines "security interest" as an interest in personal property or fixtures.*
3. *"Intent to defraud" defined, Code of Ala. 1975, § 13A-9-1(8).*

"A purpose to use deception, as defined in section 13A-8-1(1), or to injure another person's interest which has value, as defined in section 13A-8-1(14)."

4. *See note 3, supra.*
5. *See Code of Ala. 1975, former §§ 13-4-1, 13-4-2, 13-4-8, and 13-4-95.*

DESECRATION OF TOMBSTONES. Code of Ala. 1975, § 13A-7-23.1.

Charged as: Desecration of tomb, gravestone, etc.

"Any person who wilfully or maliciously injures, defaces, removes or destroys any tomb, monument, gravestone or other memorial of the dead, or any fence or any inclosure about any tomb, monument, gravestone or memorial, or who wilfully and wrongfully destroys, removes, cuts, breaks or injures any tree, shrub, plant, flower, decoration or other real or personal property within any cemetery or graveyard shall be guilty of a Class A misdemeanor."[1]

Classification.

Class A misdemeanor.

Defenses.

(1) Was not wilful or malicious.

(2) Was not within a cemetery or graveyard.

Comments.

This crime is included to prohibit the desecration of cemeteries or graveyards, conduct the legislature has labeled particularly offensive.

Cross references.

See DESECRATION OF VENERATED OBJECTS; MISCHIEF, CRIMINAL.

---

1. *See Code of Ala. 1975, former § 13-6-85. § 13A-7-23.1 was purported by the legislature to amend Code of Ala. 1975, § 13-6-85, which had already been repealed by Acts 1977, No. 607, p. 812, § 9901, as amended. However, it was included in Code of Ala. 1975, Title 13A because of the Advisory Committee's evaluation of the legislative intent.*

DESECRATION OF VENERATED OBJECTS. Code of Ala. 1975, § 13A-11-12.

"A person commits the crime of desecration of venerated objects if he intentionally:

"(1) Desecrates any public monument or structure or place of worship or burial; or

"(2) Desecrates in a public place the United States or Alabama flag or any other object of veneration by the public or a substantial segment thereof."

Classification.

Class A misdemeanor.

Comments.

The purpose of this statute is two-fold: (1) to protect property owned or utilized by the public from desecration; and (2) to cover the public desecration of a flag owned by a private person when such desecration is likely to cause a breach of the peace, or when a public flag is desecrated. While the United States Supreme Court has never reached the specific issue of the constitutionality of flag desecration statutes, the trend seems to be that a state can proscribe only those types of flag desecration that are likely to cause a breach of the peace. This approach embodies the theory that burning the flag or otherwise desecrating it is speech, albeit symbolic, and is protected by the First Amendment, unless excepted as "fighting words."

Defenses.

(1) Lack of intent to desecrate.

(2) Place of desecration is not "public."

(3) The object of desecration was not a "venerated object."

(4) The object was not venerated by a "substantial segment (of the public)."

Query.

Could a Nazi or Ku Klux Klan flag constitute "any other object of veneration"? Would the "burning in effigy of Uncle Sam" fall

DESECRATION OF VENERATED OBJECTS.—Cont'd.
within this statute if done so by American citizens or aliens? (Consider breach of peace effect.)

Cross references.
See DESECRATION OF TOMBSTONES; MISCHIEF, CRIMINAL; TAMPERING; TRESPASS, CRIMINAL.

DISORDERLY CONDUCT. Code of Ala. 1975, § 13A-11-7.

"A person commits the crime of disorderly conduct if, with intent to cause public inconvenience, annoyance or alarm, or recklessly creating a risk thereof, he:

"(1) Engages in fighting or in violent tumultuous or threatening behavior; or

"(2) Makes unreasonable noise; or

"(3) In a public place uses abusive or obscene language or makes an obscene gesture; or

"(4) Without lawful authority, disturbs any lawful assembly or meeting of persons; or

"(5) Obstructs vehicular or pedestrian traffic, or a transportation facility; or

"(6) Congregates with other person in a public place and refuses to comply with a lawful order of the police to disperse."

Classification.
Class C misdemeanor.

Comments.
This statute encompasses the common law offenses of breach of the peace and disturbing the peace. While the superseded section was oriented towards who is disturbed and the purpose of the assembly, this statute explicitly requires an intent to inconvenience, annoy, or alarm the public, or recklessly creating a risk thereof, as an element of the offense. Note that an objective standard is to be used, but even so the defendant's intent may be inferred from all the facts and surrounding circumstances. The focus on the surrounding circumstances is important. An act that would be lawful in some circumstances may amount to a breach of the peace if done under other circumstances. Abernathy v. State, 42 Ala. App. 149, 155 So. 2d 586 (1962). A number of constitutional questions arise under this statute where the purpose is to control

DISORDERLY CONDUCT.—Cont'd.
speech. Statutes that proscribe "fighting words" or "those which by their very utterance inflict injury or tend to incite an immediate breach of the peace" have been upheld by the United States Supreme Court. Chaplinsky v. New Hampshire, 315 U. S. 568, 572, 86 L. Ed. 1031 (1942). However, such statutes must be carefully drawn to punish only unprotected speech, and not be susceptible in application to protected expression. Under this test, conduct that is calculated to create a disturbance of the peace must not be proscribed. In regard to the regulation of obscenity, the United States Supreme Court's holding in Miller v. California, 413 U. S. 15, 93 S. Ct. 2607, 37 L. Ed. 2d 419 (1973), established three guidelines for the trier of fact to use in determining whether words or actions are obscene: (1) Whether "the average person, applying contemporary community standards," would find that the work, taken as a whole, appeals to the prurient interests; (2) whether the work depicts or describes, in a patently offensively way, sexual conduct specifically defined by the applicable state law; and (3) whether the work, taken as a whole, lacks serious literary, artistic, political, or scientific value. The standard to be utilized is a local standard. Accordingly, § 13A-11-7 must be authoritatively construed in such a way that freedom of speech and expression are considered under the circumstances; otherwise, the statute could be attacked on constitutional grounds as overbroad.

Defenses.
(1) Lack of requisite intent.

(2) All action and the effects of such action take place within the confines of private property.

(3) Failure to prove the conduct was of the nature of "fighting words" or "those which by their very utterance inflict injury or tend to incite an immediate breach of the peace."

(4) Failure to prove the words or acts are "obscene" or "offensive" in nature.

(5) That the gathering of persons that is charged as "obstruction" was for the

DISORDERLY CONDUCT.—Cont'd.
purpose of hearing a person speak or otherwise communicate.
(6) That an order by the police to disperse was unlawful.

Query.
Could inaction constitute "threatening behavior," which is proscribed under this statute? Could the element of intent be inferred from inaction on the part of the defendant, thereby utilizing a "tacit-admission" theory?

Cross references.
See Definition of "obstruct," § 13A-11-1(1); Obscenity and related offenses, Title 13A, chapter 12, article 4. See DISORDERLY PERSONS, FAILURE TO DISPERSE; LOITERING; INTOXICATION, PUBLIC; UNLAWFUL ASSEMBLY.

DISORDERLY PERSONS, FAILURE TO DISPERSE. Code of Ala. 1975, § 13A-11-6.
"A person commits the crime of failure of a disorderly person to disperse if he participates[1] with five or more other persons in a course of disorderly conduct[2] likely to cause substantial harm or serious inconvenience, annoyance or alarm, and intentionally[3] refuses or fails to disperse when ordered to do so by a peace officer or other public servant lawfully engaged in executing or enforcing the law."

Classification.
Class B misdemeanor.

Comments.
The elements of this offense include: (1) a group of six persons or more; (2) in a state of disorderly conduct; (3) likely to cause substantial harm or serious inconvenience, annoyance, or alarm; and (4) deliberate refusal or failure to obey a lawful order to disperse. Through this statute, there is established an interim offense between unlawful assembly, riot, and ordinary disorderly conduct. According to the commentary, the justification for creating a separate offense is that the more persons who are disorderly, the more difficult it is to control them, and thus the greater potential for harm. Therefore, this statute is designed to disperse and break up such commotions before others are attracted, in that there must be an order to disperse by an official lawfully engaged in law enforcement before one may be arrested.

Defenses.
(1) Failure to prove six or more people engaged in "a course of disorderly conduct."
(2) Failure to give notice of order to disperse.
(3) Failure to prove intent was to refuse to disperse.
(4) Order to disperse by one other than a peace officer or other public servant lawfully engaged in executing or enforcing the law.
(5) Justification for failure to disperse based on lack of accessible exit.

Cross references.
See DISORDERLY CONDUCT; HARASSMENT OR HARASSING COMMUNICATIONS; LOITERING; RIOT; UNLAWFUL ASSEMBLY.

---

1. *"Participates" implies that the accused must act in some objectively discernible manner.*
2. *See also Code of Ala. 1975, § 13A-11-7, Disorderly conduct.*
3. *Specific intent is an element of the crime.*

DIVULGING ILLEGALLY OBTAINED INFORMATION. Code of Ala. 1975, § 13A-11-35.
"A person commits the crime of divulging illegally-obtained information if he knowingly or recklessly uses or divulges information obtained through criminal eavesdropping or criminal surveillance."

Classification.
Class B misdemeanor.

Comments.
Use, as well as divulgence, of the information is criminalized. Eavesdropping is a class A misdemeanor and installation of an eavesdropping device is a class C felony. This statute is aimed at the activities of the customer/accomplice and to assist law enforcement authorities in prosecuting the actual eavesdropper/surveillant.

Defenses.
(1) Accused was "a peace officer engaged in

DIVULGING ILLEGALLY OBTAINED INFORMATION.—Cont'd.
the lawful performance of his duties." See § 13A-11-36(a)(1) of the Alabama Code.
(2) Accused was "an officer, employee or agent of a communication common carrier who, while acting in the normal course of his employment, and while engaged in any activity which was a necessary incident to the rendition of his service or to the protection of the rights or property of the carrier." See § 13A-11-36(a)(2) of the Alabama Code.
(3) Accused relied "in good faith on a lawful court order or legislative authorization." See § 13A-11-36(a)(3) of the Alabama Code.
(4) Revelation was unknowing and not reckless, i.e., simply negligent.

Cross references.
See EAVESDROPPING; EAVESDROPPING DEVICE, POSSESSION OF; LIABILITY; SURVEILLANCE; TRESPASS, CRIMINAL.

DOG RACES. See GAMBLING, LEGALIZED PARI-MUTUEL BETTING NOT AFFECTED.

DOMESTIC ANIMALS OR FOWL ON LANDING FIELDS OR OTHER AERONAUTICAL FACILITIES. See AVIATION.

DRIVING WHILE INTOXICATED. See MOTOR VEHICLE CRIMES.

DRUG PARAPHERNALIA, SALE, DISTRIBUTION, ADVERTISEMENT, ETC. See CONTROLLED SUBSTANCES — DRUG PARAPHERNALIA; SALE, DISTRIBUTION, ADVERTISEMENT, ETC.

DRUGS. See CONTROLLED SUBSTANCES.

DRUNKENNESS. See INTOXICATION, PUBLIC; MOTOR VEHICLE CRIMES.

DURESS. Code of Ala. 1975, § 13A-3-30.
The defense of duress applies where a person

DURESS.—Cont'd.
has committed a crime "because he was compelled to do so by the threat of imminent death or serious physical injury[1] to himself or another."[2] This broad provision is qualified in subsection (d)(1) and (2), which prohibits the use of this defense in prosecutions for murder or "[a]ny killing of another under aggravated circumstances, as provided by article 2 of chapter 5 of [Title 13A of the Alabama Code]," and in cases where the defendant "was negligent in placing himself in" a situation "in which it was probable that he would be subjected to duress."[3] In addition, § 13A-3-30(c) of the Alabama Code abolishes the common law presumption that a wife's acts are compelled by her husband, when committed in his presence.[4]

---

1. *See Code of Ala. 1975, § 13A-1-2(9) for definition of "serious physical injury."*
2. *Code of Ala. 1975, § 13A-3-30(a). See Haywood v. State, 43 Ala. App. 358, 190 So. 2d 725 (1966); Browning v. State, 31 Ala. App. 137, 13 So. 2d 54 (1943); Moore v. State, 23 Ala. App. 432, 127 So. 796 (1930).*
3. *The drafters of Code of Ala. 1975, § 13A-3-30 commented that "a co-partner to an offense would not escape punishment through a duress defense if the prosecution can prove that the actor recklessly placed himself in a situation where compulsion was probable."*
4. *This presumption has been held "not conclusive, . . . but . . . may be overcome by the introduction of evidence . . . tending to show that such coercion existed." Mosely v. State, 19 Ala. App. 335, 97 So. 247 (1923). See also Spencer v. State, 40 Ala. App. 93, 109 So. 2d 756 (1958); Bibb v. State, 94 Ala. 31, 10 So. 506 (1891).*

DUTY. See LIABILITY; PUBLIC DUTY; STRICT LIABILITY.

EAVESDROPPING. Code of Ala. 1975, § 13A-11-31.
Charged as: Criminal eavesdropping.
"A person commits the crime of criminal eavesdropping if he intentionally uses any device to eavesdrop,[1] whether or not he is present at the time."

EAVESDROPPING.—Cont'd.

Comments.

The elements of this crime are: (1) the use of a device; (2) the interception of a private communication; and (3) the lack of consent by at least one party to the communication. Criminal eavesdropping is basically concerned with aural interception of communications. The culpable party must use a "device" which amplifies sensitivity to the communications in question. The rationale behind this requirement, and the statute in general, is that the United States Constitution as well as the Constitution of the State of Alabama protect one's reasonable expectation of privacy.[2] Communications that can be perceived with the naked ear are not communications that one reasonably expects will remain private. The Supreme Court's logic in Katz v. United States[3] is evidenced in this statute by the fact that one can violate this statute without trespassing or being present at the situs of the subject communications. The defendant cannot be guilty of violating this statute if at least one party to the communications consents to the interception. The state must prove that defendant's conduct was intentional.[4] If the state can prove the three key elements and that the defendant's conduct was intentional, the defendant may also have committed a theft of property.[5] Persons having a statutory defense to prosecution[6] also have the burden of injecting the issue of the defense at trial.

Defenses.

(1) Communication perceived or perceptible[7] without amplifying device.

(2) Parties to communication had no reasonable expectation of privacy.

(3) Party to communications consented to defendant's interception.

(4) Defendant lacked requisite intent.

(5) Defendant's actions authorized by law.[8]

Cross references.

See Forfeiture of eavesdropping device, § 13A-11-37 of the Alabama Code. See DIVULGING ILLEGALLY OBTAINED INFORMATION; EAVESDROPPING

EAVESDROPPING.—Cont'd.

DEVICE, POSSESSION OF; THEFT OF PROPERTY.

---

1. *"To overhear, record, amplify or transmit any part of the private communication of others without the consent of at least one of the persons engaged in the communication, except as provided by law." Code of Ala. 1975, § 13A-11-30(1). As to conduct "provided by law," see note 6, infra.*
2. *See U. S. Const., Amend. IV and Ala. Const., Art. I, § 5. See also Katz v. United States, 389 U. S. 347, 88 S. Ct. 507, 19 L. Ed. 2d 576 (1967), where the Supreme Court extended the protection of the Fourth Amendment to protection of one's reasonable expectation of privacy. Justice Harlan coined the phrase "expectation of privacy" in his concurring opinion, 389 U. S. at 360.*
3. *Katz v. U. S., 389 U. S. 347, 88 S. Ct. 507, 19 L. Ed. 2d 576 (1967).*
4. *The statute expressly requires intent. "A person acts intentionally with respect to a result or to conduct described by a statute defining an offense, when his purpose is to cause that result or to engage in that conduct." Code of Ala. 1975, § 13A-2-2(1).*

   "When a statute defining an offense prescribes as an element thereof a specified culpable mental state, such mental state is presumed to apply to every element of the offense unless the context thereof indicates to the contrary." Code of Ala. 1975, § 13A-2-4(a).
5. *If ideas, thoughts, or other products are the subject of the communication and they have pecuniary value, a prosecutor could construe the statutes in Title 13, chapter 8 to argue theft.*
6. *"(a) A person does not commit a crime under this article if:*

   "(1) He was a peace officer engaged in the lawful performance of his duties; or

   "(2) He was an officer, employee or agent of a communication common carrier who, while acting in the normal course of his employment, and while engaged in any activity which was a necessary incident to the rendition of his service or to the protection of the rights or property of the carrier of such communication, intercepted, disclosed or used a communication transmitted through the facilities of that carrier; or

   "(3) He relies in good faith on a lawful court order or legislative authorization.

   "(b) The burden of injecting this issue . . . is on the defendant, but this does not shift the burden of proof." Code of Ala. 1975, § 13A-11-36.
7. *The elements of this statute are basically the*

EAVESDROPPING.—Cont'd.

same as those of the Omnibus Crime Control and Safe Streets Act of 1968 with respect to its application in the eavesdropping case of United States v. Carroll, 337 F. Supp. 1260 (D. C. D. C. 1971). In that case the defendant used a tape recorder to record a conversation he was overhearing with his unassisted ear. The recorder's microphone was no more sensitive than the human ear. The court held that there was no expectation of privacy where the conversation could be overheard by the unassisted ear and was made in nonprivate circumstances.

8. *See note 6, supra, as well as Title III, Omnibus Crime Control and Safe Streets Act of 1968, 18 U. S. C. § 2510 et seq.*

EAVESDROPPING DEVICE, POSSESSION OF. Code of Ala. 1975, §§ 13A-11-33 and 13A-11-34.

"A person commits the crime of criminal possession of an eavesdropping device if he possesses,[1] manufactures, sends or transports any device designed or commonly used for eavesdropping, and:

"(1) Intends[2] to use that device to eavesdrop;[3] or

"(2) Knows[4] that another person intends to use that device to eavesdrop." § 13A-11-34 of the Alabama Code.

Classification.

Class A misdemeanor, and upon conviction, the state may obtain a court order requiring forfeiture of the device.[5]

Comments.

This law criminalizes the possession, manufacture, or distribution of an eavesdropping device where such possession, manufacture, or distribution coincides with either an intent to use for eavesdropping or knowledge of another's intent to use for eavesdropping. However, the sale of an eavesdropping device is not criminal under §§ 13A-11-33 or 13A-11-34 of the Alabama Code.

Defenses.

(1) Lack of possession.

(2) No intent to use or no knowledge of another's intent to use.

(3) Accused was a peace officer engaged in the lawful performance of his duties.

(4) Accused was "an officer, employee or agent of a communication common carrier who, while acting in the normal course of his employment, and while engaged in any activity which was incident necessary to the rendition of his service or to the protection of the rights or property of the carrier." § 13A-11-36 of the Alabama Code.

(5) Accused relied in good faith on a lawful court order or legislative authorization.

Cross references.

See Prohibited instruments, §§ 37-8-217 through 37-8-219 of the Alabama Code. See EAVESDROPPING; SURVEILLANCE.

---

1. *To possess something in a criminal sense ordinarily requires that the actor know of its location or that the thing is under his dominion or control. See Perkins v. State, 24 Ala. App. 231, 133 So. 307 (1931).*
2. *A person acts intentionally with respect to conduct when his purpose is to engage in that conduct. Code of Ala. 1975, § 13A-2-2(1).*
3. *"To overhear, record, amplify or transmit any part of the private communication of others without the consent of at least one of the persons engaged in the communication, except as otherwise provided by law." Code of Ala. 1975, § 13A-11-30(1).*
4. *"KNOWINGLY. A person acts knowingly with respect to conduct or to a circumstance described by a statute defining an offense when he is aware that his conduct is of that nature or that the circumstance exists." Code of Ala. 1975, § 13A-2-2(2).*
5. *See Code of Ala. 1975, § 13A-11-37.*

ELECTRONIC SURVEILLANCE. See DIVULGING ILLEGALLY OBTAINED INFORMATION; EAVESDROPPING; EAVESDROPPING DEVICE, POSSESSION OF; SURVEILLANCE.

EMBEZZLEMENT. See MISAPPLICATION OF PROPERTY; THEFT OF PROPERTY.

ENTICING A CHILD FOR IMMORAL PURPOSES. See CHILD, ENTICING FOR IMMORAL PURPOSES.

ENTRAPMENT. Code of Ala. 1975, § 13A-3-31.

In 1979, the Alabama legislature adopted the present case law on entrapment,[1] "whereby the test is whether the criminal intent originated in the mind of the defendant.[2] Thus, entrapment has not been allowed when the prosecution can show that the defendant had a predisposition or prior intent to commit the crime."[3]

Comments.[4]

Alabama, like the majority[5] of courts, has developed a two-pronged, subjective test to determine entrapment.[6] This test, as enunciated by the Supreme Court in Sorrells v. United States,[7] requires first, that the defendant not be predisposed to commit the crime, and second, that the government officials induce the commission of the crime by trickery, deceit, or misrepresentation.[8] The majority's position, particularly with respect to the first prong, has been strengthened and clarified in Alabama,[9] other lower court decisions,[10] and subsequent decisions of the Supreme Court.[11] The attorney contemplating the use of the entrapment defense ought to review the background against which Chief Justice Hughes' opinion in Sorrells was founded.[12] In short, "the thrust of Chief Justice Hughes' opinion in Sorrells was that Congress did not intend the National Prohibition Act to encompass violations which resulted from temptation by government officials. Thus, the statute was simply inapplicable when its processes of detection and enforcement were abused through the instigation by government officials of an act on the part of persons otherwise innocent... Chief Justice Hughes' interpretation of 'legislative intent' was in turn based on a public policy which was stated in Butts v. United States,[13] and cited in Sorrells: 'The first duties of [the government's] officers are to prevent, not to punish crime.' Sorrells, then, asserted the defense of entrapment is allowed by the courts, not as a device for allowing the guilty to go unpunished, but to effectuate the intent of Congress in

ENTRAPMENT.—Cont'd.

enacting statutory laws and to check the abuse of these statutes by the government through the government's instigation of violations."[14]

If, as Harris[15] points out, the statutes were inapplicable in cases where government officials implanted the idea of the offense in the defendant's mind, it would seem to follow that a "searching inquiry" into the defendant's predisposition would be irrelevant and certainly not conclusive as to the likelihood of a conviction. This, in fact, would be consistent with the concurring opinion of Mr. Justice Roberts, who asserted that if entrapment were found by the court, the prosecution should not counter with proof of the defendant's predisposition. Justice Roberts' pertinent question was: "Is the statute upon which the indictment is based to be further construed as removing the defense of entrapment from such a [predisposed] defendant?"

It should not be overlooked that the possibility of a "middle ground theory" might be argued in light of the decision in United States v. Jannotti.[16] Co-defendants Jannotti and Schwartz appealed a jury verdict finding them guilty of conspiring to obstruct justice in violation of the Hobbs Act.[17] More specifically, undisputed evidence had shown that Jannotti and Schwartz accepted bribes from undercover F. B. I. agents portraying themselves as representatives of Arab investors who were considering the construction of a multi-million dollar hotel complex in Philadelphia.[18] Schwartz was also found guilty of conspiring to violate provisions of the Racketeer Influenced and Corrupt Organizations Act (RICO conspiracy).[19] The evidence showed that Schwartz and co-defendant Criden conspired to conduct the affairs of an enterprise (a law firm of which Criden was a partner) "through a pattern of racketeering activity, to wit, the payment of bribes to public officials."[20] The district court found that a jury could reasonably conclude from the evidence presented that all essential elements of the

ENTRAPMENT.—Cont'd.

crimes charged were proven by the prosecution. The court, therefore, discussed the defense of entrapment asserted by the defendants.[21]

Although the court called for a "middle ground" test in determining entrapment, in practice the test employed by the court is yet another two-pronged, subjective test. The defendant must show both government inducement and lack of predisposition in order to raise the defense. The concession given in Jannotti to the minority-subjective advocates is that if the government's conduct amounts to a violation of due process, even a predisposed defendant may not be convicted.[22] "Exactly what amounts to a violation of due process, of course, is not easily defined. In fact, the very concept of delineating entrapment from conduct . . . so egregious as to amount to a violation of due process . . . is reminiscent of the persistently confusing 'lawful' versus 'unlawful' entrapment theory."[23] Under the former view, "lawful" entrapment occurs when the officer merely affords a predisposed defendant the opportunity to commit a crime; "unlawful" entrapment occurs when the idea of committing the crime originates with the government officers, and the defendant is not predisposed.[24] A substantial number of courts have found jury charges instructing that a difference exists between "lawful" and "unlawful" entrapment are improper.[25]

Thus, the "middle ground" test announced in Jannotti is an unreliable precedent. No one can predict where the line will next be drawn between "lawful" entrapment and a denial of due process. The facts indicated reprehensible, if not ingenious, play-acting on the part of government officers and agents. The court of appeals reversed the defendants' convictions, first, on grounds that the defendants were not predisposed to commit the crimes, and alternatively, on grounds that the governmental overreaching constituted a denial of due process. It is well settled that the defense of entrapment cannot be denied to a non-predisposed defendant.[26] What if the

ENTRAPMENT.—Cont'd.

evidence had indicated that the defendants were predisposed? Would the same actions on the part of the law enforcement officers have been deemed a denial of due process, or should due process be rationed out to defendants according to their "criminal predisposition"? If the purpose of the defense is to prohibit unlawful governmental activity in fostering crime,[27] the answers to these questions are that the predisposition of the defendant is irrelevant because the scope of inquiry should focus on police conduct; and if the police conduct were so inducive as to cause a person of reasonably firm moral convictions to commit a crime, entrapment exists. If entrapment exists, there is a per se violation of the defendant's Fifth Amendment rights; and all evidence obtained through entrapment techniques is inadmissible.

The defense attorney should not overlook the use of constitutional attacks on governmental overreaching, although for the most part they have been limited to general due process and equal protection arguments. In Russell, Justice Rehnquist predicted a situation where police conduct is so outrageous that due process principles would prohibit a conviction even of a predisposed defendant.[28] In Jannotti, the United States District Court for the Eastern District of Pennsylvania held that the Philadelphia branch of the ABSCAM operation amounted to a violation of defendant's due process rights.[29] Equal protection arguments are based on the discriminatory effect of singling out certain people and inducing them to commit a crime in order to prosecute.[30] It has been argued that when congressmen or politicians are "entrapped" to commit bribery, a first amendment violation exists.[31]

Harris[32] suggested that if a person does indeed have a constitutional right not to be entrapped, the proper analysis begins with these queries:

(1) Who is the defense of entrapment intended to protect?

(2) What fundamental right should the

ENTRAPMENT.—Cont'd.

defense of entrapment be intended to protect?

(3) What specific amendments of the Constitution protect those rights?

Finally, it is worth mentioning that the entire majority-minority debate has been called an exercise in semantics.[33] However, this view is not tenable in light of the fact that such positions endeavor to achieve divergent goals: the majority view attempts to protect the unwary, innocent citizen from government temptation, while the minority view seeks to prohibit objectionable police conduct and ensure that every suspect is accorded his fair share of due process.

---

1. *See comments following Code of Ala. 1975, § 13A-3-31.*
2. *See Jackson v. State, 384 So. 2d 134 (Ala. Crim. App. 1979); Pearson v. State, 362 So. 2d 1278 (Ala. Crim. App. 1978); Hudson v. State, 335 So. 2d 208 (Ala. Crim. App. 1976), cert. denied, 335 So. 2d 211 (Ala. 1976); Suiter v. State, 57 Ala. App. 146, 326 So. 2d 675 (1975), cert. denied, 295 Ala. 424, 326 So. 2d 680 (1975); Staggs v. State, 53 Ala. App. 314, 299 So. 2d 756 (1974), cert. denied, 293 Ala. 733, 299 So. 2d 767 (1974); Johnson v. State, 291 Ala. 639, 285 So. 2d 723 (1973).*
3. *See comments following Code of Ala. 1975, § 13A-3-31.*
4. *The following comments are based largely upon "Entrapment: A Source of Continuing Confusion in the Lower Courts" by Cindy Morris Harris (Tulane Law School), appearing in The American Journal of Trial Advocacy, Volume 5, Number 2, Fall, 1981, published by the Cumberland School of Law, Birmingham, Alabama.*
5. *The defense of entrapment was not known at common law. State v. Good, 110 Ohio App. 415, 165 N. E. 2d 28 (1960) (possession and sale of narcotics). The doctrine is not recognized in some states. See, e.g., Warden v. State, 214 Tenn. 378, 381 S. W. 2d 247 (1964); People v. Schacher, 47 N. Y. S. 2d 371 (Mag. Ct. N. Y. C. 1944). See also United States ex rel. Hall v. Illinois, 329 F. 2d 354 (7th Cir. 1964) (wherein the court said there is some question whether Tennessee and New York recognize the doctrine).*
6. *The first case in which a federal court found a claim of entrapment was Woo Wai v. United States, 223 F. 412 (9th Cir. 1915).*
7. *Sorrells v. U. S., 287 U. S. 435, 53 S. Ct. 210, 77 L. Ed. 413 (1932). A prohibition agent, disguised as a tourist, persuaded the defendant to obtain a half-gallon of whiskey for him. The setting for this charade was a social gathering at the defendant's home. The agent made repeated appeals to the defendant's sense of camaraderie and perhaps even his patriotism by recounting their previous World War I days, which were spent in the same division. Eventually, the defendant yielded to the agent's requests and produced the liquor, for which the agent paid him five dollars.*

ENTRAPMENT.—Cont'd.

8. *Sorrells v. U. S., 287 U. S. 435, at 445, 53 S. Ct. 210, at 214, 77 L. Ed. 413, 418 (1932).*
9. *See Jackson v. State, 384 So. 2d 134 (Ala. Crim. App. 1979); Pearson v. State, 362 So. 2d 1278 (Ala. Crim. App. 1978); Hudson v. State, 335 So. 2d 208 (Ala. Crim. App. 1976), cert. denied, 335 So. 2d 211 (Ala. 1976); Suiter v. State, 57 Ala. App. 146, 326 So. 2d 675 (1975), cert. denied, 295 Ala. 424, 326 So. 2d 680 (1975); Staggs v. State, 53 Ala. App. 314, 299 So. 2d 756 (1974), cert. denied, 293 Ala. 733, 299 So. 2d 767 (1974); Johnson v. State, 291 Ala. 639, 285 So. 2d 723 (1973).*
10. *See Eisner v. Commonwealth, 375 S. W. 2d 825 (Ky. 1964) (engaging in prostitution); People v. Bernal, 174 Cal. App. 2d 777, 345 P. 2d 140 (1959) (sale of narcotics); People v. Outten, 13 Ill. 2d 21, 147 N. E. 2d 284 (1958) (sale of narcotic drugs); State v. Burnette, 242 N. C. 164, 87 S. E. 2d 191 (1955) (assault with intent to commit rape).*
11. *Besides Sorrells, the major cases of entrapment decided by the Supreme Court are Hampton v. United States, 425 U. S. 484, 96 S. Ct. 1646, 48 L. Ed. 2d 113 (1976); United States v. Russell, 411 U. S. 423, 93 S. Ct. 1637, 36 L. Ed. 2d 366 (1973); Sherman v. United States, 356 U. S. 369, 78 S. Ct. 819, 2 L. Ed. 2d 848 (1958).*
12. *An excellent treatment of this appears in Volume 5, Number 2 (Fall, 1981) of the American Journal of Trial Advocacy (published by the Cumberland School of Law), "Entrapment: A Source of Continuing Confusion in the Lower Courts" by Cindy Morris Harris of Tulane Law School.*
13. *Butts v. U. S., 273 F. 35, 38 (8th Cir. 1921).*
14. *Harris, C. M., "Entrapment: A Source of Continuing Confusion in the Lower Courts," Volume 5, Number 2 of the American Journal of Trial Advocacy, at page 295 (Fall, 1981). See also Trice v. U. S., 211 F. 2d 513, 518 (9th Cir. 1954) (instructions to the jury distinguishing "lawful" and "unlawful" entrapment held proper.)*
15. *Harris, C. M., "Entrapment: A Source of Continuing Confusion in the Lower Courts,"*

ENTRAPMENT.—Cont'd.

Volume 5, Number 2 of the American Journal of Trial Advocacy, at page 295 (Fall, 1981).

16. *U. S. v. Jannotti, 501 F. Supp. 1182 (E. D. Pa. 1980). The facts in Jannotti are as follows: Jannotti and Schwartz were introduced by Howard Criden to undercover agents posing as representatives of wealthy Arab investors. Jannotti was a member of the Philadelphia City Council, and Schwartz was the President of the City Council. The defendants were led to believe that the Arab investors were contemplating a multi-million dollar hotel complex, possible revitalization of Pennsylvania's coal industry, and other major improvements along the Philadelphia waterfront. Schwartz was told that the Sheik's representatives desired his expert advice concerning the mechanics of city government and the procedures for obtaining approval for the hotel project. Criden informed Schwartz that the Arabs would pay him a thirty thousand dollar consulting fee. Jannotti was also assured of the legitimacy of the project and the particular desire of the Arabs to "make friends" by paying him money. Neither defendant asked for the money that was paid them. Neither promised to sell his vote. Both asserted that no payments were necessary because the project was legitimate and that they would vote for it without payments. The idea of paying money to the councilmen originated with the undercover agents.*

There was certainly no reason for Jannotti or Schwartz to doubt that they were dealing with wealthy Arabs. The ABSCAM operation was elaborate and carefully planned. Undercover agents posing as representatives of Arab sheiks entertained on a yacht in Florida and rented a town house in Georgetown and lavish hotel suites in Philadelphia and New York. They traveled by private jet and limousines. The Chase Manhattan Bank was prepared to verify that the alleged wealthy Arabs had over four hundred million dollars on deposit in that institution. The scheme was designed, according to the court, to ascertain which city officials, given enough inducement, could be corrupted.

17. *The Hobbs Act, 18 U. S. C. § 1951(a), makes criminal the conduct of "[w]hoever in any way or degree obstructs, delays, or affects commerce or the movement of any article or commodity in commerce, by robbery or extortion or attempts or conspires so to do . . ." Extortion is "the obtaining of property from another, with his consent, induced by wrongful use of actual or threatened force, violence, or fear, or under color of official*

ENTRAPMENT.—Cont'd.

right." 18 U. S. C. § 1951(b)(2).

18. *U. S. v. Jannotti, 501 F. Supp. 1182, 1184 (E. D. Pa. 1980).*
19. *18 U. S. C. § 1962(c).*
20. *U. S. v. Jannotti, 501 F. Supp. 1182, 1185 (E. D. Pa. 1980).*
21. *U. S. v. Jannotti, 501 F. Supp. 1182, 1187 (E. D. Pa. 1980).*
22. *In Russell, the Supreme Court predicted that "we may some day be presented with a situation in which the conduct of law enforcement agents is so outrageous that due process principles would absolutely bar the . . . conviction." United States v. Russell, 411 U. S. 423, 431, 93 S. Ct. 1637, 1642, 36 L. Ed. 2d 366, 373 (1973).*
23. *Trice v. United States, 211 F. 2d 513, 518 (9th Cir. 1954) (instructions to the jury distinguishing "lawful" and "unlawful" entrapment held proper). See also Harris, C. M., "Entrapment: A Source of Continuing Confusion in the Lower Courts," Volume 5, Number 2 of the American Journal of Trial Advocacy, at page 295 (Fall, 1981).*
24. *United States v. Gardner, 516 F. 2d 334 (7th Cir. 1975), cert. denied, 423 U. S. 861, 96 S. Ct. 118, 46 L. Ed. 2d 89 (1975).*
25. *See, e.g., Government of Virgin Islands v. Cruz, 478 F. 2d 712 (3d Cir. 1973); United States v. Melchor Moreno, 536 F. 2d 1042 (1976), reh. denied, 543 F. 2d 1175 (5th Cir. 1976); United States v. Hill, 444 F. 2d 115 (10th Cir. 1971), later app., 469 F. 2d 673, cert. denied, 410 U. S. 939, 93 S. Ct. 1400, 35 L. Ed. 2d 604 (1971).*
26. *Sherman v. United States, 356 U. S. 369, 78 S. Ct. 819, 2 L. Ed. 2d 848 (1958); Sorrells v. United States, 287 U. S. 435, 53 S. Ct. 210, 77 L. Ed. 413 (1932).*
27. *United States v. Russell, 411 U. S. 423, 442, 93 S. Ct. 1637, 1648, 36 L. Ed. 2d 366, 379 (1973) (Stewart, dissenting).*
28. *U. S. v. Russell, 411 U. S. 423, 431, 93 S. Ct. 1637, 1643, 36 L. Ed. 2d 366, 373 (1973).*
29. *United States v. Jannotti, 501 F. Supp. 1182, 1204 (E. D. Pa. 1980). See also United States v. Twigg, 588 F. 2d 373 (3d Cir. 1978) (conviction reversed on due process grounds because of governmental overreaching); United States v. Archer, 486 F. 2d 670 (2d Cir. 1973); Greene v. United States, 454 F. 2d 783, 787 (9th Cir. 1972).*
30. *Orfield, The Defense of Entrapment in Federal Courts, 1967 Duke L. J. 39, 56.*
31. *United States v. Steele, 461 F. 2d 1148 (9th Cir. 1972).*
32. *Harris, C. M., "Entrapment: A Source of Continuing Confusion in the Lower Courts,"*

ENTRAPMENT.—Cont'd.

Volume 5, Number 2 of the American Journal of Trial Advocacy, at page 303 (Fall, 1981).

33. See Ortega v. United States, 348 F. 2d 847, 876 (9th Cir. 1965). See also Note, Entrapment — A Call for the Elimination of the Ninth Circuit Prohibition Against Pleading Inconsistent Defenses, 4 S. W. L. Rev. 121, 124 (1972).

ESCAPE. Code of Ala. 1975, §§ 13A-10-31 through 13A-10-33.

"(a) A person commits the crime of escape in the first degree if:

"(1) He employs physical force, a threat of physical force, a deadly weapon or a dangerous instrument in escaping or attempting to escape from custody;[1] or

"(2) Having been convicted of a felony, he escapes or attempts to escape from custody imposed pursuant to that conviction." § 13A-10-31 of the Alabama Code.

"A person commits the crime of escape in the second degree if he escapes or attempts to escape from a penal facility."[2] § 13A-10-32 of the Alabama Code.

"A person commits the offense of escape in the third degree if he escapes or attempts to escape from custody." § 13A-10-33 of the Alabama Code.

Classification.

Class B felony, first degree.

Class C felony, second and third degree.

Comments.

The classification of this crime is based upon two factors: (1) use of force, and (2) the seriousness of the crime that led to the detention. The lowest class of escape is a simple escape from custody or from a penal facility. The class is raised where at least one of the following elements is present: (1) the escapee used force or a deadly weapon, or (2) the escapee was a convicted felon. While the normal rule is that attempt of crime imposes punishment one level below that for the completed crime,[3] escape and attempted escape are treated the same.

Defenses.

(1) Forced to escape along with others due to duress.

(2) Escapee believed he was free to leave.

Cross references.

See BAIL JUMPING; ESCAPE, PERMITTING OR FACILITATING.

---

1. "A restraint or detention by a public servant pursuant to a lawful arrest, conviction or order of court, but does not include mere supervision of probation or parole, or constraint incidental to release on bail." Code of Ala. 1975, § 13A-10-30(b)(1).

2. "Any security correctional institution for the confinement of persons arrested for, charged with or convicted of a criminal offense, including but not limited to the following security facilities: the state penitentiary and any branch thereof or any county or city jail." Code of Ala. 1975, § 13A-10-30(b)(3).

3. Attempt, Code of Ala. 1975, § 13A-4-2.

ESCAPE, PERMITTING OR FACILITATING. Code of Ala. 1975, §§ 13A-10-34 and 13A-10-35.

Charged as: Permitting or facilitating escape.

"(a) A person commits the crime of permitting or facilitating escape in the first degree if:

"(1) He intentionally aids or attempts to aid in the escape of a person arrested for, charged with or convicted of a felony from a penal facility;[1] or

"(2) He is a public servant[2] of a penal facility and intentionally, knowingly or recklessly permits or facilitates the escape of a person arrested for, charged with or convicted of a felony." § 13A-10-34 of the Alabama Code.

"(a) A person commits the crime of permitting or facilitating escape in the second degree if:

"(1) He intentionally aids or attempts to aid in the escape of a person arrested for, charged with, or convicted of a misdemeanor from a penal or detentional facility; or

"(2) He is a public servant of a penal or detention facility and who intentionally, knowingly, or recklessly permits or facilitates the escape of a person arrested for, charged with, or convicted of a misdemeanor." § 13A-10-35 of the Alabama Code.

Classification.

Class C felony, first degree.

Class A misdemeanor, second degree.

ESCAPE, PERMITTING OR FACILITATING.—Cont'd.

Comments.

These sections are directed toward two situations: (1) where any person intentionally gives aid or assistance with the intent to facilitate an escape; and (2) where a public official or employee of a penal facility intentionally or recklessly permits or allows an escape. There is no criminal liability for negligently allowing or permitting an escape. The distinctions between the two sections are: (1) first degree is concerned with the escape of person arrested for, charged with, or convicted of a felony, rather than, in second degree, a misdemeanor; and (2) second degree is not restricted to escape from a penal facility.

Defenses.

(1) For those not public servants of a penal facility, lack of intent.

(2) For public servants of penal facilities, negligent instead of reckless action.

(3) For defendants not public servants of penal or detention facilities, escape was not from a penal or detentional facility.

Cross references.

See ESCAPE.

---

1. *"A restraint or detention by a public servant pursuant to a lawful arrest, conviction or order of court, but does not include mere supervision of probation or parole, or constraint incidental to release on bail." Code of Ala. 1975, § 13A-10-30(b)(1).*
2. *"Any officer or employee of government, including legislators and judges and any person or agency participating as an adviser, consultant or otherwise in performing a governmental function." Code of Ala. 1975, § 13A-10-1(7).*

ETHICS VIOLATIONS. Code of Ala. 1975, Title 36, chapter 25.

The Code of Ethics of Alabama is set out in Title 36, chapter 25, of the Code of Alabama. Title 36 is entitled Public Officers and Employees, and the official designation of chapter 25 of that title is the Code of Ethics for Public Officials, Employees, Etc. Although reflective of the central purpose of the chapter, these designations are deceptive both in scope and importance. In many instances, it is not only the conduct of the public official or employee which is regulated, but also that of his family, his business associates, and in some instances, "any person." This confusing situation is further complicated by a single all-encompassing penal provision which proscribes punishment for "any person who violates any provision of this chapter."[1] That punishment is imprisonment not to exceed 10 years and/or a fine not to exceed $10,000. What constitutes a violation of any particular provision, or the persons intended to be subject to such provision, is not clear. Many provisions appear to create strict liability offenses as culpable intent is in most instances irrelevant. Certainly no attempt should be made to evaluate or defend against a charge without a reading of the chapter information with particular attention to the interplay of definitions and the articulated purpose of the chapter. Even then, many of the provisions of this chapter may be susceptible to constitutional attack.

---

1. *Code of Ala. 1975, § 36-25-27(a).*

EXPLOSION. See ARSON; EXPLOSIVES, POSSESSION OF; GUNPOWDER, STORING.

EXPLOSIVES. See ARSON; EXPLOSIVES, POSSESSION OF; GUNPOWDER, STORING.

EXPLOSIVES, POSSESSION OF. Code of Ala. 1975, § 13A-7-44.

Charged as: Criminal possession of explosives.

"A person commits the crime of criminal possession of explosives[1] if he possesses, manufactures, buys, sells or transports any explosive, **and** intends[2] that the explosive be used in the commission of a crime involving violence to another person or destruction of another's property." (emphasis added)

Classification.

Class C felony.

EXPLOSIVES, POSSESSION OF. —Cont'd.

Comments.

This is a new crime under Alabama law to directly penalize the illicit possession, manufacture, etc. of explosives with the requisite intent that the explosives be used in the commission of a crime.

Defenses.

(1) Mere knowledge that these explosives could be used, as opposed to would be used, in the commission of a crime would not meet the requisite intent.

(2) Even if knowledge can be shown, the burden remains on the state to prove intent.

Query.

What if the manufacturer, seller, etc., has prior knowledge that a person buying the explosives had in the past used explosives to commit a crime?

Cross references.

See GUNPOWDER, STORING; NOXIOUS SUBSTANCE, USE OR POSSESSION OF.

---

1. An explosive, according to Code of Ala. 1975, § 13-7-40(2), is:

"Any chemical compound or mechanical mixture that is commonly used or intended for the purpose of producing an explosion and which contains any oxidizing and combustive units or other ingredients in such proportions, quantities or packing that an ignition by fire, by friction, by concussion, by detonator or by chemical action of any part of the compound or mixture may cause a sudden generation of highly heated gases that the resultant gaseous pressures are capable of producing destructive effects on contiguous objects or of destroying life or limb."

2. Code of Ala. 1975, § 13A-2-2(1) states that a person acts "intentionally with respect to a result or to conduct described by a statute defining an offense, when his ***purpose*** *is to cause that result or to engage in that conduct." (emphasis added)*

EXTORTION. Code of Ala. 1975, §§ 13A-8-13 through 13A-8-15.

"A person commits the crime of extortion if he knowingly obtains by threat[1] control over the property[2] of another, with intent to deprive him of the property." § 13A-8-13 of the Alabama Code.

"Extortion by means of a threat, as defined in [§ 13A-8-1(13)a. or § 13A-8-1(13)c. of the Alabama Code],[3] constitutes extortion in the first degree." § 13A-8-14 of the Alabama Code.

"Extortion by means of a threat, as defined in [§ 13A-8-1(13)b. or § 13A-8-1(13)d. through § 13A-8-1(13)k. of the Alabama Code],[4] constitutes extortion in the second degree." § 13A-8-15 of the Alabama Code.

Classification.

Class B felony, extortion in the first degree.

Class C felony, extortion in the second degree.

Comments.

Extortion is the wrongful acquisition of property by intimidation with a larcenous intent. It is a form of theft, and it includes blackmail. Classifying extortion into two degrees differentiates between effective threats of physical harm and loss of personal freedom, as compared with threats directed toward property, reputation, privacy of secrets, legal rights, and economic interests. It differs from robbery in the third degree[5] because the threat must be with regard to future, rather than imminent, harm.

Defenses.

(1) No control of the property of another obtained.

(2) Lack of intent to deprive the owner of the property.

(3) Regarding a threat of criminal prosecution[6] on a charge of extortion in the second degree, honest belief as to the rightness of such threatened prosecution.[7]

Cross references.

See ROBBERY; THEFT OF PROPERTY.

---

1. "THREAT. A menace, however communicated, to:

"a. Cause physical harm to the person threatened or to any other person; or

"b. Cause damage to property; or

"c. Subject the person threatened or any other person to physical confinement or restraint; or

"d. Engage in other conduct constituting a crime; or

"e. Accuse any person of a crime or cause criminal charges to be instituted against any person; or

"f. Expose a secret or publicize an asserted fact, whether true or false, tending to subject any

EXTORTION.—Cont'd.

person to hatred, contempt or ridicule; or

"g. Reveal any information sought to be concealed by the person threatened; or

"h. Testify or provide information or withhold testimony or information with respect to another's legal claim or defense; or

"i. Take action as an official against anyone or anything, or withhold official action, or cause such action or withholding; or

"j. Bring about or continue a strike, boycott or other similar collective action to obtain property which is not demanded or received for the benefit of the group which the actor purports to represent; or

"k. Do any other act which would not in itself substantially benefit the actor but which is calculated to harm substantially another person with respect to his health, safety, business, calling, career, financial condition, reputation or personal relationships." Code of Ala. 1975, § 13A-8-1(13).

2. *"PROPERTY. Any money, tangible or intangible personal property, property (whether real or personal) the location of which can be changed (including things growing on, affixed to or found in land and documents, although the rights represented hereby have no physical location), contract right, chose-in-action, interest in or claim to wealth, credit or any other article or thing of value of any kind.*

   "Commodities of a public utility nature, such as gas, electricity, steam and water, constitute property, but the supplying of such a commodity to premises from an outside source by means of wires, pipes, conduits or other equipment shall be deemed a rendition of a service rather than a sale or delivery of property." Code of Ala. 1975, § 13A-8-1(10). See § 13A-8-10, Theft of services.
3. *See note 1, supra, at a. and c.*
4. *See note 1, supra, at b., d., and k.*
5. *Code of Ala. 1975, § 13A-8-43(2).*
6. *See note 1, supra, at e.*
7. *"A person is not liable . . . for a threat, as defined in paragraph (13)e of Code of Ala. 1975, section 13A-8-1 [see note 1, supra], if he honestly claims the property as restitution or indemnification for harm done in the circumstances to which the threat relates, or as compensation for property or lawful services. The burden of injecting the issue of claim of right is on the defendant, but this does not shift the burden of proof." Code of Ala. 1975, § 13A-8-15(b).*

FAILING TO FILE A REQUIRED REPORT. See REPORT, REQUIRED, FAILURE TO FILE.

FALSE ADVERTISING. See ADVERTISING, FALSE.

FALSE ALARM/FALSE REPORTING TO LAW ENFORCEMENT AUTHORITIES. Code of Ala. 1975, §§ 13A-10-8 and 13A-10-9.

Charged as: Rendering a false alarm.

"A person commits the crime of rendering a false alarm if he knowingly causes a false alarm of fire or other emergency involving danger to person or property[1] to be transmitted to or within an official or volunteer fire department or any other governmental agency or to be transmitted to or within a hospital or nursing home or any building housing handicapped or immobile people." § 13A-10-8 of the Alabama Code.

"A person commits the crime of false reporting to law enforcement authorities[2] if he knowingly makes a false report or causes the transmission of a false report to law enforcement authorities of a crime[3] or relating to a crime." § 13A-10-9 of the Alabama Code.

Classification.

Class A misdemeanor.

Class C felony if false alarm concerns a hospital or nursing home or other building housing handicapped or immobile people.

Comments.

Section 13A-10-9 of the Alabama Code complements § 13A-10-8 of the Alabama Code since rendering false information concerning a crime could constitute rendering a false alarm. Section 13A-10-9 of the Alabama Code is limited to cases where the report is transmitted to law enforcement authorities, whereas § 13A-10-8 of the Alabama Code would include any organization dealing with dangerous emergencies. In both sections the alarm must be known to be false; also, both sections penalize not only the making of a false report by any person but also the

FALSE ALARM/FALSE REPORTING TO LAW ENFORCEMENT AUTHORITIES.—Cont'd.

causing of such a report or alarm to be made by another.

Defenses.

(1) Belief that a reason for report or alarm existed.

(2) Lack of intent.

Cross references.

See FALSELY REPORTING AN INCIDENT.

---

1. *"Any real or personal property, including books, records and documents." § 13A-10-1(6).*
2. *This term is broad enough to include prosecuting attorneys and other persons, rather than only peace officers.*
3. *"A misdemeanor or a felony." § 13A-1-2(5).*

FALSE INSTRUMENT OFFERED FOR RECORDING. Code of Ala. 1975, § 13A-9-12.

Charged as: Offering false instrument for recording.

"A person commits the crime of offering a false instrument for recording if, knowing that a written instrument[1] relating to or affecting real or personal property, or an interest therein, or directly affecting contractual relationships contains a material false statement or material false information, and with intent to defraud,[2] he presents or offers it to a public office or a public employee, with the knowledge that it will be registered, filed or recorded or become a part of the records of that public office or public employee."

Classification.

Class A misdemeanor.

Comments.

This section is concerned only with those instruments that are intended to become public records. It differs from forgery in the second degree[3] because the actual presentation of the instrument for recording, and not the making of the instrument, is the criminal activity regulated. It differs from criminal possession of a forged instrument in the second degree[4] because the instruments are not necessarily forged, but need only to

FALSE INSTRUMENT OFFERED FOR RECORDING.—Cont'd.

contain a material false statement or material false information. This section requires affirmative proof of the offeror's knowledge of the false information and of a specific intent to defraud.

Defenses.

(1) Lack of intent to defraud.

(2) Lack of knowledge that such instrument will be registered, filed, or recorded or become a record of a public office or public employee to which it was presented or offered.

(3) Presentation was neither to a person who is a public employee nor to a public office.

(4) Instrument does not (1) affect real or personal property or an interest therein or (2) directly affect a contractual relationship.

Cross references.

See FORGED INSTRUMENT, CRIMINAL POSSESSION OF; FORGERY.

---

1. *"Such term means:*
   "a. Any paper, document or other instrument containing written or printed matter or its equivalent; and
   "b. Any token, stamp, seal, badge, trademark or other evidence or symbol of value, right, privilege or identification,
   which is capable of being used to the advantage or disadvantage of some person." Code of Ala. 1975, § 13A-9-1(1).
2. *"A purpose to use deception, as defined in Code of Ala. 1975, section 13A-8-1(1), or to injure another person's interest which has value, as defined in section 13A-8-1(14)." Code of Ala. 1975, § 13A-9-1(8).*
3. *See Code of Ala. 1975, § 13A-9-3(a)(2).*
4. *See Code of Ala. 1975, § 13A-9-6(a).*

FALSELY REPORTING AN INCIDENT. Code of Ala. 1975, § 13A-11-11.

"A person commits the crime of falsely reporting an incident if with knowledge that the information reported, conveyed or circulated is false, he initiates or circulates a false report or warning of an alleged occurrence or impending occurrence of a fire, explosion, crime, catastrophe or emergency under circumstances in which it

FALSELY REPORTING AN INCIDENT.—Cont'd.

is likely to cause evacuation of a building, place of assembly or transportation facility, or to cause public inconvenience or alarm."

Classification.

Class A misdemeanor.

Comments.

The statute prohibits person from initiating or circulating information that he knows[1] is false about emergency situations[2] under certain circumstances. The crucial element of this crime is knowledge that the information is false. The statute imputes criminal liability to the initiator or circulator of the false report even if the unwarranted inconvenience or alarm occurs pursuant to actions of one not charged with governmental operations. False reports to school administrators or hotel managers can come within the scope of this statute. Someone who shouts "Fire!" in an assembly, when he knows such circumstance does not exist, is similarly culpable under this statute. The person need not intend to cause evacuation of facilities. Dissemination of information that one knows is false in circumstance likely to cause such public inconvenience supplies the culpable mental state.[3]

Defenses.

(1) Belief that the information is true.

(2) Failure to prove initiation or circulation of the information.

(3) Circumstance not such that it was likely to cause public inconvenience or alarm.

Cross references.

See Falsely requesting use of party line for emergency, § 13A-11-223 of the Alabama Code. See FALSE ALARM/FALSE REPORTING TO LAW ENFORCEMENT AUTHORITIES.

---

1. *"A person acts knowingly with respect to conduct or to a circumstance . . . when he is aware that his conduct is of that nature . . ." Code of Ala. 1975, § 13A-2-2(2).*

2. *The statute is broadly written to cover the following occurrences: fire, crime, explosion, catastrophe, or emergency.*

3. *When causing a particular result is a material element of an offense for which absolute liability is imposed by law, the element is not established unless the actual result is a probable consequence of the actor's conduct. Code of Ala. 1975, § 13A-2-5(c).*

FAMILY. See ABORTION; ADULTERY; BIGAMY; CHILD, ABANDONMENT OF; CHILD WELFARE, ENDANGERING; INCEST.

FELONIES. See SENTENCING.

FELONS, REGISTRATION OF. Code of Ala. 1975, §§ 13A-11-180 through 13A-11-186.

Charged as:

§ 13A-11-181: Person convicted more than twice of felony to register with sheriff of county of residence.

§ 13A-11-182: Failure to carry registration card.

§ 13A-11-183: Failure to give notice of change of address or place of residence.

§ 13A-11-184: Certain persons exempt.

§ 13A-11-185: Access to registration book.

"It shall be the duty of any person who has been convicted more than twice of a felony under the laws of any state or the United States, who has not been restored to his civil rights by competent legal authority, and who resides within any county in the state of Alabama, to register within 24 hours after his arrival in the county, in a book of registration to be kept at the county courthouse, under the supervision of the county sheriff. Such person shall make a sworn statement upon blanks to be furnished by the sheriff, stating each offense for which he has been convicted, the time and place of conviction and his address while residing in the county." § 13A-11-181 of the Alabama Code.

"Upon registration and the filing of the affidavit, as provided in [§ 13A-11-181 of the Alabama Code], the sheriff or one of his deputies shall give to such person a registration card, showing the name of such person, his address in the county and the date of registration. Such card shall be signed by the sheriff or one of his deputies.

FELONS, REGISTRATION OF.
—Cont'd.

It shall be unlawful for anyone who is required to register under the provisions of this article to be within any county in the state without having in his immediate possession a registration card as provided herein. It shall be the duty of such person to carry the card with him at all times while he is within the county and to exhibit the same to any officer of a municipality, a county or the state upon request." § 13A-11-182 of the Alabama Code.

"It shall be the duty of any person who has registered pursuant to this article and who changes his address or place of residence in the county, to inform the sheriff of such change within 24 hours after the same has been made, which shall be noted in the aforesaid book of registration and also on the registration card." § 13A-11-183 of the Alabama Code.

Classification.

"It shall be unlawful for any person subject to the provisions of this article to fail or refuse to comply with any of the provisions hereof within the time prescribed. Any person violating any provision of this article shall be subject to a fine of not less than $10.00 nor more than $50.00 for each day of violation, or imprisonment in the county jail not less than 10 nor more than 30 days for each day of violation, or both such fine and imprisonment." § 13A-11-186 of the Alabama Code.

Comments.

Convicted felons may be released from custody during the pendency of an action, but the release does not restore the felon's (full) civil rights. These statutes place a duty upon the felon to notify the sheriff in the county in which he resides[1] of his presence in that county. Not all felons who have been released from custody have the obligation; only those who have been twice convicted of a felony are required to register. The felon who is required to register must also carry a registration card which must be presented to a law officer upon request. If the felon changes his address or place of residence within the

FELONS, REGISTRATION OF.
—Cont'd.

county, the change must be brought to the attention of the sheriff. Nothing is said in the statutes as to what duty the felon has should he change his residence to a place outside the county in which he first registered. If the felon was residing in a county in Alabama and had not been convicted or served time for a felony within five years preceding September 12, 1966, this person is not required to register.[2]

Sheriffs and deputies are the only persons authorized to have access to or examine the registration books.[3] Anyone not so authorized, like felons who fail to comply with these provisions, may be subject to a fine and/or imprisonment.[4]

Defenses.

(1) Lack of two felony convictions.

(2) The provisions of this article shall not apply to any person residing in any county in the state on September 12, 1966, who has not been convicted of, or served time for, a felony within the five years next preceding such date. § 13A-11-184 of the Alabama Code.

Cross references.

See SEX OFFENDERS, REGISTRATION OF.

---

1. *"The words 'resides' or 'residing,' as used in this article, shall mean any person who remains within any county in the state for a period of more than 24 hours and maintains or uses sleeping quarters anywhere within the county." Code of Ala. 1975, § 13A-11-180.*
2. *Code of Ala. 1975, § 13A-11-184.*
3. *Code of Ala. 1975, § 13A-11-185.*
4. *Code of Ala. 1975, § 13A-11-186.*

FENCING. See RECEIVING STOLEN PROPERTY.

FINANCIAL INSTITUTIONS, FAILING, RECEIVING DEPOSITS IN. Code of Ala. 1975, § 13A-9-50.

Charged as: Receiving deposits in failing financial institutions.

"A person commits the crime of receiving[1] deposits in a failing financial institution,[2] if, as an officer, manager or other person

FINANCIAL INSTITUTIONS, FAILING, RECEIVING DEPOSITS IN.—Cont'd.

participating in the direction of a financial institution, he knowingly receives or permits the receipt of funds, a general deposit or other investment, knowing or having reason to believe that:

"(1) Due to financial difficulties the institution is about to suspend operations or go into receivership or reorganization, and

"(2) The person making the deposit or other payment is unaware of the precarious situation of the institution."

Classification.

Class A misdemeanor.

Comments.

There is no presumption of knowledge of bank failure. Culpability depends upon both knowledge of an institution's condition by a receiver and the ignorance of that condition on the part of the depositor. This section limits the sanction to those having the responsibility for directing of the institution rather than permitting liability to a mere receiving employee.

Defenses.

(1) Lack of knowledge of the failing condition of the institution.

(2) Proof that the person making the deposit knew of the precarious situation of the institution.

(3) Length of time between deposit and subsequent demise of the institution.

Cross references.

See Theft and related offenses, Title 13A, chapter 8, article 1 of the Alabama Code.

---

1. *"Receiving" as defined in Code of Ala. 1975, § 13A-8-1(11): "[A]cquiring possession, control or title and taking a security interest in the property."*
2. *"Financial institution" as defined in Code of Ala. 1975, § 13A-8-1(3): "A bank, insurance company, credit union, safety deposit company, savings and loan association, investment trust or other organization held out to the public as a place of deposit of funds or medium of savings or collective investment."*

FINANCIAL STATEMENT, ISSUING FALSE. Code of Ala. 1975, § 13A-9-49.

Charged as: Issuing false financial statement.

"A person[1] commits the crime of issuing a false financial statement if, with intent to defraud,[2] he:

"(1) Knowingly makes or utters[3] a written instrument[4] which purports to describe the financial condition or ability of himself or some other person and which is inaccurate in some material respect; or

"(2) Represents in writing that a written instrument purporting to describe a person's financial condition or ability to pay is accurate with respect to that person's current financial condition or ability to pay, knowing or having reason to believe the instrument to be materially inaccurate in that respect."

Classification.

Class B misdemeanor.

Comments.

Two distinct situations are covered by this section. The first situation covers the maker or utterer of the false financial statement, while the second covers another person who executes a writing that represents that another's financial statement is accurate. It is not necessary to prove the actor himself received any benefit. This section is directed toward a person offering a financial statement to a financial institution as a means of bolstering an application for funds.

Defenses.

(1) Lack of intent.

(2) Lack of knowledge that statement made is inaccurate.

(3) No written instrument representing an inaccurate financial condition.

Cross references.

See FORGERY; THEFT OF LOST PROPERTY; THEFT OF PROPERTY; THEFT OF SERVICES.

---

1. *"A human being, and where appropriate, a public or private corporation, an unincorporated association, a partnership, a government or a governmental instrumentality." Code of Ala. 1975, § 13A-1-2(6).*
2. *"A purpose to use deception, as defined in*

FINANCIAL STATEMENT, ISSUING FALSE.—Cont'd.

section 13A-8-1(1), or to injure another person's interest which has value, as defined in section 13A-8-1(14)." Code of Ala. 1975, § 13A-9-1(8).

3. *"To 'utter' means to directly or indirectly offer, assert, declare or put forth a forged instrument as genuine." Code of Ala. 1975, § 13A-9-1(12).*
4. *"Such term means:*
   "a. Any paper, document or other instrument containing written or printed matter or its equivalent; and
   "b. Any token, stamp, seal, badge, trademark or other evidence or symbol of value, right, privilege or identification,
   which is capable of being used to the advantage or disadvantage of some person." Code of Ala. 1975, § 13A-9-1(1).

FIRE. See ARSON.

FIREARMS, POSSESSION BY PERSONS PARTICIPATING IN, ATTENDING, ETC., DEMONSTRATIONS AT PUBLIC PLACES. Code of Ala. 1975, § 13A-11-59.

Charged as: Possession of firearms by persons participating in, attending, etc., demonstrations at public places.

"It shall be unlawful for any person, other than a law enforcement officer[1] . . . to have in his or her possession or about his or her person or in any vehicle at a point within 1,000 feet of a demonstration at a public place, any firearm after having first been advised by a law enforcement officer that a demonstration was taking place at a public place and after having been ordered by such officer to remove himself or herself from the prescribed area until such time as he or she no longer was in possession of any firearm. This subsection shall not apply to any person in possession of or having on his or her person any firearm within a private dwelling or other private building or structure."

Classification.

Class C misdemeanor.

Comments.

This section seeks to strike a balance between rights insured by the first and fourteenth amendments and the duty of the state to preserve order.[2] It has been carefully worded so as to preclude being labeled as unconstitutionally broad and overly vague. It forbids possession of a firearm[3] by a participant in a demonstration.[4] Despite the attempt at careful wording in this section, it presents some ambiguity in that it also prohibits the participant in a demonstration from having a firearm "in any vehicle" while participating in or attending any demonstration being held at a public place. Literally construed, this would impose criminal liability on the participant even if the firearm was in a vehicle miles away from the scene of the demonstration. It would be difficult indeed to show that the state had a protectable interest in preserving order that would include such sanctions.

Cross references.

See FIREARMS, USE WHILE FIGHTING IN PUBLIC PLACE.

---

1. *A law enforcement officer is: "Any duly appointed and acting federal, state, county or municipal law enforcement officer, peace officer or investigating officer, or any military or militia personnel called out or directed by constituted authority to keep the law and order, and any park ranger while acting as such on the grounds of a public park and who is on regular duty and present to actively police and control the demonstration, and who is assigned this duty by his department or agency. Such term does not include a peace officer on strike or a peace officer not on duty." Code of Ala. 1975, § 13A-11-59(a)(3).*
2. *Cox v. Louisiana, 379 U. S. 559, 85 S. Ct. 476, 13 L. Ed. 2d 487 (1965).*
3. *A firearm is defined as "[a]ny pistol, rifle, shotgun or firearm of any kind, whether loaded or not." Code of Ala. 1975, § 13A-11-59(a)(2).*
4. *Demonstration is "[d]emonstrating, picketing, speechmaking or marching, holding of vigils and all other like forms of conduct which involve the communication or expression of views or grievances engaged in by one or more persons, the conduct of which has the effect, intent or propensity to draw a crowd or onlookers. Such term shall not include casual use of property by visitors or tourists which does not have an intent*

FIREARMS, POSSESSION, ETC.—Cont'd.

or propensity to attract a crowd or onlookers." Code of Ala. 1975, § 13A-11-59(a)(1).

FIREARMS, USE WHILE FIGHTING IN PUBLIC PLACE. Code of Ala. 1975, § 13A-11-56.

Charged as: Using firearms while fighting in a public place.

A person commits the crime of using firearms while fighting in a public place if, while fighting in the streets of any city or town, or at a militia muster, or at any public place, whether public in itself, or made public at the time by an assemblage of persons, he uses or attempts to use, except in self-defense,[1] any kind of firearms.[2]

Classification.

Statutory penalty: fine of $200 to $500 and/or no more than 6 months hard labor for the county.

Comments.

The crime requires several elements: (1) use or attempt to use a firearm; (2) be a participant in a fight;[3] and (3) engage in the above-described conduct while in a "public place." The determination of what constitutes a public place is based on a facts and circumstances test. While the statute expressly carves out self-defense as a defense, other defenses and justifications provided by Title 13A, Chapter 3, of the Alabama Code are available to a defendant (see defenses below).[4] Violation of this section could be a lesser included offense under other provisions of the Code.[5]

Defenses.

(1) Self-defense.

(2) Justified by law.[6]

(3) Defendant did not use or attempt to use a firearm.

(4) Defendant was not "fighting."

(5) Incident did not occur in a "public place."

Cross references.

See FIREARMS, POSSESSION BY PERSONS PARTICIPATING IN, ATTENDING, ETC., DEMONSTRATIONS AT PUBLIC PLACES; PISTOLS, LICENSE TO

FIREARMS, USE WHILE FIGHTING IN PUBLIC PLACE.—Cont'd.

CARRY; WEAPONS, CARRYING CONCEALED.

---

1. *While the term "self-defense" is not defined, Code of Ala. 1975, § 13A-3-23(a) provides: "A person is justified in using physical force upon another person in order to defend himself or a third person from what he reasonably believes to be the use or imminent use of unlawful physical force by that other person, and he may use a degree of force which he reasonably believes to be necessary for the purpose." A person may not avail himself of this justification if he was the initial aggressor and failed to withdraw from the encounter. See Code of Ala. 1975, § 13A-3-23(c).*
2. *A firearm is "[a]ny pistol, rifle, shotgun or firearm of any kind, whether loaded or not." Code of Ala. 1975, § 13A-11-59(a)(2).*
3. *"Hostile encounter; either physical or verbal in nature. To oppose or attempt to prevent combat or battle, as hostile encounter or engagement between opposing forces . . ." Gitlow v. Kiely, 44 F. 2d 227, 232 (S. D. N. Y. 1930).*
4. *See Execution of public duty, Code of Ala. 1975, § 13A-3-22; Use of force in defense of premises, Code of Ala. 1975, § 13A-3-25; Use of force in defense of property other than premises, Code of Ala. 1975, § 13A-3-26; Use of force in making an arrest or preventing an escape; Code of Ala. 1975, § 13A-3-27; and Duress, Code of Ala. 1975, § 13A-3-30.*
5. *A defendant can be convicted of lesser included offenses that are within the offense charged. See Code of Ala. 1975, § 13A-1-9. Violating this statute could be a lesser included offense in any of the following: ASSAULT; MANSLAUGHTER; MENACING; PISTOLS, POSSESSION AND DELIVERY; RECKLESS ENDANGERMENT; RIOT; WEAPONS, CARRYING CONCEALED.*
6. *See note 4, supra.*

FIREWORKS, UNLAWFULLY DEALING IN. Code of Ala. 1975, §§ 13A-11-101 through 13A-11-105.

Note: Sections 13A-11-100 through 13A-11-105 of the Alabama Code have been repealed by Acts 1981, No. 81-409, § 18, effective May 5, 1981. As to the manufacture, sale, etc., of fireworks, see §§ 8-17-210 through 8-17-226 of the Alabama Code.

Cross references.

See EXPLOSIVES, POSSESSION OF.

FLASHING. See INDECENT EXPOSURE; LEWDNESS, PUBLIC.

FLEEING AND ELUDING. See MOTOR VEHICLE CRIMES.

FORCE BY PERSON WITH PARENTAL, CUSTODIAL, OR SPECIAL RESPONSIBILITIES.

Code of Ala. 1975, § 13A-3-24.

"The use of force upon another person is justified under any of the following circumstances:

"(1) A parent, guardian or other person responsible for the care and supervision of a minor or an incompetent person, and a teacher or other person responsible for the care and supervision of a minor for a special purpose, may use reasonable and appropriate physical force upon the minor or incompetent person when and to the extent that he reasonably believes it necessary and appropriate to maintain discipline or to promote the welfare of the minor or incompetent person.

"(2) A warden or other authorized official of a jail, prison or correctional institution may, in order to maintain order and discipline, use whatever physical force is authorized by law.

"(3) A person responsible for the maintenance of order in a common or contract carrier of passengers, or person acting under his direction, may use reasonable physical force when and to the extent that he reasonably believes it necessary to maintain order, but he may use deadly physical force only when he reasonably believes it necessary to prevent death or serious physical injury.

"(4) A person acting under a reasonable belief that another person is about to commit suicide or to inflict serious physical injury upon himself may use reasonable physical force upon that person to the extent that he reasonably believes it necessary to thwart the result.

"(5) A duly licensed physician, or a person acting under his direction, may use reasonable physical force for the purpose of administering a reasonable and recognized

FORCE BY PERSON WITH PARENTAL, CUSTODIAL, OR SPECIAL RESPONSIBILITIES. —Cont'd.

form of treatment which he reasonably believes to be adapted to promoting the physical or mental health of the patient if:

"a. The treatment is administered with the consent of the patient or, if the patient is a minor or an incompetent person, with the consent of his parent, guardian or other person responsible for his care and supervision; or

"b. The treatment is administered in any emergency when the physician reasonably believes that no one competent to consent can be consulted and that a reasonable person, wishing to safeguard the welfare of the patient, would consent."

Comments.

This section recognizes certain circumstances in which an actor, because of his parental, custodial, or professional responsibilities, may use reasonable physical force against those in his care. Parents, teachers, babysitters, camp counselors, dormitory managers, and all others who supervise minors or incompetent persons may utilize force to maintain discipline.[1] Not only may force be used against children, but wardens may control prison inmates through corporal punishment as well.

Subsection (3) extends to all common carriers the power to use reasonable force to maintain order.[2] Subsection (4) adopts traditional legal policy toward suicides. The drafters of the Code pointed out that in some suicide cases, the Alabama courts have gone so far as to charge survivors with murder.[3] Subsection (5) merely restates the Good Samaritan statute.[4]

Cross references.

See Basis for defense generally . . ., § 13A-3-21 of the Alabama Code.

---

1. *Nicholas v. State, 32 Ala. App. 574, 28 So. 2d 422 (1946) (present Alabama case law recognizes that a school teacher may administer moderate chastisement to a pupil under his care); Suits v. Glover, 260 Ala. 449, 71 So. 2d 49 (1954) (the*

FORCE BY PERSON WITH PARENTAL, CUSTODIAL, OR SPECIAL RESPONSIBILITIES. —Cont'd.

authority of teachers to discipline by force extends only to minors and does not apply to adult pupils); Moore v. Student Affairs Committee of Troy State University, 284 F. Supp. 725 (D. C. Ala. 1968) (a college does not stand, strictly speaking, in loco parentis to its students).

2. *See Code of Ala. 1975, § 37-2-115.*
3. *McMahon v. State, 168 Ala. 70, 53 So. 89 (1910).*
4. *See Code of Ala. 1975, § 6-5-332.*

FORCE IN DEFENSE OF A PERSON.

Code of Ala. 1975, § 13A-3-23.

"(a) A person is justified in using physical force upon another person in order to defend himself or a third person from what he reasonably believes to be the use or imminent use of unlawful physical force by that other person, and he may use a degree of force which he reasonably believes to be necessary for the purpose. A person may use deadly physical force if the actor reasonably believes that such other person is:

"(1) Using or about to use unlawful deadly physical force; or

"(2) Using or about to use physical force against an occupant of a dwelling while committing or attempting to commit a burglary of such dwelling; or

"(3) Committing or about to commit a kidnapping in any degree, assault in the first or second degree, burglary in any degree, robbery in any degree, forcible rape or forcible sodomy.

"(b) Notwithstanding the provisions of subsection (a), a person is not justified in using deadly physical force upon another person if it reasonably appears or he knows that he can avoid the necessity of using such force with complete safety:

"(1) By retreating, except that the actor is not required to retreat:

"a. If he is in his dwelling or at his place of work and was not the original aggressor; or

"b. If he is a peace officer or a private person lawfully assisting a peace officer at his direction.

FORCE IN DEFENSE OF A PERSON. —Cont'd.

"(c) Notwithstanding the provisions of subsection (a), a person is not justified in using physical force if:

"(1) With intent to cause physical injury or death to another person, he provoked the use of unlawful physical force by such other person; or

"(2) He was the initial aggressor, except that his use of physical force upon another person under the circumstances is justifiable if he withdraws from the encounter and effectively communicates to the other person his intent to do so, but the latter nevertheless continues or threatens the use of unlawful physical force; or

"(3) The physical force involved was the product of a combat by agreement not specifically authorized by law."

Comments.

This section allows a person to use force in defense of himself if he has a bona fide belief, and reasonable grounds for believing, that he is in danger of death or great bodily harm. The question becomes not merely what the defendant believed, but what he had the right to believe. The same test of reasonable appearances applies where a defendant goes to another person's defense. Departing from previous state law,[1] "the culpability of one who acts in defense of another is measured by the intent with which he acted and not by the intent of the person aided, unless defendant knew or might reasonably have known the intent of the other party."[2]

There are two kinds of force involved in subsection (a); ordinary physical force and "deadly physical force," i.e., readily capable of causing death or serious physical injury.[3] Section 13A-3-23(a) of the Alabama Code justifies the use of deadly physical force in a greater variety of situations than had the former code.[4]

Section 13A-3-23(b) of the Alabama Code, however, qualifies the use of deadly force by requiring the defendant to retreat as an alternative to using deadly force if he can do so without increasing the danger,[5] unless he is in his "dwelling or place of work," or "he

FORCE IN DEFENSE OF A PERSON. —Cont'd.

is a peace officer," or he is "lawfully assisting a peace officer at his direction."[6]

This defense is never available in a situation where the accused is the aggressor.[7] The aggressor may be restored to his position of defense if he attempts to withdraw from the encounter, but is pursued. Section 13A-3-23(c)(3) of the Alabama Code prohibits the use of this defense where no one person is the aggressor, for example, in a pre-arranged fist fight.[8]

Cross references.

See Basis for defense generally . . ., § 13A-3-21 of the Alabama Code.

---

1. *Previous state law required the defendant to "stand in the shoes" of the person aided. Thompson v. State, 37 Ala. App. 446, 70 So. 2d 282 (1954). If he is mistaken, he bears the fault of the apparent victim, who in fact may have been the wrongdoer. Lovejoy v. State, 31 Ala. App. 244, 15 So. 2d 300 (1943).*
2. *Mayhew v. State, 144 S. W. 229 (Texas 1912).*
3. *Code of Ala. 1975, § 13A-1-2(10).*
4. *The 1979 amendment, effective July 30, 1979:*
   (1) In subsection (a), beginning of the first sentence, deleted "Except as provided in subsections (b) and (c) of this section";
   (2) In subsection (a), beginning of the last sentence, deleted "However, deadly physical force may not be used unless" and substituted "A person may use deadly physical force";
   (3) In subsection (a), subparagraph (3), inserted "in any degree" following "kidnapping" and "robbery";
   (4) In subsection (a), subparagraph (3), deleted "mayhem" and substituted "assault in the first or second degree";
   (5) In subsection (a), subparagraph (3), following "burglary in," deleted "the first or second degree" and substituted "any";
   (6) In subsection (b), deleted subparagraph (2), which related to surrendering possession of property to a person claiming a right thereto;
   (7) In subsection (b), deleted subparagraph (3), which related to complying with a demand that one abstain from performing an act that he is not obligated to perform.
5. *Some contemporary codifications require the defendant to "know" that safe retreat is possible. The Criminal Code retains the obligation to retreat in the interest of preserving life, but gives the defendant the benefit of reasonable appearances rather than actual knowledge of an alternative.*
6. *Not requiring retreat from "in" one's dwelling or place of business conforms to present Alabama case law. Bryant v. State, 252 Ala. 153, 39 So. 2d 657 (1949); Cole v. State, 41 Ala. App. 465, 144 So. 2d 54 (1961). No requirement to give way in the face of a forceful attack is placed upon either an officer of the law or another that is lawfully assisting such an officer because the officer is under an affirmative duty. Cobb v. State, 19 Ala. App. 345, 97 So. 779 (1923). Private persons acting under police orders apparently lawful are not guilty of assaults. Watson v. State, 85 Ala. 60, 3 So. 441 (1888).*
7. *This provision codifies present Alabama law which requires one who claims self-defense to show complete freedom from fault in provoking the difficulty. Brewer v. State, 160 Ala. 66, 49 So. 336 (1909).*
8. *Galloway v. State, 28 Ala. App. 82, 178 So. 896 (1938); Russell v. State, 27 Ala. App. 10, 165 So. 256 (1936). Bodily harm incurred in the joint participation of lawful sports is not criminal. See CONSENT.*

FORCE IN DEFENSE OF PREMISES.

Code of Ala. 1975, § 13A-3-25.

"A person in lawful possession or control of premises, as defined in Section 13A-3-20, or a person who is licensed or privileged to be thereon, may use physical force upon another person when and to the extent that he reasonably believes it necessary to prevent or terminate what he reasonably believes to be the commission or attempted commission of a criminal trespass by the other person in or upon such premises." However, "[a] person may use deadly physical force . . . only [in] defense of a person, as provided in section 13A-3-23; or [when] he reasonably believes it necessary to prevent the commission of arson in the first or second degree by the trespasser."

Comments.

This section allows a legal occupant to use force to prevent a criminal trespass. The authority to use force extends not only to the legal owner or possessor but to others,

FORCE IN DEFENSE OF PREMISES. —Cont'd.

such as guests or lodgers who have a right to be on the property as well. The right to use force is subject to a "reasonable appearances" test; i.e., the person in possession must have reasonable grounds for believing that a crime is being committed.

"Premises," as defined in § 13A-3-20 of the Alabama Code, includes any "building" and any real property. "Building" is defined as "[a]ny structure which may be entered and utilized by persons for business, public use, lodging or the storage of goods and such term includes any vehicle, aircraft or watercraft used for the lodging of persons or carrying on business therein."

Section 13A-3-25(b) of the Alabama Code limits the use of deadly force to two specific situations, in defense of a person and in order to prevent arson in the first or second degree. According to § 13A-7-41 of the Alabama Code, first degree arson is a Class A felony. A person commits arson in the first degree if he "intentionally damages a building by starting or maintaining a fire or causing an explosion, and when:

"(1) Another person is present in such building at the time, and

"(2) The actor knows that fact, or the circumstances are such as to render the presence of a person therein a reasonable possibility."

Arson in the second degree, however, is only a Class B felony, and does not require the presence of a person inside the building. This section entitles a person to use deadly force if he reasonably believes it necessary to prevent damage by fire to a building or real property even when no person is threatened. This provision does not, however, permit the occupant of a house to lawfully kill an intruder who is bent on theft only. Although, if the situation deteriorates into self-defense, kidnapping, mayhem, robbery, forcible rape, or sodomy, the defendant would be protected by § 13A-3-23 of the Alabama Code.

Cross references.

See Basis for defense generally . . ., § 13A-3-21 of the Alabama Code.

FORCE IN DEFENSE OF PROPERTY (OTHER THAN PREMISES). Code of Ala. 1975, § 13A-3-26.

"A person is justified in using physical force, other than deadly physical force, upon another person when and to the extent that he reasonably believes it to be necessary to prevent or terminate the commission or attempted commission by the other person of theft or criminal mischief with respect to property other than premises as defined in Section 13A-3-20."

Comments.

This defense justifies the use of nondeadly force when there is a reasonable appearance of theft or criminal mischief[1] to personal property.[2]

Cross references.

See Basis for defense generally . . ., § 13A-3-21 of the Alabama Code.

---

1. *Code of Ala. 1975, §§ 13A-7-21, 13A-7-22, 13A-7-23.*
2. *Russell v. State, 219 Ala. 567, 122 So. 683 (1929).*

FORCE IN MAKING AN ARREST OR PREVENTING AN ESCAPE. Code of Ala. 1975, § 13A-3-27.

"(a) A peace officer is justified[1] in using that degree of physical force which he reasonably believes to be necessary, upon a person in order:

"(1) To make an arrest for a misdemeanor, violation or violation of a criminal ordinance, or to prevent the escape from custody of a person arrested for a misdemeanor, violation or violation of a criminal ordinance, unless the peace officer knows that the arrest is unauthorized; or

"(2) To defend himself or a third person from what he reasonably believes to be the use or imminent use of physical force while making or attempting to make an arrest for a misdemeanor, violation or violation of a criminal ordinance, or while preventing or attempting to prevent an escape from custody of a person who has been legally arrested for a misdemeanor, violation or

FORCE IN MAKING AN ARREST OR PREVENTING AN ESCAPE.—Cont'd.

violation of a criminal ordinance.

"(b) A peace officer is justified[2] in using deadly physical force upon another person when and to the extent that he reasonably believes it necessary in order:

"(1) To make an arrest for a felony or to prevent the escape from custody of a person arrested for a felony, unless the officer knows that the arrest is unauthorized; or

"(2) To defend himself or a third person from what he reasonably believes to be the use or imminent use of deadly physical force."

Except as provided in § 13A-3-27(f)[3] of the Alabama Code, "a person who has been directed by a peace officer to assist him to effect an arrest or to prevent an escape from custody is justified in using physical force when and to the extent that he reasonably believes that force to be necessary to carry out the peace officer's direction."[4]

"A private person acting on his own account is justified in using physical force[5] upon another person when and to the extent that he reasonably believes it necessary to effect an arrest or to prevent the escape from custody of an arrested person who he reasonably believes has committed a felony and who in fact has committed that felony, . . ."[6]

"A guard or peace officer employed in a detention facility[7] is justified:

"(1) In using deadly physical force when and to the extent that he reasonably believes it necessary to prevent what he reasonably believes to be the escape of a prisoner accused or convicted of a felony from any detention facility, or from armed escort or guard;

"(2) In using physical force, but not deadly physical force, in all other circumstances when and to the extent that he reasonably believes it necessary to prevent what he reasonably believes to be the escape of a prisoner from a detention facility."[8]

Comments.

Section 13A-3-27 reinstates the common law rules relating to the force that may be used by peace officers in making arrests or preventing escapes. The statute restores the distinction between a misdemeanor and a felony with regard to the degree of force allowed. Subsection (a) permits a peace officer to use that degree of force which he deems reasonably necessary in almost any situation that arises while making an arrest for a misdemeanor or for violation of a criminal ordinance.[9] Subsection (b) specifically justifies the use of deadly force in arresting or preventing the escape of a felon to the extent that he reasonably believes it necessary.[10] This section also provides for the use of deadly force in self-defense or in the defense of another person, subject to the reasonable appearance test.[11]

A peace officer may not rely on this statute in order to justify reckless or criminally negligent conduct, nor may a peace officer use physical force while making an unauthorized or invalid arrest.[12]

Subsection (f) establishes a defense for a citizen who uses force in assisting a peace officer to make an arrest.[13] He is justified in using deadly force in self-defense, in defense of a third person, or upon the authorization of a peace officer. This provision is in accord with present Alabama law, which imposes a duty on private citizens to assist an officer making an arrest when called upon by him.

Without an officer's authorization, a private citizen is entitled to use deadly force in self-defense, or in defense of another person, only when he reasonably believes it necessary. This represents a departure from present Alabama law, which requires the deadly force to be necessary.

Cross references.

See Basis for defense generally . . ., § 13A-3-21 of the Alabama Code.

---

1. *Note: There is no justification for reckless or criminally negligent conduct by a peace officer amounting to an offense against or with respect to persons being arrested or to innocent persons whom he is not seeking to arrest or retain in*

FORCE IN MAKING AN ARREST OR PREVENTING AN ESCAPE.—Cont'd.

custody. In addition, a peace officer who is effecting an arrest pursuant to a warrant is justified in using the physical force prescribed in Code of Ala. 1975, § 13A-3-27(a) and (b) unless the warrant is invalid and is known by the officer to be invalid.

2. *See note 1, supra.*
3. *"A person who has been directed to assist a peace officer under circumstances specified in [§ 13A-3-27(e) of the Alabama Code] may use deadly physical force to effect an arrest or to prevent an escape only when:*
   "(1) He reasonably believes that force to be necessary to defend himself or a third person from what he reasonably believes to be the use or imminent use of deadly physical force; or
   "(2) He is authorized by the peace officer to use deadly physical force and does not know that the peace officer himself is not authorized to use deadly physical force under the circumstances." Code of Ala. 1975, § 13A-3-27(f).
4. *Code of Ala. 1975, § 13A-3-27(e).*
5. *He is justified in using deadly physical force for the purpose only when he reasonably believes it necessary to defend himself or a third person from what he reasonably believes to be the use or imminent use of deadly physical force.*
6. *Code of Ala. 1975, § 13A-3-27(g).*
7. *"'Detention facility' means any place used for the confinement, pursuant to law, of a person:*
   "a. Charged with or convicted of an offense; or
   "b. Charged with being or adjudicated a youthful offender, a neglected minor or juvenile delinquent; or
   "c. Held for extradition; or
   "d. Otherwise confined pursuant to an order of a criminal court." Code of Ala. 1975, § 13A-3-27(h)(3).
8. *Code of Ala. 1975, § 13A-3-27(h)(1)(2).*
9. *Champion v. State, 35 Ala. App. 7, 44 So. 2d 616 (1949), cert. denied, 253 Ala. 436, 44 So. 2d 622 (1949).*
10. *Williams v. State, 33 Ala. App. 304, 35 So. 2d 562 (1947), aff'd, 250 Ala. 549, 35 So. 2d 567 (1948).*
11. *Green v. State, 238 Ala. 143, 189 So. 763 (1939); Holcomb v. State, 35 Ala. App. 528, 50 So. 2d 165 (1951), which, in accord with this provision of the Criminal Code, would justify the killing of a misdemeanant should he resist so as to endanger an officer's life. Holland v. State, 162 Ala. 5, 50 So. 215 (1909).*
12. *Justification extends only to a lawful arrest. Knox v. State, 42 Ala. App. 578, 172 So. 2d 787 (1964). However, under Code of Ala. 1975, § 15-10-3, an officer may arrest without a warrant "when he has reasonable cause to believe that the person arrested has committed a felony."*
13. *See note 3, supra.*

FORCE IN RESISTING ARREST (PROHIBITED). Code of Ala. 1975, § 13A-3-28.

"A person may not use physical force to resist a lawful arrest by a peace officer who is known or reasonably appears to be a peace officer."

Comments.

This section prohibits the use of physical force to resist a lawful arrest. This may imply that a person is allowed to use reasonable force to resist an unlawful arrest. Although this interpretation confirms current Alabama case law,[1] and the common law view, a minority of the drafters advocated acceptance of the New York "no sock" principle, which requires a layman to peaceably submit to arrest, regardless of whether it is lawful or unlawful and to await redress in court.[2] After much debate, the traditional Alabama rule was reinstated.

---

1. *Brown v. State, 109 Ala. 70, 20 So. 103 (1895); Spooney v. State, 217 Ala. 219, 115 So. 308 (1928); Tarwater v. State, 16 Ala. App. 140, 75 So. 816 (1917); Lowery v. State, 39 Ala. App. 659, 107 So. 2d 366 (1958); and Clark and Marshall, Crimes 486 (7th ed. 1967).*
2. *New York Penal Law § 35.27, added 1968.*

FORFEITURE AND SEIZURES. See specific headings, e.g., CONTROLLED SUBSTANCES; GAMBLING; MOTOR VEHICLE CRIMES.

FORGED INSTRUMENT, CRIMINAL POSSESSION OF. Code of Ala. 1975, §§ 13A-9-5 through 13A-9-8.

Charged as: Criminal possession of forged instrument.

"A person commits the crime of criminal possession of a forged instrument[1] in the first degree if he possesses or utters[2] any forged instrument of a kind specified in section 13A-9-2[3] with knowledge that it is

FORGED INSTRUMENT, CRIMINAL POSSESSION OF.—Cont'd.

forged and with intent to defraud."[4] § 13A-9-5 of the Alabama Code.

"A person commits the crime of criminal possession of a forged instrument in the second degree if he possesses or utters any forged instrument of a kind specified in section 13A-9-3[5] with knowledge that it is forged and with intent to defraud." § 13A-9-6 of the Alabama Code.

"A person commits the crime of criminal possession of a forged instrument in the third degree if he possesses or utters a forged instrument of a kind covered in section 13A-9-4[6] with knowledge that it is forged with intent to defraud." § 13A-9-7 of the Alabama Code.

"A person may not be punished for both the offense of forgery and the offense of criminal possession of a forged instrument with respect to the same instrument, unless arising out of separate and distinct transactions." § 13A-9-8 of the Alabama Code.

Classification.

Class B felony, criminal possession of a forged instrument in the first degree.

Class C felony, criminal possession of a forged instrument in the second degree.

Class A misdemeanor, criminal possession of a forged instrument in the third degree.

Comments.

Uttering a forged instrument is not included in the offense of forgery. Forgery is committed when the offender "falsely makes, completes or alters" an instrument. Uttering is committed simply by offering or asserting, directly or indirectly, that a forged instrument is genuine.[7] Sections 13A-9-5 through 13A-9-7 of the Alabama Code on uttering correspond to §§ 13A-9-2 through 13A-9-4 of the Alabama Code on forgery, and their grading is the same, on the premise that similar culpable conduct should receive similar treatment. If all persons involved in the forgery and distribution of a forged instrument have the same criminal knowledge and intent, the same sanction should be applied. Under

FORGED INSTRUMENT, CRIMINAL POSSESSION OF.—Cont'd.

prior law, guilty knowledge with intent to defraud was required only for first degree possession. The current statutes have eliminated this inconsistency. The requirement of actual knowledge protects the innocent possessor. There may be no double conviction for conduct that is part of the same transaction.

Defenses.

(1) Knowledge that the instrument is a forgery.

(2) Lack of intent to defraud.

(3) The quality of the forged instrument is so poor that it could not be mistaken for the real item.

Cross references.

See FORGERY; FORGERY DEVICE, CRIMINAL POSSESSION OF.

---

1. *"A written instrument which has been falsely made, completed or altered." Code of Ala. 1975, § 13A-9-1(7).*
2. *"To 'utter' means to directly or indirectly offer, assert, declare or put forth a forged instrument as genuine." Code of Ala. 1975, § 13A-9-1(12).*
3. *"A person commits the crime of forgery in the first degree if, with intent to defraud, he falsely makes, completes or alters a written instrument which is or purports to be, or which is calculated to become or to represent if completed:*
   "(1) Part of an issue or series of stamps, securities or other valuable instruments issued by a government or governmental agency; or
   "(2) Part of an issue or series of stock, bonds or other instruments representing interests in or claims against a business enterprise or its property." Code of Ala. 1975, § 13A-9-2.
4. *"A purpose to use deception, as defined in section 13A-8-1(1), or to injure another person's interest which has value, as defined in section 13A-8-1(14)." Code of Ala 1975, § 13A-9-1(8).*
5. *"A person commits the crime of forgery in the second degree if, with intent to defraud, he falsely makes, completes or alters a written instrument which is or purports to be, or which is calculated to become or to represent if completed:*
   "(1) A deed, will, codicil, contract, assignment or a check, draft, note or other commercial instrument which does or may evidence, create, transfer, terminate or otherwise affect a legal right, interest, obligation or status; or

FORGED INSTRUMENT, CRIMINAL POSSESSION OF.—Cont'd.

"(2) A public record, or an instrument filed or required or authorized by law to be filed in a public office or with a public employee; or

"(3) A written instrument officially issued or created by public office, public employees or government agency." Code of Ala. 1975, § 13A-9-3.

6. *"A person commits the crime of forgery in the third degree if, with intent to defraud, he falsely makes, completes or alters a written instrument." Code of Ala. 1975, § 13A-9-4.*
7. *Terry v. State, 29 Ala. App. 340, 197 So. 44 (1940), cert. denied, 240 Ala. 51, 197 So. 46 (1940).*

FORGERY. Code of Ala. 1975, §§ 13A-9-2 through 13A-9-4.

"A person commits the crime of forgery in the first degree if, with intent to defraud,[1] he falsely makes,[2] completes[3] or alters[4] a written instrument[5] which is or purports to be, or which is calculated to become or to represent if completed:[6]

"(1) Part of an issue or series of stamps, securities or other valuable instruments issued by a government[7] or governmental agency; or

"(2) Part of an issue or series of stock, bonds or other instruments representing interests in or claims against a business enterprise or its property."[8] § 13A-9-2 of the Alabama Code.

"A person commits the crime of forgery in the second degree if, with intent to defraud, he falsely makes, completes or alters a written instrument which is or purports to be, or which is calculated to become or to represent if completed:

"(1) A deed, will, codicil, contract, assignment or a check, draft, note or other commercial instrument which does or may evidence, create, transfer, terminate or otherwise affect a legal right, interest, obligation or status; or

"(2) A public record, or an instrument filed or required or authorized by law to be filed in a public office or with a public employee; or

"(3) A written instrument officially issued or created by a public office, public employees or government agency." § 13A-9-3 of the Alabama Code.

FORGERY.—Cont'd.

"A person commits the crime of forgery in the third degree if, with intent to defraud, he falsely makes, completes or alters a written instrument." § 13A-9-4 of the Alabama Code.

Classification.

Class B felony, forgery in the first degree.

Class C felony, forgery in the second degree.

Class A misdemeanor, forgery in the third degree.

Comments.

Forgery in all three degrees requires intent to defraud with a written instrument. The degrees are determined by the contents of the forged instruments. (Note: A charge of a higher degree does not include a lesser degree.)[9]

The statute on first degree forgery punishes conduct that would impair public trust and confidence in governmental or commercial papers. Second degree forgery refers to deeds, wills, and contractual instruments. Third degree forgery covers forged writings not the subject of the first or second degree statutes. The 1979 Legislature added "a check, draft, note or other" commercial instrument to the second degree.

Where the forgery consists of a signature, it may be accomplished by a defendant who himself affixes another's signature to a writing or by obtaining the proper signature of the signer to a writing that does not accord with the signer's understanding of its contents. Where forgery is accomplished by obtaining the proper signature, defendant's conduct is the equivalent of obtaining a signature by deception as defined by § 13A-9-11 of the Alabama Code.

Defenses.

(1) Lack of intent to defraud.

(2) The written instrument could not be mistaken for the real item due to some flaw in its production.

(3) Incapability of the written instrument to be used to the advantage or disadvantage of any person.

(4) Although not a complete defense, a person charged with forgery in the first or second degree should consider the

FORGERY.—Cont'd.

possibility of having the charge reduced to "obtaining a signature by deception" where the forgery consists of a signature.

Cross references.

See FORGED INSTRUMENT, CRIMINAL POSSESSION OF; FORGERY DEVICE, CRIMINAL POSSESSION OF; SIGNATURE OBTAINED BY POSSESSION.

---

1. *Code of Ala. 1975, § 13A-9-1(8): "A purpose to use deception, as defined in section 13A-8-1(1), or to injure another person's interest which has value, as defined in section 13A-8-1(14)."*
2. *"To 'falsely make' a written instrument means to make or draw a complete written instrument in its entirety, or an incomplete written instrument, which purports to be authentic creation of its ostensible maker, but which is not either because the ostensible maker is fictitious or because, if real, he did not authorize the making or drawing thereof." Code of Ala. 1975, § 13A-9-1(4).*
3. *"To 'falsely complete' a written instrument means to transform, by adding, inserting or changing matter, an incomplete written instrument into a complete one, without lawful authority, so that the completed written instrument falsely appears or purports to be in all respects an authentic creation of its ostensible maker or authorized by him." Code of Ala. 1975, § 13A-9-1(5).*
4. *"To 'falsely alter' a written instrument means to change, without lawful authority, a written instrument, whether complete or incomplete, by means of erasure, obliteration, deletion, addition or transportation of matter, or in any other manner, so that the instrument so changed falsely appears or purports to be in all respects an authentic creation of its ostensible maker or authorized by him." Code of Ala. 1975, § 13A-9-1(6).*
5. *"Written instrument" means:*

   "a. Any paper, document or other instrument containing written or printed matter or its equivalent; and

   "b. Any token, stamp, seal, badge, trademark or other evidence or symbol of value, right, privilege or identification,

   which is capable of being used to the advantage or disadvantage of some person." Code of Ala. 1975, § 13A-9-1(1).
6. *"One which purports to be a genuine written instrument fully drawn with respect to every essential feature thereof." Code of Ala. 1975, § 13A-9-1(2).*

FORGERY.—Cont'd.

7. *"The United States, any state or any county, municipality or other political unit within territory belonging to the United States, or any department, agency or subdivision of any of the foregoing, or any corporation or other association carrying out the functions of government, or any corporation or agency formed pursuant to interstate compact or international treaty.*

   "As used in this definition 'state' includes any state, territory or possession of the United States, the District of Columbia and the Commonwealth of Puerto Rico." Code of Ala. 1975, § 13A-8-1(5).
8. *"Any money, tangible or intangible personal property, property (whether real or personal) the location of which can be changed (including things growing on, affixed to or found in land and documents, although the rights represented hereby have no physical location), contract right, chose-in-action, interest in or claim to wealth, credit or any other article or thing of value of any kind.*

   "Commodities of a public utility nature, such as gas, electricity, steam and water, constitute property, but the supplying of such a commodity to premises from an outside source by means of wires, pipes, conduits or other equipment shall be deemed rendition of a service rather than a sale or delivery of property. Code of Ala. 1975, § 13A-8-1(10). See Code of Ala. 1975, § 13A-8-10, Theft of services.
9. *Hamilton v. State, 35 Ala. App. 570, 50 So. 2d 449 (1951); Martin v. State, 354 So. 2d 1151 (1978).*

FORGERY DEVICE, CRIMINAL POSSESSION OF. Code of Ala. 1975, § 13A-9-9.

Charged as: Criminal possession of forgery device.

"A person commits the crime of criminal possession of a forgery device if he makes or possesses with knowledge of its character any plate, die or other device, appliance, apparatus, equipment or article specifically designed or adapted for use in forging written instruments[1] with intent to use it himself, or to aid or permit another to use it for purposes of forgery."

Classification.

Class C felony.

Comments.

This section requires affirmative proof of the offender's knowledge of the illegal potential

FORGERY DEVICE, CRIMINAL POSSESSION OF.—Cont'd.
of the device, and he must have made or possessed it with the specific intent to use it for purposes of forgery. Those who supply or furnish the forger with the means to carry out his purpose, and the forger himself, fall within the limits of this section.

Defenses.
(1) No intent to use or allow to be used for the purpose of forgery.
(2) Lack of knowledge of the character of the possible forgery device possessed.
(3) No capability of the written instrument produced to be used to the advantage or disadvantage of any person.

Cross references.
See BURGLAR'S TOOLS, POSSESSION OF; FORGED INSTRUMENT, CRIMINAL POSSESSION OF; FORGERY.

---

1. *"Such term means:*
"a. Any paper, document or other instrument containing written or printed matter or its equivalent; and
"b. Any token, stamp, seal, badge, trademark or other evidence or symbol of value, right, privilege or identification,
which is capable of being used to the advantage or disadvantage of some person." Code of Ala. 1975, § 13A-9-1(1).

FRAUD IN INSOLVENCY. Code of Ala. 1975, § 13A-9-48.
"A person commits the crime of fraud in insolvency if, with the intent to defraud[1] a creditor and with knowledge or reason to believe either that proceedings have been or are about to be instituted for the appointment of a receiver[2] or that a composition agreement or other arrangement for the benefit of creditors has been or is about to be made, he:
"(1) Conveys, transfers, removes, conceals, destroys, encumbers or otherwise disposes of any part of or any interest in the debtor's estate; or
"(2) Presents to any creditor or to the receiver any writing or record relating to the debtor's estate, not otherwise within the coverage of sections 13A-10-101,[3] 13A-10-102[4] or 13A-10-109,[5] knowing or having reason to believe that it contains a false material statement; or
"(3) Misrepresents or refuses to disclose to the receiver, under circumstances not amounting to a violation of section 13A-10-4,[6] the existence, amount or location of any part of or in interest in debtor's estate, or any other information that he is legally required to furnish to the administrator."

Classification.
Class B misdemeanor.

Comments.
This section extends the protection given to secured and judgment creditors, §§ 13A-9-46 and 13A-9-47, respectively, of the Alabama Code, to unsecured creditors. It requires an intent to defraud a creditor. It also requires knowledge or a reason to believe either that proceedings have been instituted for the appointment of a receiver or that another arrangement for the benefit of the creditors has been made. This section protects the creditor or receiver in situations not covered by other sections on business records or perjury.

Defenses.
(1) Lack of intent.
(2) Lack of knowledge or reason to believe that proceedings have started or are about to commence.
(3) Belief that any false statements are true.

Cross references.
See BUSINESS RECORDS, FALSIFYING; DEFRAUDING SECURED AND JUDGMENT CREDITORS; FAILING TO FILE A REQUIRED REPORT; PERJURY.

---

1. *A purpose to use deception, defined in (1) below, or to injure another person's interest which has value, defined in (2) below. (See Code of Ala. 1975, § 13A-9-1(8).)*
"(1) DECEPTION occurs when a person knowingly:
"a. Creates or confirms another's impression which is false and which the defendant does not believe to be true; or
"b. Fails to correct a false impression which the defendant previously has created or confirmed; or

FRAUD IN INSOLVENCY.—Cont'd.

"c. Fails to correct a false impression when the defendant is under a duty to do so; or

"d. Prevents another from acquiring information pertinent to the disposition of the property involved; or

"e. Sells or otherwise transfers or encumbers property, failing to disclose a lien, adverse claim or other legal impediment to the enjoyment of the property when the defendant is under a duty to do so, whether that impediment is or is not valid, or is not a matter of official record; or

"f. Promises performance which the defendant does not intend to perform or knows will not be performed. Failure to perform, standing alone, however, is not proof that the defendant did not intend to perform.

"The term 'deception' does not, however, include falsity as to matters having no pecuniary significance, or puffing by statements unlikely to deceive ordinary persons. 'Puffing' means an exaggerated commendation of wares or services." Code of Ala. 1975, § 13A-8-1(1).

(2) Value is defined as "[t]he market value of the property at the time and place of the criminal act."

"Whether or not they have been issued or delivered, certain written instruments, not including those having a readily ascertainable market value such as some public and corporate bonds and securities shall be evaluated as follows:

"a. The value of an instrument constituting an evidence of debt, such as a check, draft or promissory note, shall be deemed the amount due or collectible thereon or thereby, that figure ordinarily being the face amount of the indebtedness less any portion thereof which has been satisfied.

"b. The value of any other instrument that creates, releases, discharges or otherwise affects any valuable legal right, privilege or obligation shall be deemed the greatest amount of economic loss which the owner of the instrument might reasonably suffer by virtue of the loss of the instrument.

"When the value of property cannot be ascertained pursuant to the standards set forth above, its value shall be deemed to be an amount not exceeding $100.00.

"Amounts involved in thefts committed pursuant to one scheme or course of conduct, whether from the same person or several persons, may be aggregated in determining the grade of the offense; provided, that only one conviction may be had and only one sentence enforced for all thefts included in such aggregate." Code of Ala. 1975, § 13A-8-1(14).

2. *" 'Receiver' means an assignee or trustee for the benefit of creditors, a conservator, a liquidator or any other person legally entitled to administer property for the benefit of creditors." Code of Ala. 1975, § 13A-9-48(b).*
3. *See Perjury in the first degree, Code of Ala. 1975, § 13A-10-101.*
4. *See Perjury in the second degree, Code of Ala. 1975, § 13A-10-102.*
5. *See Unsworn falsification to authorities, Code of Ala. 1975, § 13A-10-109.*
6. *See Failing to file required report, Code of Ala. 1975, § 13A-10-4.*

GAMBLING. Code of Ala. 1975, § 13A-12-21.

"A person commits the crime of simple gambling[1] if he knowingly advances[2] or profits[3] from unlawful[4] gambling activity as a player."[5]

Classification.

Class C misdemeanor.

Comments.

Section 13A-12-20 of the Alabama Code comprehensively defines gambling in one statute and clarifies "at risk" as not being limited to just loss or gain of money, but includes anything of value.[6]

Section 13A-12-21(b) of the Alabama Code expressly provides a defense to the charge of gambling, stating that "a person charged with being a player . . . engaged in a social game in a private place" has a complete defense. Keeping paraphernalia has been dropped as a chargeable offense.

Defenses.

(1) Section 13A-12-21(b) of the Alabama Code expressly provides that if the person charged with being a player was engaged in a social game in a private place, he has a complete defense.

(2) The person did not have the requisite intent ("knowingly advances or profits").

(3) Bona fide business transactions valid under the law of contracts, including securities, commodities, contracts of indemnity or guaranty, and life, health or accident insurance. See § 13A-12-20(4) of the Alabama Code.

(4) The person did not profit or advance within the meaning of the statute.

GAMBLING.—Cont'd.

Cross references.

See COCKFIGHTING OR KEEPING A COCKPIT; GAMBLING, CONSPIRACY TO PROMOTE; GAMBLING, LEGALIZED PARI-MUTUEL BETTING NOT AFFECTED; GAMBLING, POSSESSION OF DEVICE; GAMBLING, POSSESSION OF RECORDS; GAMBLING, POSSESSION, ETC., OF STAMP PRIMA FACIE EVIDENCE OF VIOLATION OF GAMBLING LAWS; GAMBLING PLACES; LOTTERY PARAPHERNALIA, TRANSPORTATION; SOLICITATION.

---

1. *"A person engages in gambling if he stakes or risks something of value upon the outcome of a contest of chance or a future contingent event not under his control or influence, upon an agreement or understanding that he or someone else will receive something of value in the event of a certain outcome. Gambling does not include bona fide business transactions valid under the law of contracts, including but not limited to contracts for the purchase or sale at a future date of securities or commodities, and agreements to compensate for loss caused by the happening of chance, including but not limited to contracts of indemnity or guaranty and life, health or accident insurance." Code of Ala. 1975, § 13A-12-20(4).*
2. *"A person 'advances gambling activity' if he engages in conduct that materially aids any form of gambling activity. Conduct of this nature includes but is not limited to conduct directed toward the creation or establishment of the particular game, contest, scheme, device or activity involved, toward the acquisition or maintenance of premises, paraphernalia, equipment or apparatus therefor, toward the solicitation or inducement of persons to participate therein, toward the actual conduct of the playing phases thereof, toward the arrangement of any of its financial or recording phases or toward any other phase of its operation. A person advances gambling activity if, having substantial proprietary control or other authoritative control over premises being used with his knowledge for purposes of gambling activity, he permits that activity to occur or continue or makes no effort to prevent its occurrence or continuation." Code of Ala. 1975, § 13A-12-20(1).*
3. *"A person 'profits from gambling activity' if he accepts or receives money or other property pursuant to an agreement or understanding with any person whereby he shares or is to share in the proceeds of gambling activity." Code of Ala. 1975, § 13A-12-20(9).*
4. *"UNLAWFUL. Not specifically authorized by law." Code of Ala. 1975, § 13A-12-20(12).*
5. *"PLAYER. A person who engages in any form of gambling solely as a contestant or bettor, without receiving or becoming entitled to receive any profit therefrom other than personal gambling winnings, and without otherwise rendering any material assistance to the establishment, conduct or operation of the particular gambling activity." Code of Ala. 1975, § 13A-12-20(8).*
6. *"SOMETHING OF VALUE. Any money or property, any token, object or article exchangeable for money or property or any form of credit or promise directly or indirectly contemplating transfer of money or property or of any interest therein, or involving extension of a service entertainment or a privilege of playing at a game or scheme without charge." Code of Ala. 1975, § 13A-12-20(11).*

GAMBLING, CONSPIRACY TO PROMOTE. Code of Ala. 1975, § 13A-12-23.

Charged as: Conspiracy to promote gambling.

"A person commits the crime of conspiracy to promote gambling[1] if he conspires to advance[2] or profit[3] from gambling activity otherwise than as a player."[4]

Classification.

Class A misdemeanor.

Comments.

Section 13A-12-23(b) of the Alabama Code defines "conspire" as engaging "in activity constituting a criminal conspiracy as defined in section 13A-4-3."[5] A criminal conspiracy for purposes other than "to advance or profit from gambling activity," should be charged under the general criminal conspiracy statute.

Section 13A-12-23 of the Alabama Code does not expressly provide for any defenses. However, since it specifically refers to § 13A-4-3 of the Alabama Code for definitions, it should be argued that the defense of renunciation (as provided for therein)[6] would be viable.

GAMBLING, CONSPIRACY TO PROMOTE.—Cont'd.

Defenses.

(1) Although he agreed with one or more persons to engage in certain conduct, he did not intend that that conduct be criminal.

(2) The person did not "conspire" to advance or profit from gambling activity.

(3) The person was **only** a player.

(4) Renunciation.

Cross references.

See GAMBLING; GAMBLING, LEGALIZED PARI-MUTUEL BETTING NOT AFFECTED; GAMBLING, POSSESSION, ETC. OF STAMP PRIMA FACIE EVIDENCE OF VIOLATION OF GAMBLING LAWS; GAMBLING, POSSESSION OF DEVICE; GAMBLING, POSSESSION OF RECORDS, GAMBLING, PROMOTING; LOTTERY PARAPHERNALIA, TRANSPORTATION; SOLICITATION.

---

1. *Gambling: "A person engages in gambling if he stakes or risks something of value upon the outcome of a contest of chance or a future contingent event not under his control or influence, upon an agreement or understanding that he or someone else will receive something of value in the event of a certain outcome. Gambling does not include bona fide business transactions valid under the law of contracts, including but not limited to contracts for the purchase or sale at a future date of securities or commodities, and agreements to compensate for loss caused by the happening of chance, including but not limited to contracts of indemnity or guaranty and life, health or accident insurance." Code of Ala. 1975, § 13A-12-20(4).*
2. *Advance a gambling activity: "A person 'advances gambling activity' if he engages in conduct that materially aids any form of gambling activity. Conduct of this nature includes but is not limited to conduct directed toward the creation or establishment of the particular game, contest, scheme, device or activity involved, toward the acquisition or maintenance of premises, paraphernalia, equipment or apparatus therefor, toward the solicitation or inducement of persons to participate therein, toward the actual conduct of the playing phases thereof, toward the arrangement of any of its financial or recording phases or toward any other phase of its operation. A person advances gambling activity if, having substantial proprietary control or other authoritative control over premises being used with his knowledge for purposes of gambling activity, he permits that activity to occur or continue or makes no effort to prevent its occurrence or continuation." Code of Ala. 1975, § 13A-12-20(1).*
3. *Profit: "A person 'profits from gambling activity' if he accepts or receives money or other property pursuant to an agreement or understanding with any person whereby he shares or is to share in the proceeds of gambling activity." Code of Ala. 1975, § 13A-12-20(9).*
4. *Player: "A person who engages in any form of gambling solely as a contestant or bettor, without receiving or becoming entitled to receive any profit therefrom other than personal gambling winnings, and without otherwise rendering any material assistance to the establishment, conduct or operation of the particular gambling activity." Code of Ala. 1975, § 13A-12-20(8).*
5. *"A person is guilty of criminal conspiracy if, with the intent that conduct constituting an offense be performed, he agrees with one or more persons to engage in or cause the performance of such conduct, and any one or more of such persons does an overt act to effect an objective in the agreement." Code of Ala. 1975, § 13A-4-3(a).*
6. *"A person is not liable under this section if, under circumstances manifesting a voluntary and complete renunciation of his criminal purpose, he gave a timely and adequate warning to law enforcement authorities or made a substantial effort to prevent the enforcement of the criminal conduct contemplated by the conspiracy. Renunciation by one conspirator, however, does not affect the liability of another conspirator who does not join in the abandonment of the conspiratorial objective. The burden of presenting the issue of renunciation is on the defendant, but this does not shift the burden of proof." Code of Ala. 1975, § 13A-4-3(c).*

GAMBLING, LEGALIZED PARI-MUTUEL[1] BETTING NOT AFFECTED. Code of Ala. 1975, § 13A-12-31.

Defend as: Legalized pari-mutuel betting not affected.

"All presently effective state statutes and laws and locally adopted ordinances and laws pursuant thereto legalizing, authorizing or allowing greyhound races

GAMBLING, LEGALIZED PARI-MUTUEL BETTING NOT AFFECTED.—Cont'd.

and betting or wagering thereon are hereby expressly and specifically preserved, saved and excepted from any repealer provisions contained anywhere in the Criminal Code."

This exemption also applies to both the promotion or conspiracy to promote and the possession of records or devices.

Cross references.

See GAMBLING.

---

1. Pari-mutuel: "A form of lottery in which the winning chances or plays are not determined upon the basis of a drawing or other act on the part of persons conducting or connected with the scheme, but upon the basis of the outcome of a future contingent event or events otherwise unrelated to the particular scheme." Code of Ala. 1975, § 13A-12-20(7).

GAMBLING, POSSESSION, ETC., OF STAMP PRIMA FACIE EVIDENCE OF VIOLATION OF GAMBLING LAWS. Code of Ala. 1975, § 13A-12-90.

"The holding, owning, having in possession of, or paying the tax of a wagering occupational tax stamp issued by the internal revenue authorities of the United States shall be held in all the courts of this state as prima facie evidence against the person holding such stamp in any prosecution of such person for violation of the gambling laws of this state."

Comments.

Although not a crime in itself, the defense attorney concerned with a gambling charge must be aware that "[i]n cases where the proper prosecuting officers shall produce said stamp or certified copy, the grand jury may indict the holder of such stamp or the proper prosecuting officer may file information against the holder of such stamp without further proof, charging such holder with the violation of the Alabama gambling laws."[1] And "[u]pon the trial of such person, proof of the owning, holding or possession of such stamp may be made by two witnesses who have seen such stamp in the place of business of the holder or on his person, or by the production of the original

GAMBLING, POSSESSION, ETC., OF STAMP PRIMA FACIE EVIDENCE OF VIOLATION OF GAMBLING LAWS.—Cont'd.

stamp with proof by one or more witnesses that it is the property of the defendant, or by production by the state of a copy of such stamp certified by the director of the issuing federal internal revenue district as being a copy of the stamp originally issued to the defendant. Proof made as herein provided shall be sufficient evidence, without explanation, to convict of violation of the gambling laws."[2]

Cross references.

See GAMBLING.

---

1. Code of Ala. 1975, § 13A-12-91.

2. Code of Ala. 1975, § 13A-12-92.

GAMBLING, POSSESSION OF DEVICE. Code of Ala. 1975, § 13A-12-27.

"A person commits the crime of possession of a gambling device[1] if with knowledge of the character thereof he manufactures, sells, transports, places or possesses, or conducts or negotiates any transaction affecting or designed to affect ownership, custody or use of:

"(1) A slot machine;[2] or

"(2) Any other gambling device, with the intention that it be used in the advancement of unlawful[3] gambling activity."[4]

Classification.

Class A misdemeanor.

Comments.

This statute requires that the person have knowledge that the character of the device is for gambling. Section 13A-12-28 of the Alabama Code establishes a presumption of knowledge; once there is proof of possession, it is "prima facie evidence of possession thereof with knowledge of its character or contents." Thereafter, the defendant has the burden of overcoming the presumption of knowledge.

The manufacture, sale, possession, etc., of a slot machine with knowledge of its character is a per se violation; however, if the device is "any other gambling device,"

GAMBLING, POSSESSION OF DEVICE.—Cont'd.

the state must prove, additionally, that the person intended to use it to advance unlawful gambling activities.

Defenses.

(1) The device does not fit the definition of a slot machine, and there is not proof that he intended to use it to advance gambling activities.

(2) The person had no knowledge of the character of the device.

(3) The item possessed does not fit the definition of a gambling device (e.g., lottery tickets, which would warrant a charge of possession of gambling records).

(4) The device is being used, or is to be used, in a legal pari-mutuel operation.

Cross references.

See GAMBLING; GAMBLING, LEGALIZED PARI-MUTUEL NOT AFFECTED; GAMBLING, POSSESSION, ETC., OF STAMP PRIMA FACIE EVIDENCE OF VIOLATION OF GAMBLING LAWS; GAMBLING, POSSESSION OF RECORDS; LOTTERY PARAPHERNALIA, TRANSPORTATION; SOLICITATION.

---

1. *Gambling device: "Any device, machine, paraphernalia or equipment that is normally used or usable in the playing phases of any gambling activity, whether that activity consists of gambling between persons or gambling by a person involving the playing of a machine. However, lottery tickets, policy slips and other items used in the playing phases of lottery and policy schemes are not gambling devices within this definition." Code of Ala. 1975, § 13A-12-20(5).*
2. *Slot machine: "A gambling device that, as a result of the insertion of a coin or other object, operates, either completely automatically or with the aid of some physical act by the player, in such a manner that, depending upon elements of chance, it may eject something of value. A device so constructed or readily adaptable or convertible to such use is no less a slot machine because it is not in working order or because some mechanical act of manipulation or repair is required to accomplish its adaptation, conversion or workability. Nor is it any less a slot machine because apart from its use or adaptability as such it may also sell or deliver something of value on a basis other than chance. Code of Ala. 1975, § 13A-12-20(10).*
3. *Unlawful: "Not specifically authorized by law." Code of Ala. 1975, § 13A-12-20(12).*
4. *Advancing a gambling activity: "A person 'advances gambling activity' if he engages in conduct that materially aids any form of gambling activity. Conduct of this nature includes but is not limited to conduct directed toward the creation or establishment of the particular game, contest, scheme, device or activity involved, toward the acquisition or maintenance of premises, paraphernalia, equipment or apparatus therefor, toward the solicitation or inducement of persons to participate therein, toward the actual conduct of the playing phases thereof, toward the arrangement of any of its financial or recording phases or toward any other phase of its operation. A person advances gambling activity if, having substantial proprietary control or other authoritative control over premises being used with his knowledge for purposes of gambling activity, he permits that activity to occur or continue or makes no effort to prevent its occurrence or continuation." Code of Ala. 1975, § 13A-12-20(1).*

GAMBLING, POSSESSION OF RECORDS. Code of Ala. 1975, §§ 13A-12-24 and 13A-12-25.

Charged as: Possession of gambling records.

"A person commits the crime of possession of gambling[1] records in the first degree if with knowledge of the contents thereof, he possesses any writing, paper, instrument or article:

"(1) Of a kind commonly used in the operation or promotion of a bookmaking[2] scheme or enterprise, and constituting, reflecting or representing more than five bets, or more than $500.00; or

"(2) Of a kind commonly used in the operation, promotion or playing of a lottery[3] or mutuel[4] scheme or enterprise, and constituting, reflecting or representing more than five plays or chances therein." § 13A-12-24(a) of the Alabama Code.

"A person commits the crime of possession of gambling records in the second degree if with knowledge of the contents thereof, he possesses any writing, paper, instrument or article:

GAMBLING, POSSESSION OF RECORDS.—Cont'd.

"(1) Of a kind commonly and peculiarly used in the operation or promotion of a bookmaking scheme or enterprise; or

"(2) Of a kind commonly and peculiarly used in the operation, promotion or playing of a lottery or mutuel scheme or enterprise." § 13A-12-25(a) of the Alabama Code.

Classification.

Class A misdemeanor, (both first and second degree).

Comments.

To fall within the scope of these statutes, the person must have had knowledge of the contents of the writings, paper, etc., that he had in his possession. However, § 13A-12-28(a) of the Alabama Code creates the presumption that the possession of any gambling record is prima facie evidence that the possession was with knowledge of its character or contents. Therefore, the burden is on the defendant to overcome this presumption of knowledge.

The writings, papers, etc., must have also been actually used, or were intended to be used, in the operation or promotion of a bookmaking scheme or enterprise, or in the playing of a lottery or mutuel scheme or enterprise. It is a complete defense that the papers, writings, etc., were not used, or were never intended to be so used. The burden of injecting this issue is on the defendant; however, the burden of proof does not shift.[5]

Both statutes require that the writings, papers, etc., be of a kind that is "commonly" used in the operation or promotion of such offenses. What is "commonly" used is not defined but is left to be determined on a case by case basis with the aid of expert testimony.[6]

Just as any other illegally used or possessed item is confiscated and forfeited to the state, so too are gambling devices, records and any and all money or vehicles used in furtherance thereof.[7]

Prior to 1979, first degree possession of gambling records was a Class C felony and second degree possession was a Class A misdemeanor. However, under the present statute an individual charged with possession of records reflecting $1 is subject to the same punishment as an individual whose records show $1,000,000 (both are Class A misdemeanors).

Defenses.

(1) The person is able to overcome the "presumption of knowledge" as to the contents of the writings, papers, etc.

(2) The writings, papers, etc., were not used and not intended to be used in the operation or promotion of bookmaking or playing a lottery/mutuel.

(3) The person is able to prove that the items possessed were not of the character that is "commonly" used for bookmaking or lottery/mutuel purposes.

(4) Keep in mind that a charge for first degree may not be given unless the number of bets/plays or monetary amount surpasses the minimum designated in the statute.

(5) The person possesses writings, papers, etc., from a legal pari-mutuel.

Cross references.

See GAMBLING; GAMBLING, CONSPIRACY TO PROMOTE; GAMBLING, LEGALIZED PARI-MUTUEL BETTING NOT AFFECTED; GAMBLING, POSSESSION, ETC., OF STAMP PRIMA FACIE EVIDENCE OF VIOLATION OF GAMBLING LAWS; GAMBLING, POSSESSION OF DEVICE; LOTTERY PARAPHERNALIA, TRANSPORTATION; SOLICITATION.

---

1. *"GAMBLING. A person engages in gambling if he stakes or risks something of value upon the outcome of a contest of chance or a future contingent event not under his control or influence, upon an agreement or understanding that he or someone else will receive something of value in the event of a certain outcome. Gambling does not include bona fide business transactions valid under the law of contracts, including but not limited to contracts for the purchase or sale at a future date of securities or commodities, and agreements to compensate for loss caused by the happening of chance, including but not limited to*

GAMBLING, POSSESSION OF RECORDS.—Cont'd.

contracts of indemnity or guaranty and life, health or accident insurance." Code of Ala. 1975, § 13A-12-20(4).

2. *"BOOKMAKING. Advancing gambling activity by unlawfully accepting bets from members of the public as a business, rather than in a casual or personal fashion, upon the outcome of future contingent events." Code of Ala. 1975, § 13A-12-20(2).*
3. *"LOTTERY or POLICY. An unlawful gambling scheme in which:*

"a. The players pay or agree to pay something of value for chances, represented and differentiated by numbers or by combinations of numbers or by some other medium, one or more of which chances are to be designated by the winning ones; and

"b. The winning chances are to be determined by a drawing or by some other fortuitous method; and

"c. The holders of the winning chances are to receive something of value."

"[T]here are three elements to a lottery: '(1) A prize, (2) awarded by chance, (3) for a consideration.'" Opinion of the Justices, 397 So. 2d 546, 547 (Ala. 1981). Code of Ala. 1975, § 13A-12-20(6).

4. *"PARI-MUTUEL, MUTUEL, or THE NUMBERS GAME. A form of lottery in which the winning chances or plays are not determined upon the basis of a drawing or other act on the part of persons conducting or connected with the scheme, but upon the basis of the outcome of a future contingent event or events otherwise unrelated to the particular scheme." Code of Ala. 1975, § 13A-12-20(7).*
5. *Code of Ala. 1975, § 13A-12-26.*
6. *Smith v. State, 273 Ala. 183, 136, So. 2d 911 (1962).*
7. *Code of Ala. 1975, § 13A-12-30.*

GAMBLING, PROMOTING. Code of Ala. 1975, § 13A-12-22.

"A person commits the crime of promoting gambling if he knowingly advances or profits from unlawful gambling activity otherwise than as a player."

Classification.

Class A misdemeanor.

Defenses.

(1) Knowingly particpated only as a player.

Cross references.

See COCKFIGHTING OR KEEPING A COCKPIT; GAMBLING, CONSPIRACY TO PROMOTE; GAMBLING, LEGALIZED PARI-MUTUEL BETTING NOT AFFECTED; GAMBLING, POSSESSION OF DEVICE; GAMBLING, POSSESSION OF RECORDS; GAMBLING, POSSESSION, ETC., OF STAMP PRIMA FACIE EVIDENCE OF VIOLATION OF GAMBLING LAWS; GAMBLING PLACES; LOTTERY PARAPHERNALIA, TRANSPORTATION; SOLICITATION.

GAMBLING PLACES; GAMBLING DEVICES IN BARRED HOUSE. Code of Ala. 1975, § 13A-12-52.

Charged as: Exhibiting gambling devices in barred house or where speaking tubes or electric signals are used.

"No person or persons shall exhibit or expose to view in any barred or barricaded house or room, in any place built or constructed in such manner as to make it difficult of access or ingress to police officers or other oficers, or protected, furnished or equipped with speaking tubes, dumbwaiters, electric wires or bells, or other apparatus for giving alarm from the outside or from the inside of such house, or room when two or more persons are present, any cards, dice, roulette wheel or any gambling implements whatever."

Classification.

"Any person violating the provisions of this section shall be guilty of a felony and shall be punished by imprisonment in the penitentiary for not less than one nor more than five years; and all persons who visit or resort to any such barred or barricaded house or room or other place that is built or protected or equipped in the manner descirbed in this section and where any cards, dice, roulette wheel or any gaming implements whatever are kept or exhibited or exposed to view when said persons visit or resort to such place for the purpose of gaming, shall be guilty of a misdemeanor and, upon conviction, shall be fined not less than $50.00 nor more than $300.00 and may also be imprisoned in the county jail or sentenced to hard labor for the county for not more than six months." § 13A-12-52 of the Alabama Code.

GAMBLING PLACES; GAMBLING DEVICES IN BARRED HOUSE. —Cont'd.

Comments.

The focus of the defense attorney should be on the question of intent relative to "exhibiting or exposing to view" and relative to the intent behind the construction of the building (i.e., "to make it difficult of access or ingress to police officers"). He should not overlook the constitutional implications of what is a rather vague statement.

Defenses.

(1) Did not exhibit or expose to view.
(2) The room was not barricaded in any way.
(3) The house was not constructed in such a manner as to make access or ingress difficult for the police.
(4) The house was not constructed with the intent to make access or ingress difficult for the police.
(5) Two or more persons were not present.

GAMBLING PLACES; MAINTAINING ELECTRIC BELLS. Code of Ala. 1975, § 13A-12-50.

Charged as: Unlawful to maintain electric bells, etc.

"No person or persons shall maintain or use any electric bells, wires or signals or any elevators or dumbwaiters or other implements or appliances connected with any gaming place or rooms used for gaming, which may be used for the purpose of communicating with the occupants of such gaming house or rooms used for gaming or with those who may be within. . ."

Classification.

"[A]ny person who erects, maintains or uses any such bells, wires, signals or elevators or dumbwaiters or other implements or appliances or devices of like kind for said purpose shall be guilty of a felony and shall be punished by imprisonment in the penitentiary for not less than one nor more than five years." § 13A-12-50 of the Alabama Code.

Comments.

It is of constitutional significance that there is no specific intent or purpose attached to

GAMBLING PLACES; MAINTAINING ELECTRIC BELLS. —Cont'd.

the bells, wires, signals, etc. It is possible to fall victim to § 13A-12-50 of the Alabama Code by maintaining a fire alarm system, a telephone, etc.

Defenses.

(1) Consider a constitutional attack based on vagueness.
(2) Electric bells, etc., cannot be used for communicating with occupants.
(3) Not a gaming or gambling place.

GAMBLING PLACES; OWNER PERMITTING PERSON TO EQUIP ROOM. Code of Ala. 1975, § 13A-12-53.

Charged as: Owner permitting any person to equip any room, etc.

"Any person who, being the owner, proprietor, or keeper, or superintendent of any tavern, inn, restaurant, billiard room, poolroom or other public house, permits or suffers any person or persons on or about the premises to provide a barred or barricaded room or rooms to which persons resort for gaming or who knowingly or wilfully permits or knowingly or wilfully suffers any person or persons to equip any room or rooms on or about the premises with electric bells, wires or signals, or elevators, dumbwaiters or other implements or appliances connected with such rooms used or to be used for the purpose of communicating with an occupant or occupants of such gambling room or rooms, shall likewise be guilty of a felony . . ."

Classification.

A felony, and punishable by imprisonment in the penitentiary for not less than one nor more than five years.

Defenses.

(1) Owner did not know, permit, or suffer the establishment of a gambling room.
(2) The equipment was not for gaming or warning purposes.

Note: The attorney reviewing §§ 13A-12-50 through 13A-12-58 of the Alabama Code should note that § 13A-12-58 of the Alabama Code provides the "[t]he presence

GAMBLING PLACES; OWNER PERMITTING PERSON TO EQUIP ROOM.—Cont'd.

of electric bells, wires or signals or dumbwaiters or of other implements or appliances that may be used for the purpose of communicating with persons who are occupying a barred or barricaded room on or about the premises of a hotel, restaurant, billiard room, poolroom or any room above the grade floor in the business district of any town or city is prima facie evidence that gaming was being there carried on by such parties in any prosecution against them, if they have the general reputation of being gamblers, and in all such cases, proof of such general reputation is admissible in evidence."

Cross references.

See GAMBLING; GAMBLING, POSSESSION OF DEVICES; GAMBLING, POSSESSION OF RECORDS.

GOVERNMENTAL OPERATIONS. See OBSTRUCTING GOVERNMENTAL OPERATIONS.

GOVERNMENTAL RECORDS, TAMPERING WITH. Code of Ala. 1975, § 13A-10-12.

Charged as: Tampering with governmental records.

"A person commits the crime of tampering with governmental records[1] if:

"(1) He knowingly[2] makes a false entry in or falsely alters any governmental record; or

"(2) Knowing he lacks the authority to do so, he intentionally[3] destroys, mutilates, conceals, removes or otherwise substantially impairs the verity or availability of any governmental record; or

"(3) Knowing he lacks the authority to retain a governmental record he refuses to deliver up the record in his possession upon proper request of a person lawfully entitled to receive such record for examination or other purposes."

Classification.

Class A misdemeanor.

Comments.

This section covers: (1) falsely altering governmental records; (2) substantially impairing the availability of governmental records; and (3) refusing to deliver up such records on request. Governmental records includes not only records belonging to the government but also records required by law to be kept by others for information of the government.

Defenses.

(1) Lack of knowledge that entry made was false.

(2) Belief of authority to retain records.

(3) Belief of authority to impair such records.

Cross references.

See OBSTRUCTING GOVERNMENTAL OPERATIONS.

---

1. *"Any record, paper, document or thing belonging to, or received or kept by, the government for information or record, or required by law to be kept by others for information of the government." Code of Ala. 1975, § 13A-10-1(4).*
2. *"A person acts knowingly with respect to conduct or to a circumstance described by a statute defining an offense when he is aware that his conduct is of that nature or that the circumstance exists." Code of Ala. 1975, § 13A-2-2(2).*
3. *"A person acts intentionally with respect to a result or to conduct described by a statute defining an offense, when his purpose is to cause that result or to engage in that conduct." Code of Ala. 1975, § 13A-2-2(1).*

GRATUITIES, OFFER TO, OR RECEIPT OF, BY MEMBER OR EMPLOYEE OF GOVERNMENTAL AGENCY, BOARD, OR COMMISSION. Code of Ala. 1975, § 36-25-12.

Charged as: Promise of future employment, favors, etc., for members of governmental regulatory agencies, boards, etc.

"No person shall offer or give to a member or employee of a governmental agency, board or commission that regulates a business with which such person is associated, and no member or employee of a governmental

GRATUITIES, ETC.—Cont'd.

regulatory agency, board or commission shall solicit or accept from any such person anything of value including a promise of future employment or a favor or service while the member or employee is associated with the regulatory agency, board or commission."

Comments.

Actually, this section creates two offenses:

(1) The offer or giving of a gratuity to a member or employee of a governmental regulatory agency, board or commission, and

(2) The solicitation or receipt by the same of such gift.

The first can be committed by "any person" where as only members or employees of such agencies, board or commission may be charged with the latter. Unlike § 36-25-6 of the Alabama Code, there is no requirement of any agreement or understanding that the member or employee would be influenced or take action. All that is required is that (1) such member or employee (2) be offered or receive, or solicitor accept (3) anything of value (4) while a member or employee. The lack of any intent requirement makes this a strict liability offense. Expenses incident to social occasions afforded such members or employees are specifically prohibited from constituting a thing of value.

Defenses.

(1) No employee or member of an agency or commission (specified in § 36-25-12 of the Alabama Code) was involved.

(2) There was no offer, giving, soliciting, or accepting.

(3) Nothing of value was involved.

(4) Was not during the tenure of the employee or member in question.

Cross references.

See Alderman not to hold other municipal offices or have interest, etc., in municipal contract, etc., § 11-43-53 of the Alabama Code; employment of municipal officers by corporations holding franchises as to use of streets, § 11-43-11 of the Alabama Code. See ETHICS VIOLATIONS.

GRATUITIES, OFFER TO, OR RECEIPT OF, BY PUBLIC OFFICIAL OR EMPLOYEE. Code of Ala. 1975, § 36-25-6.

Charged as: Offering, receiving, etc., gifts, favors, etc.

"No person shall offer to or give to a public official or employee or his family, and none of the aforenamed shall solicit or receive anything of value, including a gift, favor or service or a promise of future employment, based on any understanding that the vote, official actions, decisions or judgment of the intended recipient or family member would be influenced thereby."

Comments.

Actually, this section creates two offenses:

(1) The offer or giving of a gratuity to a public official, employee or family member thereof, and

(2) The solicitation or receipt by the same of such gift.

The first can be committed by "any person" whereas only public officials, employees or their family members may be charged with the latter. Requisite to either charge is an understanding that the benefit conferred would influence the vote, action, decision or judgment of **"the intended recipient or family member."** The language of the statute is deceptive in that if read literally, it does not make an influenced official's or employee's conduct culpable where he was not in fact the intended recipient of the benefit. (The official or employee cannot be a family member — see Definitions, § 36-25-1(10), (12)). Similarly, it would seem that the statute is over broad unless it was the drafter's intention to make culpable the influencing of the family member's vote, judgment or decision. The wording defies any alternative construction, and the magnitude of the language is such as would seem to preclude judicial repair of the statute. Expenses incident to social occasions afforded public officials and employees (and presumably the benefit received by any official or employee incident to a social occasion) is specifically prohibited from constituting a thing of value. Actual influence of the official or employee does not seem to be required.

GRATUITIES, OFFER TO, OR RECEIPT OF, BY PUBLIC OFFICIAL OR EMPLOYEE.—Cont'd.

Defenses.

(1) Lack of an understanding.

(2) Official or employee was not the **"intended recipient."**

Cross references.

See BRIBERY OF PUBLIC SERVANT; CONFIDENTIAL INFORMATION, MISUSE OF; CONFLICT OF INTEREST, FAILURE TO DISCLOSE; ETHICS VIOLATIONS; TRADING IN PUBLIC OFFICE.

GUNPOWDER, STORING. Code of Ala. 1975, § 13A-11-224.

Charged as: Storing gunpowder, etc., in city or town.

"Any person who keeps on hand, at any one time, within the limits of any incorporated city or town, for sale or for use, more than 50 pounds of gunpowder or other explosives[1] shall," be guilty of illegally storing gunpowder.

Classification.

Statutory penalty: a fine of not less than $100.00.

Comments.

This statute regulates the amount of explosives that may be legally stored within a populated area. Because possession and storage can occur simultaneously, this section should be read in conjunction with the prohibition on possession of explosives.[2]

Defenses.

(1) Material stored is not an explosive intended to be regulated by the legislature, e.g., fireworks for agricultural use.

(2) Place of storage is not within the limits of an incorporated city or town.

(3) Quantity is less than 50 pounds.

Cross references.

See EXPLOSIVES, POSSESSION OF; FIREWORKS, UNLAWFULLY DEALING IN.

---

1. *An explosive is: "Any chemical compound or mechanical mixture that is commonly used or intended for the purpose of producing an*

GUNPOWDER, STORING.—Cont'd.

explosion and which contains any oxidizing and combustive units or other ingredients in such proportions, quantities or packing that an ignition by fire, by friction, by concussion, by detonator or by chemical action of any part of the compound or mixture may cause a sudden generation of highly heated gases that the resultant gaseous pressures are capable of producing destructive effects on contiguous objects or of destroying life or limb." Code of Ala. 1975, § 13A-7-40(2).

2. *"A person commits the crime of criminal possession of explosives if he possesses, manufactures, buys, sells or transports any explosive, and intends that the explosive be used in the commission of a crime involving violence to another person or destruction of another's property." This is a Class C felony. Code of Ala. 1975, § 13A-7-44.*

HABITUAL FELONY OFFENDER. Code of Ala. 1975, § 13A-5-9.

The Alabama Code[1] provides additional penalties in all cases when it is shown that a criminal defendant has been previously convicted of a felony. Only prior felony convictions can be used for enhancement purposes and can only be applied to a subsequent felony conviction.[2] When it is shown that the defendant does in fact have a prior felony conviction,[3] the application of the statute is mandatory[4] and cannot be circumvented by use of a plea bargain.[5]

Although the statute speaks in terms of the use of any previous felony convictions, the United States Supreme Court has held that Gideon v. Wainwright[6] is retroactive and any prior convictions in violation thereof cannot be used for enhancement purposes.[7] The Alabama courts have followed the counsel requirement and have held that the burden is on the State to show that the defendant did have, or waived, counsel at each prior proceeding.[8] This may be proved by entering in the record a certified copy of the prior conviction.[9]

The actual determination of whether the statute will apply is made by the court after a finding of guilt.[10] The indictment need not allege the application of the habitual offender statute.[11]

The United States Supreme Court has

HABITUAL FELONY OFFENDER. —Cont'd.

recently held that a defendant sentenced under a habitual offender statute subsequently found unconstitutional, is entitled to re-sentencing.[12] Additionally, the Alabama Legislature recently amended § 13A-5-6 of the Alabama Code, providing for enhancement of sentences for the commission of felonies when a firearm or deadly weapon is used or attempted to be used.[13] When a person is convicted of a Class A felony committed in the proscribed manner, the sentence shall not be less than 20 years; and for either a Class B or C felony, not less than 10 years.

Comments.

The United States Supreme Court has recently held that, under federal law, a defendant convicted and sentenced under a statute that itself contains an enhancement clause, cannot also be sentenced under 18 U. S. C. § 924, the general enhancement statute. In Busic v. United States, 446 U. S. 398, 100 S. Ct. 1747, 64 L. Ed. 2d 381 (1980), the defendant was convicted and sentenced specifically under 18 U. S. C. § 111 (armed assault on federal officers) and § 924(c). On remand, 639 F. 2d 940 (3rd Cir. 1981), the court held that since the District Court had sentenced under the belief that § 924(c) and § 111 applied, the sentences should be vacated and remanded for sentencing under either, but not both, of the statutes. In Simpson v. United States, 435 U. S. 6, 98 S. Ct. 909, 55 L. Ed. 2d 70 (1978), the defendant was convicted and sentenced specifically under 18 U. S. C. § 2113(d) (bank robbery by the use of a dangerous weapon or device) and § 924(c).

Cross references.

See N. Chiarkas, Alabama Criminal Trial Practice, §§ 26-4 through 26-8. See SENTENCING.

---

1. *Code of Ala. 1975, § 13A-5-9. Habitual felony offenders:*

"(a) In all cases when it is shown that a criminal defendant has been previously convicted of any felony and after such conviction has committed another felony, he must be punished as follows:

"(1) On conviction of a Class C felony, he must be punished for a Class B felony;

"(2) On conviction of a Class B felony, he must be punished for a Class A felony;

"(3) On conviction of a Class A felony, he must be punished by imprisonment for life or for any term of not more than 99 years but not less than 15 years.

"(b) In all cases when it is shown that a criminal defendant has been previously convicted of any two felonies and after such convictions has committed another felony, he must be punished as follows:

"(1) On conviction of a Class C felony, he must be punished for a Class A felony;

"(2) On conviction of a Class B felony, he must be punished by imprisonment for life or for any term of not more than 99 years but not less than 15 years;

"(3) On conviction of a Class A felony, he must be punished by imprisonment for life or for any term of not less than 99 years.

"(c) In all cases when it is shown that a criminal defendant has been previously convicted of any three felonies and after such convictions has committed another felony, he must be punished as follows:

"(1) On conviction of a Class C felony, he must be punished by imprisonment for life or for any term not more than 99 years but not less than 15 years;

"(2) On conviction of a Class B felony, he must be punished for life in the penitentiary;

"(3) On conviction of a Class A felony, he must be punished for imprisonment for life without parole."

See also the comment to § 26-3, N. Chiarkas, Alabama Criminal Trial Practice.

2. *Misdemeanors cannot be used for enhancement purposes and cannot be enhanced.*

3. *The defendant need not have actually been imprisoned on any of the prior convictions for them to apply. Watson v. State, 392 So. 2d 1274 (Ala. Cr. App. 1980), cert. denied, 392 So. 2d 1280 (Ala. 1981).*

4. *"In all cases when [a prior conviction] is shown . . . he must be punished" as per the habitual offender act. § 13A-5-9. Watson v. State, 392 So. 2d 1274 (Ala. Cr. App. 1980), cert. denied, 392 So. 2d 1280 (Ala. 1981).*

5. *Milner v. State, 7 Div. 1839 (Ala. Cr. App. 1981), wherein the court spoke of the district attorney's obligation, as an officer of the court, to "show" the defendant's prior convictions to the court, but did not refer to any such duty to the court on the part of the defense attorney.*

HABITUAL FELONY OFFENDER.—Cont'd.

6. *Gideon v. Wainwright, 372 U. S. 335, 83 S. Ct. 792, 9 L. Ed. 2d 799 (1963), the Sixth Amendment right to counsel applies to state felony cases unless it is waived.*
7. *United States v. Tucker, 404 U. S. 443, 92 S. Ct. 589, 30 L. Ed. 2d 592 (1972); Burgett v. Texas, 389 U. S. 109, 88 S. Ct. 258, 19 L. Ed. 2d 319 (1967); Greer v. Beto, 384 U. S. 269, 86 S. Ct. 1477, 16 L. Ed. 2d 526 (1966).*
8. *Thatch v. State, 397 So. 2d 246 (Ala. Cr. App. 1981), cert. denied, 397 So. 2d 253 (Ala. 1981); Watson v. State, 392 So. 2d 1274 (Ala. Cr. App. 1980), cert. denied, 392 So. 2d 1280 (Ala. 1981); Williams v. State, 393 So. 2d 492 (Ala. Cr. App. 1981).*
9. *Thatch v. State, 397 So. 2d 246 (Ala. Cr. App. 1981), cert. denied, 397 So. 2d 253 (Ala. 1981); Thomas v. State, 395 So. 2d 1105 (Ala. Cr. App. 1981).*
10. *Code of Ala. 1975, § 13-5-10.*
11. *Coker v. State, 396 So. 2d 1094 (Ala. Cr. App. 1981); Thatch v. State, 397 So. 2d 246 (Ala. Cr. App. 1981), cert. denied, 397 So. 2d 253 (Ala. 1981); Thomas v. State, 395 So. 2d 1105 (Ala. Cr. App. 1981).*
12. *Hicks v. Oklahoma, 447 U. S. 343, 100 S. Ct. 2227, 65 L. Ed. 2d 175 (1980).*
13. *Act 81-840, Alabama Legislature, Regular Session 1981, effective May 27, 1981.*

HARASSMENT OR HARASSING COMMUNICATIONS. Code of Ala. 1975, § 13A-11-8.

"(1) A person commits the crime of harassment if, with intent to harass, annoy or alarm another person, he:

"a. Strikes, shoves, kicks or otherwise touches a person or subjects him to physical contact; or

"b. Directs abusive or obscene language or makes an obscene gesture towards another person." § 13A-11-8(a) of the Alabama Code.

"(1) A person commits the crime of harassing communications if, with intent to harass or alarm another person he:

"a. Communicates with a person, anonymously or otherwise, by telephone, telegraph, mail or any other form of written or electronic communication, in a manner likely to harass or cause alarm; or

"b. Makes a telephone call, whether or not a conversation ensues, with no purpose of legitimate communication; or

"c. Telephones another person and addresses to or about such other person any lewd or obscene words or language.

Nothing in this section should apply to legitimate business telephone communications." § 13A-11-8(b) of the Alabama Code.

Classification.

Class C misdemeanor, harassment or harassing communication.

Comments.

Under §§ 13A-6-20 through 13A-6-25 of the Alabama Code, assault does not occur until there is some physical injury. Thus, mere physical touching does not fall within the provisions covered by assault. This statute supplements the assault provisions by covering nonconsensual physical touching that does not cause a physical injury, but is intentionally done to harass, annoy or alarm another person. It is not clear why the drafters of this statute rejected a proposal making the following of a person in or about a public place, with intent to harass, annoy or alarm an offense. A "catch-all" provision was rejected that would have covered any course of conduct or repeated acts that alarm or seriously annoy and serve no legitimate purpose.

Defenses.

(1) Lack of intent.

(2) Within the scope and in furtherance of a business purpose.

Query.

Are legitimate business communications other than those by telephone also exempted from the coverage of this statute?

Cross references.

See DISORDERLY CONDUCT.

HAZARD, CREATING. Code of Ala. 1975, § 13A-11-220.

Charged as: Creating a hazard.

"A person commits the crime of creating a hazard if:

"(1) Having discarded, in any place

HAZARD, CREATING.—Cont'd.

accessible to children, a container having a compartment of more than one and one half cubic feet capacity and a door or lid that locks or fastens automatically when closed and cannot easily be opened from the inside, he fails to remove the door, lid or locking or fastening device; or

"(2) Being the owner or otherwise having possession of land upon which there is an abandoned well, cistern or cesspool of a depth of four feet or more and a top width of 12 inches or more, he fails to fill, cover or fence it with a suitable protective construction."

Classification.

Class B misdemeanor.

Comments.

This statute is divided into two subsections, neither of which require a culpable mental state on the part of an actor:

(1) The actor is criminally liable for conduct that is similar to creating an "attractive nuisance" in the law of torts.[1] A person can be criminally liable although a child[2] was not actually entrapped. A person whose conduct causes a child to become entrapped in a container whose dimensions meet those of the statute can be charged with reckless endangerment[3] and/or unlawful imprisonment.[4] If the entrapped child dies due to the proscribed conduct, the defendant can be found guilty of manslaughter,[5] or criminally negligent homicide.[6]

(2) An owner or possessor of land is required to fill, cover, or enclose an abyss. No person has to suffer actual harm for liability to attach to a person whose acts or omissions fall within the scope of the statute. One who violates this statute and causes actual harm or death to another person can also be charged with reckless endangerment, unlawful imprisonment, manslaughter, or criminally negligent homicide.[7] This subsection is based on a theory similar to the torts concept of maintaining abnormally dangerous conditions on the land.[8]

Defenses.

(1) Regarding hazardous containers:

(a) Did not discard a container.

(b) Area not accessible to children.

(c) Door or lid did not lock or fasten automatically.

(d) Door or lock could easily be opened from inside.

(e) Door or lid or fastening device had been removed.

(f) Container did not have dimensions specified to fall within scope of statute.

(2) Regarding hazardous conditions on land:

(a) Person charged not owner or possessor of land.

(b) Abyss covered, filled or enclosed.

(c) Abyss less than four feet deep or top less than 12 inches wide.

Cross references.

See LITTERING.

---

1. *See generally W. Prosser, Law of Torts § 59 (4th ed. 1971).*
2. *"Children" is not defined within the statute but may include those under 14 years of age who have a defense to prosecution as an adult, Code of Ala. 1975, § 13A-3-3, or those under seven years of age who are conclusively presumed incapable of committing a crime. See Blocker v. State, 40 Ala. App. 658, 120 So. 2d 924 (1960) and cases cited therein. Cf. Code of Ala. 1975, § 13A-11-170, which defines minor as an unmarried person under 18 years of age.*
3. *"A person commits the crime of reckless endangerment if he recklessly engages in conduct which creates a substantial risk of serious physical injury to another person." Code of Ala. 1975, § 13A-6-24.*
4. *"A person commits the crime of unlawful imprisonment in the first degree if he restrains another person under circumstances which expose the latter to a risk of serious physical injury." Code of Ala. 1975, § 13A-6-41.*

   "A person commits the crime of unlawful imprisonment in the second degree if he restrains another person." Code of Ala. 1975, § 13A-6-42. The official commentary states that the person must cause interference with the victim's liberty intentionally or knowingly, but these are not elements listed in the statutes.
5. *"A person commits the crime of manslaughter if he recklessly causes the death of another person." Code of Ala. 1975, § 13A-6-3(a)(1). See Garret v. State, 268 Ala. 299, 105 So. 2d 541 (1958), stating the theory upon which this statute is based.*

HAZARD, CREATING.—Cont'd.

6. *"A person commits the crime of criminally negligent homicide if he causes the death of another person by criminal negligence." Code of Ala. 1975, § 13A-6-4. Though negligence is a culpable mental state included by the statute under subsection (b), the jury is permitted to consider statutes regulating defendant's conduct in determining whether he departed from the standard of conduct appropriate for him under the circumstances. The violation of some statutes does not establish a prima facie case of criminal negligence or the presumption of criminal negligence but is one factor having a bearing upon the existence of such negligence.*
7. *See notes 3, 4, 5, and 6, supra.*
8. *See Restatement of Torts 2d, § 519.*

HEROIN. See CONTROLLED SUBSTANCES.

HINDERING PROSECUTION/ HINDERING APPREHENSION OF ESCAPEE.

Code of Ala. 1975, §§ 13A-10-43 and 13A-10-44.

A person commits the crime of hindering prosecution if with the intent to hinder the apprehension, prosecution, conviction or punishment of another for conduct constituting a murder or a Class A or B felony (Hindering Prosecution in the First degree, § 13A-10-43 of the Alabama Code), or a Class C felony or a Class A misdemeanor (Hindering Prosecution in the Second degree, § 13A-10-44 of the Alabama Code), he renders criminal assistance[1] to such person.

A person commits the crime of hindering the apprehension of an escapee (§ 13A-10-45 of the Alabama Code) if, with the intent to hinder the apprehension of a person known to have escaped from a detention facility,[2] he renders criminal assistance to such person.

Classification.

Class C felony, hindering prosecution, first degree.

Class A misdemeanors, hindering prosecution, second degree, and hindering apprehension of escapee.

Comments.

In these sections the theory of obstructing justice is employed instead of the "accomplice" or "accessory after the fact" theories. A person who intentionally aids another to elude apprehension or trial is interfering with the process of government. § 13A-10-42 of the Alabama Code, which defines "criminal assistance," sets forth five specific acts that incur liability (see note 1, infra). The first two sections differ concerning the degree of the offense with which the offender being assisted is charged. § 13A-10-45 of the Alabama Code was included to cover hindering apprehension of persons who have escaped from custody, no matter where they were held, including mental institutions.

Defenses.

(1) Lack of intent. One may furnish aid without intending to hinder the apprehension or conviction of an offender.

(2) Lack of knowledge that the person you are helping is an offender.

Cross references.

See COMPOUNDING; OBSTRUCTING GOVERNMENTAL OPERATIONS.

---

1. *"For purposes of sections 13A-10-43 through 13A-10-45, a person renders 'criminal assistance' to another if he:*
   "(1) Harbors or conceals such person;
   "(2) Warns such person of impending discovery or apprehension; except that this subdivision does not apply to a warning given in connection with an effort to bring another into compliance with the law;
   "(3) provides such person with money, transportation, weapon, disguise or other means of avoiding discovery or apprehension;
   "(4) Prevents or obstructs, by means of force, deception or intimidation, anyone except a trespasser from performing an act that might aid in the discovery or apprehension of such person; or
   "(5) Suppresses, by an act of concealment, alteration or destruction, any physical evidence that might aid in the discovery or apprehension of such person." Code of Ala. 1975, § 13A-10-42.
2. *"Any place used for the confinement, pursuant to*

HINDERING PROSECUTION/ HINDERING APPREHENSION OF ESCAPEE.—Cont'd.

law, of a person:

"a. Charged with or convicted of a criminal offense; or

"b. Charged with being or adjudicated a youthful offender, or a neglected minor or juvenile delinquent; or

"c. Held for extradition; or

"d. Otherwise confined pursuant to an order of court." Code of Ala. 1975, § 13A-10-30(b)(2).

HOLIDAYS. See SUNDAY, CERTAIN ACTS PROHIBITED; SUNDAY, HOLDING PUBLIC MARKETS AND TRADING.

HOMICIDE. See HOMICIDE, CRIMINALLY NEGLIGENT; MANSLAUGHTER; MOTOR VEHICLE CRIMES; MURDER.

HOMICIDE, CRIMINALLY NEGLIGENT. Code of Ala. 1975, § 13A-6-4.

"A person commits the crime of criminally negligent[1] homicide if he causes the death of another person by criminal negligence."

Classification.

Class A misdemeanor.

Comments.

As in all criminal charges, the facts of the incident determine what the charge will be. However, there is a thin line between this offense and manslaughter, § 13A-6-3 of the Alabama Code. Both offenses are predicated upon there having been created "a substantial and unjustifiable risk." If the person was aware of the risk and consciously disregarded it and a death occurs because of his "reckless" conduct, he will be charged with manslaughter. If the person was not aware of the "substantial and unjustifiable risk," he could not have consciously disregarded it, and there is a lesser degree of intent.

The statute, so as to clarify Alabama case law, does not recognize the misdemeanor-manslaughter rule.

HOMICIDE, CRIMINALLY NEGLIGENT.—Cont'd.

However, § 13A-6-4(b) of the Alabama Code states that "[t]he jury may consider statutes and ordinances regulating the actor's conduct in determining whether he is culpably negligent." Therefore, if a person violates a statute which is classified as a misdemeanor and a death results, the actor is not automatically culpable for the homicide (as would be the effect with a misdemeanor-manslaughter rule).

With the adoption of § 32-5A-192 of the Alabama Code in 1980 (homicide by vehicle), there is the possibility that a person could be charged under either statute. The comments following that statute state that it is not to be a lesser included offense to § 13A-6-4 of the Alabama Code, or for a prosecution under one to be a bar to a prosecution under the other.

Defenses.

(1) Defendant's actions did not constitute gross negligence.

(2) Involuntary intoxication.

(3) Insanity.

(4) Accident.

Cross references.

See N. Chiarkas, Alabama Criminal Trial Practice, § 14-36 (Special plea of insanity).

See INSANITY; INTOXICATION; MANSLAUGHTER; MOTOR VEHICLE CRIMES; RECKLESS ENDANGERMENT.

---

1. *Code of Ala. 1975, § 13A-2-2(4) defines criminal negligence: "A person acts with criminal negligence with respect to a result or to a circumstance which is defined by statute as an offense when he fails to perceive a substantial and unjustifiable risk that the result will occur or that the circumstance exists. The risk must be of such nature and degree that the failure to perceive it constitutes a gross deviation from the standard of care that a reasonable person would observe in the situation. A court or jury may consider statutes or ordinances regulating the defendant's conduct as bearing upon the question of criminal negligence."*

HOOKER. See PROSTITUTION.

HUNTING, USE OF AIRCRAFT, PROHIBITION. See AVIATION.

ILLEGALLY OBTAINED INFORMATION. See DIVULGING ILLEGALLY OBTAINED INFORMATION; EAVESDROPPING; EAVESDROPPING DEVICE, POSSESSION OF; SURVEILLANCE.

IMMATURITY. Code of Ala. 1975, § 13A-3-3.

Prosecution as an adult is barred if the defendant was less than 14 years old[1] when the crime was committed. Defendants less than 14 years old are conclusively presumed incapable of committing a crime[2] under this section. Age at the time of the alleged offense determines whether there is juvenile court jurisdiction.[3] This is a change from current case law.

---

1. *Pending legislation could change this age limit.*
2. *Alabama has followed the common law doctrine that children below the age of seven are conclusively presumed incapable of committing a crime of any type. A child from seven to fourteen years is rebuttably presumed incapable of committing any crime. Children older than fourteen have no presumption of incapacity.*
3. *Juvenile courts have original and exclusive jurisdiction over children under eighteen; however, a child of fourteen or more years of age at the time of the offense charged (felony) may be transferred for criminal prosecution if, after a hearing, the juvenile court finds this to be in the best interest of the child or the public. Code of Ala. 1975, Title 12, chapter 15, article 2.*

   States that have recently revised their criminal codes have unanimously adopted the "age at the time of the offense" position. Calif. Penal Code § 26; Proposed Federal Criminal Code § 501; Criminal Code of Georgia § 26-710; Ill. Revised Criminal Code § 6-1; Mich. Revised Criminal Code § 701; Minn. Criminal Code § 609.055; N. J. Penal Code § 2B:4010; New York Revised Penal Law § 30.00; Proposed Ore. Criminal Code § 53; Proposed Revision Texas Penal Code § 8.06.

IMPERSONATING PEACE OFFICER. Code of Ala. 1975, § 13A-10-11.

"A person commits the crime of impersonating a peace officer[1] if he falsely pretends to be a peace officer and does any act in that capacity."

Classification.

Class C misdemeanor, impersonating public servant.

Class C felony, impersonating peace officer.

Comments.

The objective of these sections is to prevent imposition by the pretense of authority. Both sections require a specific act performed in the capacity of the respective office impersonated. While a peace officer falls within the definition of a public servant, the greater potential for harm necessitates the separate, more severe section.

Defenses.

(1) No specific act while pretending to be a public servant or police officer.

(2) Honest belief by the accused that he was such an official.

(3) Note, it is no defense to a prosecution under this section that the office the actor pretended to hold did not in fact exist.

---

1. *"Any public servant vested by law with a duty to maintain public order or to make arrests for crime, whether that duty extends to all crimes or is limited to specific crimes." Code of Ala. 1975, § 13A-10-1(5).*

IMPERSONATING PUBLIC SERVANT. Code of Ala. 1975, § 13A-10-10.

"A person commits the crime of impersonating a public servant[1] if he falsely pretends to be a public servant and does any act in that capacity."

---

1. *"Any officer or employee of government, including legislators and judges and any person or agency participating as an adviser, consultant, or otherwise in performing a governmental function." Code of Ala. 1975, § 13A-10-1(7).*

IMPERSONATION, CRIMINAL. Code of Ala. 1975, § 13A-9-18.

Charged as: Criminal impersonation.

"A person commits the crime of criminal impersonation if he:

IMPERSONATION, CRIMINAL. —Cont'd.

"(1) Assumes a false identity and does an act in his assumed character with intent to gain an economic benefit for himself or another or to injure or defraud[1] another; or

"(2) Pretends to be a representative of some person or organization and does an act in his pretended capacity with intent to gain an economic benefit for himself or another or to injure or defraud another."

Classification.

Class B misdemeanor.

Comments.

In the past, various criminal statutes dealt with false identity; these have now been combined in § 13A-9-18 of the Alabama Code. This section provides criminal sanctions against those who assume a false indentity (i.e., pretending to be the named beneficiary of a will), or whose assumed identity adversely affects the public regard for fraternal orders or veteran's organizations (i.e., collecting money as a member of the Veterans of Foreign Wars).

The element of intent must be established; the actor must have intended to either gain an economic benefit, such as filing a financial statement, or to injure or defraud another, such as impersonating an officer and delivering a complaint.

Defenses.

(1) No intent to assume false identity (i.e., person was under the belief that he was beneficiary to the will).

(2) No intent to gain an economic benefit or defraud or injure another.

(3) Note, wearing the insignia of orders and societies without the requisite intent as explained above is no longer a criminal violation and should be dealt with through civil remedies.

Cross references.

See CLERGYMAN, FRAUDULENTLY PRETENDING TO BE; THEFT OF PROPERTY; THEFT OF SERVICES.

---

1. *Intent to defraud. Code of Ala. 1975, § 13A-9-1(8).*

IMPRISONMENT. See UNLAWFUL IMPRISONMENT.

INCAPACITY. See IMMATURITY; INSANITY; JUVENILE PROCEEDINGS.

INCEST. Code of Ala. 1975, § 13A-13-3.

"[A] person commits incest if he marries or engages in sexual intercourse[1] with a person he knows to be, either legitimately or illegitimately: [h]is ancestor or descendant[2] . . . or [h]is brother or sister[3] . . . or [h]is stepchild or stepparent[4] . . . or [h]is aunt, uncle, nephew or niece[5] . . .".

Classification.

Class C felony.

Comments.

As is stated in the comments following § 13A-13-3 of the Alabama Code, notwithstanding the fact that "[s]exual intercourse [or marriage] between closely related persons is almost universally regarded as a grave offense[6] . . . [there seems to be little justification for retaining the incest sanction against] relationships between stepparents and stepchildren, and adoptive parents and adopted children [which is already covered under 'bigamy', or between brother and sister by adoption] . . . where [all parties are] over the age of 21 years and [in the stepparent/stepchild and adoptive-parent/adoptive-child cases, the child] . . . is not financially dependent on the parent."

Defenses.

In addition to the defenses of knowledge, ignorance, intent, etc., (see specific defenses), § 13A-13-3(b) states that "[a] person [will] not be convicted of incest or . . . attempt to commit incest upon the uncorroborated testimony of the person with whom the offense is alleged to have been committed."

Query.

It is difficult to create a situation that would be violative of § 13-13-3(a)(3) of the Alabama Code and not also violate the bigamy statute, § 13A-13-1 of the Alabama Code.

Cross references.

See ADULTERY; BIGAMY.

---

1. *Exactly what the drafters mean by "sexual intercourse" is not clear. See the explanation in ADULTERY, note 3, supra.*

INCEST.—Cont'd.

2. *By blood or adoption.*
3. *Whole or half blood or adoption.*
4. *This is restricted only while the marriage creating the relationship exists; thus, one might find it difficult to separate this from bigamy.*
5. *Whole or half blood.*
6. *In the comments following § 13A-13-3, the drafters point out that "[t]here are various explanations as to why the state should punish such activity which may be carried on in private, by mutual intelligent consent of the participants, and without obvious impact on the community."*

INCITING TO RIOT. See RIOT, INCITING TO.

INDECENT EXPOSURE. Code of Ala. 1975, § 13A-6-68.

"A person commits the crime of indecent exposure if, with intent to arouse or gratify sexual desire of himself or of any person other than his spouse,[1] he exposes his genitals under circumstances in which he knows his conduct is likely to cause **affront** or **alarm**[2] in any public place or on the private premises of another or so near[3] thereto as to be seen from such private premises."

Classification.

Class A misdemeanor.

Comments.

One reading of § 13A-6-68 of the Alabama Code could lead to the conclusion that if one exposes his genitals in public to arouse or gratify the sexual desire of his spouse, he cannot be charged with indecent exposure. In addition, one must wonder how any one could be found to "knowingly" engage in conduct that is likely to cause "affront or alarm" when even the drafters confess that they don't know what "affront or alarm" means.[4] Anyone confronted by this charge would have to, at the very least, attack it as being void on its face. This crime requires both an "intent" and a "knowing".

Defenses.

(1) Actor did not intend to arouse or gratify any sexual desire of himself or anyone else. (See Comments, supra). It would seem that he is permitted to act in the fashion described in § 13A-6-68 of the Alabama Code if his intent was to arouse a sexual desire in his spouse.

(2) He did not know his conduct was likely to cause affront or alarm.

(3) Statute is vague; it does not give proper or clear notice as to what constitutes "affront or alarm," and since the actor must act knowingly, we must not define the issue ex post facto.

(4) Statute is vague and irrational as to the exclusion of spouse while including the self. See Query, infra.

Query.

(1) Bill and Jane are married. While in public and knowing that his conduct was likely to cause "affront or alarm", Bill exposes his genitals. Now if his intent was to arouse his own sexual desire, he could fall within the meaning of "indecent exposure". However, under the same circumstances as above except that Bill's intent was not to arouse his own sexual desire but to arouse Jane's sexual desire, he would fall outside the meaning of "indecent exposure". One must ask what difference that makes? What is the rationale behind this distinction? In fact, if Bill exposed himself to arouse Jane, and Jane exposed herself to arouse Bill, both would still fall outside the meaning of § 13A-6-68 of the Alabama Code.

(2) How could you ever find that someone knew his conduct would cause "X" when "X" is undefined?

Cross references.

See DISORDERLY CONDUCT; LEWDNESS, PUBLIC.

---

1. *I would assume that this would include someone who was living in cohabitation with the actor. See Code of Ala. 1975, § 13A-6-60(4).*
2. *The comments following Code of Ala. 1975, § 13A-6-68 confess that " '[a]ffront' is undefined in Alabama, nor is it defined in any other jurisdiction. 'Alarm' is undefined in this context. The Michigan Draft Commentary suggests that the purpose of the exposure and the likelihood of psychological harm to others determines criminality. It is clear, however, that 'affront and alarm' do not mean the same thing as 'vulgar and indecent,' with which the courts have struggled repeatedly. Although technical definitions and reported examples of 'affront and alarm' are not*

INDECENT EXPOSURE.—Cont'd.

available, the words as used in this section suggest a subjective test of what would likely cause one of those reactions in the observer of the exposure, whereas 'vulgar and indecent,' as presently used, have produced an objective test regarding the nature of the act, regardless of its likely effect upon observers."

3. *The drafters have not made clear just "how" near is "so" near.*
4. *See comments following Code of Ala. 1975, § 13A-6-68. See also note 2, supra.*

INSANITY. Code of Ala. 1975, § 13A-3-1.

Defend as: Mental disease or defect.

"[A] person is not responsible[1] for criminal conduct if at the time of such conduct as a result of mental disease or defect[2] he lacks substantial capacity to appreciate the criminality of his conduct or to conform his conduct to the requirements of law."

Comments.

As do all other states, Alabama provides a defense to a criminal charge described as legal insanity. The essence of this defense is that while the defendant may have committed the acts complained of in the indictment that would normally be criminal, he was legally irresponsible for his acts because of his mental capacity at the time. Acceptance of this defense by the jury, however, is unlike the acceptance of all other criminal law defenses because the acquitted defendant is likely to be committed to a mental institution rather than be free to return home.[3]

The rationale of the insanity defense has been variously stated by commentators,[4] but it seems to serve the purpose of separating out the criminally culpable who ought to be sentenced to effectuate the purposes of the criminal law from those who are ill and in need of medical treatment without the stigma of criminality attaching.[5] It has been suggested that punishment of insane people would not further the usually expressed purposes of the criminal law.[6]

As the commentary following § 13A-3-1 of the Alabama Code points out, "[t]he criteria of insanity, or mental responsibility, that prevails in most American jurisdictions is the old English M'Naghten rule, i.e., a person is not criminally liable if:

" 'at the time of the committing of the act, the party accused was labouring under such a defect of reason, from disease of mind, as not to know the nature and quality of the act he was doing; or, if he did know it, that he did not know he was doing what was wrong.' M'Naghten's Case, 10 Clark & Fin. 200, 210 (1843).

"The M'Naghten, or 'right or wrong,' test was followed in Alabama as the sole criterion of responsibility until Parsons v. State, 81 Ala. 577, 2 So. 854 (1886) where the court supplemented M'Naghten with the so-called 'irresistible impulse' test. There the court considered the 'right or wrong' test valid but not sufficiently comprehensive to cover all situations as there is ample medical evidence of the existence of knowledge of the nature of one's act and yet such person may be insane; that many insane persons have no power or capacity to choose between right and wrong; that under M'Naghten's Case the court charges the jury one thing, but receives expert testimony on something else; that unconsciousness of right and wrong and powerlessness to do right are separate; that the uncontrollable impulse test, in addition to the universal test, is in accord with modern knowledge and no more difficult to apply than the 'right or wrong' test.

"The law in Alabama on insanity as a defense in a criminal case[7] has been well recognized:

" 'Under a plea of not guilty by reason of insanity, the burden is on the defendant to clearly prove to the reasonable satisfaction of the jury that he was so affected by disease of the brain when the offense was committed as to render him so insane that he did not know right from wrong with respect to the particular offense charged, or by reason of such mental disease he could not resist doing the wrong; and the crime must have been the product solely of such diseased mind.' Steeter v. State, 278 Ala. 272, 177 So. 2d 826 (1965); Aaron v. State, 271 Ala. 70, 122 So. 2d 360 (1960); Lee v.

INSANITY.—Cont'd.

State, 265 Ala. 623, 93 So. 2d 757 (1957); Lakey v. State, 258 Ala. 116, 61 So. 2d 117 (1952) and cases cited; Parsons v. State, 81 Ala. 577, 2 So. 854 (1886).

"The M'Naghten rule has been caustically criticized for many years. Some major criticisms are: (1) It fails to identify many persons accused of crime who suffer from serious mental disorders and who are not responsible. The rule unduly emphasizes the intellect or cognitive element and de-emphasizes, or ignores, the volitional and emotional facets of personality. (2) The 'right and wrong' concept is essentially a moral or ethical judgment, not a medical determination. (3) The test emerged before the advancement of modern psychiatry and is concerned with a compartmentalized "brain" or mind" rather than recognizing man as an integrated personality. Witnesses, courts, and juries should be free to consider all information advanced by relevant scientific disciplines. For detailed criticism, see Frank T. Lindman & Donald M. McIntyre, Jr., The Mentally Disabled and the Law (1961)."

---

1. *Title 13A provides two general defenses: Code of Ala. 1975, chapter 3, article 1 deals with responsibility and Code of Ala. 1975, chapter 3, article 2 deals with justification and excuse.*
2. *According to Code of Ala. 1975, § 13A-3-1(b), " '[m]ental disease or defect' does not include an abnormality manifested only by repeated criminal or otherwise antisocial conduct."*
3. *See generally Goldstein, The Insanity Defense 145 (1967); LaFave & Scott, Criminal Law § 51 (1972) (hereinafter LaFave & Scott).*
4. *It has been suggested, for example, that the real purpose of the insanity defense is not to acquit those who would otherwise be held criminally responsible, but, rather, to "authorize the state to hold those 'who must be found not to possess the guilty mind mens rea' even though the criminal law demands that no person be held criminally responsible if doubt is cast on any material element of the offense charged." Goldstein & Katz, Abolish the "Insanity Defense" — Why Not?, 72 Yale L. J. 853, 864 (1963).*
5. *M. P. C. § 4.01, Comment (Tent. Draft No. 4, 1955).*
6. *LaFave & Scott, § 36 at pp. 271-72.*

INSANITY.—Cont'd.

7. *See N. Chiarkas, Alabama Criminal Trial Practice.*

INSOLVENCY. See FRAUD IN INSOLVENCY.

INSPECTION, REFUSAL TO PERMIT. Code of Ala. 1975, § 13A-10-3.

Charged as: Refusal to permit inspection.

"A person commits the crime of refusing to permit inspection of property[1] that is owned, possessed or otherwise subject to his control if, knowing that a public servant[2] is legally authorized to inspect[3] such property and an attempt is being made to exercise that authority, he:

"(1) Refuses to produce the property for a reasonable inspection; or

"(2) Refuses to permit a reasonable inspection."

Classification.

Class C misdemeanor.

Comments.

This offense has elements of strict liability because a belief that refusal is lawful is not a defense. Where the refusal to permit inspection takes the form of a physical obstruction, the section on OBSTRUCTING GOVERNMENTAL OPERATIONS should be utilized. Knowledge of the public servant's legal authority to inspect is not required. This section implies that a person should know or be aware of the attempt to inspect his property.

Defenses.

(1) Unreasonable inspection.

(2) Property sought for inspection not actually in accused's control or possession.

(3) No legal authorization to inspect property.

Cross references.

See OBSTRUCTING GOVERNMENTAL OPERATIONS.

---

1. *"Any real or personal property, including books, records and documents." Code of Ala. 1975, § 13A-10-1(6).*
2. *"Any officer or employee of government, including legislators and judges and any person or agency participating as an adviser, consultant or otherwise in performing a governmental*

INSPECTION, REFUSAL TO PERMIT.—Cont'd.

function." Code of Ala. 1975, § 13A-10-1(7).

3. *"For the purposes of this section, 'legally authorized inspection' includes any lawful search, sampling, testing or other examination of property, in connection with the regulation of the defendant's business or occupation, that is authorized by law." Code of Ala. 1975, § 13A-10-3(b).*

INTERESTS OF PUBLIC OFFICIALS AND EMPLOYEES; DISCLOSURE REQUIRED. Code of Ala. 1975, § 36-25-14.

Charged as: Failure to disclose economic interests.

"No person elected or employed to serve as a public offical or employee shall be allowed to take the oath of office or enter upon his duties unless he has previously filed a statement of economic interests . . ."

Comments.

Within this section is a detailed list of facts refquired to be disclosed.[1] However, this action specifically provides that if the required information is not filed, the state ethics commission must notify the individual of any deficiency. After notification, the individual has 10 days to file.

Query.

The vagueness of this statute raises two critical issues;

(1) Whether failure to file (first time . . . second time . . .) is a violation subject to the penalty provisions of this chapter? and

(2) If so, whether this is a strict liability offense?

The first issue arises from the language "No person . . . **shall be allowed** to take the oath of office or enter upon his duties unless he has previously filed . . ." Implicit in the words "shall be allowed" is the notion that the impetus is upon someone other than the official to act (that the official or employee shall be prohibited by someone — the state ethics commission, the courts, etc. — from entering office. Therefore, failure to file can only be a violation by the implied intent of this section, which, of course, would be subject to a constitutional attack.

INTERESTS OF PUBLIC OFFICIALS AND EMPLOYEES; DISCLOSURE REQUIRED.—Cont'd.

Assuming that failure to file is a violation, the next question, which is raised by the second issue, is whether such a violation is a strict liability offense? At first blush it would seem to be. However, there is a notification requirement in § 36-25-14(7) of the Alabama Code which casts some doubt on that conclusion. It provides that if the required information is not filed, the state ethics commission must notify the individual of his failure to file as required and thereafter the public official or employee shall have 10 days to so file. Additionally, it should be noted that supplemental filing is required annually.

Defenses.

(1) Not a public official or employee.

(2) Has filed the required statement.

(3) Never notified by state ethics commission of any deficiency.

Cross references.

See CONFLICT OF INTEREST, FAILURE TO DISCLOSE; ETHICS VIOLATIONS.

---

1. *The statement of economic interest must be filed at the office of the state ethics commission. "Such statement shall be made on a form provided by the commission and shall contain the following information on the person making such filing:*

"(1) Name, residential address, business; name and address of living spouse, minor and dependent children, adult children, parents, brothers and sisters, and to the best of his knowledge the principal occupation of each of these persons;

"(2) A list of occupation(s) to which one third or more of working time was given during previous reporting year by the filing offical or employee and spouse;

"(3) A listing of total combined family income of the public official or employee during the most recent reporting year as to income from salaries, fees, dividends, profits, commissions and other compensation from any business doing business in Alabama and listing the names of each business and the income derived from such business in the following categorical amounts: less than $1,000.00; at least $1,000.00 and less than $10,000.00; $10,000.00 or more; further, the person reporting shall name any business or

INTERESTS OF PUBLIC OFFICIALS AND EMPLOYEES; DISCLOSURE REQUIRED.—Cont'd.

subsidiary thereof in which he or his spouse or dependents, jointly or severally, own one tenth or more of the stock or in which he or his spouse serves as an officer, director, trustee or consultant where such service provides income of more than $1,000.00 for the reporting period;

"(4) If the filing public offical or employee, or his spouse, has engaged in a business during the last reporting year which provides legal, accounting, medical or health related, real estate, banking, insurance, educational, farming, engineering, architectural management or other professional services or consultations, then the filing party shall report the number of clients of such business in each of the following categories and the income in categorical amounts received during the reporting period from the combined number of clients in each catergory: electric utilities, gas utilities, telephone utilities, water utilities, cable television companies, intrastate transportation companies, pipeline companies, oil and/or gas exploration companies, oil and gas retail companies, banks, savings and loan associations, loan and/or finance companies, manufacturing firms, mining companies, life insurance companies, casualty insurance companies and other insurance companies, retail companies, beer, wine and/or liquor companies or distributors, trade associations, professional associations, governmental associations, associations of public employees or public officials, counties and any other businesses or associations that the commission may deem appropriate. Amounts received from combined clients in each category shall be reported as: less than $1,000.00; more than $1,000.00 but less than $10,000.00; $10,000.00 or above;

"(5) If retainers are in existence or contracted for in any of the above categories of clients, a listing of the categories along with the anticipated income to be expected annually from each category of clients shall be shown in the following amounts: less than $1,250.00; $1,250.00 or more;

"(6) If real estate that is held for investment or is revenue producing is held by a public offical, his spouse or dependents, then a listing thereof by the following categories of fair market value: under $50,000.00; at least $50,000.00 but less than $250,000.00; $250,000.00 or more; and the following categories of annual gross rent and lease income on real estate: less than $10,000,00; at least $10,000.00 and less than $50,000.00;

INTERESTS OF PUBLIC OFFICIALS AND EMPLOYEES; DISCLOSURE REQUIRED.—Cont'd.

$50,000.00 or more. Furthermore, if a public offical or a business in which he is associated receives rent or lease income from any governmental agency in Alabama, specific details of the lease or rent agreement shall be filed with the commission;

"(7) A listing of indebtedness to businesses operating in Alabama showing types and number of each as follows: banks, savings and loan associations, insurance companies, mortgage firms and stockbrokers (the commission shall add additional categories as it deems necessary); and the indebtedness to combined organizations in each category in amounts as follows: less than $25,000.00; $25,000.00 but less than $50,000.00; $50,000.00 but less than $100,000.00; $100,000.00 or more. Indebtedness associated with the homestead of the person filing is exempted from this disclosure requirement. Filing required by this section shall reflect information and facts in existence at the end of the reporting year. In the event that said information required herein is not filed as required, the commission shall notify the public official or employee concerned as to his failure to so file and the public official shall have 10 days to file said report after receipt of said notification." Code of Ala. 1975, § 36-25-14.

INTERFERENCE. See CUSTODY, INTERFERENCE WITH; JUDICIAL PROCEEDINGS, INTERFERENCE WITH.

INTIMIDATING A JUROR. Code of Ala. 1975, § 13A-10-127.

"A person commits the crime of intimidating a juror if he attempts, by the use of a threat,[1] to influence a juror's vote, opinion, decision or other action as a juror."

Classification.

Class C felony.

Comments.

This crime can only be committed by the use of a threat, as defined in § 13A-6-25 of the Alabama Code, to influence a juror's vote, opinion, decision or other action as a juror.

This crime, unlike its counterpart crime of intimidating a witness, § 13A-10-123 of the Alabama Code, requires the person either to have been summoned as a juror or to have

INTIMIDATING A JUROR.—Cont'd.

had his name drawn to attend as a prospective juror; nothing is mentioned of "persons believed to be jurors."

Defenses.

(1) No threat was made.

(2) Although not a defense in the real sense at least, one ought to look at "Jury tampering", § 13A-10-128 of the Alabama Code (Class B misdemeanor), for a possible reduction in the charge.

Cross references.

See ATTEMPT; BRIBERY OF PUBLIC SERVANTS; COERCION; JURY TAMPERING; SOLICITATION.

---

1. *"Threat" is used in the same context as in Code of Ala. 1975, § 13A-6-25, Criminal Coercion: "A person commits the crime of criminal coercion, if, without legal authority, he threatens to confine, restrain, or to cause physical injury to the threatened person or another, or to damage the property or reputation of the threatened person or another with intent thereby to induce the threatened person or another against his will to do an unlawful act or refrain from doing a lawful act."*

INTIMIDATING A WITNESS. Code of Ala. 1975, § 13A-10-123.

"A person commits the crime of intimidating a witness if he attempts, by use of a threat[1] directed to a witness or a person he believes will be called as a witness in any official proceedings,[2] to:

"(1) Corruptly influence the testimony[3] of that person;

"(2) Induce that person to avoid legal process summoning him to testify; or

"(3) Induce that person to absent himself from an official proceeding to which he has been legally summoned."

Classification.

Class C felony.

Comments.

Intimidation of a witness is distinguished from other sections of Title 13A of the Alabama Code by virtue of the use of threats to corruptly influence or induce action on the part of the witnesses to avoid summons or proceedings.

The Code raised the classification from a misdemeanor to a Class C felony, thus

INTIMIDATING A WITNESS.—Cont'd.

placing it on the same level as bribery. Also, as in bribery, the person the threat is directed towards does not have to be a witness; all that is required is that the person making the threat believe the person will be called as a witness.[4]

Defenses.

(1) No threat was made.

(2) Although not a defense in itself, one might want to consider, at least, the possibility of reducing the crime to tampering with a witness, § 13-10-124 of the Alabama Code (Class B misdemeanor); or to criminal coercion, § 13A-6-25 of the Alabama Code (Class A misdemeanor), if the person making the threats had no reason to believe the person threatened would be a witness.

Cross references.

See ATTEMPT; BRIBERY OF PUBLIC SERVANTS; COERCION; SOLICITATION.

---

1. *According to Code of Ala. 1975, § 13A-10-123(b), " '[t]hreat,' as used in this section, means any threat proscribed by section 13A-6-25 on criminal coercion." Threat is defined in Code of Ala. 1975, § 13A-8-1(13) as "A menance, however communicated, to:*

"a. Cause physical harm to the person threatened or to any other person; or

"b. Cause damage to property; or

"c. Subject the person threatened or any other person to physical confinement or restraint; or

"d. Engage in other conduct constituting a crime; or

"e. Accuse any person of a crime or cause criminal charges to be instituted against any person; or

"f. Expose a secret or publicize an asserted fact, whether true or false, tending to subject any person to hatred, contempt or ridicule; or

"g. Reveal any information sought to be concealed by the person threatened; or

"h. Testify or provide information or withhold testimony or information with respect to another's legal claim or defense; or

"i. Take action as an official against anyone or anything, or withhold offical action, or cause such action or withholding; or

"j. Bring about or continue a strike, boycott or other similar collective action to obtain property which is not demanded or received for the benefit of the group which the actor purports to represent; or

INTIMIDATING A WITNESS.—Cont'd.

"k. Do any other act which would not in itself substantially benefit the actor but which is calculated to harm substantially another person with respect to his health, safety, business, calling, career, financial condition, reputation or personal relationships."

2. *"Official proceedings" as defined in Code of Ala. 1975, § 13A-10-100(b)(5) is "[a]ny proceeding heard before any legislative, judicial, administrative, or other government agency or offical authorized to hear evidence under oath."*
3. *"Testimony", according to Code of Ala. 1975, § 13A-10-120(b)(2), is defined as: ". . . includ[ing] oral or written statements, documents or any other material that may be offered as evidence in an official proceeding."*
4. *Wallace v. State, 27 Ala. App. 545, 176 So. 310 (1937).*

INTOXICATION. Code of Ala. 1975, § 13A-3-2.

Intoxication[1] is a defense if it is involuntary and "as a result the actor lacks the capacity to appreciate the criminality of his conduct or to conform his conduct to the requirements of law." Whether voluntary[2] or involuntary, intoxication "is admissible in evidence whenever it is relevant to negate[3] an element of the offense charged."[4] However, "[w]hen recklessness establishes an element of an offense and the actor is unaware of a risk because of voluntary intoxication, his unawareness is immaterial in a prosecution for that offense."[5]

Note, according to § 13A-3-2(d) of the Alabama Code, "[i]ntoxication in itself does not constitute mental disease or defect within the meaning of section 13A-3-1 [of the Alabama Code]."

---

1. *According to Code of Ala. 1975, § 13A-3-2(e)(1), " '[i]ntoxication' includes a disturbance of mental or physical capacities resulting from the introduction of any substance into the body."*
   "The definition of intoxication is not limited to alcohol but is sufficiently broad to include other personality altering substances, e.g., marijuana, L. S. D., glue sniffing, etc." Code of Ala. 1975, § 13A-3-2 Commentary.
2. *According to Code of Ala. 1975, § 13A-3-2(e)(1), " '[v]oluntary intoxication' means intoxication caused by substances that the actor knowingly introduced into his body, the tendency of which*

INTOXICATION.—Cont'd.

to cause intoxication he knows or ought to know, unless he introduces them under circumstances that would afford a defense to a charge of crime."

3. *Gautorey v. State, 284 Ala. 82, 222 So. 2d 175 (1969). Hamilton v. City of Birmingham, 396 So. 2d 121 (1980).*
4. *See Code of Ala. 1975, § 13A-3-2(b). See also, e.g., Patterson v. State, 30 Ala. App. 217, 24 So. 2d 228 (1945) (larceny); Ray v. State, 257 Ala. 418, 59 So. 2d 582 (1952) (may negate premeditation and deliberation and reduce first degree murder to second degree, or negate the specific intent essential to a malicious killing and reduce it to manslaughter); Walker v. State, 31 Ala. App. 345, 17 So. 2d 428 (1944) (assault with intent to murder); Moran v. State, 34 Ala. App. 238, 39 So. 2d 419 (1949) (assault with intent to rape).*
5. *See Code of Ala. 1975, § 13A-3-2(b). See also Johnson v. Louisville & N. R. Co., 104 Ala. 241, 16 So. 75 (1893).*

INTOXICATION, PUBLIC. Code of Ala. 1975, § 13A-11-10.

Charged as: Public intoxication.

"A person commits the crime of public intoxication if he appears in a public place under the influence of alcohol, narcotics or other drugs to the degree that he endangers himself or another person or property, or by boisterous and offensive conduct annoys another person in his vicinity."

Classification.

Class A violation.

Comments.

This crime has three basic elements and punishes two types of behavior. All three elements must be present if criminal liability is to attach. The defendant must: (1) appear in public, and (2) be under the influence of alcohol, narcotics or other drugs.[1] The third element relates to the defendant's behavior when the other two elements are present. Culpable behavior can consist of being in a physical or mental condition that creates a risk of danger to persons or property.

Alternatively, culpable behavior can consist of offensive or boisterous conduct by defendant which annoys another person in defendant's vicinity. The defendant is not culpable under this statute if, while under

INTOXICATION, PUBLIC.—Cont'd.

the influence of alcohol or drugs, he publicly annoys another in his vicinity but the alcohol or drugs did not cause this behavior.[2] Specific intent is not a prerequisite to criminal liability.

Defenses.

(1) Place of defendant's appearance was not public.

(2) Defendant was not under the influence of alcohol, narcotics, or any other drug.

(3) Defendant's conduct could not reasonably be perceived as endangering himself, another or property.

(4) Defendant's conduct in respect of another person would not prove annoying to a reasonable person similarly situated.

(5) Person annoyed by defendant was not in "his vicinity."

(6) Defendant's endangering or annoying conduct was not the product of the influence of alcohol or drugs.

(7) "Involuntary intoxication," which provides a defense under § 13A-3-2(c)[3] of the Alabama Code.

Cross references.

See DURESS; INTOXICATION.

---

1. *The statute makes no distinction between those situations in which defendant is under the influence of prescribed drugs, or over-the-counter drugs legitimately being used for medical purposes, and situations where defendant is under the influence of controlled substances. The conduct of a person under the influence of medication may also endanger persons or property. It is not certain whether such conduct is criminally culpable. A person whose conduct was induced by medication could use defense 7.*

   The statute does not measure a specific quantity of intoxicants that is prohibited. The determination of culpability is based on the extent to which the defendant's intoxication and resultant conduct pose a risk of harm to persons or property. Read in this light, the crime is one of strict liability. It does not require a culpable mental state on the part of the actor. See Code of Ala. 1975, § 13A-2-3.

2. *The statute states that the culpable defendant "appears in public under the influence . . . to the degree that . . . by boisterous and offensive conduct [he] annoys another . . . ." Although the statute is not clearly worded, the language strongly implies that influence of alcohol or drugs must have a causal relationship to the annoying conduct. Counsel should consider Code of Ala. 1975, § 13A-2-5 on rules governing causation. Generally, if the actual result is not within the contemplation of the actor, or within the area of risk of which he should have been aware, he is not deemed to have caused the result.*

3. *Involuntary intoxication is not defined, but voluntary intoxication is "intoxication caused by a substance that the actor* ***knowingly*** *introduced into his body, the tendency of which to cause intoxication he* ***knows or ought to know,*** *unless he introduces them under circumstances that would afford a defense to a charge of crime" (emphasis added). Code of Ala. 1975, § 13A-3-2(e)(2).*

JOY RIDING. See MOTOR VEHICLE CRIMES; UNAUTHORIZED USE OF VEHICLE/UNLAWFUL BREAKING AND ENTERING A VEHICLE.

JUDICIAL PROCEEDINGS, INTERFERENCE WITH. Code of Ala. 1975, § 13A-10-130.

Charged as: Interfering with judicial proceedings.

"A person commits the crime of interfering with judicial proceedings if:

"(1) He engages in disorderly, contemptuous or insolent behavior, committed during the sitting of a court in its immediate view and presence, and directly tending to interrupt its proceedings or impair the respect due its authority;

"(2) He intentionally creates a breach of the peace or disturbance under circumstances directly tending to interrupt a court's proceedings;

"(3) As an attorney, clerk or other officer of the court, he knowingly fails to perform or violates a duty of his office, or knowingly disobeys a lawful directive or order of a court;

"(4) Knowing that he is not authorized to practice law, he represents himself to be an attorney and acts as such in a court proceeding; or

"(5) He records or attempts to record the deliberation of a jury."

JUDICIAL PROCEEDINGS, INTERFERENCE WITH.—Cont'd.

Classification.

Class B misdemeanor.

Comments.

The courts have discretion to punish specific behavior as contempt of court. This section provides an alternative method for punishment through a normal criminal process; however, its use is not required and is subject to double jeopardy limitations.

Subsection (1) relates only to disturbances during the court proceedings and in the court's immediate view.

Subsection (2) does not require that the disturbance be within the view of the court, but only that the disturbance be intentional and reasonably calculated to disturb the court.

Subsection (3) is limited to any "attorney, clerk or other officer of the court." It does not include jurors, witnesses, etc. The offender must have knowledge that he is violating a lawful directive order.

Subsection (4) relates to § 34-3-1 of the Alabama Code, dealing with the unlawful practice of law. Subsection (4) covers only unlawful practice performed in some judicial proceeding.

Subsection (5) is not the offense of jury tampering but, rather an offense against judicial proceedings since a defendant possesses no intent to influence the jury.

Defenses.

(1) A person already held in contempt of court by a judge is not subject to this provision due to the double jeopardy limitation.

(2) To subsection (1): The disorderly behavior was not during the sitting of the court or not within its immediate view.

(3) To subsection (2): Defendant lacked the intent to disturb the peace for the purpose of interrupting the court.

(4) To subsection (3):

a. Person is juror, witness, etc., not an attorney, clerk, or officer of the court.

b. Offense was not done knowingly.

c. The directive was not lawful.

(5) To subsection (4): Person has to know he was not authorized to practice, and the act

had to occur in a court proceeding. Otherwise, see unlawful practice of law, § 34-3-1 of the Alabama Code.

(6) To subsection (5): Did not attempt to record.

Cross references.

See Contempt and similar offenses generally, §§ 12-1-7 through 12-1-11, 12-3-11, 12-11-30, 12-15-12, 12-16-82, 12-16-89, 12-16-213, 28-4-316 and 34-3-1 of the Alabama Code; Unlawful Practice of Law, § 34-3-1 of the Alabama Code. See HINDERING PROSECUTION/HINDERING APPREHENSION OF ESCAPEE; OBSTRUCTING GOVERNMENTAL OPERATIONS.

JUMPING BAIL. See BAIL JUMPING.

JURY TAMPERING. Code of Ala. 1975, § 13A-10-128.

"A person commits the crime of jury tampering if, with intent to influence a juror's[1] vote, opinion, decision or other action in the case, he attempts directly or indirectly to communicate with a juror other than as part of the proceedings in the trial of the case."

Classification.

Class B misdemeanor.

Comments.

Communication with a juror during a judicial proceeding concerning the subject matter under consideration is not allowed. This section does not cover conversations among jurors or any lawful means to influence jurors, such as in an argument in the open courtroom. Otherwise, any communication, direct or indirect, for the purpose of influencing a juror is prohibited. Prior to this revised section a person engaged in "innocent conversation" concerning the case could be punished. Now the burden of proving an intent to influence the juror's vote is upon the prosecution.

Defenses.

(1) That only "innocent conversation" was engaged in.

JURY TAMPERING.—Cont'd.

(2) That the conversation was by lawful means.

(3) No intent to influence, directly or indirectly.

Cross references.

See Contempt, § 12-1-8 of the Alabama Code. See ATTEMPT; BRIBERY OF PUBLIC SERVANTS; COERCION; INTIMIDATING A JUROR; JUDICIAL PROCEEDINGS, INTERFERENCE WITH; SOLICITATION.

---

1. *"Any person who is a member of any jury, including a grand jury, impaneled by any court of this state or by any public servant authorized by law to impanel a jury. The term juror also includes any person who has been summoned or whose name has been drawn to attend as a prospective juror." Code of Ala. 1975, § 13A-10-120.*

JUVENILE DELINQUENTS. See JUVENILE PROCEEDINGS.

JUVENILE PROCEEDINGS. Code of Ala. 1975, Title 12, chapter 15.

I. Definitions. Code of Ala. 1975, § 12-15-1.

"(1) ADULT. An individual 19 years of age or older.

* * *

"(3) CHILD.

"a. Such term, before January 1, 1978, means an individual under the age of 17 or under 19 years of age who committed the act of delinquency with which he is charged before reaching the age of 17 years.

"b. Such term, after December 31, 1977, means an individual under the age of 18 or under 19 years of age and who committed the act of delinquency with which he is charged before reaching the age of 18 years.

"(4) CHILD IN NEED OF SUPERVISION. A child who:

"a. Being subject to compulsory school attendance, is habitually truant from school; or

"b. Disobeys the reasonable and lawful demands of his parents, guardian or other custodian and is beyond their control; or

"c. Has committed an offense established by law but not classified as criminal or one applicable only to children; and

"d. In any of the foregoing, is in need of care or rehabilitation.

* * *

"(7) COURT OR JUVENILE COURT.[1] The juvenile division of the district court or the juvenile division of the circuit court as established by this chapter.

"(8) DELINQUENT ACT. An act designated a crime under the law of this state or of another state if the act occurred in another state or under federal law or a violation of a municipal ordinance; provided, however, that traffic offenses committed by one 16 years of age or older shall be excepted unless transferred to the juvenile court by the court having jurisdiction.

"(9) DELINQUENT CHILD. A child who has committed a delinquent act and is in need of care or rehabilitation.

"(10) DEPENDENT CHILD. A child:

"a. Who, for any reason is destitute, homeless or dependent on the public for support; or

"b. Who is without a parent or guardian able to provide for his support, training or education; or

"c. Whose custody is the subject of controversy; or

"d. Whose home, by reason of neglect, cruelty or depravity on the part of his parent, parents, guardian or other person in whose care he may be, is an unfit and improper place for him; or

"e. Whose parent, parents, guardian or other custodian neglects or refuses, when able to do so or when such service is offered without charge, to provide or allow medical, surgical or other care necessary for such child's health or well-being; or

"f. Who is in such condition or surroundings or is under such improper or insufficient guardianship or control as to endanger his morals, health or general welfare; or

"g. Who has no proper parental care or guardianship; or

"h. Whose parent, parents, guardian or custodian fail, refuse or neglect to send such child to school in accordance with the terms

JUVENILE PROCEEDINGS.—Cont'd.

of the compulsory school attendance laws of this state; or

"i. Who has been abandoned by his parents, guardian or other custodian; or

"j. Who is physically, mentally or emotionally abused by his parents, guardian or other custodian or who is without proper parental care and control necessary for his well-being because of the faults or habits of his parents, guardian or other custodian or their neglect or refusal, when able to do so, to provide them; or

"k. Whose parents, guardian or other custodian are unable to discharge their responsibilities to and for the child; or

"l. Who has been placed for care or adoption in violation of the law; or

"m. Who for any other cause is in need of the care and protection of the state; and

"n. In any of the foregoing, is in need of care or supervision.

"(11) DETENTION CARE. The temporary care of delinquent children or children alleged to be delinquent in secure custody pending court disposition or transfer to a residential facility or further care of a child adjudicated a delinquent; provided, however, that detention care may also include temporary care of children in need of supervision until January 1, 1978.

"(12) GUARDIAN AD LITEM. A licensed lawyer appointed by a court to defend or represent a child in any action to which such child may be a party.

"(13) INTAKE OFFICE. The office in the probation service or designee of the judge with the duty of primary contact with the law enforcement agency and complainants of children coming under the jurisdiction of the court.

"(14) JUDGE. Judge of the juvenile court as prescribed by this chapter.

"(15) LAW ENFORCEMENT OFFICER. Any person, however denominated, who is authorized by law to exercise the policy powers of the state or local governments.

"(16) LEGAL CUSTODIAN. A person, agency or department, other than a parent or legal guardian, to whom legal custody of the child has been given by court order or

JUVENILE PROCEEDINGS.—Cont'd.

who is acting in loco parentis.

"(17) LEGAL CUSTODY. A legal status created by court order which vests in a custodian the right to have physical custody of the child and to determine where and with whom he shall live within the state and the right and duty to protect, train and discipline him and to provide him with food, shelter, clothing, education and ordinary medical care, all subject to the powers, rights, duties and responsibilities of the guardian of the person of the child and subject to any residual parental rights and responsibilities. An individual granted legal custody shall exercise the rights and responsibilities personally unless otherwise authorized by the juvenile court.

"(18) MINOR. An individual who is under the age of 19 years and who is not a "child" within the meaning of this chapter.

"(19) PROBATION. The legal status created by court order following an adjudication of delinquency or in need of supervision whereby a child is permitted to remain in a community subject to supervision and return to court for violation of probation at any time during the period of probation.

"(20) PROTECTIVE SUPERVISION. A legal status created by court order following an adjudication of dependency whereby a child is permitted to remain in his home subject to supervision and to return to the court for violation of protective supervision at any time during the period of protective supervision."

II. Sentences and Fines.

Just as the juvenile laws are separate and distinct from the criminal laws, likewise the juvenile courts have their own sentencing and fine schedules. All violations are classified as misdemeanor violations. Unlike the criminal code, wherein §§ 13A-5-6, 13A-5-7, 13A-5-11 and 13A-5-12 of the Alabama Code set out the possible sentences and fines for all criminal violations, the juvenile chapter has no all encompassing statute; each statute, where appropriate, delineates what will be the maximum possible sentence and/or fine for

JUVENILE PROCEEDINGS.—Cont'd.

violating its provisions.

Section 12-15-14 of the Alabama Code empowers the juvenile courts with authority to convict "any person who knowingly and willfully disregards or fails to obey any lawful order made by the court under the provisions of this chapter or who knowingly and willfully interferes with the custody of any child under the jurisdiction of said court." The possible sanctions are a fine of not more than $500 and/or hard labor for the county for not more than 6 months.

III. Child Support, Treatment, Etc., Failure To Pay. Code of Ala. 1975, § 12-15-9.

"Whenever legal custody of a child is vested in someone other than his parents, after due notice to the parents or other persons legally obligated to care for and support the child and after a hearing, the court may order that the parent or other legally obligated person shall pay in such manner as the court may direct a reasonable sum that will cover in whole or in part the support and treatment of the child after the order is entered and including support, treatment, costs and legal fees from the commencement of the proceeding.

"If the parent or other legally obligated person willfully fails or refuses to pay such sum, the court may proceed against him for contempt or the order may be filed and shall constitute a civil judgment."

Classification.

Contempt of Court or a civil judgment.

Comments.

This statute applies only when the child is in the legal custody of someone other than the child's parents. The parents are not the only persons liable for the support payments, for the statute also places the burden on any "other persons legally obligated to care for and support the child."

The choice of remedies for nonpayment rests within the discretion of the court, either contempt of court or the entry of a civil judgment against the individual.

Section 13A-13-4 of the Alabama Code provides for criminal liability for

JUVENILE PROCEEDINGS.—Cont'd.

nonsupport, violation of which is a Class A misdemeanor. The comments following that section state that the "[n]onsupport must also be proven to be 'willful' which means 'intentional or designed failure or refusal to provide pursuant to intention or design, without just cause.' St. John v. State, 22 Ala. App. 115, 113 So. 321 (1927)." Such would also apply to § 12-15-9 of the Alabama Code.

The statute states that the court "may" order the payments. The individual's ability to pay will be considered. This is also the procedure in § 13A-13-4 of the Alabama Code.

Defenses.

(1) Not the child's parent nor legally obligated to provide for the child's support and treatment.

(2) Inability to pay when also considering the person's own minimal needs.

Cross references.

See CHILD, ABANDONMENT OF; CHILD WELFARE, ENDANGERING; NONSUPPORT.

IV. Contributing To The Delinquency Of A Minor. Code of Ala. 1975, § 12-15-13.

"(a) It shall be unlawful for any parent, guardian or other person to willfully aid, encourage or cause any child to become or remain delinquent, dependent or in need of supervision or by words, acts, threats, commands or persuasions, to induce or endeavor to induce, aid or encourage any child to do or perform any act or to follow any course of conduct which would cause or manifestly tend to cause such child to become or remain delinquent, dependent or in need of supervision or by the neglect of any lawful duty or in any other manner contribute to the delinquency, dependency or need of supervision of a child. The employment of any child in violation of any of the provisions of the child labor law, or permitting, conniving at, aiding or abetting such employment shall be held to be encouraging, causing and contributing to the delinquency, dependency or need of supervision of such child. Failure on the

JUVENILE PROCEEDINGS.—Cont'd.

part of any parent, guardian or other person having custody of the child to cause such child to attend school as required by the compulsory attendance law shall be held to be encouraging, causing and contributing to the delinquency, dependency or need of supervision of such child.

"(b) Whenever, in the course of any proceedings under this chapter or when, by affidavit as provided in this subsection, it shall appear to the juvenile court that a parent, guardian or other person having custody, control or supervision of a child or any other person not standing in any such relation to such child has aided, encouraged or caused such child to become delinquent, dependent or in need of supervision, as defined in this chapter, or has by words, act or omission contributed thereto or has, by threats, commands or persuasion, induced or endeavored to induce, aided or encouraged such child to do or perform any act or to follow any course of conduct which would cause or manifestly tend to cause such child to become or remain delinquent, dependent or in need of supervision, the court shall, for the protection of such child from such influences, have jurisdiction in such matters, as provided in this section. The court shall cause such parent, guardian or other person to be brought before it upon either summons or a warrant, affidavit of probable cause having first been made."

Classification.

Misdemeanor: A fine of not more than $500 and/or not more than 12 months hard labor for the county.

Comments.

Section 12-15-13(a) of the Alabama Code proscribes all willful conduct on the part of anyone (not just parents or guardians) that causes, induces or threatens any child to become or remain delinquent, etc. The section also applies to persons who neglect to perform any lawful duty that contributes to the delinquency, etc. It may include all persons, from police officers to the Director of Youth Services, and everyone in-between (probation officers, juvenile court judges, etc.).

JUVENILE PROCEEDINGS.—Cont'd.

The person charged under this section need not have specifically intended to contribute to the delinquency, etc.

Cross references.

See CHILD, ABANDONMENT OF; CHILD WELFARE, ENDANGERING; CIGARETTES, SELLING TO MINOR.

V. Removal, Concealment, Of Delinquent Child. Code of Ala. 1975, § 12-15-15.

"(a) It shall be unlawful for any person to remove, conceal or cause to be removed or concealed, or attempt so to do, any delinquent or dependent child or one in need of supervision, as defined in this chapter, or one alleged in a petition or order of transfer filed in said court to be so or any child whose custody is the subject of controversy in said court, or for any person to interfere with the custody of or remove or attempt to remove any delinquent or dependent child or one in need of supervision or one alleged so to be or any child whose custody is the subject of controversy in said court who is in the custody of the court or of a probation officer or any other officer or person designated by the court as a special officer or any child who has been by said court committed to a department of state government, any person, persons, institution, association or corporation, under the terms of this chapter or by virtue of its general equity jurisdiction.

"(b) It shall be unlawful for any person to interfere knowingly with or oppose or otherwise obstruct any probation officer or representative of the department of pensions and security in the performance of his duties under this chapter."

Classification.

Misdemeanor. A fine of not more than $500 and/or not more than 12 months hard labor for the county.

Comments.

This section prosecutes persons causing, attempting, successfully concealing or "child-snatching" children who are delinquent, etc., or who are the subject of any juvenile court proceeding, or children

JUVENILE PROCEEDINGS.—Cont'd.
who are in the custody of persons designated by the court as their legal custodian. The section applies to both the procurer who pays someone to "grab" the child as well as to the "child-snatcher." § 12-15-15(a) of the Alabama Code is a strict liability statute. It makes no provision that the person must have acted "knowingly."

Defenses.

(1) Section 12-15-15(b) of the Alabama Code requires that the person must have knowingly interfered with the probation officer.

Cross references.

See CUSTODY, INTERFERENCE WITH; UNLAWFUL IMPRISONMENT.

---

1. *"The judge of the district court shall serve as the juvenile court judge in those districts having only one district judge. In those districts having more than one district court judge, the presiding circuit court judge shall designate from time to time a district court judge or circuit court judge who shall serve as the judge hearing juvenile cases." Code of Ala. 1975, § 12-15-3(a).*
"The circuit court and the district court shall exercise original concurrent juvenile jurisdiction sitting as the juvenile court." Code of Ala. 1975, § 12-15-2(a).

KIDNAPPING. Code of Ala. 1975, § 13A-6-43 and § 13A-6-44.

"A person commits the crime of kidnapping in the first degree if he abducts[1] another person with intent to

"(1) Hold him for ransom or reward; or

"(2) Use him as a shield or hostage; or

"(3) Accomplish or aid the commission of any felony or flight therefrom; or

"(4) Inflict physical injury upon him, or to violate or abuse him sexually; or

"(5) Terrorize him or a third person; or

"(6) Interfere with the performance of any governmental or political function." § 13A-6-43(a) of the Alabama Code.

"A person commits the crime of kidnapping in the second degree if he abducts another person." § 13A-6-44(a) of the Alabama Code.

Classification.

Class A felony, kidnapping in the first degree.

KIDNAPPING.—Cont'd.

Class B felony, kidnapping in the second degree.

Comments.

Kidnapping is an aggravated form of false imprisonment. Second degree covers the entire spectrum of kidnapping, and first degree covers six of the most aggravated purposes of abduction.

None of the six purposes of abduction listed in § 13A-6-43(a) of the Alabama Code has to be accomplished. The crime is considered complete when there is an abduction.

Because of the substantial danger to the life of the kidnapped victim, § 13A-6-43(b) of the Alabama Code provides that "A person does not commit the crime of kidnapping in the first degree if he voluntarily releases the victim alive, and not suffering from serious physical injury, in a safe place prior to apprehension." No definition is given for "serious", but it appears to be left to the discretion of the court. The offender would not be absolved from prosecution. He could be charged with second degree kidnapping. The burden of injecting the issue of a voluntary safe release is on the defendant, but this does not shift the burden of proof.

Note that when an unintentional death occurs during the act of kidnapping in the first degree,[2] the felony-murder rule, § 13A-6-2(a)(3), of the Alabama Code, will be applicable.

Section 13A-6-44 expressly states when an abduction is not considered kidnapping:[3]

"(1) The abduction is not coupled with intent to use or to threaten to use deadly force,

"(2) The actor is a relative[4] of the person abducted, and

"(3) The actor's sole purpose is to assume lawful control of that person."

It appears that this is to be taken as one defense, the elements to be read in conjunction with each other even though the conjunctive word "and" is not included following the first element. Again, the burden of injecting this issue of defense is on the defendant, but this does not shift the burden of proof.

Special note should be made to the crime "Interference with custody" (§ 13A-6-45 of

KIDNAPPING.—Cont'd.

the Alabama Code), which appears to have been intended to be a "lesser-related" offense to kidnapping. However, the purpose of the statutes is not the same; kidnapping statutes are designed to protect persons from physical danger, whereas the interference with custody statute is designed to protect parental custody against unlawful interruption. Therefore, there are two separate victims, the person abducted and the parent (assuming the abductee was under the age of 18). Just as a defendant can be charged with two murders if in a single shotgun blast two people are killed, it appears that an abductor could be convicted under both the kidnapping and the interference with custody statutes, although I would not hesitate to bring a constitutional attack against such a prosecution.

Defenses.

(1) The victim voluntarily accompanied the defendant.[5]

(2) The voluntary release of the victim alive, not suffering from serious physical injury, in a safe place, and prior to apprehension. This is a defense to the extent that it could reduce the charge to kidnapping in the second degree.

(3) No attempted or successful abduction within the meaning of § 13A-6-40(2) of the Alabama Code.

(4) For second degree kidnapping: the abduction was not coupled with the intent to use or to threaten to use deadly force, and the actor is a relative of the person abducted, and the actor's sole purpose was to assume lawful control of that person.[6]

Query.

(1) Section 13A-6-43(b) of the Alabama Code refers only to "serious physical injury" for reducing first degree to second degree kidnapping. What about mental anguish and suffering? What about brainwashing?

(2) What is "serious physical injury"?

Cross references.

See Felony-murder rule, § 13A-6-2(a)(3) of the Alabama Code. See CUSTODY,

KIDNAPPING.—Cont'd.

INTERFERENCE WITH; MURDER; UNLAWFUL IMPRISONMENT.

---

1. Code of Ala. 1975, § 13A-6-40(2) defines abduct as "To restrain a person with intent to prevent his liberation by either:

"(a) Secreting or holding him in a place where he is not likely to be found, or

"(b) Using or threatening to use deadly physical force."

2. If the kidnapped victim were to die, second degree kidnapping would not apply, because of the physical injury.

3. Code of Ala. 1975, § 13A-6-44(b).

4. Code of Ala. 1975, § 13A-6-40(3) defines relative as "A parent or stepparent, ancestor, sibling, uncle or aunt or other lawful custodian, including an adoptive relative of the same degree through marriage or adoption."

5. Hubbard v. State, 23 Ala. App. 537, 128 So. 587 (1930). However, there can be no valid acquiescence by the victim if he is less than 16 years old or an incompetent person and the person or institution having legal custody or control has not acquiesced. See definition of "Restrain", Code of Ala. 1975, § 13A-6-40(1).

6. If the abductor does not have the right to assume lawful control over the person abducted, he cannot claim this defense.

L. S. D. See CONTROLLED SUBSTANCES.

LARCENY. See THEFT OF PROPERTY.

LEGAL PROCESS, SIMULATING.

Code of Ala. 1975, § 13A-10-131.

Charged as: Simulating legal process.

"A person commits the crime of simulating legal process if he knowingly delivers or causes to be delivered to another person any demand, request or claim for the payment of money or the delivery or transfer of property that in form and substance simulates any legal process issued by any court of this state."

Classification.

Class B misdemeanor.

Comments.

This is a new section of the Code. Adopted to prevent creditors, bill collectors, landlords, bailors, etc., from sending a "dun"[1] that was meant to mislead the receiver into thinking

LEGAL PROCESS, SIMULATING.—Cont'd.

legal proceedings had been instituted against him.

There is a specific requirement of mens rea by the sender, thus protecting the sender from a misinterpretation of a bill simply requesting payment of a debt or return of property.

Defenses.

(1) The specific mens rea requirement (of the sender) is missing.

---

1. *A demand for payment to a delinquent debtor. Black's Law Dictionary 451 (5th ed., 1979).*

LEWDNESS, PUBLIC. Code of Ala. 1975, § 13A-12-130.

Charged as: Public lewdness.

"A person commits the crime of public lewdness if:

"(1) He exposes his anus or genitals in a public place and is reckless about whether another may be present who will be offended or alarmed by his act; or

"(2) He does any lewd act in a public place which he knows is likely to be observed by others who would be affronted or alarmed."

Classification.

Class C misdemeanor.

Comments.

This section is concerned with open lewdness and obscenity and does not require an intent to arouse or gratify sexual desire, as does § 13A-6-68 of the Alabama Code (Indecent exposure).[1]

Acts such as "streaking" or "mooning" would be covered by this section. Participating in a nudist colony, where no person present or observing would be affronted or alarmed, wouldn't be covered. Note, no age factors are given here.

Some types of conduct could be charged under either this statute or § 13A-11-7(a)(3) of the Alabama Code (disorderly conduct).[2] Both are Class C misdemeanors.

Defenses.

(1) The exposure or act was conducted on private property where no one was likely to be present or observe it (sun bathing in backyard that is enclosed).

LEWDNESS, PUBLIC.—Cont'd.

(2) The persons present were neither offended, alarmed or affronted[3] by the exposure or act.

(3) The act or exposure was not done intentionally or recklessly.

Query.

Subsection (1)[4] refers to exposing the anus or genitals. Subsection (2)[5] states that there must be a "lewd act." Because a female's breasts are not considered genitals, merely exposing them without also performing "any lewd act," even if doing so would cause others to be offended, affronted or alarmed[6] (but not with intent to arouse or gratify sexual desires — see INDECENT EXPOSURE), is not a crime under this statute.

Cross references.

See DISORDERLY CONDUCT; INDECENT EXPOSURE.

---

1. *"A person commits the crime of indecent exposure if, with intent to arouse or gratify sexual desire of himself or of any other person other than his spouse, he exposes his genitals under circumstances in which he knows his conduct is likely to cause affront or alarm in any public place or on the private premises of another or so near thereto as to be seen from such private premises."*
2. *"A person commits the crime of disorderly conduct if, with intent to cause public inconvenience, annoyance or alarm, or recklessly creating a risk thereof, he: . . . In a public place uses abusive or obscene language or makes an obscene gesture."*
3. *The comments following Code of Ala. 1975, § 13A-6-68 confess that " '[a]ffront' is undefined in Alabama, nor is it defined in any other jurisdiction. 'Alarm' is undefined in this context. The Michigan Draft Commentary suggests that the purpose of the exposure and the likelihood of psychological harm to others determines criminality. It is clear, however, that 'affront and alarm' do not mean the same thing as 'vulgar and indecent,' with which the courts have struggled repeatedly. Although technical definitions and reported examples of 'affront and alarm' are not available, the words as used in this section suggest a subjective test of what would likely cause one of those reactions in the observer of the exposure, whereas 'vulgar and indecent,' as presently used, have produced an objective test regarding the nature of the act, regardless of its likely effect upon observers."*

LEWDNESS, PUBLIC.—Cont'd.

4. *Code of Ala. 1975, § 13A-12-130(a)(1).*
5. *Code of Ala. 1975, § 13A-12-130(a)(2).*
6. *See note 3, supra.*

LIABILITY. Code of Ala. 1975, § 13A-2-20.

This section states that: "[a] person is criminally liable for an offense if it is committed by his own behavior or by the behavior of another person[1] for which he is legally accountable."[2]

Classification.

In the comments following § 13A-2-23 of the Alabama Code the drafters make clear that "[r]egarding the extent of liability as a consequence of the principal's actions, Alabama case law has held that as a general rule each person entering upon an unlawful purpose is responsible for everything which may consequently and proximately flow from the unlawful purpose (whether committed by defendant or not, and whether specifically intended or not)."[3]

Comments.

Generally, a person is liable for his own behavior. In addition the Alabama Code provides three situations under which one person can be held liable for the behavior of another person. The first situation is when liability is imposed by statute. More specifically, § 13A-2-21 of the Alabama Code states that "[a] person is legally accountable for the behavior of another person if he is made accountable for the behavior of such person by the statute defining the offense or by specific provision of . . . title [13A]."

The second situation[4] is where "[a] person . . . acting with the culpable mental state sufficient for the commission of the offense in question, . . . causes an innocent[5] person to engage in such behavior."

The third situation[6] is where "[a] person . . . with the intent to promote or assist [in] the commission of [an] offense . . . procures, induces or causes [another] person to commit the offense; or [h]e aids or abets [another] person in committing the offense; or [h]aving a legal duty to prevent the commission of the offense, he fails to make an effort he is legally required to make."

LIABILITY.—Cont'd.

Of course, as is stated in § 13A-2-26 of the Alabama Code, "[a] person is criminally liable for conduct constituting an offense which he performs or causes to be performed in the name of or in behalf of a corporation to the same extent as if such conduct were performed in his own name or behalf."

Defenses.

§ 13A-2-24 of the Alabama Code.

This section states that "[u]nless otherwise provided by the statute defining the offense, a person shall not be legally accountable for behavior of another constituting a criminal offense if:

"(1) He is a victim of that offense;[7] or

"(2) The offense is so defined that his conduct is inevitably incidental to its commission;[8] or

"(3) Prior to the commission of the offense, he voluntarily terminated his effort to promote or assist its commission and either gave timely and adequate warning to law enforcement authorities, or to the intended victim, or wholly deprived his complicity of its effectiveness in the commission of the offense. The burden of injecting this issue is on the defendant, but this does not shift the burden of proof."

But note, "[i]n a prosecution for an offense in which criminal liability is based upon the behavior of another person . . . it is no defense that . . . [s]uch other person has not been prosecuted for or convicted of any offense based upon the behavior in question, or has been previously acquitted thereof, or has been convicted of a different offense or degree of offense; [or] [t]he defendant belongs to a class of persons who, by definition of the offense, are legally incapable of committing the offense in an individual capacity."[9]

---

1. *Stokley v. State, 254 Ala. 534, 49 So. 2d 284 (1950). And note, "[a] person is criminally liable for conduct constituting an offense which he performs or causes to be performed in the name of or in behalf of a corporation to the same extent as if such conduct were performed in his own name or behalf." Code of Ala. 1975, § 13A-2-26.*
2. *See Code of Ala. 1975, §§ 13A-2-21 through 13A-2-26.*

LIABILITY.—Cont'd.

3. *Mabry v. State, 40 Ala. App. 129, 110 So. 2d 250 (1969), cert. denied, 268 Ala. 660, 110 So. 2d 260; Leonard v. State, 43 Ala. App. 454, 192 So. 2d 461 (1966); Fuller v. State, 43 Ala. App. 632, 198 So. 2d 625 (1966); Pugh v. State, 42 Ala. App. 499, 169 So. 2d 27 (1964); White v. State, 42 Ala. App. 249, 160 So. 2d 496 (1964); Berness v. State, 40 Ala. App. 198, 113 So. 2d 178 (1959), cert. denied, 269 Ala. 694, 113 So. 2d 183; Stokley v. State, 254 Ala. 534, 49 So. 2d 284 (1950); Ray v. State, 32 Ala. App. 556, 28 So. 2d 116 (1946); but see Fairbanks v. State, 46 Ala. App. 110, 239 So. 2d 908 (1970); and see People v. Chapman, 62 Mich. 280, 28 N. W. 896 (1886).*
4. *Code of Ala. 1975, § 13A-2-22.*
5. *Blocker v. State, 40 Ala. App. 658, 120 So. 2d 924 (1960); Berness v. State, 38 Ala. App. 1, 83 So. 2d 607 (1953) (reversed on other grounds), aff'd, 40 Ala. App. 198, 113 So. 2d 178, cert. denied, 269 Ala. 694, 113 So. 2d 183 (1958); Jones v. State, 31 Ala. App. 504, 19 So. 2d 81 (1944); Johnson v. State, 142 Ala. 70, 38 So. 182 (1904); see also, Boushea v. United States, 173 F. 2d 131 (8th Cir. 1949).*
6. *Code of Ala. 1975, § 13A-2-23.*
7. *Alldredge v. State, 45 Ala. App. 171, 227 So. 2d 803 (1969); Mahone v. State, 44 Ala. App. 372, 209 So. 2d 435 (1968); Blocker v. State, 40 Ala. App. 658, 120 So. 2d 924 (1960); Fuller v. State, 39 Ala. App. 90, 94 So. 2d 788 (1957).*
8. *Fuller v. State, 40 Ala. App. 297, 115 So. 2d 110 (1958), cert. denied, 361 U. S. 936; Bodiford v. State, 86 Ala. 67, 5 So. 559 (1888); Smith v. State, 39 Ala. 554 (1865).*
9. *Code of Ala. 1975, § 13A-2-25.*

LIBEL AND DEFAMATION. Code of Ala. 1975, §§ 13A-11-160 through 13A-11-164.

Charged as: § 13A-11-160: Libel tending to provoke breach of peace; § 13A-11-163: Defamation; § 13A-11-164: Refusal to testify by printer of libel or defamation.

(1) "Any person who publishes a libel of another which may tend to provoke a breach of the peace . . ." is guilty of criminal libel. § 13A-11-160 of the Alabama Code.

(2) "Any person who writes, prints or speaks of and concerning any woman, falsely imputing to her a want of chastity; and any person who speaks, writes or prints of and concerning another any accusation falsely and maliciously importing the commission by such a person of a felony or any other indictable offense involving moral turpitude . . ." is guilty of criminal defamation. § 13A-11-163 of the Alabama Code.

Classification.

Statutory penalty: fine not to exceed $500.00 or sentence for not more than six months hard labor for the county (one or both, at the discretion of the jury for criminal defamation).

Comments.

The sections covered here impose criminal sanctions on libelous and certain kinds of defamatory acts. Libel that would give or provoke a breach of the peace is a question for the trier of fact based on reasonable man principles. Publication of certain documents have historically been considered privileged in civil actions.[1] This classification is retained in this article and covers such documents as indictments, warrants, affidavits, and court proceedings.[2] The publisher of the privileged documents can still be found guilty if (1) he denies a request for a reasonable explanation or a contradiction; (2) actual malice is proven; or (3) the publisher refuses a written request to publish the subsequent determination of such a suit, action or investigation.[3] It is sufficient in an indictment for libel that the party alleging libel state generally the matter published concerning him.[4] The printer or proprietor of the medium used to publish the libelous statement may be found guilty of contempt, and a misdemeanor, if he refuses to testify before a grand or petit jury concerning the publication at issue.[5]

Two general areas of conduct constitute criminal defamation. They are: (1) a false accusation concerning a woman's lack of chastity; and (2) a false accusation concerning commission of a felony or other offense involving moral turpitude concerning any other person.

Defenses.

(1) Truth.

LIBEL AND DEFAMATION.—Cont'd.

(2) Privileged publication.[6]

(3) Lack of actual malice on a charge concerning a defamation importing the commission of a felony or offense involving moral turpitude.

(4) Failure of libeled person to make written request to publish a subsequent determination of the suit, action or investigation at issue.

(5) Party alleging libel did not present a reasonable explanation or contradiction of the publication at issue.

Cross references.

See BLACKLIST, MAINTAINING.

---

1. *See, for example, Lawson v. Hicks, 38 Ala. 279 (1862).*
2. *Code of Ala. 1975, § 13A-11-161.*
3. *Code of Ala. 1975, § 13A-11-161.*
4. *Code of Ala. 1975, § 13A-11-162.*
5. *Code of Ala. 1975, § 13A-11-164.*
6. *Code of Ala. 1975, § 13A-11-161.*

LINES. See PARTY LINES.

LITTERING. Code of Ala. 1975, § 13A-7-29.

"A person commits the crime of criminal littering if he:

"(1) Knowingly deposits in any manner litter[1] on any public or private property or in any public or private waters, having no permission to do so; or

"(2) Negligently deposits in any manner glass or other dangerously pointed or edged objects on or adjacent to water to which the public has lawful access for bathing, swimming or fishing, or on or upon a public highway, or within the right of way thereof; or

"(3) Discharges sewage, oil products or litter from a watercraft vessel of more than 25 feet in length into a river, inland lake or stream within the state or within three miles of the shoreline of the state; or

"(4)a. Drops or permits to be dropped or thrown upon any highway any destructive or injurious material and does not immediately remove the same or cause it to be removed; or

"b. Removes a wrecked or damaged vehicle from a highway and does not remove glass or other injurious substance dropped upon the highway from such vehicle.

Classification.

Class C misdemeanor.

Comments.

This crime may be committed in three different ways: (1) knowingly, (2) negligently or (3) in accordance with the concept of strict liability. If the offender makes a knowing deposit, the description of the matter littered is more encompassing. For the knowing deposit to constitute a criminal act, there is the additional requirement that there be no consent. Where the deposit is only negligent, the matter littered must be likely to cut or puncture persons. Negligent deposit is further limited in that it must occur in a public bathing, swimming or fishing area. In this instance, the criminality of the act is not dependent upon lack of consent. There are two other acts which constitute an offense regardless of intent or state of mind. These are the discharge of sewage, oil products or litter from a watercraft over 25 feet in length and the dropping of destructive or injurious material. The offense contains a specific provision that imposes an affirmative duty upon wrecker operators to remove such material from the highway or they will be held strictly liable.

There is considerable overlapping of the provisions of this section. Local ordinances should be consulted to see how local jurisdictions have supplemented the act.

Defenses.

(1) Consent to knowing deposit under § 13A-7-29(c)(1) of the Alabama Code.

Query.

The commentators state that provision (a)(3), which deals with the discharge of matter from watercraft over 25 feet in length, "may become unnecessary." This is an invitation to argue to the court that the provision is in fact unnecessary and unreasonable. They point out that it is the act in a certain environment that is criminal rather than the act alone. Additionally, the distinction of vessels according to length invites an equal protection argument. In

LITTERING.—Cont'd.

this day of concentrated toxic waste, a vessel of 25 feet or less could easily dump toxic wastes as easily as a larger vessel. The intent of the statute, expressed by the drafters, is to prohibit conduct harmful to the environment, but not to be concerned with "trivial" cases. The identification of acts that may be harmful or trivial is not related to the length of vessels. An injunction against enforcement or a dismissal might be obtained on this basis.

Cross references.

See HAZARD, CREATING A; MISCHIEF, CRIMINAL; NOXIOUS SUBSTANCE, USE OR POSSESSION; TRESPASS, CRIMINAL.

---

1. *Code of Ala. 1975, § 13A-7-29(b): " 'Litter' means rubbish, refuse, waste material, garbage, dead animals or fowl, offal, paper, glass, cans, bottles, trash, scrap metal, debris or any foreign substance of whatever kind and description, and whether or not it is of value."*

LOBBYING AND CONTRACTING BY FORMER OFFICIAL OR EMPLOYEE, DISCLOSURE REQUIRED. Code of Ala. 1975, § 36-25-13.

Charged as: Failure to disclose lobbying or contracting, etc.

"(a) No former state official or employee shall serve for a fee as a lobbyist or represent clients before the body of which he is a former member or employee for a period of three years after he leaves such membership or employment, unless notice of such representation is given within five days after such appearance to the state ethics commission in the manner prescribed by the commission and,

"(b) No former public official or employee shall enter into a contract with any governmental agencies unless within five days of entering into said contract notice is filed with the commission of his previous status as a public official or employee and a copy of the contract provided."

Comments.

Disclosure regarding contracting with governmental agencies is a lifetime burden incurred as a result of public service, whereas disclosure of lobbying is only required for a period of 3 years immediately following termination of membership or employment. Similarly, contracts with **any** agency and the official or employee must be disclosed, whereas only lobbying before the body of which the official or employee was a member or employee need be reported. It is not discernible whether by use of the term "state" official the statute was intended to exclude lobbying activities before county or city bodies.

Defenses.

To § 36-25-13(1) of the Code of Alabama:

(1) Was never a state official or employee.
(2) No fee.
(3) Not acting as a lobbyist or representative.
(4) Not before the same agency (where previously employed).
(5) More than three (3) years since last employed by the agency in question.
(6) Required notice was given.

To § 36-25-13(2) of the Code of Alabama:

(1) Was never a public official or employee.
(2) Agreement did not constitute a contract.
(3) Contract is not with any government agency.
(4) Required notice was given.

Cross references.

See ETHICS VIOLATIONS.

LOITERING. Code of Ala. 1975, § 13A-11-9.

"A person commits the crime of loitering if he:

"(1) Loiters, remains or wanders about in a public place for the purpose of begging; or

"(2) Loiters or remains in a public place for the purpose of gambling; or

"(3) Loiters or remains in a public place for the purpose of engaging or soliciting another person to engage in prostitution or deviate sexual intercourse;[1] or

"(4) Being masked, loiters, remains or

LOITERING.—Cont'd.

congregates in a public place; or

"(5) Loiters or remains in or about a school, college or university building or grounds after having been told to leave by any authorized official of such school, college or university, and not having any reason or relationship involving custody of or responsibility for a pupil or any other specific, legitimate reason for being there, and not having written permission from a school, college or university administrator; or

"(6) Loiters or remains in any transportation facility, unless specifically authorized to do so, for the purpose of soliciting or engaging in any business, trade or commercial transactions involving the sale of merchandise or services; or

"(7) Loiters or remains in any place with one or more persons for purpose of unlawfully using or possessing a dangerous drug."[2]

Classification.

A violation.

Comments.

This statute utilizes "probable cause" as the basis for arrest. It abandons the "status" approach of the superceded statute (§ 13-6-16 of the Alabama Code), which set out thirteen classifications that constituted vagrancy, all of which relied upon the status of the individual as the determining factor relative to punishment. These statutes were held unconstitutional in Broughton v. Brewer, 298 F. Supp. 260 (S. D. Ala. 1969) on the grounds that they were so vague that they violated the fair notice requirements of due process guaranteed by the Fourteenth Amendment to the United States Constitution. This statute punishes identifiable "conduct" rather than "status" and protects individuals from the operation of the statute by requiring proof of criminal intent. Sections 13A-11-9(a)(1)-(3), (a)(6) and (a)(7) of the Alabama Code require proof that the alleged conduct was "for the purpose of" facilitating or promoting some specific conduct. Sections 13A-11-9(a)(4) and (a)(5) of the Alabama Code do not require proof of intent. The conduct itself is specified. It is interesting that the

LOITERING.—Cont'd.

Commentary to § 13A-11-9 of the Alabama Code points out that begging by "those who have suffered some misfortune" is not to fall within the scope of this statute, yet there is no provision for such an exemption in the wording of the statute. Conduct "for the purpose of" gambling, prostitution, deviate sexual intercourse, and use or possession of a dangerous drug are also specified. Note that the element of criminal intent that is required in some sections presents an insurmountable burden of proof. If Russ "loiters or waits in a place with one or more persons" who are suspected or known to deal in the "unlawful use or possession of dangerous drugs", should Russ be culpable on the presentation of such proof? Such "guilty by association" convictions should fall victim to a constitutional attack. § 13A-11-9(a)(5) of the Alabama Code, requires the school to prove the individual did not have "any other specific, legitimate reason for being there." According to the commentary, §§ 13A-11-9 (a)(4) and (b) of the Alabama Code merely restate the penalty for wearing masks and the attendant exceptions. However, § 13A-11-9(b) of the Alabama Code makes no reference to persons "participating in the celebration of a legal holiday" as did old § 13-6-16 of the Alabama Code. Therefore, a person standing on a street corner wearing a mask on Halloween night is not exempt from the new statute. (But see defense (4), infra).

Defenses.

(1) To subsection (1): failure to prove the individual loitered, remained, or wandered about.

(2) To subsection (1): failure to prove the proscribed conduct was engaged in a "public place."

(3) To subsections (1), (2), (3), (6), (7): failure to prove criminal intent.

(4) To subsection (4): a person does not commit a crime if he is going to or from or staying at a masquerade party, or is participating in a public parade or presentation of an educational, religious, or historical character or in an event as

LOITERING.—Cont'd.
defined in § 13A-11-140(a)(1) of the Alabama Code.
(5) To subsection (5): "any specific, legitimate reason" for presence.
(6) To subsection (7): failure to prove the drug was "dangerous."

Query.
If subsection (1) were enforced only against those not "suffering some misfortune," there might be an equal protection argument. If otherwise legal and permissible conduct is engaged in, can that conduct become illegal due to an "illegal purpose"?

Cross references.
See ASSAULT; CONTROLLED SUBSTANCES.

---

1. "Deviate sexual intercourse" is defined in § 13A-6-60(2) as "[a]ny act of sexual gratification between persons not married to each other, involving the sex organs of one person and the mouth or anus of another."

2. "Dangerous drug"... means any narcotic, drug or controlled substance as defined in chapter 2 of Title 20 of this Code and any schedule incorporated therein." § 13A-11-9(d).

LOTTERY PARAPHERNALIA, TRANSPORTATION OF. Code of Ala. 1975, § 13A-12-70.

Charged as: Transportation by certain persons; seizures of vehicles used.

"Any transportation or conveyance within this state of any slip, ticket, card, paper, writing, article, thing or other device or paraphernalia which is customarily or usually used in the operation of a form or type of lottery commonly known as a numbers (or number) game or policy game (herein called "lottery paraphernalia") or any possession thereof in any vehicle of transportation by any person who is or has been within three years next preceding actually engaged in or connected with the setting up, conducting or operation of any such game, or who is or has been within three years preceding an employee of a person or persons who are or have been engaged in setting up, conducting or

LOTTERY PARAPHERNALIA, TRANSPORTATION OF.—Cont'd.
operating of any such game is hereby declared to be a misdemeanor."

Classification.
Misdemeanor, and "[a]ll conveyance or vehicles of transportation which have been within three years next preceding or are used by such persons for the conveying or transporting of such prohibited lottery paraphernalia into this state or from one point in the state to another point within the state, or in which conveyance any such lottery paraphernalia may be contained or found while such conveyance is in the custody or control of such person shall be contraband and shall be forfeited to the state of Alabama and shall be seized by any sheriff or other person acting under authority of the law in the enforcement of the laws of this state who become cognizant of the facts or who finds such prohibited lottery paraphernalia being transported, stored or contained as aforesaid in such conveyance or vehicle. And such officer or person shall report the seizure and the facts connected therewith to a district attorney in the county where seizure is made, or, in default thereof, to the attorney general of the state, giving full description of the vehicle or conveyance seized and detained, the person in whose possession it was found, the person making a claim to the same, or any interest therein, if the name can be ascertained or is known, and the date of seizure."

Comments.
Section 13A-12-70 of the Alabama Code deals strictly with the transportation of "lottery" paraphernalia and not other types of gambling paraphernalia or any objects not commonly used in lotteries. In addition, there are two elements that must be satisfied under § 13A-12-70 of the Alabama Code. First, the person charged must be actually engaged in or connected with the setting up, conducting or operating a lottery (or an employee of such a person). And second, he must be either presently involved, or been involved within the last three (3) years, with setting up, conducting

LOTTERY PARAPHERNALIA, TRANSPORTATION OF.—Cont'd.

or operating a lottery. Note, according to § 13A-12-71 of the Alabama Code, the actual movement of a vehicle does not have to be shown prior to confiscation. The mere presence of the lottery paraphernalia in the vehicle is sufficient. § 13A-12-73 of the Alabama Code dictates the condition for the sale of confiscated vehicles. In fact, "[t]he court in condemnation proceedings shall sell the rights of all interested persons in and to said conveyance or vehicle who aided or assisted any such person as described in section [13A-12-70] in the illegal transportation or who had knowledge or notice thereof, or who had knowledge of the presence thereof in said vehicle or conveyance, or who could by reasonable diligence have obtained knowledge or notice thereof. Any bona fide bailor or conditional vendor or chattel mortgagee who shall, prior to bailing, selling or accepting a mortgage upon such conveyance or vehicle, make inquiry of the sheriff and chief of police of the county and city of the residence of such bailee, vendee or mortgagor and of the sheriff and chief of police of the county and city of the place of business of the bailor, vendor or mortgagee, or of any recognized or licensed agency which makes a systematic check of court records of convictions for violations of the law and furnishes credit reports, and in answer to such inquiry shall be informed in writing that the prospective bailee, conditional vendee or mortgagor has no reputation as a person who has been engaged in operating or connected with lotteries, gambling or gaming and that such person has not according to their records been convicted of a violation of any of the laws of this state, any other state or of any municipal ordinance relating to gaming, gambling or lotteries, shall be presumed to be entitled to such conveyance or vehicle or to be protected to the extent of his interest therein."

Defenses.

(1) Not lottery paraphernalia.

LOTTERY PARAPHERNALIA, TRANSPORTATION OF.—Cont'd.

(2) Not engaged in, or employer of, a lottery operation, presently or within the last three (3) years.

Cross references.

See GAMBLING; GAMBLING, POSSESSION OF DEVICE; GAMBLING, POSSESSION OF RECORDS.

MAIMING ONE'S SELF TO ESCAPE DUTY OR OBTAIN ALMS. Code of Ala. 1975, § 13A-14-1.

"Every person who, with design to disable himself from performing a legal duty, existing or anticipated, shall inflict upon himself an injury whereby he is so disabled and every person who shall so injure himself with intent to avail himself of such injury to excite sympathy or to obtain alms or some charitable relief shall be guilty of a felony."

Classification.

Felony.

Comments.

This section might be more easily understood if divided into two separate offenses:

(1) "Every person who, with design to disable himself from performing a legal duty, existing or anticipated, shall inflict upon himself an injury whereby he is so disabled," contains three elements to be established by the state:

1. Intent — to disable one's self; and
2. Intent (motive) — to avoid a legal duty; and
3. Result — he must be so disabled as to avoid the specific legal duty (existing or anticipated).

(2) "Every person who shall so injure himself with intent to avail himself of such injury to excite sympathy or to obtain alms or some charitable relief," contains three elements to be established by the state:

1. Intent — to injure one's self; and
2. Intent (motive) —
   a. to excite sympathy, or
   b. to obtain alms, or
   c. to obtain charitable relief; and
3. Result — he must be injured.

At first blush, the major difference, relative to burden of proof (for the state), is that

MAIMING ONE'S SELF TO ESCAPE DUTY OR OBTAIN ALMS.
—Cont'd.

under the second offense, the injured person need not have received sympathy, alms, or charity. Nor is it necessary that his injury be such that would excite sympathy or likely to gain alms or charity. Thus, if I injure myself by cutting off the small toe on my left foot with the intent to gain sympathy, I have committed a felony under § 13A-14-1 of the Alabama Code, notwithstanding the fact that I never received sympathy and notwithstanding the fact that I changed my mind and never showed the injury to anyone. The crime may be complete when the injury is inflicted.

On the other hand, the first offense requires not only the intent to injure one's self to avoid a legal duty and the actual injury, but, additionally, requires that such injury must avoid the specific legal duty.

The major difference between the first offense and the second offense is that the former requires the actor to be successful in his design, whereas the latter does not require success; however, both require an actual injury.

Defenses.

(1) Lack of intent to injure.
(2) Lack of intent to avoid a legal duty at the time the injury was inflicted (first offense).
(3) Lack of intent to excite sympathy, obtain alms or obtain charitable relief at the time the injury was inflicted (second offense).
(4) No actual injury.
(5) Injury not serious enough to avoid the specific legal duty (first offense).
(6) Mental illness.
(7) Intoxication.

MANSLAUGHTER. Code of Ala. 1975, § 13A-6-3.

"A person commits the crime of manslaughter if:

"(1) He recklessly[1] causes the death of another person,[2] or

"(2) He causes the death of another person under circumstances that would constitute murder under section 13A-6-2; except, that he causes the death due to a sudden heat of passion caused by provocation recognized by law, and before a reasonable time for the passion to cool and for reason to reassert itself."

Classification.

Class C felony.

Comments.

The offense of manslaughter is no longer divided into degrees, as it was under former § 13A-1-90 of the Alabama Code. The former first degree manslaughter, voluntary manslaughter,[3] is now § 13A-6-3(a)(2) of the Alabama Code; and former second degree manslaughter, involuntary manslaughter,[4] is now § 13A-6-3(a)(1) of the Alabama Code.

Prior to the adoption of § 32-5A-192 of the Alabama Code in 1980 (homicide by vehicle), most charges of manslaughter arising out of motor vehicle accidents were charged under § 13A-6-3 of the Alabama Code. It should be noted that the possible sentence is considerably less under 32 of the Alabama Code.[5]

If the homicide occurred due to the "heat of passion," the defendant could be charged under either § 13A-6-2 of the Alabama Code (murder) or this manslaughter statute. To remove the case from the murder statute, there must be four elements proven: (1) the death was due to a sudden heat of passion; (2) the heat of passion was caused by provocation; (3) such provocation is that which is recognized by law; and (4) the killing was before a reasonable time for the passion to cool. Adequate legal provocation has been found where there was a blow inflicting considerable pain or injury,[6] or a felonious attack with a gun or similar deadly weapon.[7] Insufficient legal provocation would be mere abusive or opprobrious words or insulting gestures,[8] or a minor, or technical, assault or battery.[9]

The burden of injecting the issue of legal provocation is on the defendant; however, once injected, the burden is on the state to disprove the defense.

Defenses.

(1) Defendant's action did not constitute "recklessness" or "wantonness," only

MANSLAUGHTER.—Cont'd.

negligence or even criminal or gross negligence.

(2) Involuntary intoxication.

(3) Insanity.

(4) Self-defense.

Cross references.

See N. Chiarkas, Alabama Criminal Trial Practice, § 14-36 (Special plea of insanity). See also HOMICIDE, CRIMINALLY NEGLIGENT; INSANITY; INTOXICATION; MOTOR VEHICLE CRIMES; MURDER.

---

1. *Code of Ala. 1975, 13A-2-2(3) defines recklessly as: "A person acts recklessly with respect to a result or to a circumstance described by a statute defining an offense when he is aware of and consciously disregards a substantial and unjustifiable risk that the result will occur or that the circumstance exists. The risk must be of such nature and degree that disregard thereof constitutes a gross deviation from the standard of conduct that a reasonable person would observe in the situation. A person who creates a risk but is unaware thereof solely by reason of voluntary intoxication, as defined in subdivision (e)(2) of section 13A-3-3, acts recklessly with respect thereto."*
2. *Code of Ala. 1975, § 13A-6-1(2) defines a person as: "when referring to the victim of a criminal homicide, means a human being who had been born and was alive at the time of the homicidal act."*
3. *The unlawful killing of another, feloniously, without any expressed or implied malice, by voluntarily depriving him of life. Clarke v. State, 117 Ala. 1, 23 So. 671 (1897).*
4. *An unintentional killing due to gross, criminal or culpable negligence. Fitzgerald v. State, 112 Ala. 34, 20 So. 966 (1895).*
5. *Manslaughter is a class C felony, punishable by fine of not more than $5,000 and/or imprisonment for not more than 10 years or less than 1 year. Homicide by vehicle is punishable by fine from $50—$2,000 and/or imprisonment from 3 months—1 year, or in the alternative, imprisonment in the state penitentiary for 1—5 years.*

   See MOTOR VEHICLE CRIMES.
6. *Easley v. State, 246 Ala. 359, 20 So. 2d 519 (1945).*
7. *Robertson v. State, 217 Ala. 696, 117 So. 412 (1928).*
8. *Cates v. State, 50 Ala. 166 (1874).*
9. *Easley v. State, 246 Ala. 359, 20 So. 2d 519 (1945).*

MARATHON CONTESTS. Code of Ala. 1975, § 13A-14-3.

Charged as: Promoting, advertising or conducting a marathon contest.

"It shall be unlawful for any person, firm, association or corporation to promote, advertise or conduct any marathon dance contests, walkathon contests or similar endurance contests, by whatever name called, of walking, dancing, riding or running, and it shall be unlawful for any person to participate in any marathon dance contest, walkathon contest or similar physical endurance contest by walking, dancing, riding or running continuing or intended to continue for a period of more than eight consecutive hours, whether or not an admission is charged or a prize awarded, and it shall be unlawful for any person to participate in more than one such contest or performance within any period of 48 hours."

Classification.

Unclassified misdemeanor with specific provision for a fine of not less than $50.00 nor more than $500.00; or imprisonment of not less than 30 days nor more than 90 days; or both.

Comments.

The continuation of the activity to another day shall constitute another separate and distinct offense, § 13A-14-3(c) of the Alabama Code. This law is an anomaly from another era, and its utility is questionable. The offense is not predicated upon the awarding of a prize, or an admission charge. The drafter's intent remains a mystery. There are inherent vagueness problems and a potential infringement upon basic rights. Ultimately the state may bear the burden of establishing exactly what the intent of the statute is and how the provisions are rationally related to its end.

Defenses.

(1) Among the more obvious are some interesting first amendment questions.

MARIJUANA. See CONTROLLED SUBSTANCES.

MENACING. Code of Ala. 1975, § 13A-6-23.

"A person commits the crime of menacing if by physical action,[1] he intentionally[2] places or attempts[3] to place another person in fear of imminent serious physical injury."[4]

Classification.

Class B misdemeanor.

Comments.

This statute is intended to cover some situations that do not fall directly within the scope of the three basic assault provisions or within the scope of the harassment provision. The classic example of menacing is a person, intending to frighten another, points an unloaded gun at him, though not known by the victim to be unloaded. McArdle v. State, 372 So. 2d 901 (1979). Chapman v. State, 78 Ala. 463 (1885). Technically, such conduct does not constitute either assault or attempted assault under the Criminal Code because "physical injury," within the meaning of those statutes, is neither inflicted nor intended. Menacing may be distinguished from criminal harassment, which covers, inter alia, any nonconsensual physical contact that does not produce physical injury. Any threat of physical injury accompanied by both an intent and an attempt to carry out that intent is an attempted assault.

Defenses.

(1) The action charged was physical in nature.
(2) No intent to place another in fear.
(3) Not imminent.
(4) Not serious.
(5) Did not place or attempt to place another person in fear of serious physical injury.

Query.

Could the circumstances be sufficient to confer the meaning and effect of "physical action" upon mere physical inaction? For example, at 1:00 in the morning it is announced that restaurant (or bar) is closing; everyone leaves except for one person who refuses to rise from his seat or to

MENACING.—Cont'd.

communicate in any manner. Consider the physical size of the person, his mode of dress, the time of day, the presence or lack of presence of other customers, the number of employees present, his failure to communicate, etc. Are the criteria for determining if fear exists objective or subjective in nature?

Cross references.

See Assault, §§ 13A-6-20 through 13A-6-22 of the Alabama Code; Harassment, § 13A-11-8 of the Alabama Code. See RECKLESS ENDANGERMENT.

---

1. *There is no statutory definition of "physical action," but Code of Ala. 1975, § 13A-2-1(5) states that "TO ACT" is "[e]ither to perform an act or to omit to perform an act." Code of Ala. 1975, § 13A-2-1(1) defines an "ACT" as "[a] bodily movement, and such term includes possession of property." A "VOLUNTARY ACT" is defined as: "[a]n act performed consciously as a result of effort or determination, and such term includes the possession of property if the actor was aware of his physical possession or control thereof for a sufficient time to have been able to terminate it." Code of Ala. 1975, § 13A-2-1(2).*
2. *According to Code of Ala. 1975, § 13A-2-2(1): "A person acts intentionally with respect to a result or to conduct described by a statute defining an offense, when his purpose is to cause that result or to engage in that conduct."*
3. *"A person is guilty of an attempt to commit a crime if, with the intent to commit a specific offense, he does any overt act towards the commission of such offense." Code of Ala. 1975, § 13A-4-2(a).*
4. *Serious physical injury, as defined in Code of Ala. 1975, § 13A-1-2(9), is: "Physical injury which creates a substantial risk of death, or which cause serious and protracted disfigurement, protracted impairment of health or protracted loss or impairment of the function of any bodily organ."*

Physical injury, as defined in Code of Ala. 1975, § 13A-1-2(8), is "[i]mpairment of physical condition or substantial pain."

MENTAL DISEASE OR DEFECT. See INSANITY.

MENTAL ILLNESS. See INSANITY.

MINORS. See CHILD WELFARE, ENDANGERING; CIGARETTES, SELLING TO MINOR; JUVENILE PROCEEDINGS; NONSUPPORT; OBSCENE MATERIALS DISPLAYING OR DEPICTING CHILDREN; OBSCENE MATERIALS, SALE, EXHIBITION, ETC. TO MINORS.

MISAPPLICATION OF PROPERTY.

Code of Ala. 1975, § 13A-9-51.

"A person commits the crime of misapplication[1] of property[2] if, with knowledge that he is misapplying and that the misapplication involves substantial risk of loss or detriment to the owner[3] of the property or to a person for whose benefit the property was entrusted, he misapplies or disposes of property that has been entrusted to him as a fiduciary[4] or that is property of the government[5] or a financial institution."[6]

Classification.

Class A misdemeanor.

Comments.

Even though the individual is entrusted with the property as a fiduciary (or the property is owned by the government or financial institution) and he knowingly misapplies the property, such action does not fall within the scope of this statute unless the misapplication involved "substantial risk of loss or detriment to the owner of the property or to a person for whose benefit the property was entrusted."

Defenses.

(1) Lack of knowledge that a misapplication has occurred.

(2) Lack of knowledge that a substantial risk of loss may occur.

(3) Lack of fiduciary duty and the property is not that of a financial institution or the government.

Cross references.

See Theft and related offenses, §§ 13A-8-1 through 13A-8-22 of the Alabama Code. See THEFT OF PROPERTY.

---

1. *"To 'misapply' means to deal with the property contrary to law or governmental regulation of the custody or disposition of that property; 'governmental regulation' includes administrative and judicial rules and orders as well as statutes and ordinances." Code of Ala. 1975, § 13A-9-51(c).*
2. *"Any money, tangible or intangible personal property, property (whether real or personal) the location of which can be changed (including things growing on, affixed to or found in land and documents, although the rights represented hereby have no physical location), contract right, chose-in-action, interest in a claim to wealth, credit or any other article or thing of value of any kind." Code of Ala. 1975, § 13A-8-1(10).*
3. *Owner is defined as: "A person, other than the defendant, who has possession of or any other interest in the property involved, even though that interest or possession is unlawful, and without whose consent the defendant has no authority to exert control over the property.*
   "A secured party, as defined in section 7-9-105(i), is not an owner in relation to a defendant who is a debtor, as defined in section 7-9-105(d), in respect of property in which the secured party has a security interest, as defined in section 7-1-201(37)." Code of Ala. 1975, § 13A-8-1(8).
4. *" 'Fiduciary' includes a trustee, guardian, executor, administrator, receiver or any other person acting in a fiduciary capacity, or any person carrying on fiduciary functions on behalf of a corporation or other organization which is a fiduciary." Code of Ala. 1975, § 13A-9-51(b).*
5. *"The United States, any state or any county, municipality or other political unit within territory belonging to the United States, or any department, agency or subdivision of any of the foregoing, or any corporation or other association carrying out the functions of government, or any corporation or agency formed pursuant to interstate compact or international treaty.*
   "As used in this definition 'state' includes any state, territory or possession of the United States, the District of Columbia and the Commonwealth of Puerto Rico." Code of Ala. 1975, § 13A-8-1(5).
6. *"A bank, insurance company, credit union, safety deposit company, savings and loan association, investment trust or other organization held out to the public as a place of deposit of funds or medium of savings or collective investment." Code of Ala. 1975, § 13A-8-1(3).*

MISCHIEF, CRIMINAL. Code of Ala. 1975, §§ 13A-7-21 through 13A-7-23.

Charged as: Criminal mischief.

"A person commits the crime of criminal mischief in the first degree if, with intent to damage property,[1] and having no right to do so or any reasonable ground to believe that he has such a right, he inflicts damages to property:

"(a) In an amount exceeding $1,000.00; or

"(b) By means of an explosion." § 13A-7-21(a) of the Alabama Code.

"A person commits the crime of criminal mischief in the second degree if, with intent to damage property, and having no right to do so or any reasonable ground to believe that he has such a right, he inflicts damages to property in an amount which exceeds $250.00 but does not exceed $1,000.00." 13A-7-22(a) of the Alabama Code.

"A person commits the crime of criminal mischief in the third degree if, with intent to damage property, and having no right to do so or any reasonable ground to believe that he has such a right, he inflicts damages to property in an amount not exceeding $250.00." § 13A-7-23(a) of the Alabama Code.

Classification.

Class C felony, criminal mischief in the first degree.

Class A misdemeanor, criminal mischief in the second degree.

Class B misdemeanor, criminal mischief in the third degree.

Comments.

This law seeks to prohibit: (1) the intentional (2) infliction of damage to property (3) where there is no right to do so or reasonable ground to believe such a right exists. (See § 13A-2-6[2] of the Alabama Code.) The differentiation of degrees is determined by the following breakdown of the value of the damage inflicted:

First degree — Over $1,000

Second degree — Over $250 but not over $1,000

Third degree — Not over $250

Additionally, use of an explosive as the

MISCHIEF, CRIMINAL.—Cont'd.

means of inflicting the damage constitutes an act in the first degree. No matter the amount of the damage, the offender must intend to damage the property. Hollinger v. State, 40 So. 2d 220 (1959). Intent includes the reasonably foreseeable result of one's voluntary act. Note, the Advisory Committee intentionally rejected a provision that would have criminalized "reckless" damage.

Defenses.

(1) No intent to damage property.

(2) Right, or reasonable ground to believe a right, to damage exists. (Note, under a strict construction, even though the offender believed he had no right to damage, if he had reasonable grounds to believe that he had such a right, it would be complete defense.)

(3) Damage did not exceed $1,000, and no explosive was used (first degree).

(4) Damage did not exceed $250 (second degree).

Query.

Consider the implications if there is no loss of value (i.e., burn vacant derelict house, higher or equal value to property).

Cross references.

See DESECRATION OF TOMBSTONE.

1. *"Injury or harm to property that lowers its value or involves loss of efficiency." Code of Ala. 1975, § 13A-7-23.*
2. *See Code of Ala. 1975, § 13A-2-6.*

MISDEMEANORS. See SENTENCING.

MISTAKE. Code of Ala. 1975, § 13A-2-6.

A person may not be convicted of a crime if the act or omission constituting the crime was induced by the actor's misapprehension of fact which, if true, would have justified the act or omission. Although the draftsmen of the Alabama Criminal Code did not explain the rationale of this provision, it is presumably based upon the notion that such a mistake of fact would negate the mens rea necessary to the commission of a crime. More specifically, § 13A-2-6(a) of the Alabama Code, states that:

MISTAKE.—Cont'd.

"A person is not relieved of criminal liability for conduct because he engages in that conduct under a mistaken belief of fact unless:

"(1) His factual mistake negatives the culpable mental state required for the commission of an offense; or

"(2) The statute defining the offense or a statute related thereto expressly provides that such a factual mistake constitutes a defense or exemption; or

"(3) The factual mistake is of a kind that supports a defense of justification as defined in article 2 of chapter 3 of this title."

Section 13A-2-6(b) of the Alabama Code, states that "[a] person is not relieved of criminal liability for conduct because he engages in that conduct under a mistaken belief that it does not, as a matter of law, constitute an offense, unless his mistaken belief is founded upon an official statement of the law contained in a statute or the latest judicial decision of the highest state or federal court which has decided on the matter."

Although the burden of injecting the issue of mistake of law is on the defendant, § 13A-2-6(c) of the Alabama Code provides that the burden of proof does not shift.

Finally, under § 13A-2-6(d) of the Alabama Code, "[a] mistake of law, other than as to the existence or meaning of the statute under which the defendant is prosecuted, is relevant to disprove the specific state of mental culpability required by the statute under which the defendant is prosecuted."

Comments.

Mistake of fact may or may not negate criminal liability depending on whether the crime charged requires proof of any particular mental element. Mistake of fact, therefore, is a defense to crimes requiring criminal intent or some particular mental element such as "knowingly" and "willfully." The Drafters of the Code cite the crime of larceny as an example. A defendant is not guilty of larceny if he believed, albeit mistakenly, that the property taken was his own because larceny requires proof of an intent to wholly deprive

MISTAKE.—Cont'd.

the owner of his property.[1] In crimes which require no mental element, the defendant is liable irrespective of his intentions or lack of mens rea.[2]

Under § 13A-2-6(a)(3) of the Alabama Code, a person may not be convicted of a crime if the act or omission constituting the crime was induced by the actor's misapprehension of fact which, if true, would have justified the act or omission.[3]

---

1. *Reed v. State, 32 Ala. App. 338, 27 So. 2d 22 (1946), cert. denied, 248 Ala. 196, 27 So. 2d 25 (1946). Also see Gordon v. State, 52 Ala. 308 (1875).*
2. *United States v. Parfait Powder Puff Co., Inc., 163 F. 2d 1008 (7th Cir. 1947), cert. denied, 332 U. S. 851, 68 S. Ct. 355, 92 L. Ed. 421 (1948); United States v. Balint, 258 U. S. 250, 42 S. Ct. 301, 66 L. Ed. 604 (1922).*
3. *See Code of Ala. 1975, § 13A-3 for the defense(s) of justification generally. See also PUBLIC DUTY.*

MISUSE OF CONFIDENTIAL INFORMATION. See CONFIDENTIAL INFORMATION, MISUSE OF.

MOTOR VEHICLE CRIMES. Code of Ala. 1975, Title 32 (Motor vehicles and traffic).

I. Generally.

All the statutes concerning the use of and regulation of motor vehicles in Alabama are in Title 32 of the Alabama Code. It is divided into eighteen chapters, but virtually all the sections with criminal provisions are found in Chapters 32-5, 32-5A (Rules of the Road), and 32-8 (Uniform Certificate of Title and Antitheft Act) of the Alabama Code. Most of the remaining criminal provisions are found in Chapter 32-10 (Motor Vehicle Accidents) of the Alabama Code. All of the chapters contain some provisions that have criminal implications.

The violation of any provision in Title 32 of the Alabama Code is a misdemeanor, unless specifically classified as a felony.[1] The possible fines and/or sentences are usually set forth within each chapter in a general

MOTOR VEHICLE CRIMES.—Cont'd.

penalty section. Many statutes, however, provide for their own specific maximum penalty.

II. Rules Of The Road. Code of Ala. 1975, Chapter 32-5A.

—A. Generally.

Enacted in 1980, the Rules of the Road repealed and superceded most of the previous Chapter 32-5. The chapter regulates all behavior on the state's roads and is divided into twelve articles: general provisions,[2] traffic signs and signals,[3] operation and use of vehicles,[4] driving on roadways and passing,[5] right of way,[6] turns,[7] special stops,[8] speed restrictions,[9] serious traffic offenses,[10] pedestrians,[11] motorcycles[12] and bicycles.[13]

Section 32-5A-8(b) of the Alabama Code sets forth the possible sentences and/or fines for violators and increases the maximum sanctions for repeat offenders.[14] To qualify for enhancement purposes, the prior conviction must have occurred within one year of the present one and must have been a misdemeanor; prior felonies cannot be used. The prior conviction need not have been for the same offense currently charged. § 32-5A-9 of the Alabama Code provides the sanctions for felonies.[15]

The four most serious traffic offenses are in Chapter 32-5A of the Alabama Code. They are reckless driving, § 32-5A-190 of the Alabama Code; driving under the influence, § 32-5A-191 of the Alabama Code; homicide by vehicle, § 32-5A-192 of the Alabama Code; and fleeing or attempting to elude police officer, § 32-5A-193 of the Alabama Code. These four statutes apply not only to highways, but also "elsewhere throughout the state."[16] This changes the prior law under Chapter 32-5 of the Alabama Code.

—B. Reckless Driving.

"[A]ny person who drives any vehicle carelessly and heedlessly in willful or wanton disregard for the rights or safety of persons or property, or without due caution and circumspection and at a speed or in a manner so as to endanger or be likely to endanger any person or property shall be guilty of reckless driving." § 32-5A-190(a)

MOTOR VEHICLE CRIMES.—Cont'd.

of the Alabama Code. The only change of significance from the superceded § 32-5-50 of the Alabama Code is that the provision is no longer limited to driving a vehicle "upon the highway." The statute is concerned with whether defendant's conduct was "likely to endanger any person or property." Actual damage or injury is not necessary.

Wantonness is a "conscious doing of some act or omission of some duty under knowledge of existing conditions and conscious that from the doing of such act or omission of such duty injury will likely or probably result."[17] Wantonness can only be proved when it is shown that there was actual knowledge (wantonness "does not result from the mere negligence in the failure to have that knowledge and consciousness"[18]), and the act was "done with reckless indifference as to the consequences."[19] A person is not guilty of wanton negligence in assuming "that another will exercise due care and caution for his safety."[20] Reckless driving is not a "lessor included offense under a charge of driving while under the influence of alcohol or drugs."[21]

If a person is convicted of reckless driving, his drivers license may be suspended for a period not exceeding 6 months. Further sanctions are enhanced for repeat offenders: first conviction — imprisonment from 5—90 days and/or a fine from $25—$500; second and any subsequent conviction — imprisonment from 10 days—6 months and/or a fine from $50—$500.[22]

—C. Driving While Under The Influence Of Alcohol Or Controlled Substances (D. U. I.).

The ability of a driver or person in actual physical control of a vehicle is impaired by alcohol or other drugs while:

"(1) There is 0.10 percent or more by weight of alcohol in his blood;

"(2) Under the influence of alcohol;

"(3) Under the influence of a controlled substance to a degree which renders him incapable of safely driving; or

"(4) Under the combined influence of

MOTOR VEHICLE CRIMES.—Cont'd.

alcohol and a controlled substance to a degree which renders him incapable of safely driving."[23]

Although a D. U. I. conviction can be obtained without introducing the results of chemical tests of bodily substances,[24] most prosecutions include such evidence. The admissibility of the results of chemical tests is governed by § 32-5A-194 of the Alabama Code, which applies to civil, criminal and quasi-criminal proceedings. The chemical analysis must be performed by an individual licensed by the State Board of Health and conducted according to methods approved by said Board.[25] If the bodily substance being tested is blood, it must have been withdrawn by "a physician or a registered nurse (or other qualified person)."[26] The request for such test must be made in writing by a law enforcement officer.[27] The individual may, at his own expense, have an additional test made by a qualified person of his own choosing. The failure or inability to do so does not affect the admissibility of the test that was requested by the law enforcement officer.[28] The person subjected to chemical tests has the right to "full information concerning the tests" if he makes a request in writing for such records.[29]

There is a presumption that any person who drives on the roads of Alabama consents to be subjected to chemical or similar tests when suspected of D. U. I.[30] When a law enforcement officer requests a driver suspected of D. U. I. to submit to such a test, he shall also advise the individual that refusal to submit results in an automatic suspension of all driving privileges for a 45 day period. If the officer does not advise the defendant, and the unadvised motorist is subjected to tests, the results of the tests are admissible against the defendant. The officer's failure to properly inform the defendant affects only the validity of the suspension of his driving privileges.[31] If a defendant refuses to submit to a test, no test shall be given.[32] This is admissible against him.[33] Because there is a presumption of consent, the results are admissible even when the defendant is unconscious or otherwise incapable of refusing; there is no implied withdrawal of consent even in death.[34]

MOTOR VEHICLE CRIMES.—Cont'd.

Historically, Alabama case law held that a defendant could not be made to incriminate himself with either testimonial or physical evidence. "The accused cannot, directly or indirectly, be compelled to do an affirmative act, or to affirmatively say anything which may tend to criminate him."[35] In 1966, the United States Supreme Court in Schmerber v. California[36] distinguished between testimonial and physical evidence as applied to the Fifth Amendment right against self-incrimination. The Court stated that "the privilege is a bar against compelling 'communications' or 'testimony' but that compulsion which makes a suspect or accused the source of 'real or physical evidence' does not violate it." The Court held that the extraction of blood by a doctor to determine its alcohol content did not violate the defendant's privilege against self-incrimination. Alabama followed Schmerber's testimonial/physical evidence distinction and abolished the historical rule.[37]

Punishment for a first conviction of D. U. I. is imprisonment for not more than 1 year and/or a fine of $100—$1,000 and mandatory completion of a D. U. I. court-referred program. The court has the discretion to suspend the defendant's driving privileges for up to 6 months.[38] Subsequent convictions within five years are punishable by fine of $200—$1,500 and/or imprisonment for not more than 1 year, and suspension of driving privileges for a 6 month period is mandatory.[39] "Neither reckless driving nor any other traffic infraction" will be a lesser included offense. § 32-5A-191(c) of the Alabama Code.

Even though a person is in one of the four conditions listed in § 32-5A-191(a) of the Alabama Code, a valid defense to the charge of D. U. I. is that he was not driving or in actual physical control of the vehicle. To

MOTOR VEHICLE CRIMES.—Cont'd.

sustain a charge based on driving the vehicle, there must be some movement of the vehicle. There need not be any movement if the charge is based on actual physical control. Actual physical control requires the person to be able to drive the vehicle. If the person is found asleep in a parked vehicle, even though the motor is not running, he could awake at any time and drive off, but if he did not have the means of putting the vehicle in motion (no keys, engine, transmission, drive shaft, etc), he may not be subject to this statute.

—D. Homicide By Vehicle.

Section 32-5A-192 of the Alabama Code is similar to that of the felony-murder doctrine. The commission of a felony that results in death is felony-murder. If the proximate cause of a death is due to "the violation of any state law or municipal ordinance applying to the operation or use of a vehicle or to the regulation of traffic," it is homicide by vehicle.

The statute requires that the violation be committed unlawfully and unintentionally. Because of the latter element, homicide by vehicle could be a lesser included offense to the homicide statutes — murder, manslaughter and criminally negligent homicide.[40] The official commentary following the vehicular homicide statute states that a prosecution under the statute is not a bar to prosecution under one of the homicide statutes.

A violation of the statute is not classified as a felony or misdemeanor. It provides its own sanctions: a fine from $500 — $2,000 and/or imprisonment from 3 months — 1 year, or in the alternative, imprisonment in the state penitentiary for 1—5 years.

The statute applies to any person who causes the death of another person as a result of violating a traffic law. This statute does not apply if the underlying operation or use of the vehicle was not a violation of a state law or city ordinance. Self-defense would be a defense.

The violator need not have been operating a vehicle, only violating a law or ordinance that regulates traffic or the operation or use

MOTOR VEHICLE CRIMES.—Cont'd.

of a vehicle. If a person violates any state law that applies to the regulation of vehicles and, as a result, a death occurs, he would be within the broad wording of this statute (i.e., a person removes a stop sign without lawful authority, § 32-5A-37 of the Alabama Code, and, as a proximate cause, a death occurs in a traffic accident at that intersection).

—E. Fleeing Or Attempting To Elude Police Officers.

Alabama had no comparable statute prior to the adoption of § 32-5A-192 of the Alabama Code. This new statute creates a violation if any driver of a motor vehicle willfully fails or refuses to stop his vehicle after being given a signal to stop or otherwise flees or attempts to elude the police after being given such a signal. The signal given by the police may be by hand, voice, emergency light or siren.

The sanctions for this offense are a fine of $100 — $500 and/or imprisonment of 30 days — 6 months. This penalty is comparable to the maximum fine for a Class C misdemeanor and to the maximum imprisonment for a Class B misdemeanor under § 13A of the Alabama Code.

The wording of the statute is broad enough to include those situations where an officer is directing traffic and by hand motions instructs a driver to stop. If the driver willfully fails to do so and drives on, he could be charged under this statute. The same conduct could be charged as disobeying a police officer's lawful order, § 32-5A-4 of the Alabama Code, which carries a much lesser penalty, even for a repeat offender.[41] This statute could be used as a plea bargaining tool to force a guilty plea to the statute with the lesser sanctions.

—F. Other Crimes.

Speed restrictions are established in § 32-5A of the Alabama Code. The two most important statutes are § 32-5A-171 and 32-5A-173 of the Alabama Code. The former statute sets the maximum highway speed at 55 mph, and the latter authorizes local authorities to set speed limits within their respective jurisdictions. Additionally,

MOTOR VEHICLE CRIMES.—Cont'd.

drivers may not drive at a speed that is "greater than is reasonable and prudent under the circumstances." § 32-5A-170 of the Alabama Code. This statute can be used against drivers who, even though driving well under the stated maximum speed limit, are traveling at a speed that is dangerous because of poor road conditions, such as fog, rain, snow, ice, etc.

The speeding statute that carries with it the greatest sanctions is Racing on Highways, § 32-5A-178 of the Alabama Code. This statute is violated when any person participates, in any manner, in any "race, speed competition or contest, drag race of acceleration contest, test of physical endurance, exhibition of speed or acceleration, or for the purpose of making a speed record." The statute's applicability is restricted to races or contests that occur on a highway.[42] Drag racing on private property would not be covered. However, the statute is not restricted to drivers of the vehicles but includes any person who "in any manner participates in such race". Query: would this also include a person who is there merely watching?

The possible sanctions escalate after the first conviction: first conviction — fine $25—$500 and/or imprisonment from 5—90 days; second and subsequent convictions — fine $50—$500 and/or imprisonment from 10 days—6 months. Whether or not to suspend all driving privileges is left to the discretion of the judge. Any suspension, however, cannot exceed 6 months.

A motorcycle driver is subject to the same rights and duties as a driver of any other vehicle.[43] This part of Rules of the Road contains special provisions that apply to motor-driven cycles[44] and bicycles with a motor attached.

III. Uniform Certificate Of Title And Antitheft Laws. Code of Ala. 1975, Chapter 32-8.

—A. Generally.

This chapter is modeled on its counterpart in the Uniform State Laws. The subject matter of the chapter can be divided into

MOTOR VEHICLE CRIMES.—Cont'd.

two areas: certificate of title and security interests, and antitheft laws.

Misdemeanor violations are punishable by a fine of not more than $500 and/or imprisonment for not more than 6 months. Felony violations are punishable by fine of $500 — $5,000 and/or 1 — 10 years.[45] A violation of any provisions in Chapter 32-8 of the Alabama Code is a misdemeanor unless otherwise specified.[46]

—B. Certificate Of Title.

Most of the "crimes" involving a certificate of title are in two statutes. The following violations are misdemeanors: (1) to fraudulently allow another to use or possess a certificate of title; (2) to willfully fail to mail a certificate of title to the Alabama Department of Revenue within 10 days; (3) to willfully fail to deliver to the transferee such a certificate; and (4) to knowingly or willfully make a fraudulent application for title or registration. § 32-8-13 of the Alabama Code.

It is also a misdemeanor for a dealer to transfer in any manner any vehicle that is required to be titled when there has not been compliance with any provision of this chapter.[47] The statute applies only to dealers. It does not matter whether the dealer was acting for himself or for another.

It is a felony for anyone, with fraudulent intent, to alter, forge or counterfeit a certificate of title, or an assignment thereof, or possess a certificate knowing it is such, or, in an application for a certificate of title, to conceal or falsify any material fact. § 32-8-12 of the Alabama Code.

If a person aids, abets, etc., another to violate provision of this chapter, they are guilty of the same act, be it a misdemeanor or a felony.[48]

—C. Antitheft Laws.

The antitheft laws can be divided into two categories: (1) those dealing with the defendant's "unauthorized" conduct, and (2) those concerning a vehicle's identification number. The only "unauthorized" conduct that is punishable as a misdemeanor is the "unauthorized damaging or tampering with vehicles":

MOTOR VEHICLE CRIMES.—Cont'd.

when anyone, willfully and without right to do so, damages or tampers with a vehicle or any of it parts or components. § 32-8-83 of the Alabama Code.

There are two felony statutes: (1) the possession, concealment, sale or disposal of any vehicle knowing that it was stolen or unlawfully converted, § 32-8-82 of the Alabama Code; and (2) the taking, use, or driving of any vehicle without the owner's consent and with the intent to temporarily or otherwise deprive him of the vehicle or its possession, § 32-8-81 of the Alabama Code. This statute overlaps § 13A-8-11 of the Alabama Code (unauthorized use of vehicle), in which the required intent is to temporarily deprive the owner of his vehicle; and § 13A-8-3 through § 13A-8-5 of the Alabama Code (the theft statutes), in which the required intent is to permanently deprive the owner of his vehicle.

The two sections dealing with vehicle identification numbers (VIN) are §§ 32-8-86 and 32-8-87 of the Alabama Code. It is a misdemeanor for anyone to willfully remove or falsify the VIN, or to buy, receive, possess, sell or dispose of such an altered vehicle or engine. If either was performed with the intent to conceal or misrepresent the identity of the vehicle or engine, it is a felony. It is also a felony, punishable by a fine up to $5,000 and/or 5 years imprisonment, for anyone[49] to possess, sell or exchange or offer to do so, or to give away any certificate of title or VIN plates. Included is any owner, agent or employee of any junkyard, salvage yard or scrap metal processing plant, to have in their possession any motor vehicle that is junk or salvage or a total loss when the VIN or license plates have been unlawfully removed.

It is a misdemeanor for anyone to knowingly file a false report on the theft or conversion of a vehicle. § 32-8-85 of the Alabama Code.

IV. Motor Vehicle Accidents. Code of Ala. 1975, Chapter 32-8.

There are four duties that may, depending upon the circumstances, apply to every driver of a vehicle that is involved in an accident: (1) The driver must always return

MOTOR VEHICLE CRIMES.—Cont'd.

to the vehicle he struck; (2) If the vehicle struck was occupied or attended to by any person, or if anyone sustained an injury, the driver has the duty to give to the other person his name, address, registration number, and if requested, exhibit his driver license; (3) If there was any injury sustained, he must provide transportation to the hospital, if needed, and also provide reasonable medical assistance;[50] (4) If the vehicle was unattended, and its operator/owner cannot be located or contacted, a note containing the above information must be left in or on the struck vehicle in a conspicuous place.[51]

If a motor vehicle damages any fixture that is legally upon or adjacent to the highway, the driver must take reasonable steps to locate the owner. If the owner cannot be located, the same information required in accidents involving vehicles must be left, and an accident report filed with the local police department.[52]

If any accident results in injury to anyone, by the quickest means of communication, the local police, county sheriff or highway patrol must be notified of such accident.[53] The penalties for these violations are a fine not to exceed $5,000 and/or imprisonment for 30 days — 1 year in the county/city jail or 1 — 5 years in the state penitentiary.[54]

The Motor Vehicle Safety-Responsibility Act, § 32-7 of the Alabama Code, has provisions that apply to traffic accidents. If a person knowingly files a false or forged accident report, he is subject to a fine of up to $1,000 and/or 1 year imprisonment.[55] If the accident involved any personal injury or more than $50 property damage, a report must be filed with the Director of Public Safety within 10 days.[56] Failure to do so can result in a fine of up to $25 and a mandatory suspension of driving privileges for up to 30 days.[57]

V. Revocations And Suspensions.

The revocation of a drivers license is the termination of all driving privileges that are not subject to renewal or restoration, except by application for a new license, the disposition of which is left to the discretion

MOTOR VEHICLE CRIMES.—Cont'd.

of the Director of Public Safety.[58] Revocation is mandatory if the driver is convicted of one of seven offenses: (1) manslaughter or homicide by vehicle resulting from the operation of a motor vehicle; (2) upon a second or subsequent conviction within five years for D. U. I. (upon first conviction, revocation is within the discretion of the court); (3) any felony in which a motor vehicle is used; (4) failure to stop, render aid or identify himself when involved in a motor vehicle accident in which someone is injured; (5) perjury or the making of a false affidavit or statement under oath to the Director of Public Safety; (6) three reckless driving convictions within 12 months; and (7) unauthorized use of a motor vehicle that is not a felony.[59]

The suspension of a drivers license is the temporary withdrawal of all driving privileges for a specified period of time.[60] Suspension is authorized, without a preliminary hearing, when a driver's record shows any of the following: (1) commission of an offense for which revocation is mandatory if convicted; (2) frequent convictions of serious traffic offenses; (3) he is a "habitually reckless or negligent driver" as shown by a record of accidents or otherwise; (4) he is incompetent to drive a motor vehicle; (5) he has permitted an unlawful or fraudulent use of his vehicle; (6) he has committed a revocable or suspendable offense in another state; (7) he is convicted of fleeing or attempting to elude police officers; or (8) he is convicted of racing on the highways.[61]

Cross references.

See CONTROLLED SUBSTANCES; HOMICIDE, CRIMINALLY NEGLIGENT; OBSCURING IDENTITY OF VEHICLE; RECKLESS ENDANGERMENT; UNAUTHORIZED USE OF VEHICLE/UNLAWFUL BREAKING AND ENTERING A VEHICLE.

---

1. *Code of Ala. 1975, § 32-5A-8(A).*
2. *Code of Ala. 1975, §§ 32-5A-1 through 32-5A-13.*
3. *Code of Ala. 1975, §§ 32-5A-30 through 32-5A-37.*
4. *Code of Ala. 1975, §§ 32-5A-50 through 32-5A-62.*
5. *Code of Ala. 1975, §§ 32-5A-80 through 32-5A-92.*
6. *Code of Ala. 1975, §§ 32-5A-110 through 32-5A-116.*
7. *Code of Ala. 1975, §§ 32-5A-130 through 32-5A-139.*
8. *Code of Ala. 1975, §§ 32-5A-150 through 32-5A-155.*
9. *Code of Ala. 1975, §§ 32-5A-170 through 32-5A-178.*
10. *Code of Ala. 1975, §§ 32-5A-190 through 32-5A-195.*
11. *Code of Ala. 1975, §§ 32-5A-210 through 32-5A-222.*
12. *Code of Ala. 1975, §§ 32-5A-240 through 32-5A-245.*
13. *Code of Ala. 1975, §§ 32-5A-260 through 32-5A-266.*
14. *The first conviction of a misdemeanor is punishable by fine not to exceed $100 or imprisonment not to exceed 10 days; for the second conviction within one year, by fine not to exceed $200 and/or imprisonment not to exceed 30 days; for any subsequent conviction, by fine not to exceed $500 and/or imprisonment not to exceed 3 months.*
15. *"Imprisonment for not less than one year nor more than 10 years, or by a fine of not more than $5,000," or both. This penalty is equal to a Class C felony under Code of Ala. 1975, § 13A. See also Code of Ala. 1975, § 32-8-14.*
16. *Code of Ala. 1975, § 32-5A-2(2).*
17. *Graves v. Wildsmith, 278 Ala. 228, 117 So. 2d 448 (1965).*
18. *Buffalo Rock Co. v. Davis, 228 Ala. 603, 154 So. 2d 556 (1934).*
19. *Buffalo Rock Co. v. Davis, 228 Ala. 603, 154 So. 2d 556 (1934).*
20. *Wunderlich v. Franklin, 100 F. 2d 164 (5th Cir. 1938).*
21. *Code of Ala. 1975, § 32-5A-190(c).*
22. *Code of Ala. 1975, § 32-5A-190(b).*
23. *Code of Ala. 1975, § 32-5A-191(a).*
24. *The police officer's testimony as to the field sobriety tests may be sufficient for a D. U. I. conviction.*
25. *Code of Ala. 1975, § 32-5A-194(a)(1).*
26. *Such a person will not incur any civil or criminal liability if they properly administer a blood test. Code of Ala. 1975, § 32-5A-194(a)(2).*
27. *Code of Ala. 1975, § 32-5A-194(d).*
28. *Code of Ala. 1975, § 32-5A-194(a)(3).*
29. *Code of Ala. 1975, § 32-5A-194(a)(4).*
30. *Code of Ala. 1975, § 32-5-192(a).*
31. *Redus v. State, 398 So. 2d 757 (Ala. Crim. App. 1981), cert. denied, 398 So. 2d 762 (Ala. Crim. App. 1981).*

MOTOR VEHICLE CRIMES.—Cont'd.

32. Code of Ala. 1975, § 32-5-192(c).
33. Hill v. State, 366 So. 2d 318 (Ala. 1979).
34. Code of Ala. 1975, § 32-5-192(b).
35. Davis v. State, 131 Ala. 10, 31 So. 569 (1902).
36. Schmerber v. California, 384 U. S. 757, 86 S. Ct. 1826, 16 L. Ed. 2d 908 (1966).
37. Hubbard v. State, 283 Ala. 183, 215 So. 2d 267 (1968), judgment vacated at 408 U. S. 934, 92 S. Ct. 2851, 33 L. Ed. 2d 747 (1972), resentencing at 290 Ala. 118, 274 So. 2d 298 (1973).
38. Code of Ala. 1975, § 32-5A-191(c).
39. Code of Ala. 1975, § 32-5A-191(d).
40. Code of Ala. 1975, §§ 13A-6-2 through 13A-6-4.
41. The minimum punishment that may be imposed if sentenced according to Code of Ala. 1975, § 32-5A-8 could be as little as $1.00 or 1 day. The minimum sanction that can be imposed under the fleeing statute, even for a first offender, would be for **not less** than 30 days.
42. Highway is defined as the "entire width between the boundary lines of every way publicly maintained when any part thereof is open to the use of the public for purposes of vehicular travel." Code of Ala. 1975, § 32-1-1.1(23).
43. Code of Ala. 1975, § 32-5A-24.
44. A motor-driven cycle is a motorcycle that has a "motor which produces not to exceed five brake horsepower nor to exceed 150 cubic centimeter engine displacement, and weighs less than 200 pounds fully equipped." Code of Ala. 1975, § 32-1-1.1(34).
45. Code of Ala. 1975, § 32-8-14.
46. Code of Ala. 1975, § 32-8-13(5).
47. Code of Ala. 1975, § 32-8-30(b).
48. Code of Ala. 1975, § 32-8-11.
49. Including a firm or corporation and its officers, agents or employees.
50. Code of Ala. 1975, § 32-10-2. However, the statute does not abrogate the duty to provide such assistance in a nonnegligent manner.
51. Code of Ala. 1975, § 32-10-3.
52. Code of Ala. 1975, § 32-10-4.
53. Code of Ala. 1975, § 32-10-5.
54. Code of Ala. 1975, § 32-10-6.
55. Code of Ala. 1975, § 32-7-37(b).
56. Code of Ala. 1975, § 32-7-5.
57. Code of Ala. 1975, § 32-7-37(a).
58. Code of Ala. 1975, § 32-1-1.1(53).
59. Code of Ala. 1975, § 32-5A-195(j).
60. Code of Ala. 1975, § 32-1-1.1(71).
61. Code of Ala. 1975, § 32-5A-195(k).

MULTIPLE CONVICTIONS. Code of Ala. 1975, § 13A-1-8.

"When the same conduct of a defendant may establish the commission of more than one offense, the defendant may be prosecuted for each such offense. He may not, however, be convicted of more than one offense if:

"(1) One offense is included in the other, as defined in section 13A-1-9 [Lesser included offenses]; or

"(2) One offense consists only of a conspiracy or other form of preparation to commit the other; or

"(3) Inconsistent findings of fact are required to establish the commission of the offenses; or

"(4) The offenses differ only in that one is defined to prohibit a designated kind of conduct generally and the other to prohibit a specific instance of such conduct."

And, according to § 13A-1-9(a) of the Alabama Code, "[a] defendant may be convicted of an offense included in an offense charged." Section 13A-1-9(a)(1) through (4) of the Alabama Code goes on to define a "lesser included offense" by stating that "[a]n offense is an included one if:

"(1) It is established by proof of the same or fewer than all the facts required to establish the commission of the offense charged; or

"(2) It consists of an attempt or solicitation to commit the offense charged or to commit a lesser included offense; or

"(3) It is specifically designated by statute as a lesser degree of the offense charged; or

"(4) It differs from the offense charged only in the respect that a less serious injury or risk of injury to the same person, property or public interests, or a lesser kind of culpability suffices to establish its commission."

Note, the attorney must keep in mind, as stated in § 13A-1-9(b) of the Alabama Code, that "[t]he court shall not charge the jury with respect to an included offense unless there is a rational basis for a verdict convicting the defendant of the included offense."

Comments.

Sections 13A-1-8 and 13A-1-9 of the Ala-

MULTIPLE CONVICTIONS.—Cont'd.
bama Code codify and expand the double jeopardy protection afforded criminal defendants by the United States and the Alabama Constitution.[1] The notion that a person shall not be twice placed in jeopardy for the same offense actually includes two separate prohibitions: (1) an individual shall not be subjected to successive prosecutions for the same offense and (2) an individual shall not receive two punishments for the same offense. The former may be described as the procedural bar of double jeopardy. It is based on a policy of judicial economy, avoiding harassment of defendants and the "furtherance of psychological security."[2] The issues faced within the successive prosecution rubric are collateral estoppel,[3] joinder of prosecution,[4] determination of manifest necessity to terminate an initial trial[5] and the determination of whether jeopardy had attached at the first trial.[6] Because they are essentially procedural protections, the reader is referred elsewhere for treatment of these issues.[7] The double jeopardy prohibition of multiple convictions, on the other hand, is an aspect of the substantive criminal law. According to the Supreme Court of the United States, "[t]he legislature remains free under the Double Jeopardy guarantee to define crimes and fix punishments; but once the legislature has acted courts may not impose more than one punishment for the same offense."[8] The substantive aspect of double jeopardy has been described as "a limitation upon judicial interpretation of the substantive criminal law."[9]

The attempt to determine whether a particular defendant is being punished twice for the "same offense" has occupied a great deal of judicial time. The narrowest kind of definition would protect the defendant only when the evidence showed that only one violation of one statute had occurred.[10] Under this kind of analysis, the only protection that would be provided a defendant under the multiple conviction bar would be against being sentenced, for example, twice for the murder of the same

MULTIPLE CONVICTIONS.—Cont'd.
person. But the courts have not restricted "same offense" so completely, and "[i]t has long been understood that separate statutory crimes need not be identical . . . in order to be the same within the meaning of the constitutional prohibition."[11]

Various types of tests have been developed to answer the question of whether the defendant is being twice punished for the same offense. Under a required evidence approach, two offenses are the same if the required elements of one are all included in the other.[12] If each crime requires an element not required by the other, there are two different crimes and both can be punished constitutionally. Under the actual evidence approach, the focus is on the evidence actually presented and whether the same evidence is being used to return two convictions.[13] If the "same" evidence is the only evidence of two crimes, they are constitutionally the same crimes, and double conviction is not allowed. Under a transactional or behavioral approach, multiple punishment will be barred if the court determines that the conduct involved constituted a single episode or transaction.[14] This latter test is the most defendant-oriented. The majority of courts apply the required evidence standard, which was defined as follows by the United States Supreme Court in Blockburger v. United States: ". . . where the same act or transaction constitutes a violation of two distinct statutory provisions, the test to be applied to determine whether there are two offenses or only one, is whether each provision requires proof of an additional fact which the other does not."[15]

This Blockburger required-evidence test has been the Supreme Court's standard analysis of the protection afforded to criminal defendants under the federal Double Jeopardy Clause and any application of the other, more defendant-protective standards is based on state constitutional or statutory provisions.

Alabama's rule against multiple punishments is stated in § 13A-1-8(b) of the Alabama Code, which provides, as a general

MULTIPLE CONVICTIONS.—Cont'd.

rule, that where the defendant's conduct establishes the violation of more than one statute, he may be prosecuted for each crime. The statute also provides, however, that a defendant cannot be convicted of both (1) a greater and lesser included offense or (2) a general prohibition and a specific prohibition of the same conduct. While the latter provision forbids conviction of, for example, both theft by taking and motor vehicle theft, reference must be made to § 13A-1-9(a)(1) through (4) of the Alabama Code to determine what is a lesser included offense.

---

1. *U. S. Const., Amend. V; Ala. Const., Art. I, § 9.*
2. *Note, "Statutory Implementation of the Double Jeopardy clauses: New Life for a Moribund Constitutional Guarantee", 65 Yale L. J. 339, 341 (1956).*
3. *See Ashe v. Swenson, 397 U. S. 436, 90 S. Ct. 1189, 25 L. Ed. 2d 469 (1970).*
4. *See People v. White, 390 Mich. 245, 212 N. W. 2d 222 (1973); see also Note, "Double Jeopardy: Multiple Prosecutions From the Same Transaction", 15 Am. Crim. L. Rev. 259, 286-89 (1978).*
5. *See, e.g., Arizona v. Washington, 434 U. S. 487, 98 S. Ct. 824, 54 L. Ed. 2d 717 (1978) and cases cited therein. See also, N. Chiarkas, Alabama Criminal Trial Practice.*
6. *See N. Chiarkas, Alabama Criminal Trial Practice.*
7. *See N. Chiarkas, Alabama Criminal Trial Practice.*
8. *Brown v. Ohio, 432 U. S. 161, 165, 97 S. Ct. 2221, 53 L. Ed. 2d 197 (1977).*
9. *Schwartz, "Multiple Punishment for the 'Same Offense:' Michigan Grapples With the Definitional Problem", 25 Wayne L. Rev. 825 (1979).*
10. *There is a great deal of precedent dealing with the question of how many violations of a statute have been proven. This is particularly relevant in the area of multiple victims of a single accident or theft. Usually, an act that has several victims constitutes several violations of the same statute. But see Corson v. State, 144 Ga. App. 559, 241 S. E. 2d 454 (1978).*
11. *Brown v. Ohio, 432 U. S. 161, 164, 97 S. Ct. 2221, 53 L. Ed. 2d 187 (1977).*
12. *This test derives from an early Massachusetts case. Morey v. Commonwealth, 108 Mass. 433 (1871).*

MULTIPLE CONVICTIONS.—Cont'd.

13. *See, e.g., Estep v. State, 11 Okla. Crim. 103, 143 P. 64 (1914).*
14. *See, e.g., Crumbley v. City of Atlanta, 68 Ga. App. 69, 22 S. E. 2d 181 (1942).*
15. *Blockburger v. United States, 284 U. S. 299, 304, 52 S. Ct. 180, 76 L. Ed. 306 (1932).*

MURDER. Code of Ala. 1975, § 13A-6-2.

"A person commits the crime of murder if:

"(1) With intent to cause the death of another person,[1] he causes the death of that person or of another person; or

"(2) Under circumstances manifesting extreme indifference to human life, he recklessly engages in conduct which creates a grave risk of death to a person other than himself, and thereby causes the death of another person; or

"(3) He commits or attempts to commit arson in the first degree, burglary in the first or second degree, escape in the first degree, kidnapping in the first degree, rape in the first degree, robbery in any degree, sodomy in the first degree or any other felony clearly dangerous to human life and, in the course of and in furtherance of the crime that he is committing or attempting to commit, or in immediate flight therefrom, he, or another participant if there be any, causes the death of any person."

Classification.

Class A felony.

Comments.

Note that the present statute eliminates the various degrees of murder, and sets down criteria for three types of criminal homicide.[2]

In simplifying criminal homicide, the four culpable mental states[3] have been included. (But see Strict liability, § 13A-2-4 of the Alabama Code).

Excluded from this section are: the fictional types of expressed and implied malice, the "transferred intent" doctrine, the "depraved mind" concept, and the deliberate, malicious and premeditated mental state concepts. The legal effect of a homicide committed during the commission of felony (not included under the felony-murder rule) has been clarified.

MURDER.—Cont'd.

In the 17th century, Coke defined common law murder as: "When a man of sound memory and of the age of discretion unlawfully kills any reasonable creature in being, and under the King's peace, with malice aforethought, either expressed or implied by the law, the death taking place within a year and a day." Common law first degree murder in Alabama is defined in Mitchell v. State.[4] All other homicides are second degree murder. There were no degrees of murder at common law, as law provided for the death penalty for all types of murder.

Section 13A-6-2 of the Alabama Code differs from the former murder statute, § 13-1-70 of the Alabama Code, by eliminating the degree distinction based on deliberation and premeditation. Statutory homicide does not demand that the act be well thought out or planned, nor does it demand that the act be committed while the perpetrator is in a cool state.[5]

Section 13A-6-2 of the Alabama Code states that reckless endangerment resulting in homicide is murder.[6]

This statute voids the former need to establish transferred intent. The anachronistic rule that "the law follows the bullet" is replaced by § 13A-6-2(a)(1) of the Alabama Code (intent to cause the death of another) and § 13A-6-2(a)(2) of the Alabama Code (the reckless engagement in conduct that creates a grave risk of death).

At early common law, death occurring during the attempt of any felony was deemed murder. But later, this was refined to apply to only felonies dangerous to life and likely to cause death (i.e., arson, burglary, rape, robbery and kidnapping). § 13A-6-2(a)(3) of the Alabama Code presents a broader felony-murder rule than the past Alabama Code section with the addition of escape, kidnapping in the first degree, sodomy in the first degree, and "any other felony clearly dangerous to human life" and includes "immediate flight."

Defenses.

(1) Section 13A-6-2(b) of the Alabama Code speaks directly to what circumstances will take the killing out of the murder concept — the legal provocation of a killing committed in a sudden heat of passion without a reasonable "cooling-off" period.

(2) Self-defense.

(3) Accident.

(4) Defense of others.

(5) Public authority.

(6) Defense of property.[7]

(7) Prevention of crime.[8]

(8) Insanity.

(9) Other mitigating factors, such as infancy, incapacity or intoxication.

Query.

Under § 13A-6-2(a)(3) of the Alabama Code, when does a felony begin and end? At the end of the immediate escape? Is this to be a question of fact?

Cross references.

See N. Chiarkas, Alabama Criminal Trial Practice, §§ 14-36 (Special plea of insanity) and 26-9 (Capital punishment). See also ARSON; ASSAULT; BURGLARY; HOMICIDE, CRIMINALLY NEGLIGENT; INSANITY; INTOXICATION; MANSLAUGHTER; ROBBERY; SODOMY.

---

1. *Code of Ala. 1975, § 13A-6-1(2) defines "person": "Such term, when referring to the victim of a criminal homicide, means a human being who had been born and was alive at the time of the homicidal act."*

2. *Code of Ala. 1975, § 13A-6-1(3) defines "criminal homicide": "Murder, manslaughter, or criminally negligent homicide."*

3. *As defined in § 13A-2-2:*

"(1) INTENTIONALLY. A person acts intentionally with respect to a result or to conduct described by a statute defining an offense, when his purpose is to cause that result or to engage in that conduct.

"(2) KNOWINGLY. A person acts knowingly with respect to conduct or to a circumstance described by a statute defining an offense when he is aware that his conduct is of that nature or that the circumstance exists.

"(3) RECKLESSLY. A person acts recklessly with respect to a result or to a circumstance described by a statute defining an offense when he is aware of and consciously disregards a substantial and unjustifiable risk that the result will occur or that the circumstance exists. The

MURDER.—Cont'd.

risk must be of such nature and degree that disregard thereof constitutes a gross deviation from the standard of conduct that a reasonable person would observe in the situation. A person who creates a risk but is unaware thereof solely by reason of voluntary intoxication, as defined in subdivision (e)(2) of section 13A-3-3, acts recklessly with respect thereto.

"(4) CRIMINAL NEGLIGENCE. A person acts with criminal negligence with respect to a result or to a circumstance which is defined by statute as an offense when he fails to perceive a substantial and unjustifiable risk that the result will occur or that the circumstance exists. The risk must be of such nature and degree that the failure to perceive it constitutes a gross deviation from the standard of care that a reasonable person would observe in the situation. A court or jury may consider statutes or ordinances regulating the defendant's conduct as bearing upon the question of criminal negligence."

4. *Mitchell v. State, 60 Ala. 26 (1877).*
5. *"Premeditation and deliberation" may exist while the defendant is still holding the deadly weapon. White v. State, 236 Ala. 124, 181 So. 109 (1938).*
6. *Reed v. State, 25 Ala. App. 18, 142 So. 441 (1932), wherein driver was intoxicated and recklessly driving on a highway with knowledge of the presence of others; Gautney v. State, 284 Ala. 82, 222 So. 2d 175 (1969), wherein the court found murder in the intent to recklessly fire a pistol.*
7. *See Code of Ala. 1975, § 13A-3-23(a)(3), burglary in any degree and robbery in any degree, and § 13A-3-25(b)(2), prevention of the commission of arson in the first or second degree.*
8. *See Code of Ala. 1975, §§ 13A-3-23 to 13A-3-25.*

NARCOTICS. See CONTROLLED SUBSTANCES.

NEGOTIABLE INSTRUMENT, NEGOTIATING A WORTHLESS.

Code of Ala. 1975, §§ 13A-9-13.1 through 13A-9-13.3.

Charged as: Negotiating worthless negotiable instrument.

"(a) A person commits the crime of negotiating a worthless negotiable instrument[1] if he negotiates[2] or delivers[3] a negotiable instrument for a thing of value and with the intent, knowledge or expectation that it will not be honored by the drawee.

"(b) For the purposes of this section, it is prima facie evidence that the maker or drawer[4] intended, knew or expected that the instrument would not be honored if:

"(1) The maker or drawer had no such account with the drawee at the time the negotiable instrument was negotiated or delivered,[5] . . . or

"(2) Payment was refused by the drawee for lack of funds, upon presentation within 30 days after delivery,[6] and the maker or drawer shall not have paid the holder thereof the amount due thereon, together with a service charge of not more than $10.00, within 10 days after receiving written notice from the holder of the instrument that payment was refused upon such instrument,[7] . . . or

"(3) Notice that payment was refused is mailed by certified or registered mail and is returned undelivered to the sender, when such notice is mailed within a reasonable time after dishonor[8] to the address printed on the instrument or given by the maker or drawer at the time of issuance of the instrument."

Classification.

Class A misdemeanor.

Comments.

While usually referred to as the bad check statute, § 13A-9-13.1 of the Alabama Code applies to any negotiable instrument. This statute punishes the negotiation or delivery of the negotiable instrument even without a present exchange to promote and maintain public confidence. Intent is presumed if the instrument is not honored by the drawee on presentment. Whether there were sufficient funds in the account when the paper was executed is irrelevant. The offense is classified without regard to the face amount of the instrument or the number of instruments passed within a stated time. If the passer actually receives property, he may be prosecuted for the higher offenses of theft or attempted theft.

NEGOTIABLE INSTRUMENT, NEGOTIATING A WORTHLESS. —Cont'd.

Defenses.

(1) Lack of intent, knowledge or expectation that the instrument will not be honored by the drawee.

(2) Presentation later than 30 days after delivery.

(3) Failure of the receiving party to obtain proper identification.

(4) Lack of initials signifying that the receiving party witnessed the signature or endorsement of the party presenting the instrument.

Cross references.

See "Deception by promised performance" defined, § 13A-8-1(1)f of the Alabama Code; "Theft by deception" defined, § 13A-8-2(2) of the Alabama Code.

---

1. *Code of Ala. 1975, § 7-3-104.*
2. *Code of Ala. 1975, § 7-3-202.*
3. *Code of Ala. 1975, § 7-1-201(14).*
4. *Prima facie evidence of identity.*

"(a) In any prosecution or action under the provisions of section 13A-9-13.1, a negotiable instrument for which the information required in subsections (b) and (c) of this section is available at the time of issuance shall constitute prima facie evidence of the identity of the party issuing the negotiable instrument and that such person was a party authorized to draw upon the named account.

"(b) To establish this prima facie evidence, the following information regarding the identity of the party presenting the negotiable instrument shall be requested by the party receiving such instrument: the presenter's name, residence address, and home phone number. Such information may be provided by either of two methods:

"(1) It may be recorded upon the negotiable instrument itself; or

"(2) The number of a check-cashing identification card issued by the receiving party may be recorded on the negotiable instrument. Such check-cashing identification card shall be issued only after the information required in this subsection has been placed on file by the receiving party.

"(c) In addition to the information required in subsection (b) of this section, the party receiving a negotiable instrument shall witness the signature or endorsement of the party presenting such negotiable instrument and, as evidence of such, the receiving party shall initial the negotiable instrument." Code of Ala. 1975, § 13A-9-13.3.

5. *Code of Ala. 1975, § 7-3-503(2).*
6. *Code of Ala. 1975, § 7-1-201(14).*
7. *"(a) Notice mailed by certified or registered mail, evidenced by return receipt, to the address printed on the instrument or given at the time of issuance shall be deemed sufficient and equivalent to notice having been received by the person making, drawing, uttering or delivering said instrument.*

"(b) The form of notice shall be substantially as follows:

'This statutory notice is provided pursuant to section 13A-9-13.2. You are hereby notified that a check or instrument numbered ———, apparently issued by you on ——— (date), drawn upon ——— (name of bank), and payable to ———, has been dishonored. Pursuant to Alabama law, you have 10 days from receipt of this notice to tender payment of the full amount of such check or instrument plus a service charge of not more than $10.00, the total amount due being $———. Unless this amount is paid in full within the specified time above the holder of such check or instrument may assume that you delivered the instrument with intent to defraud and may turn over the dishonored instrument and all other available information relating to this incident to the proper authorities for criminal prosecution.'

"(c) Any party holding a worthless negotiable instrument and giving notice in substantially similar form to that provided in subsection (b) of this section shall be immune from civil or criminal liability for the giving of such notice and for proceeding under the forms of such notice." Code of Ala. 1975, § 13A-9-13.2.

8. *Code of Ala. 1975, § 7-3-508.*

NONSUPPORT. Code of Ala. 1975, § 13A-13-4.

"A man or woman commits the crime of nonsupport if he or she intentionally[1] fails to provide support which that person is able to provide[2] and which that person knows[3] he or she is legally obligated to provide to a dependent spouse or child less than 19 years of age."

Classification.

Class A misdemeanor.

NONSUPPORT.—Cont'd.

Comments.

Under this section, Alabama law now recognizes nonsupport as a crime separate and distinct from that of abandonment or desertion. The elements of nonsupport are: (1) a legal obligation to support (either the spouse or a child under 19 years); (2) the ability to support; (3) an intentional failure to support; and (4) knowledge of the obligation (which is inferred as a matter of law regarding a spouse and legitimate children). The statute does not define support, but instead lists "food, shelter, clothing, medical attention and other necessary care" as examples.[4]

Subdivision (c) of this section specifically includes in the classification "children," those "born out of wedlock and whose paternity has been admitted by the actor or has been established in a civil suit." This clarifies the requirement that the offender "know" of the legal obligation.

Although the statute supposedly eliminates discrimination based on wealth by recognizing the concept of the "ability to support", its practical effect is to protect the offender who, because of passion or emotion, intentionally remains idle, unproductive, and steadfastly refuses to render support. (At best the burden of proof required for conviction is increased significantly). The commentary to the statute reflects a concern for the minimum needs of the husband, as well as for the needs of any illegitimate children he may have. However, the apparent intent of the statute may be thwarted by the construction of the "ability to pay" loophole provided by the drafters. While the statute does not discriminate between the sexes, and it is careful to place the obligation of support of children on both the husband and wife, it does not articulate the criteria for establishing whether or not spousal support is owed.

Defenses.

(1) Unintentional failure to provide support.

(2) Lack of knowledge that accused was legally obligated.

(3) Lack of legal obligation to provide

NONSUPPORT.—Cont'd.

support.

(4) Lack of ability to provide support.

(5) Ascertain that the accused is being prosecuted for failing to provide support to a person that does not fall within the classifications of either a "spouse" or "child" as defined under this chapter.

(6) Section 13A-13-6(b) states that a person doesn't commit an offense under the nonsupport statute for the "sole reason he provides a child under the age of 19 years . . . with remedial treatment by spiritual means alone in accordance with the tenets and practices of a recognized church or religious denomination by a duly accredited practitioner thereof in lieu of medical treatment."

Query.

While the statute indicates that a man and a woman will not be treated differently on the basis of sex in regard to nonsupport of a child, there is no indication of the factors to be considered where spousal nonsupport is concerned. The common law version of this crime relied upon the differences between the sexes as the basis for granting spousal nonsupport, and without further elaboration, this statute establishes the same common law result. In addition, there is some question as to the need for a criminal sanction for spousal nonsupport where the civil contempt order can accomplish the same end in the case of one able, but unwilling, to pay.

Cross references.

See CHILD, ABANDONMENT OF; CHILD WELFARE, ENDANGERING; JUVENILE PROCEEDINGS.

---

1. *Intentionally means a willful failure or willful refusal without just cause. St. John v. State, 22 Ala. App. 115, 113 So. 2d 321 (1927).*
2. *"Inability to provide" support recognizes the principle that indigents cannot be incarcerated for the inability to pay. Tate v. Short, 401 U. S. 395, 91 S. Ct. 668, 28 L. Ed. 2d 130 (1971). It is settled Alabama law that imprisonment for contempt should never be imposed by a judge where the failure to pay alimony, etc., is not from contumacy, but from inability to comply with the order. Muery v. Muery, 46 Ala. App. 617, 247 So.*

NONSUPPORT.—Cont'd.

2d 123 (1971), cert. denied, 287 Ala. 737, 247 So. 2d 128 (1971).

3. *Knowledge of the obligation to pay is an element of the crime that must be proved by the prosecution. Knowledge of paternity of the child must be admitted or determined by a civil court decree in order to obtain a conviction for nonsupport of a child.*
4. *Code of Ala. 1975, § 13A-13-4(b).*

NOXIOUS SUBSTANCE, USE OR POSSESSION OF. Code of Ala. 1975, §§ 13A-7-27 and 13A-7-28.

Charged as: Criminal use or possession of noxious substance.

"A person commits the crime of criminal use of a noxious substance if he knowingly deposits on the land or in the building or vehicle of another, without his consent, any stink bomb or device, irritant or offensive-smelling substance, with the intent to interfere with another's use of the land, building or vehicle." § 13A-7-27(a) of the Alabama Code.

"A person commits the crime of criminal possession of noxious substances if he possesses, manufactures or transports any stink bomb or device, irritant, offensive-smelling or injurious substance, and intends that the injurious article or substance be used in the commission of any crime."[1] § 13A-7-28(a) of the Alabama Code.

Classification.

Class A misdemeanor, criminal use of noxious substance.

Class A misdemeanor, criminal possession of noxious substance.

Comments.

These statutes are intended to prohibit the intentional interference with another's use of his land, building or vehicle by the use of a stink bomb, tear gas or similar substance. The commentary indicates that the offense can be committed against the general public as well as against the individual. Particular note should be taken that an element of the crime requires the substance be "deposited on" the land, or "in" the building or vehicle of another. A less technical, but perhaps more important, point is whatever physical act is required, there must be a specific intent to interfere with the use of land, building or vehicle. Possession includes the manufacture and transportation of the substance. For unknown reasons it does not include sale or distribution. The basic elements of criminal possession are possession and an intent to use the substance in the commission of any crime. This makes the scope of possession relatively broader.

Defenses.

Relative to use:

(1) Consent.
(2) Lack of intent to interfere.
(3) Did not knowingly deposit.
(4) Defendant's own land, building, or vehicle.

Relative to possession:

(1) Did not possess, manufacture or transport.
(2) Did not intend substance be used in the commission of a crime.

---

1. *Regarding the unconstitutionality of the old law in this area, see Bolin v. State, 266 Ala. 256, 96 So. 2d 582 (1957).*

OBSCENE MATERIALS, SALE, EXHIBITION, ETC., TO MINORS. Code of Ala. 1975, §§ 13A-12-171 and 13A-12-172.

Charged as: Display, distribution, exhibition or possession with intent to display, distribute or exhibit obscene works to minors prohibited.

Section 13A-12-171 of the Alabama Code, provides:

"It shall be unlawful for any person[1] knowingly[2] to show, exhibit, display, sell or distribute[3] to a minor[4] any obscene[5] work,[6] or knowingly to possess any obscene work with the intent to show, exhibit, display, sell or distribute it to a minor, or knowingly to display for sale,[7] in any business establishment frequented by minors or where minors are or may be invited as part of the general public, any obscene work or

OBSCENE MATERIALS, SALE, EXHIBITION, ETC., TO MINORS.—Cont'd.

any portion whatsoever of any obscene work."

Section 13A-12-172 of the Alabama Code provides:

"It shall be unlawful for any person knowingly by any method or means to exhibit, or aid or abet in the exhibition of, any obscene performance[8] with knowledge that a minor is present in the audience, or knowingly by any method or means to exhibit, or aid or abet in the exhibition of, any obscene performance with reckless disregard as to whether a minor is present in an audience, or knowingly by any method or means to exhibit, or aid or abet in the exhibition of, any obscene performance where it is likely or probable that a minor is present in an audience."

Classification.

"Any person who violates [these sections] shall be guilty of a misdemeanor and, upon conviction, must be fined not more than $10,000.00 and may also be imprisoned in the county jail or sentenced to hard labor for the county for not more than one year." § 13A-12-178 of the Alabama Code.

Comments.

The key to successful prosecution under this division is proving requisite knowledge. Consider what must be proven to convict an actor of selling obscene material to a minor. First, it must be shown that the actor intentionally sold the work. Second, the state must show that the work is one that the actor knew was obscene with respect to minors. Third, the state must prove that the actor knew that the person to whom he sold the work was a minor.

The second and third aspects of the actor's conduct are difficult to establish, at best. The meaning of obscenity will vary vis-à-vis the "contemporary community standard." The state has the burden of proving that the work is obscene as it relates to minors, and that the actor "knew" it was obscene as it relates to minors.

Finally, the state must prove the actor knew that the person to whom he sold the obscene

OBSCENE MATERIALS, SALE, EXHIBITION, ETC., TO MINORS.—Cont'd.

work was a minor. And, honest mistake as to the age of a minor will constitute a defense to prosecution.

Persons acting in furtherance of a bona fide scientific or educational purpose are exempt from prosecution under these provisions.[9] Parents or guardians are similarly exempt from prosecution. Parents or guardians who accompany minors waive application of these provisions with respect to transactions occurring in their presence.[10]

Note, either with the normal procedure of issuing a search warrant, or with the judge or magistrate actually viewing the obscene work or material and authorizing a search warrant, the materials can be seized and must be returned within 24 hours unless criminal prosecution has begun.[11]

An advisory hearing can occur after prosecution has begun to determine if the performance or work is obscene; this cannot be used in the criminal prosecution.[12]

The work used in violation of this Code can not only be forfeited but also destroyed. The work and the owner[13] must be made a party if possible.[14]

The government is given the power to extradite persons charged with these crimes.[15]

Defenses.

(1) Honest mistake as to age of minor (have to show person charged made a reasonable, bona fide attempt to ascertain true age). § 13A-12-174 of the Alabama Code.

(2) Person charged did not possess intent, had no reason to believe further inspection was needed, and did not act recklessly.

(3) Material or performance was not open to general public and there was no reason to believe a minor would be present.

(4) Material was not considered obscene for minors by the average person.

(5) Material was for scientific, educational, etc., purposes. § 13A-12-173(1) of the Alabama Code.

(6) Person committing act is minor's parent

OBSCENE MATERIALS, SALE, EXHIBITION, ETC., TO MINORS. —Cont'd.

or guardian. § 13A-12-173(2) of the Alabama Code.

(7) Minor was accompanied by parent or guardian who gave their consent. § 13A-12-173(3) of the Alabama Code.

(8) Owner was not a consenting party in display, exhibit, etc. § 13A-12-179 of the Alabama Code.

Query.

Is an actor culpable for sale, distribution, etc., of a "portion" of an obscene work under § 13A-12-171 of the Alabama Code?

Cross references.

See CHILD WELFARE, ENDANGERING; OBSCENE MATERIALS DISPLAYING OR DEPICTING CHILDREN.

---

1. *"PERSON. Any individual and, except where inappropriate, any partnership, firm, association, corporation or other legal entity." Code of Ala. 1975, § 13A-12-170(9).*
2. *"KNOWINGLY. The intentional doing of an act involving a work or performance when a person knows the nature of the work or performance when he has knowledge of, or good reason to know, or a reasonable ground for belief which warrants further inspection or inquiry of the character and content of the work or performance." Code of Ala. 1975, § 13A-12-170(10).*
3. *"DISTRIBUTE. To transfer possession of or title to, whether with or without monetary consideration." Code of Ala. 1975, § 13A-12-170(11).*
4. *"MINOR. Any unmarried person under the age of 18 years." Code of Ala. 1975, § 13A-12-170(1).*
5. *"OBSCENE. a. To the average person, applying contemporary community standards, the work or performance, taken as a whole, appeals to the prurient interest of minors; and b. The work or performance depicts or describes, in a patently offensive way for minors, sexual conduct, actual or simulated, normal or perverted; and c. The work or performance, taken as a whole, lacks serious literary, artistic, political or scientific value for minors." Code of Ala. 1975, § 13A-12-170(2).*
6. *"WORK. Any book, magazine, newspaper or other printed or written material, or any picture, drawing, photograph, film, videotape, motion picture or other pictorial representation, or any sound recording, or any statue or other figure, or any other article, device or material." Code of Ala. 1975, § 13A-12-170(3).*
7. *"DISPLAY FOR SALE. To expose, place, exhibit or in any fashion display any work for the purpose of the sale of such work to any person in such a manner that the work can be physically examined or seen." Code of Ala. 1975, § 13A-12-170(13).*
8. *"PERFORMANCE. Any film, videotape, motion picture, sound recording, play, dance or other exhibition or presentation, whether pictured, animated or live, presented or performed before any audience of one or more persons." Code of Ala. 1975, § 13A-12-170(4).*
9. *Code of Ala. 1975, §§ 13A-12-171 through 13A-12-173.*
10. *Code of Ala. 1975, § 13A-12-173(2) and (3).*
11. *Code of Ala. 1975, § 13A-12-176.*
12. *Code of Ala. 1975, § 13A-12-177.*
13. *"OWNER. Any person who owns or has legal right to possession of any work." Code of Ala. 1975, § 13A-12-170(12).*
14. *Code of Ala. 1975, § 13A-12-179.*
15. *Code of Ala. 1975, § 13A-12-175.*

OBSCENE MATERIALS DISPLAYING OR DEPICTING CHILDREN. Code of Ala. 1975, §§ 13A-12-191 through 13A-12-198.

Charged as: Dissemination or public display of obscene matter depicting persons under 17 years of age involved in obscene acts.

Section 13A-12-191 of the Alabama Code states:

"Any person who shall knowingly[1] disseminate[2] or display publicly[3] any obscene[4] matter[5] displaying or depicting in any way a person under the age of 17 years engaged in or involved in any way in any obscene act of sado-masochistic abuse,[6] sexual intercourse,[7] sexual excitement,[8] masturbation,[9] nudity[10] or other sexual conduct shall be guilty of a Class C felony."

Charged as: Possession with intent to disseminate obscene matter depicting persons under 17 years of age involved in obscene acts.

Section 13A-12-192 of the Alabama Code states:

"Any person who knowingly possesses with intent to disseminate any obscene matter

OBSCENE MATERIALS DISPLAYING OR DEPICTING CHILDREN.—Cont'd.

displaying or depicting in any way a person under the age of 17 years engaged in or involved in any way in any obscene act of sado-masochistic abuse, sexual intercourse, sexual excitement, masturbation, nudity or other sexual conduct[11] shall be guilty of a Class C felony. Possession of six or more copies of the same obscene material is prima facie evidence of possession with intent to disseminate the same."

Charged as: Parents or guardian permitting children to engage in production of obscene matter.

Section 13A-12-196 of the Alabama Code states:

"Any parent or guardian who knowingly permits or allows any person under the age of 17 years to engage in the production of any obscene matter displaying or depicting in any way such person under the age of 17 years engaged in or involved in any way in any obscene act of sado-masochistic abuse, sexual excitement, masturbation, nudity or other sexual conduct shall be guilty of a Class B felony."

Charged as: Production of obscene matter depicting persons under 17 years of age involved in obscene acts.

Section 13A-12-197 of the Alabama Code states:

"Any person who knowingly films, prints, records, photographs or otherwise produces any obscene matter displaying or depicting in any way a person under the age of 17 years engaged in or involved in any way in any obscene act of sado-masochistic abuse, sexual intercourse, sexual excitement, masturbation, nudity or other sexual conduct shall be guilty of a Class A felony."

Classification.

Class C felony, dissemination of obscene matter depicting person under 17. § 13A-12-191 of the Alabama Code.

Class C felony, possession with intent to disseminate. § 13A-12-192 of the Alabama Code.

OBSCENE MATERIALS DISPLAYING OR DEPICTING CHILDREN.—Cont'd.

Class B felony, parent or guardian permitting child to engage in obscene matters. § 13A-12-196 of the Alabama Code.

Class A felony, production of obscene matter depicting persons under 17 years of age. § 13A-12-197 of the Alabama Code.

Comments.

The sections sanction the use of children under 17 years of age in obscene materials, by finding the parent or guardian who knowingly permits his child to engage in pornographic acts and the person who knowingly films, records, etc., guilty of a felony. Those persons who knowingly disseminate, place on public display or possess with intent to disseminate[12] are also guilty of a felony.

The key factors here are "knowingly," which for this section means awareness or reckless disregard, the age of the child, and whether the material is in fact obscene according to the definitions in § 13A-12-190 of the Alabama Code.[13]

Note that the state does not have to establish the identity of the child used in the obscene matter.[14] In addition, actual proof of the age of the child is not required. However, if a genuine copy of a birth certificate shows that the child is over 16 years of age the case should be dismissed.[15] In addition, several factors can be observed by the jury to determine the approximate age of the child. These factors include the general body growth and bone structure of the person; development of pubic hair and body hair; development of the sexual organs, and the context in which the person is placed.[16]

Defenses.

(1) Person had no knowledge that the child was under 17 years of age.

(2) Parents did not give their consent or did not know child was involved.

(3) Possessor did not possess six copies of the same material.

(4) Person was, in fact, over 16 years of age.

(5) Material was not obscene.

(6) Material was for literary, scientific or educational purposes.

OBSCENE MATERIALS DISPLAYING OR DEPICTING CHILDREN.—Cont'd.

Query.

Sections 13A-12-191 and 13A-12-192 of the Alabama Code are not clear whether they are concerned with the **idea** of depicting children engaged in sexual conduct; i.e., person depicted is not really a child, but looks like a child; or perhaps, is even an **imagined** child; or rather, is concerned with protecting **actual** children from being used in obscene materials.

Cross references.

See CHILD WELFARE, ENDANGERING; OBSCENE MATERIALS, SALE, EXHIBITION, ETC., TO MINORS; OBSCENE MATTER, IMPORTATION, DISPLAY, DISTRIBUTION, ETC.

---

1. *"KNOWINGLY. A person knowingly disseminates or publicly displays obscene matter when the person knows the nature of the matter. A person knows the nature of the matter when either of the following circumstances exist:*
   "a. The person is aware of the character and content of the matter; or
   "b. The person recklessly disregards circumstances suggesting the character and content of the matter." Code of Ala. 1975, § 13A-12-190(4).
2. *"DISSEMINATE. To sell, lend or show for monetary consideration or to offer or agree to do the same." Code of Ala. 1975, § 13A-12-190(1).*
3. *"DISPLAY PUBLICLY. The exposing, placing, posting, exhibiting or in any fashion displaying in any location, whether public or private, an item in such a manner that it may be readily seen and its content or character distinguished by normal unaided vision viewing it from a public thoroughfare, depot or vehicle." Code of Ala. 1975, § 13A-12-190(2).*
4. *"OBSCENE. When used to describe any act or matter which contains a depiction of an act of sado-masochistic abuse, sexual intercourse, sexual excitement, masturbation, nudity or other sexual conduct, such term means such an act or matter which:*
   "a. Applying contemporary local community standards, on the whole, appeals to the prurient interest; and
   "b. Is patently offensive; and
   "c. On the whole, lacks serious literary, artistic, political or scientific value." Code of Ala. 1975, § 13A-12-190(12).

OBSCENE MATERIALS DISPLAYING OR DEPICTING CHILDREN.—Cont'd.

5. *"MATTER. Any book, magazine, newspaper or other printed or written material, or any picture, drawing, photograph, motion picture or other pictorial representation or electrical or electronic reproduction or any other articles, equipment, machines or materials." Code of Ala. 1975, § 13A-12-190(11).*
6. *"SADO-MASOCHISTIC ABUSE. Such terms means either of the following:*
   "a. Flagellation or torture, for the purpose of sexual stimulation, by or upon a person who is nude or clad in undergarments or in a revealing or bizarre costume; or
   "b. The condition of a person who is nude or clad in undergarments or in a revealing or bizarre costume being fettered, bound or otherwise physically restrained for the purpose of sexual stimulation." Code of Ala. 1975, § 13A-12-190(5).
7. *"SEXUAL INTERCOURSE. Intercourse, real or simulated, whether genital-genital, oral-genital, anal-genital or oral-anal, whether between persons of the same or opposite sex or between a human and an animal." Code of Ala. 1975, § 13A-12-190(7).*
8. *"SEXUAL EXCITEMENT. The condition of human male or female genitals when in a state of sexual stimulation." Code of Ala. 1975, § 13A-12-190(6).*
9. *"MASTURBATION. Manipulation, by hand or instrument, of the human genitals, whether one's own or another's, for the purpose of sexual stimulation." Code of Ala. 1975, § 13A-12-190(8).*
10. *"NUDITY. The lewd showing of the genitals or pubic areas, or the lewd showing of the post-pubertal human female breasts below a point immediately above the top of the areola, or the lewd showing of covered human male genitals in a discernibly turgid state. For purposes of this definition, a female breast is considered uncovered if the nipple only or the nipple and the areola only are uncovered." Code of Ala. 1975, § 13A-12-190(10).*
11. *"OTHER SEXUAL CONDUCT. Any touching of the genitals, pubic areas or buttocks of the human male or female, or the breasts of the female, whether alone or between members of the same or opposite sex or between humans and animals in an act of apparent sexual stimulation or gratification." Code of Ala. 1975, § 13A-12-190(9).*
12. *Six or more copies of the same material indicates "possession with intent to disseminate."*

OBSCENE MATERIALS DISPLAYING OR DEPICTING CHILDREN.—Cont'd.

13. See notes 1 through 11, supra.
14. Under Code of Ala. 1975, § 13A-12-194, identity of persons depicted not required.
15. Code of Ala. 1975, § 13A-12-193(a).
16. Code of Ala. 1975, § 13A-12-193(b).

OBSCENE MATTER, IMPORTATION, DISPLAY, DISTRIBUTION, ETC.

Code of Ala. 1975, §§ 13A-12-150 through 13A-12-159.

Charged as: Importation, public display, sale, distribution, manufacture or possession with intent to exhibit or distribute obscene works prohibited (§ 13A-12-151 of the Alabama Code).

"It shall be unlawful for any person knowingly:[2]

"(1) To send or cause to be sent, or bring or cause to be brought, into this state, for sale or distribution,[3] any obscene[4] work;[5] or

"(2) Within this state, to display publicly,[6] sell or distribute any obscene work, or to possess any obscene work with intent to exhibit it for monetary consideration, or to make, manufacture, print, prepare, publish, produce or possess any obscene work with intent to sell or distribute it."

Charged as: Exhibition or aiding or abetting in exhibition of obscene performances (§ 13A-12-152 of the Alabama Code).

"It shall be unlawful for any person knowingly, for any monetary consideration, to exhibit by any method or means any obscene performance, or knowingly, for any monetary consideration, to aid or abet in the exhibition of any obscene performance."[7]

Classification.

"Any person who violates [section 13A-12-151 or 13A-12-152] shall be guilty of a misdemeanor and, upon conviction, must be fined not more than $10,000.00 and may also be imprisoned in the county jail or sentenced to hard labor for the county for not more than one year."[8] § 13A-12-157 of the Alabama Code.

OBSCENE MATTER, IMPORTATION, DISPLAY, DISTRIBUTION, ETC.—Cont'd.

Comments.

The defendant must have acted intentionally or at least had reasonable grounds to believe that the character and content of the work was obscene. The intent must be to sell, distribute, or exhibit publicly or to possess with intent to exhibit for monetary consideration. No mention is made concerning persons obtaining such material for their personal use or possessing such material in their home.

Whether the work or performance is obscene is based on the view of the average person applying contemporary community standards. The obscene work or performance must depict sexual conduct,[9] including sexual intercourse,[10] masturbation, urination, bestiality, sado-masochistic abuse,[11] etc.

When a person is charged with § 13A-12-151 or 13A-12-152 of the Alabama Code, the governor has the power to request extradition if said person is located out of state.[12] Defendant, owner,[13] or state can file for an advisory hearing.[14]

Defenses.

(1) The crime was not done intentionally, or there was no reasonable basis for further inquiry. [A "friend" asks you to deliver a couple of packages to another one of his friends on your way through the state.]

(2) The possession of the obscene work or performance was for personal use.

(3) The planned exhibition was private; the general public was not invited.

(4) The average person in the particular community would not find the material offensive.

(5) The distribution of the material involved no monetary consideration.

(6) Performance or work when taken as a whole, had literary, artistic, political, or scientific value, thus was not obscene. § 13A-12-150(1) of the Alabama Code.

(7) This section does not apply to broadcast or telecasts through licensed FCA facilities. § 13A-12-159 of the Alabama Code.

OBSCENE MATTER, IMPORTATION, DISPLAY, DISTRIBUTION, ETC.
—Cont'd.

(8) The defendant was acting in furtherance of a bona fide scientific or educational endeavor. § 13A-12-153 of the Alabama Code.

(9) Section 13A-12-158 of the Alabama Code permits forfeiture and destruction of works used in violation of these sections. The work and the owner should be made a party. The defense of the owner is not being either a consenting party or in privy to the violation.

Cross references.

See Title 47 U. S. C. A.; Construction and punishment of offenses, § 13A-1-7 of the Alabama Code; Fugitives from justice and extradition generally, § 15-9-1 et seq. of the Alabama Code; Punishment generally, §§ 13A-5-1, 13A-5-6, 13A-5-7, 13A-5-11, 13A-5-12 of the Alabama Code; Search and seizure, § 15-5-1 et seq. of the Alabama Code. See OBSCENE MATERIALS DISPLAYING OR DEPICTING CHILDREN; OBSCENE MATERIALS, SALE, EXHIBITION, ETC., TO MINORS.

---

1. *"PERSON. Any individual and, except where inappropriate, any partnership, firm, association, corporation or other legal entity." Code of Ala. 1975, § 13A-12-150(7).*
2. *"KNOWINGLY. The intentional doing of an act involving a work or performance when a person knows the nature of the work or performance. A person knows the nature of the work or performance when he has knowledge of, or good reason to know, or a reasonable ground for belief which warrants further inspection or inquiry of, the character and content of the work or performance." Code of Ala. 1975, § 13A-12-150(8).*
3. *"DISTRIBUTE. To transfer possession of or title to for any monetary consideration." Code of Ala. 1975, § 13A-12-150(10).*
4. *"OBSCENE. Such term means that: a. To the average person, applying contemporary community standards, the work or performance, taken as a whole, appeals to the prurient interest; and b. The work or performance depicts or describes, in a patently offensive way, sexual conduct, actual or simulated, normal or perverted; and c. The work or performance, taken as a whole, lacks serious literary, artistic, political or scientific value." Code of Ala. 1975, § 13A-12-150(1).*

OBSCENE MATTER, IMPORTATION, DISPLAY, DISTRIBUTION, ETC.
—Cont'd.

5. *"WORK. Any book, magazine, newspaper or other printed or written material, or any picture, drawing, photograph, film, videotape, motion picture or other pictorial representation, or any sound recording, or any statue or other figure, or any other article, device or material." Code of Ala. 1975, § 13A-12-150(2).*
6. *"DISPLAY PUBLICLY. To expose, place, exhibit or in any fashion display, in any location, public or private, any work in such a manner that the work can either be readily seen and its content or character distinguished by normal unaided vision or be physically examined, by viewing it or examining it from any place to which members of the general public are invited." Code of Ala. 1975, § 13A-12-150(9).*
7. *"PERFORMANCE. Any film, videotape, motion picture, sound recording, play, dance or other exhibition or presentation, whether pictured, animated or live, presented or performed before any audience of one or more persons." Code of Ala. 1975, § 13A-12-150(3).*
8. *Code of Ala. 1975, § 13A-12-157.*
9. *"SEXUAL CONDUCT. Such term means: a. Any act of masturbation, urination, defecation, sado-masochistic abuse, sexual intercourse or any other physical contact with a person's unclothed genitals, pubic area, buttocks or the breast or breasts of a female, whether alone or between members of the same or opposite sex or between a human and an animal, in an apparent act of sexual stimulation, gratification or perversion; or b. Lewd exhibition of the genitals." Code of Ala. 1975, § 13A-12-150(4).*
10. *"SEXUAL INTERCOURSE. Intercourse, whether genital-genital, oral-genital, anal-genital or oral-anal, and whether between persons of the same or opposite sex or between a human and an animal." Code of Ala. 1975, § 13A-12-150(5).*
11. *"SADO-MASOCHISTIC ABUSE. Flagellation or torture, in an apparent act of sexual stimulation, by or upon a person who is nude or clad in undergarments or in a revealing or bizarre costume, or the binding or physical restraining of a person who is so clothed, for the apparent purpose of sexual stimulation." Code of Ala. 1975, § 13A-12-150(6).*
12. *Code of Ala. 1975, § 13A-12-154.*
13. *"OWNER. Any person who owns or has legal right to possession of any work." Code of Ala.*

OBSCENE MATTER, IMPORTATION, DISPLAY, DISTRIBUTION, ETC. —Cont'd.

1975, § 13A-12-150(11).

14. *Code of Ala. 1975, § 13A-12-156.*

OBSCURING IDENTITY OF VEHICLE. Code of Ala. 1975, § 13A-8-22.

"(a) A person commits the crime of obscuring identity of a vehicle if:

"(1) He obscures[1] the manufacturer's serial number or any other distinguishing identification number or mark upon any vehicle[2] or component part thereof, except tires, with intent to render it unidentifiable; or

"(2) He possesses a vehicle or component part thereof knowing that the manufacturer's serial number or other identification number or mark has been obscured unless he legally acquired ownership of the vehicle or part before the manufacturer's serial number was obscured or before he knew it was obscured.

* * *

"(d) Proof that a person has obscured the manufacturer's serial number or other distinguishing identification number or mark on a vehicle is prima facie evidence that he did so with the intent to render it unidentifiable within the meaning of subdivision (a)(1) of this section.

"(e) Possession of a vehicle held for sale in the course of business on which the serial number or other identification number or mark has been obscured is prima facie evidence of knowledge of that fact."

Classification.

Class C felony.

Comments.

This statute is a precautionary sanction. By making the obscuring of identity numbers a crime in itself, the marketability of such items is hampered. Prima facie cases are provided and do away with the necessity for the state to prove any criminal intent or knowledge.

Defenses.

A report by the defendant to the police or other appropriate government[3] agency before arrest is a defense to a charge of violating subdivision (2) of this section. The burden of injecting this issue is on the defendant, but it does not shift the burden of proof.[4]

Cross references.

See MOTOR VEHICLE CRIMES; RECEIVING STOLEN PROPERTY; THEFT OF PROPERTY.

---

1. *" 'Obscure' means to remove, deface, cover, alter, destroy or otherwise render unidentifiable." Code of Ala. 1975, § 13A-8-22(b).*
2. *" 'Vehicle' means any propelled device in, upon or by which any person or property is transported on land, water or in the air, including stationary rails or tracks, and includes motor vehicles, motorboats, vessels and aircraft." Code of Ala. 1975, § 13A-8-22(c).*
3. *"GOVERNMENT. The United States, any state or any county, municipality or other political unit within territory belonging to the United States, or any department, agency or subdivision of any of the foregoing, or any corporation or other association carrying out the functions of government, or any corporation or agency formed pursuant to interstate compact or international treaty.*

   "As used in this definition 'state' includes any state, territory or possession of the United States, the District of Columbia and the Commonwealth of Puerto Rico." Code of Ala. 1975, § 13A-8-1(5).
4. *Code of Ala. 1975, § 13A-8-22(f).*

OBSTRUCTING GOVERNMENTAL OPERATIONS. Code of Ala. 1975, § 13A-10-2.

"(a) A person commits the crime of obstructing governmental operations if, by means of intimidation, physical force or interference or by any other independently unlawful act, he:

"(1) Intentionally obstructs, impairs or hinders the administration of law or other governmental function;[1] or

"(2) Intentionally prevents a public servant[2] from performing a governmental function.

"(b) This section does not apply to the obstruction, impairment or hindrance of the making of an arrest."[3]

Classification.

Class A misdemeanor.

OBSTRUCTING GOVERNMENTAL OPERATIONS.—Cont'd.

Comments.

This section establishes a general offense, whereas other sections deal with specific methods of interfering with governmental functions. To prevent the section from being overly broad, the obstruction must be the result of intimidation, physical force or interference or other independently unlawful act. Due to the definition of "governmental function," this section would not apply to illegal action by a public servant in performing an unauthorized function.

Defenses.

(1) Lack of intent.

(2) No intimidation, physical force, interference or independently unlawful act done by the accused.

Cross references.

See BRIBERY OF PUBLIC SERVANTS; BRIBING A JUROR; BRIBING A WITNESS; ESCAPE; ESCAPE, PERMITTING OR FACILITATING; GOVERNMENTAL RECORDS, TAMPERING WITH; HINDERING PROSECUTION/HINDERING APPREHENSION OF ESCAPEE; INSPECTION, REFUSAL TO PERMIT; INTIMIDATING A JUROR; INTIMIDATING A WITNESS; PERJURY.

---

1. *"Any activity which a public servant is legally authorized to undertake on behalf of a government." Code of Ala. 1975, § 13A-10-1(3).*
2. *"Any officer or employee of government, including legislators and judges and any person or agency participating as an adviser, consultant or otherwise in performing a governmental function." Code of Ala. 1975, § 13A-10-1(7).*
3. *Resisting arrest, Code of Ala. 1975, § 13A-10-41.*

OBSTRUCTING JUSTICE. See FALSE ALARM/FALSE REPORTING TO LAW ENFORCEMENT AUTHORITIES; GOVERNMENTAL RECORDS, TAMPERING WITH; HINDERING PROSECUTION/HINDERING APPREHENSION OF ESCAPEE; IMPERSONATING PUBLIC SERVANT; OBSTRUCTING GOVERNMENTAL OPERATIONS;

OBSTRUCTING JUSTICE.—Cont'd. PEACE OFFICER, REFUSING TO AID; RESISTING ARREST.

P. C. P. See CONTROLLED SUBSTANCES.

PARI-MUTUEL. See GAMBLING, LEGALIZED PARI-MUTUEL BETTING NOT AFFECTED.

PARTY LINES. Code of Ala. 1975, §§ 13A-11-222 and 13A-11-223.

Charged as: § 13A-11-222: Unlawfully refusing to yield party line; § 13A-11-223: Falsely requesting use of party line for emergency.

"A person commits the crime of refusing to yield a party line[1] if he intentionally refuses immediately to yield a party line after he is informed that it is needed for an emergency call."[2] § 13A-11-222(a) of the Alabama Code.

"A person commits the crime of falsely requesting use of party line for emergency if he states that a party line is needed for an emergency call knowing such statement to be false." § 13A-11-223(a) of the Alabama Code.

Classification.

Class B misdemeanor.

Defenses.

(1) At the time of the request to yield for an emergency call, the line was being used for another emergency call.[3]

(2) Belief that the call to be made is an emergency would serve as a defense for falsely requesting use of a party line.

Cross references.

See FALSELY REPORTING AN INCIDENT.

---

1. *"The term 'party line' means a subscriber's line telephone circuit consisting of two or more main telephone stations connected therewith, each having a distinctive ring or telephone number." Code of Ala. 1975, § 13A-11-222(b).*
2. *"The term 'emergency call' means a telephone call to a police or fire department, or for medical aid or ambulance service, necessitated by a situation in which human life or property is in jeopardy and prompt summoning of aid is essential." Code of Ala. 1975, § 13A-11-222(c).*
3. *Code of Ala. 1975, § 13A-11-222(d).*

PEACE OFFICER, REFUSING TO AID. Code of Ala. 1975, § 13A-10-5.

Charged as: Refusing to aid peace officer.

"(a) A person commits the crime of refusing to aid a peace officer if,[1] upon command by a peace officer identified to him as such, he fails or refuses to aid such peace officer in:

"(1) Effecting or securing a lawful arrest; or

"(2) Preventing the commission by another person of any offense.

"(b) A person is not liable under this section if the failure or refusal to aid the officer was reasonable under the circumstances. The burden of injecting this issue is on the defendant, but this does not shift the burden of proof."

Classification.

Class C misdemeanor.

Comments.

Section 13A-10-5 of the Alabama Code applies only to commands for assistance in making a lawful arrest or preventing a crime. § 13A-10-6 of the Alabama Code affects the conduct of persons in the vicinity of a fire. Both sections require that the person requesting assistance identify himself and that the request be reasonable. The commentary indicates that there is not an affirmative duty to assist in the "complicated and hazardous" work of modern fire fighting. Whether the complexity or hazards of aiding a peace officer in a lawful arrest or prevention of crime might be considered as to the reasonableness of the request is not known at this time. Prior law had no element of reasonableness. It was no excuse that a citizen thought his assistance would be futile or dangerous.[2]

Defenses.

(1) Lack of identification.
(2) Unreasonable request.
(3) Lack of intent to disobey.

Cross references.

See ARSON; FORCE IN MAKING AN ARREST OR PREVENTING AN ESCAPE; OBSTRUCTING GOVERNMENTAL OPERATIONS.

PEACE OFFICER, REFUSING TO AID.—Cont'd.

---

1. *"Any public servant vested by law with a duty to maintain public order or to make arrests for crime, whether that duty extends to all crimes or is limited to specific crimes." Code of Ala. 1975, § 13A-10-1(5).*
2. *Dougherty v. State, 106 Ala. 63, 17 So. 393 (1895).*

PERJURY. Code of Ala. 1975, §§ 13A-10-101 through 13A-10-108.

"A person commits the crime of perjury in the first degree when in any official proceeding[1] he swears falsely[2] and his false statement is material[3] to the proceeding in which it is made." § 13A-10-101(a) of the Alabama Code.

"A person commits the crime of perjury in the second degree when he swears with intent to mislead a public servant[4] in the performance of his duty and his false statement is material to the action, proceeding or matter involved." § 13A-10-102(a) of the Alabama Code. "A person commits the crime of perjury in the third degree when he swears falsely." § 13A-10-103(a) of the Alabama Code.

Classification.

Class C felony, first degree.
Class A misdemeanor, second degree.
Class B misdemeanor, third degree.

Comments.

Perjury in the first degree consists of making a "materially false statement" in an official proceeding; perjury in the second degree consists of making a "materially false statement" with the intent to mislead a public servant in the performance of his duty; and perjury in the third degree covers making a false statement, but the element of materiality is not required. Both first and second degree perjury also require that the defendant not believe his statement to be true. All three sections require the statement to be made under oath.[5] Third degree perjury relates to situations in private transactions where oaths are required. This section imposes a less severe penalty that is designed to encourage its frequent application and discourage the practice of perjury.

Situations may arise where a person has

PERJURY.—Cont'd.

made statements under oath that are inconsistent to the degree that one of them must be false.[6] These statements must be made within the same jurisdiction since the statement made in the jurisdiction where the perjury action is brought may be the jurisdiction in which the true statement was made. The requirement that both statements be made within the period of the statute of limitations is to allow a witness to tell the truth the second time without fear of being prosecuted for telling the truth. If the second statement is the untrue one, then perjury charges can be brought directly under §§ 13A-10-101 through 13A-10-103 of the Alabama Code. If the prosecutor cannot prove which statement was false, the lesser offense must be the one used for conviction. This is based upon the assumption that the lesser of the two statements was false.

Except for a prosecution based upon inconsistent statements,[7] uncorroborated testimony of a single witness may not be used.[8] This rule provides a definite line of demarcation between what is and what is not reasonable doubt. Charges of perjury may not be brought based upon a defendant's testimony in a previous criminal proceeding[9] if the substance of his statement was to deny his guilt.[10] This is based upon the principle that double jeopardy should prohibit a retrial of essentially the same substantive offense through the guise of a perjury trial. On the other hand res judicata should not preclude such action since perjury would be a different offense from the original prosecution.

If a person retracts his false statement in the course of the same proceeding in which it was made, so long as the retraction was made before it became manifest that the falsification was or would be exposed,[11] that person cannot be charged under these sections. This rule encourages a witness to admit a false statement and change the statement instead of taking the chance his false statement will not be discovered.

PERJURY.—Cont'd.

Defenses.

(1) Statement was not material (1st & 2nd degree).

(2) Belief statement was true (1st & 2nd degree).

(3) Lack of intent to mislead.

(4) But, note according to § 13A-10-108 of the Alabama Code:

"It is no defense to prosecution for perjury:

"(1) That the oath was administered in an irregular manner.

"(2) That there was some irregularity in the appointment or qualification of the person who administered the oath, if the taking of the oath was required or authorized by law.

"(3) That the document was not sworn to if the document contains a recital that it was made under oath, the declarant was aware of the recital when he signed the document and the document contains the signed jurat[12] of a public servant authorized to administer oaths.

"(4) That the defendant mistakenly believed the false statement to be immaterial.

"(5) That the statement was inadmissible under the law of evidence."

Cross references.

See Accomplice liability, § 13A-2-23 of the Alabama Code. See FORGERY; OBSTRUCTING GOVERNMENTAL OPERATIONS; SOLICITATION; THEFT OF PROPERTY; UNSWORN FALSIFICATION TO AUTHORITIES.

---

1. *"OFFICIAL PROCEEDING. Any proceeding heard before any legislative, judicial, administrative or other government agency or official authorized to hear evidence under oath." Code of Ala. 1975, § 13A-10-100(b)(5).*

2. *"SWEARS FALSELY AND FALSE SWEARING. The making of a false statement under oath required or authorized by law, or the swearing or affirming the truth of such statement previously made, which the declarant does not believe to be true. A false swearing in a subscribed written instrument shall not be deemed complete until the instrument is delivered by its subscriber, or by someone acting in his behalf, to another person with intent that it be uttered or published as true." Code of Ala. 1975, § 13A-10-100(b)(1).*

3. *"MATERIAL. A statement is 'material,'*

PERJURY.—Cont'd.

regardless of the admissibility of the statement under the rules of evidence, if it could have affected the course or outcome of the official proceeding. It is no defense that the declarant mistakenly believed the falsification to be immaterial. Whether a falsification is material in a given factual situation is a question of law." Code of Ala. 1975, § 13A-10-100(b)(2).

4. *"PUBLIC SERVANT. Any officer or employee of government, including legislators and judges and any person or agency participating as an adviser, consultant or otherwise in performing a governmental function." § 13A-10-1(7).*
5. *"OATH. Such term includes an affirmation and every other mode authorized by law of attesting to the truth of that which is stated. For the purposes of this article, written statements shall be treated as if made under oath if:*

"a. The statement was made on or pursuant to form bearing notice, authorized by law, to the effect that false statements made therein are punishable; or

"b. The statement recites that it was made under oath, the declarant was aware of such recitation at the time he made the statement and intended that the statement should be represented as a sworn statement, and the statement was in fact so represented by its delivery or utterance with the signed jurat of an officer authorized to administer oaths appended thereto." Code of Ala. 1975, § 13A-10-100(b)(3).

6. *Code of Ala. 1975, § 13A-10-104. Perjury prosecution for inconsistent statements; highest degree of perjury for which conviction may be had:*

"(a) Where a person has made statements under oath which are inconsistent to the degree that one of them is necessarily false, each having been made within the jurisdiction of this state and within the period of the statute of limitations, the prosecution may proceed by setting forth the inconsistent statements in a single count alleging in the alternative that one or the other was false and not believed by the defendant to have been true when made. In such case, it shall not be necessary for the prosecution to prove which statement was false, but only that one or the other was false and not believed by the defendant to be true.

"(b) The highest degree of perjury of which the defendant may be convicted shall be determined by hypothetically assuming each statement to be false and perjurious. If perjury of the same degree would be established by the making of each statement, the accused may be convicted of that degree at most. If perjury of different degrees would be established by the making of the two statements, the accused may be convicted of the lesser degree at most."

7. *See Code of Ala. 1975, § 13A-10-104, note 6, supra.*
8. *Corroboration is required for perjury conviction:*

"In any prosecution for perjury, except a prosecution based upon inconsistent statements pursuant to section 13A-10-104, the falsity of a statement may not be established by the uncorroborated testimony of a single witness." Code of Ala. 1975, § 13A-10-105.

9. *Criminal proceeding was used instead of "trial", thus including previous preliminary hearings, habeas corpus, and possible coram nobis proceedings in which defendant denied his guilt.*
10. *Code of Ala. 1975, § 13A-10-106. Denial of guilt in previous trial not to be prosecuted as perjury:*

"No prosecution shall be brought under this article if the substance of the defendant's false statement was a denial of his guilt in a previous criminal proceeding."

11. *Code of Ala. 1975, § 13A-10-107. When retraction of false statement is a bar to perjury conviction:*

"No person shall be convicted of perjury if he retracted his false statement in the course of the same proceeding in which it was made before it became manifest that the falsification was or would be exposed. Statements made in separate hearings at separate stages of the same trial or administrative proceeding shall be deemed to have been made in the course of the same proceeding. The burden of injecting the issue of retraction is on the defendant, but this does not shift the burden of proof."

12. *"JURAT. A clause wherein a notary public or other attesting officer authorized by law to administer oaths in connection with affidavits, depositions and other subscribed written instruments certifies that the subscriber has appeared before him and sworn to the truth of contents thereof." Code of Ala. 1975, § 13A-10-100(b)(6).*

PHONE. See HARASSMENT OR HARASSING COMMUNICATIONS; PARTY LINES.

PHYSICAL EVIDENCE, TAMPERING WITH. Code of Ala. 1975, § 13A-10-129.

Charged as: Tampering with physical evidence.

"A person commits the crime of tampering

PHYSICAL EVIDENCE, TAMPERING WITH.—Cont'd.

with physical evidence[1] if, believing that an official proceeding[2] is pending or may be instituted, and acting without legal right or authority, he:

"(1) Destroys, mutilates, conceals, removes or alters physical evidence with intent to impair its use, verity or availability in the pending or prospective official proceeding; or

"(2) Knowingly makes, presents or offers any false physical evidence with intent that it be introduced in the pending or prospective official proceeding."

Classification.

Class A misdemeanor.

Comments.

This offense has not been previously covered in the Alabama Code, and there have been no Alabama cases on point. The prosecution has the burden of proving either an intent to impair the use of evidence or the intent to introduce false evidence.

This section does not require that a proceeding be pending or be instituted. It only requires that the person committing the crime believe such. It also does not require that the evidence be admitted.

Defenses.

(1) No intent to impair the use, verity or availability of physical evidence.

(2) Person had no reason to believe such material (that was tampered with) would end up in court.

(3) Accidental destruction or loss of material.

Cross references.

See ATTEMPT; FORGERY; GOVERNMENTAL RECORDS, TAMPERING WITH; HINDERING PROSECUTION; HINDERING APPREHENSION OF ESCAPEE; OBSTRUCTING GOVERNMENTAL OPERATIONS.

---

1. " 'Physical evidence,' as used in this section, includes any article, object, document, record or other thing of physical substance." Code of Ala. 1975, § 13A-10-129(b).

2. An "official proceeding" includes "[a]ny proceeding heard before any legislative, judicial, administrative, or other government agency authorized to hear evidence under oath." Code of Ala. 1975, § 13A-10-100(b)(5)

PILOT. See AVIATION.

PIMPING. See PROSTITUTION.

PISTOL, BOWIE KNIFE, SELLING TO MINORS. Code of Ala. 1975, § 13A-11-57.

Charged as: Selling a pistol (or bowie knife) to a minor.

No person shall give or lend to any minor[1] any pistol,[2] or bowie knife,[3] or other knife of like kind or description.

Classification.

Statutory penalty: a fine of not less than $50 nor more than $500.

Comments.

The transfer of possession to a minor of a pistol, bowie knife "or other knife of like kind" is prohibited by this section. The means of transfer expressly prohibited by this section (give, sell, lend) indicate that the actor's conduct must be intentional.[4] Based on rules of construction applicable to statutes within the criminal code,[5] the state should be required to established that the actor knew that the transferee was a minor. If the weapon transferred is a pistol, the accused is also culpable of violating § 13A-11-76 of the Alabama Code.[6]

Defenses.

(1) Actor did not give, lend, or sell prohibited weapon.

(2) Weapon not one expressly prohibited by this statute.

(3) Transferee not a minor.

(4) Transferor did not "know" transferee was a minor.

Query.

What is a knife of like kind in reference to a bowie knife? And, who makes this determination?

Cross references.

See JUVENILE PROCEEDINGS; PISTOLS, LICENSE TO CARRY; PISTOLS, POSSESSION AND DELIVERY.

PISTOL, BOWIE KNIFE, SELLING TO MINORS.—Cont'd.

---

1. *"Minor" is not defined in this section. It is defined in other sections of this title, but resorting to other provision makes the statute's construction even more difficult. See, e.g., Code of Ala. 1975, § 13A-3-3 (Immaturity for one less than 14 years of age); Code of Ala. 1975, § 13A-6-69 (Enticing a child under 16 years of age); Code of Ala. 1975, § 13A-11-76 (Pistols, delivery to minor under age of 18 years of age); Code of Ala. 1975, § 13A-11-103 (Fireworks, sale to minors under 10 years of age); Code of Ala. 1975, § 13A-12-170 (Obscenity, display, sale, etc. to minor under 18 years of age); Code of Ala. 1975, § 13A-12-191 (Obscenity, dissemination to minors under 17 years of age); Code of Ala. 1975, § 13A-13-4 (Nonsupport of dependent child under 19 years of age).*
2. *Pistol is not defined in this division. § 13A-11-70(1) of the Alabama Code defines pistol as "[a]ny firearm with a barrel less than 12 inches in length."*
3. *Bowie knife is not defined in this title. This is especially troublesome when a person can be criminally liable for transfer of bowie knives or knives of "like kind" to minors.*
4. *Although no culpable mental state is expressly designated in a statute defining an offense, an appropriate mental state may nevertheless be required for the commission of that offense. The same may be true with respect to some or all of the material elements, if the proscribed conduct necessarily involves such culpable mental state. A statute defining a crime, unless clearly indicating a legislative intent to impose strict liability, provides for mental culpability. Code of Ala. 1975, § 13A-2-5(b).*
5. *Code of Ala. 1975, § 13A-2-5(b).*
6. *The accused could be in this situation if the prosecutor charged him with violation of Code of Ala. 1975, § 13A-11-76 because no penalty is provided for violating that statute.*

PISTOLS, LICENSE TO CARRY. Code of Ala. 1975, §§ 13A-11-73 through 13A-11-75, and § 13A-11-83.

Charged as: § 13A-11-73: Violation of license to carry pistol in vehicle or concealed on person — Required.

"No person shall carry a pistol in any vehicle or concealed on or about his person, except on his land, in his own abode or fixed place

PISTOLS, LICENSE TO CARRY. —Cont'd.

of business, without a license therefor as hereinafter provided."

Classification.[1]

Imprisonment for any term less than one year or by a fine of not more than $500.00, or both.

Comments.

A person can obtain a license to carry a pistol in a vehicle or concealed on his person from the sheriff in the county in which he resides. The license, which lasts one year, may be a "qualified or unlimited license"[2] issued to the suitable[3] applicant who convinces the sheriff that he has reason to fear injury to his person or property or has "any other proper reason for carrying a pistol" and pays a fee of $1.00. The license itself, which is completed in triplicate, must bear the name, address, description and signature of the applicant.[4] The sheriff keeps a copy (for 6 years), sends one to the licensee and one to the director of public safety. The licenses can be revoked if the sheriff determines that the applicant is not suitable to possess the same.[5] Certain persons are exceptions to the rule that a license from the state must be obtained to carry a pistol. Typical of the members of this exempt group are law enforcement officers of any state or political subdivision thereof; officers, employees and members of the armed forces of the United States; merchants and repairers of pistols and specially exempt organizations.[6] Antique pistols[7] can be transported or possessed without a license if unloaded in a box, bag or securely wrapped package and not on the transporter's person.

Carrying a pistol in a vehicle or concealed on one's person without a license carries a punishment of a prison term for less than one year or a fine of not more than $500.00, or both.[8] A like punishment applies to those persons covered by the section on exceptions. The punishment is only applicable to those persons who are not on duty and, therefore, not covered by the exceptions. Any person violating this section will have his pistol seized by the law

PISTOLS, LICENSE TO CARRY.
—Cont'd.

officer observing the violation. Seized pistols may be destroyed or otherwise disposed of by the state unless defendants having any interest in the property are able to prevail in the proceedings.[9]

Defenses.

(1) A state license is not required when the person is on foot and the weapon is not concealed. But city ordinances should be consulted for prohibitions in the same areas of conduct.

(2) The weapon is not a pistol, because its barrel is less than 12 inches long.

(3) The vehicle where the pistol is located is the person's fixed abode or place of business for which a license is not required.

(4) The person is exempt by §§ 13A-11-74, 13A-11-83 or 13A-11-52 of the Alabama Code.

Cross references.

See FIREARMS, POSSESSION BY PERSONS PARTICIPATING IN, ATTENDING, ETC., DEMONSTRATIONS AT PUBLIC PLACES; PISTOLS, POSSESSION AND DELIVERY; WEAPONS, CARRYING CONCEALED.

---

1. *Note, in addition to Code of Ala. 1975, § 13A-11-73 (License to carry pistol in vehicle or concealed on person — Required), Code of Ala. 1975, § 13A-11-84 lists the various penalties for the other violations within Code of Ala. 1975, Title 13A, chapter 11, article 3, division 2. Specifically, Code of Ala. 1975, § 13A-11-84(a) (Penalties; seizure and disposition of pistols involved in violations of certain sections) provides that "[e]very violation of subsection (a) of section 13A-11-72 ['No person who has been convicted in this state or elsewhere of committing or attempting to commit a crime of violence shall own a pistol or have one in his possession or under his control.'] or of section 13A-11-81 ['No person shall in purchasing or otherwise securing delivery of a pistol or in applying for a license to carry the same, give false information or offer false evidence of his identity'] or section 13A-11-82, ['No person shall change, alter, remove or obliterate the name of the maker, model, manufacturer's number or other mark of identification of any pistol. Possession of any pistol upon which any such mark shall have been changed, altered, removed or obliterated shall be prima facie evidence that the possessor has changed, altered, removed or obliterated the same.'] shall be punishable by imprisonment for not more than five years. Every violation of subsection (b) of section 13A-11-72 ['No person who is a drug addict or an habitual drunkard shall own a pistol or have one in his possession or under his control'], or of sections 13A-11-73, 13A-11-74 ['The provisions of section 13A-11-73 shall not apply to marshals, sheriffs, prison and jail wardens and their regularly employed deputies, policemen and other law enforcement officers of any state or political subdivision thereof, or to the members of the army, navy or marine corps of the United States or from the national guard, organized reserves or state guard organizations when on duty or going to or from duty, or to the regularly enrolled members of any organization duly authorized to purchase or receive such weapons from the United States or from this state; provided, that such members are at or are going to or from their places of assembly or target practices, or to officers or employees of the United States duly authorized to carry a pistol, or to any person engaged in manufacturing, repairing or dealing in pistols, or the agent or representative of such person possessing, using, or carrying a pistol in the usual or ordinary course of such business, or to any common carrier, except taxicabs, licensed as a common carrier, or to any person permitted by law to possess a pistol while carrying it unloaded in a secure wrapper, from the place of purchase to his home or place of business, or to or from a place of repair or in moving from one place of abode or business to another'] and sections 13A-11-77 through 13A-11-80 ['§ 13A-11-77. Sales regulated; application for purchase. No seller shall deliver a pistol to the purchaser thereof until 48 hours shall have elapsed from the time of the application for the purchase thereof, and, when delivered, the pistol shall be securely wrapped and shall be unloaded. At the time of applying for the purchase of a pistol, the purchaser shall sign in triplicate and deliver to the seller a statement containing his full name, address, occupation, color, place of birth, the date and hour of application, the caliber, make, model and manufacturer's number of the pistol to be purchased and a statement that he has*

PISTOLS, LICENSE TO CARRY. —Cont'd.

never been convicted in this state or elsewhere of a crime of violence. The seller shall within six hours after such application, sign and attach his address and forward by registered or certified mail one copy of such statement to the chief of police of the municipality or the sheriff of the county of which the seller is a resident; the duplicate duly signed by the seller shall within seven days be sent by him with his address to the director of public safety; and he shall retain the triplicate for six years. This section shall not apply to purchases by licensed retailers from manufacturers, wholesalers or jobbers, or to purchases by wholesalers or jobbers from manufacturers; § 13A-11-78. Dealers' licenses — Required. No retail dealer shall sell or otherwise transfer, or expose for sale or transfer, or have in his possession with intent to sell, or otherwise transfer, any pistol without being licensed as hereinafter provided; § 13A-11-79. Same — Issuance; conditions; display; fees. The duly constituted licensing authorities of any city, town or political subdivision of this state may grant licenses in forms prescribed by the secretary of state, effective for not more than one year from date of issue, permitting the licensee to sell pistols at retail within this state subject to the following conditions, in addition to those specified in section 13A-11-77 for breach of any of which the license shall be forfeited and the licensee subject to punishment as provided in this division. The business shall be carried on only in the building designated in the license. The license or a copy thereof, certified by the issuing authority, shall be displayed on the premises where it can easily be read. No pistol shall be sold in violation of any provisions of this division, nor shall a pistol be sold under any circumstances unless the purchaser is personally known to the seller or shall present clear evidence of his identity. A true record in triplicate shall be made of every pistol sold, in a book kept for the purpose, the form of which may be prescribed by the secretary of state and shall be personally signed by the purchaser and by the person effecting the sale, the caliber, make, model and manufacturer's number of the weapon, the name, address, occupation, color and place of birth of purchaser and a statement signed by the purchaser that he has never been convicted in this state or elsewhere of a crime of violence. One copy shall be sent within six hours by registered or certified mail to the chief of police of the municipality or the sheriff of the county of which the dealer is a resident; the dealer shall within seven days send the duplicate to the secretary of state; and the dealer shall retain the triplicate for six years. No pistol or imitation thereof or placard advertising the sale thereof shall be displayed in any part of any premises where it can readily be seen from the outside. The fee for issuing said license shall be $.50, which fee shall be paid into the state treasury; § 13A-11-80. Loans secured by deposit, etc., of pistol prohibited; certain transfers prohibited. No person shall make any loan secured by a mortgage, deposit or pledge of a pistol contrary to this division, nor shall any person lend or give a pistol to another or otherwise deliver a pistol contrary to the provisions of this division.'] shall be punishable by imprisonment for any term less than one year or by a fine of not more than $500.00, or both. The punishment for violating sections 13A-11-78 or 13A-11-79 may include revocation of license."

In addition, Code of Ala. 1975, § 13A-11-84(b) establishes the "duty of any sheriff, policeman or other peace officer of the state of Alabama, arresting any person charged with violating sections 13A-11-71 through 13A-11-73 or any one or more of said sections, to seize the pistol or pistols in the possession or under the control of the person or persons charged with violating said section or sections, and to deliver said pistol or pistols to one of the following named persons: if a municipal officer makes the arrest, to the city clerk or custodian of stolen property of the municipality employing the arresting officer; if a county, state or other peace officer makes the arrest, to the sheriff of the county in which the arrest is made. The person receiving the pistol or pistols from the arresting officer shall keep it in a safe place in as good condition as received until disposed of as hereinafter provided. Within five days after the final conviction of any person arrested for violating any of the above-numbered sections, the person receiving possession of the pistol or pistols, seized as aforesaid, shall report the seizure and detention of said pistol or pistols to the district attorney within the county where the pistol or pistols are seized, giving a full description thereof, the number, make and model thereof, the name of the person in whose possession it was found when seized, the person making claim to same or any interest therein, if

PISTOLS, LICENSE TO CARRY. —Cont'd.

the name can be ascertained or is known, and the date of the seizure. Upon receipt of the report from the person receiving possession of the pistol or pistols as aforesaid, it shall be the duty of the district attorney within the county wherein the pistol or pistols were seized to forthwith file a complaint in the circuit court of the proper county, praying that such seized pistol or pistols be declared contraband, be forfeited to the state and be destroyed. Any person, firm or corporation or association of persons in whose possession said pistol or pistols may be seized or who claim to own the same or any interest therein shall be made a party defendant to said complaint, and thereupon such matter shall proceed and be determined in the circuit court of the proper county in the same form and manner, as near as may be, as in the forfeiture and destruction of gaming devices, except as herein otherwise provided. When any judgment of condemnation and forfeiture is made in any case filed under the provisions of this section, the judge making such judgment shall direct therein the destruction of the pistol or pistols by the person receiving possession of said pistol or pistols from the arresting officer in the presence of the clerk or register of the court, unless the judge is of the opinion that the nondestruction thereof is necessary or proper in the ends of justice, in which event and upon recommendation of the district attorney, the judge shall award the pistol or pistols to the sheriff of the county or to the sheriff or the chief of police of the municipality to be used exclusively by the sheriff or the chief of police in the enforcement of law, and the sheriff of the county and the chiefs of police of the municipalities shall keep a permanent record of all pistols awarded to them as provided for herein, to be accounted for as other public property, and said order, in the event that no appeal is taken within 15 days from the rendition thereof, shall be carried out and executed before the expiration of 20 days from the date of the judgment. The court, at its discretion, shall direct in said judgment that the costs of the proceedings be paid by the person in whose possession said pistol or pistols were found when seized, or by any party or parties who claim to own said pistol or pistols, or any interest therein, and who contested the condemnation and forfeiture thereof."

Finally, note that Code of Ala. 1975, § 13A-11-76, "[n]o person shall deliver a pistol to any person under the age of 18 or to one who he has reasonable cause to believe has been convicted of a crime of violence or is a drug addict, an habitual drunkard or of unsound mind", does not provide a specific penalty.

2. *This term is not defined by the Code.*
3. *The sheriff has some discretion in issuing a license. Even though a person has not been convicted of a crime of violence or a felony, the sheriff may refuse to issue a license if he deems the applicant unsuitable. Mandamus is not appropriate if it is determined that the sheriff did not abuse his discretion nor act arbitrarily or capriciously. Conviction for violation of obscenity laws may be sufficient to justify a refusal. Hess v. Butler, 379 So. 2d 1259 (Ala. 1980).*
4. *A license may be no defense for carrying a concealed weapon if the licensee had a prior conviction. Such a license is void, as the sheriff had no power to issue it.*
5. *Giving false information or false evidence of identity is punishable by imprisonment for not more than 5 years.*
6. *Code of Ala. 1975, § 13A-11-74.*
7. *"This division shall not apply to the purchase, possession or sale of pistols as curiosities or ornaments or to the transportation of such pistols unloaded and in a bag, box or securely wrapped package, but not concealed on the person." Code of Ala. 1975, § 13A-11-83.*
8. *Code of Ala. 1975, § 13A-11-73. Compare this provision to Code of Ala. 1975, § 13A-11-50, which prohibits a person from carrying a pistol concealed about his person. The punishment provided under that section is a fine of at least $50.00 and not more than $500.00 and, possibly, a 6 month term of hard labor for the county. A person who has good reason to apprehend an attack is allowed to submit evidence of these grounds to the jury in mitigating the punishment or justification of the offense. See Code of Ala. 1975, § 13A-11-51.*
9. *Code of Ala. 1975, § 13A-11-84(b).*

PISTOLS, POSSESSION AND DELIVERY. Code of Ala. 1975, §§ 13A-11-72 and 13A-11-76.

Charged as: § 13A-11-72: Certain persons forbidden to possess pistol; § 13A-11-76: Delivery to minors, habitual drunkards, etc.

"(a) No person who has been convicted in this state or elsewhere of committing or

PISTOLS, POSSESSION AND DELIVERY.—Cont'd.

attempting to commit a crime of violence shall own a pistol or have one in his possession or under his control."

"(b) No person who is a drug addict or an habitual drunkard shall own a pistol or have one in his possession or control." § 13A-11-72 of the Alabama Code.

"No person shall deliver a pistol to any person under the age of 18 or to one who he has reasonable cause to believe has been convicted of a crime of violence or is a drug addict, an habitual drunkard or of unsound mind." § 13A-11-76 of the Alabama Code.

Classification.

See Comment, infra.

Comments.

These sections regulate the ownership, control, possession or delivery of pistols.[1]

One who has been convicted of committing or attempting to commit a crime of violence[2] in any state is prohibited to own, possess, or have a pistol under his control. § 13A-11-72(a) of the Alabama Code.[3] Violation of this section subjects the defendant to punishment by imprisonment for not more than five years.

A drug addict or an habitual drunkard is not allowed to possess, own, or have a pistol under his control. § 13A-11-72(b) of the Alabama Code. An addict or habitual drunkard whose conduct violates this statute can be imprisoned for a term of less than one year, and/or fined a maximum of $500.00.

There is a special statute prohibiting the delivery of pistols to minors or habitual drunkards.[4] The most significant feature of this statute is that there is no punishment for violation.[5] The sale of pistols to persons prohibited to own, possess or have a pistol under their control is discussed in §§ 13A-11-77 through 13A-11-79 of the Alabama Code.

Defenses.

(1) The firearm is not a pistol (barrel more than 12 inches in length).

(2) The person in possession, though convicted of a crime of violence, received a pardon.

PISTOLS, POSSESSION AND DELIVERY.—Cont'd.

(3) The person in possession was not convicted of a crime of violence.

(4) The possessor is not a drug addict or an habitual drunkard.

(5) The pistol qualifies as an antique possession which is exempt from the prohibitions of the divisions on pistols.

Cross references.

See PISTOLS, BOWIE KNIFE, SELLING TO MINORS; PISTOLS, LICENSE TO CARRY.

---

1. *A pistol is "[a]ny firearm with a barrel less than twelve inches in length." "Firearm" is not defined within this division. Code of Ala. 1975, § 13A-11-70(1).*
2. *As used in this division, a crime of violence means any of the following crimes, or an attempt to commit any of them: murder, manslaughter, (except manslaughter arising out of the operation of a vehicle), rape, mayhem, assault with intent to rob, assault with intent to ravish, assault with intent to murder, robbery, burglary, kidnapping and larceny.*
3. *This provision preempts in part Code of Ala. 1975, § 13A-11-58, which authorizes sale and delivery and purchase by residents of states adjoining Alabama.*
4. *See Code of Ala. 1975, § 13A-11-76.*
5. *Declaration or denouncement of conduct as unlawful does not make it a crime unless provision is made for punishment. Embry v. City of Montgomery, 41 Ala. App. 568, 140 So. 2d 291 (1962).*

POISON. See NOXIOUS SUBSTANCE, USE OR POSSESSION OF.

PORNOGRAPHY. See OBSCENE MATERIALS, SALE, EXHIBITION, ETC. TO MINORS; OBSCENE MATERIALS DISPLAYING OR DEPICTING CHILDREN; OBSCENE MATTER, IMPORTATION DISPLAY, DISTRIBUTION, ETC.

POSSESSION OF. See specific title (e.g. BURGLAR'S TOOLS, FORGED INSTRUMENT, ETC.).

PRESCRIPTION, ADMINISTRATION, ETC. OF CONTROLLED SUBSTANCES BY PRACTITIONERS OF VETERINARY MEDICINE FOR USE OF HUMAN BEINGS OR BY PRACTITIONERS OF DENTISTRY FOR PERSONS NOT UNDER TREATMENT IN REGULAR PRACTICE OF PROFESSION. See CONTROLLED SUBSTANCES — USE BY VETERINARIANS AND DENTISTS.

PRISON CONTRABAND, PROMOTING. Code of Ala. 1975, §§ 13A-10-36 through 13A-10-38.

Charged as: Promoting prison contraband.

A person is guilty of promoting prison contraband[1] in the first degree if:

"(1) He intentionally and unlawfully introduces within a detention facility,[2] or provides an inmate with, any deadly weapon, instrument, tool or other thing which may be useful for escape;

"(2) Being a person confined in a detention facility, he intentionally and unlawfully makes, obtains or possesses any deadly weapon, instrument, tool or other thing which may be useful for escape." § 13A-10-36(a) of the Alabama Code.

A person is guilty of promoting prison contraband in the second degree if:

"(1) He intentionally and unlawfully introduces within a detention facility, or provides an inmate with, any narcotic, dangerous drug or controlled substance as defined in the 'Alabama Controlled Substances Act,' or any amendments thereto; or

"(2) Being a person confined in a detention facility, he intentionally and unlawfully makes, obtains or possesses any narcotic, dangerous drug, or controlled substance as defined in chapter 2 of Title 20 of this Code." § 13A-10-37(a) of the Alabama Code.

A person is guilty of promoting prison contraband in the third degree if:

"(1) He intentionally and unlawfully

PRISON CONTRABAND, PROMOTING.—Cont'd.

introduces within a detention facility, or provides an inmate with, any contraband or thing which the actor knows or should know it is unlawful to introduce or for the inmate to possess; or

"(2) Being a person confined in a detention facility, he intentionally and unlawfully makes, obtains or possesses any contraband." § 13A-10-38(a) of the Alabama Code.

Classification.

Class C felony, first and second degree.

Class B misdemeanor, third degree.

Comments.

The first subdivision of each part is confined to persons who intentionally and unlawfully introduce contraband into a detention facility or supply it to inmates. The second subdivision concerns persons confined who intentionally make, obtain or possess contraband. These sections are distinguished by the nature of the contraband. The offense in the third degree encompasses all items not specifically mentioned in §§ 13A-10-36 and 13A-10-37 of the Alabama Code that inmates are prevented from possessing by statute or regulation.

Defenses.

(1) Lack of intent.

(2) Lawful introduction.

(3) Providing item to a person not an inmate who subsequently supplied the item to an inmate.

(4) Lack of knowledge or reasons person should know an item supplied under § 13A-10-38 of the Alabama Code is considered contraband. The official commentary refers to § 13A-10-1(5) of the Alabama Code, which defines peace officer, and § 13A-10-30 of the Alabama Code, which defines contraband.

Cross references.

See CONTROLLED SUBSTANCES; ESCAPE, PERMITTING OR FACILITATING.

---

1. *"Any article or thing which a person confined in a detention facility is legally prohibited from*

PRISON CONTRABAND, PROMOTING.—Cont'd.

obtaining or possessing by statute, rule, regulation or order." Code of Ala. 1975, § 13A-10-30(b)(4).

2. *"Any place used for the confinement, pursuant to law, of a person:*

"a. Charged with or convicted of a criminal offense; or

"b. Charged with being or adjudicated a youthful offender, or a neglected minor or juvenile delinquent; or

"c. Held for extradition; or

"d. Otherwise confined pursuant to an order of court." Code of Ala. 1975, § 13A-10-30(b)(2).

PROSTITUTION. Code of Ala. 1975, §§ 13A-12-110 to 13A-12-113.

Charged as: Promoting prostitution.

"A person commits the crime of promoting prostitution in the first degree if he knowingly:

"(1) Advances prostitution[1] by compelling a person by force or intimidation to engage in prostitution, or profits from such coercive conduct by another; or

"(2) Advances or profits from prostitution[2] of a person less than 16 years of age." § 13A-12-111(a) of the Alabama Code.

"A person commits the crime of promoting prostitution in the second degree if he knowingly:

"(1) Advances or profits from prostitution by managing, supervising, controlling or owning, either alone or in association with others, a house of prostitution or a prostitution business[3] or enterprise involving prostitution activity by two or more prostitutes other than the defendant; or

"(2) Advances or profits from prostitution of a person less than 18 years of age." § 13A-12-112(a) of the Alabama Code.

"[A] person commits the crime of promoting prostitution in the third degree if he knowingly advances or profits from prostitution." § 13A-12-113(a) of the Alabama Code.

Classification.

Class B felony, first degree.

Class C felony, second degree.

PROSTITUTION.—Cont'd.

Class A misdemeanor, third degree.

Comments.

These sections penalize the promotion of prostitution but not the patronizing of a prostitute or the act of prostitution itself. There is no current Alabama statute that forbids prostitution. Inconsistent and varied barriers to prostitution can be found in municipal ordinances.[4] Prostitution can also be attacked through the civil remedy of abatement of nuisance, but this is limited to defining houses of prostitution as nuisances per se. Persons connected with a house of prostitution can be found guilty of maintaining a nuisance.[5] Prostitution is considered presumptive evidence of venereal disease, requiring those in the trade to be examined by a health officer.[6] The health officer is to use every "proper means" for the suppression of venereal disease. No statute, however, fails to define "proper means."[7]

Case law has been of little help in providing a clear definition of prostitution. Definitional foundations for prostitution in Alabama have ranged from economic gain to indiscriminate lewdness. At least one decision labeled all women, who associated with women of bad character, prostitutes.[8]

The original draft of this Code incorporated both prostitution and the patronizing of a prostitute. The enacted sections grew out of the controversy that purged all sanctions save those for promoting prostitution. Thus, foregoing sections are directed toward those person (pimps, madams, business organizers, etc.) who knowingly promote prostitution.

Section 13A-12-111(a) of the Alabama Code, promoting prostitution in the first degree, is distinguished by the use of force or intimidation or the fact that the prostitute is less than 16 years old. This age is consistent with Alabama's age of consent.

Section 13A-12-112(a)(1) of the Alabama Code deals with those promoting a house of prostitution or a prostitution business employing those who engage in prostitution willingly and voluntarily; and there must be two or more prostitutes other than the defendant.

PROSTITUTION.—Cont'd.

Section 13A-12-112(a)(2) of the Alabama Code makes any advancing or profiteering from the prostitution of a person less than 18 years of age a second degree offense.

Section 13A-13-113 of the Alabama Code makes all promoting of prostitution not covered by a higher degree, a class A misdemeanor.

Defenses.

A. First degree:

(1) Not done knowingly (i.e., answering service).

(2) No force or intimidation used.

(3) If the person prostituted is 16 years of age or older, the charge should be reduced to the second or third degree.

(4) Did not advance prostitution or profit from it according to definition in § 13A-10-110 of the Alabama Code.

(5) Person prostituted willingly and was over 16 years of age. However, this could still leave open a charge in the second or third degree.

B. Second degree:

(1) Not done knowingly.

(2) Did not advance or profit from the prostitution.

(3) Only one prostitute involved.

(4) If person is 18 years of age or older, the charge should be, at least, reduced to the third degree.

C. Third degree:

(1) Not done knowingly.

(2) Person prostituted is 18 years of age or older, willingly prostitutes, without working through a house or business organization.

Note: Entrapment ought to be considered as a possible defense to this charge (see Entrapment).

Cross references.

See Forcible compulsion, § 13A-6-60(8) of the Alabama Code; Lack of consent, § 13A-6-70 of the Alabama Code; Mentally defective, § 13A-6-60(5) of the Alabama Code; Mentally incapacitated, § 13A-6-60(6) of the Alabama Code; Physically helpless, § 13A-6-60(7) of the Alabama Code. See ADULTERY;

PROSTITUTION.—Cont'd.

ENTRAPMENT; RAPE; SEXUAL ABUSE; SEXUAL MISCONDUCT; SODOMY.

---

1. "ADVANCE PROSTITUTION. A person 'advances prostitution' if, acting other than as a prostitute or a patron of a prostitute, he knowingly causes or aids a person to commit or engage in prostitution, procures or solicits patrons for prostitution, provides persons or premises for prostitution purposes, operates or assists in the operation of a house of prostitution or a prostitution enterprise." Code of Ala. 1975, § 13A-12-110.

2. "PROFIT FROM PROSTITUTION. A person 'profits from prostitution' if, acting other than as a prostitute receiving compensation for personally-rendered prostitution services, he accepts or receives money or other property pursuant to a prior agreement with any person whereby he participates or is to participate in the proceeds of prostitution activity."

3. Civil remedies of abatement of nuisances, Code of Ala. 1975, §§ 6-5-140 through 6-5-154.

4. Power is granted to municipalities to prohibit houses of prostitution and punish the inmates as vagrants or otherwise in Code of Ala. 1975, § 11-47-113.

5. Code of Ala. 1975, §§ 6-5-140 to 6-5-154.

6. Code of Ala. 1975, § 22-16-18.

7. Code of Ala. 1975, § 22-16-18.

8. See Stokes v. State, 92 Ala. 73, 9 So. 40 (1890); Wilson v. State, 17 Ala. App. 307, 84 So. 783 (1920); Kelly v. State, 31 Ala. App. 201, 14 So. 2d (1943); State of Kansas v. Dodson, 565 P. 2d 296 (1977).

PUBLIC DUTY. Code of Ala. 1975, § 13A-3-22.

Defend as: Execution of public duty.

If not inconsistent with another statute, "conduct which would otherwise constitute an offense is justifiable and not criminal when it is required or authorized by law or by a judicial decree or is performed by a public servant in the reasonable exercise of his official powers, duties or functions."

PUBLIC INTOXICATION. See INTOXICATION, PUBLIC.

PUBLIC SERVANTS. See BRIBERY OF PUBLIC SERVANTS; ETHICS VIOLATIONS; IMPERSONATING PUBLIC SERVANT; TRADING IN PUBLIC OFFICE.

RAPE. Code of Ala. 1975, §§ 13A-6-61 and 13A-6-62.

A male[1] commits rape when he engages in sexual intercourse[2] with a female[3] by forcible compulsion[4] or when she is incapable[5] of giving consent[6] or by reason of the ages of the parties.[7] There is rape in the first degree (§ 13A-6-61 of the Alabama Code) and rape in the second degree (§ 13A-6-62 of the Alabama Code). "Rape" by forcible compulsion is always rape in the first degree. Without forcible compulsion there are two distinctions: (1) whether the female was incapable of consent; and (2) ages of the of the parties. First, a female was incapable of giving consent if she was (at the time) physically helpless,[8] mentally incapacitated,[9] or mentally defective.[10] If she was physically helpless or mentally incapacitated, the rape was in the first degree. If she was mentally defective, the rape was in the second degree. Second, if the male was at least sixteen years of age and the female was less than sixteen years of age, there are two issues: (1) if she was under twelve years old, the rape is of the first degree; (2) if she was more than twelve years old (but less than sixteen) and he was at least two years older than she, the rape is of the second degree; if neither age categories are matched there is no rape based on ages of the parties.

Classification.

Rape in the first degree is a Class A felony.

Rape in the second degree is a Class C felony.

Comments.

The comments following §§ 13A-6-61 and 13A-6-62 of the Alabama Code state the intention to continue defining rape as "the unlawful carnal knowledge of a woman forcibly **and**[11] without her consent," established by Owens v. State.[12] The woman must demonstrate that she was legally incapable of giving consent; **or** that she refused consent **and** "earnestly resisted."

RAPE.—Cont'd.

Fear of (immediate) death or (serious) physical injury will excuse the failure to "earnestly resist." In addition, the statute limits the possible victims of a rape to women, except women married to, or "living in cohabitation" with, the actor. This could raise some good equal protection arguments (depending on the nature of the case), as well as some notice or vagueness problems. See the query following the defenses below.

Defenses.

(1) Consent.

(2) Marriage to the woman claiming the rape.

(3) Living (cohabitation) with the woman claiming the rape (see Query, infra).

(4) He is less than 16 years old. (Also look at the relative ages of both, under rape in the second degree).

(5) It would also seem possible to defend by showing that, although she did not explicitly give consent, she was capable of consenting and did not "resist in earnest." The comment indicates that it may be a successful defense even if she said "no."

(6) No penetration.

(7) Additional defenses might include attacks on the statute as being vague or violative of equal protection (see Query, infra).

Query.

(1) In § 13A-6-61(a)(3) of the Alabama Code a female who is "**less**[13] than 12 years old" is protected; and, in § 13A-6-62(a)(1) of the Alabama Code, a female who is "**more**[14] than 12 years old is protected"; however, there is no mention of the female who **is** 12 years old. Of course, there is the argument that "more than 12 years old" includes the "12 year old." This might be convincing if the drafters did not go to such pains in defining the age of the suspect. Note, in the same Code sections (§§ 13A-6-61(a)(3) and 13A-6-62(a)(1) of the Alabama Code), the accused's age is defined as "being 16 years or older." I could assume that if the drafters (in § 13A-6-62(a)(1) of the Alabama Code) intended that she be 12 years or older they would have stated that she be "more than

RAPE.—Cont'd.

12 years old." This could, of course, raise a question of vagueness, assuming the drafters did not intend to exclude 12 year olds from the protection of the statute (which otherwise would raise an even more important defense).

(2) The possible victims of rape are limited to "any female person who is not married to the actor." Additionally, "[p]ersons living together in cohabitation are married for purposes of [sexual offenses]." See § 13A-6-60(4) of the Alabama Code. It would appear that the statute would not require that the husband and wife be living together for the husband to defend on this ground to the charge of rape. What of the "living in cohabitation" situation? Under adultery, "living in cohabitation" would exist if there was a weekly interaction, that is, he visits her once a week on a regular basis (or intending it to be on a regular basis). Can he raise this defense? Would it matter if he was "living in cohabitation" with several women (although separately)? If he were married and "living in cohabitation" with one or more other women, could he make use of this defense? Can he (like his married counterpart) after an absence of a week (month, year) still claim that they are "living in cohabitation" and, thereby, defend against the charge of rape. It would appear that no matter how one answers the questions presented above, the issue of vagueness is apparent.

(3) Another group that may not be protected by the statutes (see §§ 13A-6-60(6) and 13A-6-61(a)(2) of the Alabama Code), would be any female person who is temporarily incapable of appraising or controlling her conduct owing to the influence of a narcotic or intoxicating substance, or to any other incapacitating act committed upon her, as long as it was **not** without her consent (this could be less than "with her consent"). Note, this would appear to be the case even if the person administering the narcotic, intoxicant, etc., did so with the intent of rendering her incapable of appraising or controlling her conduct so that, in the words of the drafters,

RAPE.—Cont'd.

"he may gain access to her."

Cross references.

See SEXUAL ABUSE; SEXUAL MISCONDUCT; SODOMY.

---

1. *Although the charge of rape is specifically aimed at men, a woman aiding a man in committing rape could be charged as an accomplice.*
2. *Sexual intercourse is defined by Code of Ala. 1975, § 13A-6-60(1) as having "its ordinary meaning and occurs upon any penetration, however slight; emission is not required." See also ADULTERY, note 3, supra.*
3. *Female is defined and restricted by Code of Ala. 1975, § 13A-6-60(4) as "any female person who is not married to the actor. Persons living together in cohabitation are married for purposes of this article, regardless of the legal status of their relationship otherwise."*
4. *Forcible compulsion is defined by Code of Ala. 1975, § 13A-6-60(8) as "[p]hysical force that overcomes earnest resistance or a threat, express or implied, that places a person in fear of immediate death or serious physical injury to [herself] or another person."*
5. *She is incapable of giving consent if she was, at the time, mentally defective (Code of Ala. 1975, § 13A-6-60(5); see also note 10, infra); or she was, at the time, mentally incapacitated (Code of Ala. 1975, § 13A-6-60(6) ; see also note 9, infra); or she was, at the time physically helpless (Code of Ala. 1975, § 13A-6-60(7); see also note 8, infra.)*
6. *Consent or rather the lack of consent is defined by Code of Ala. 1975, § 13A-6-70. It states that "[w]hether or not specifically stated, it is an element of every offense defined in this article, with the exception of subdivision (a)(3) of § 13A-6-65 that the sexual act was committed without consent of the victim." Code of Ala. 1975, § 13A-6-70(b) establishes that the "lack of consent results from either forcible compulsion, or incapacity to consent." Note that "[i]f the offense charged is [not rape but rather] sexual abuse, any circumstances, in addition to forcible compulsion or incapacity to consent, in which the victim does not expressly or impliedly acquiesce in the actor's conduct," constitute lack of consent. And, Code of Ala. 1975, § 13A-6-70(c) establishes that "[a] person is deemed incapable of consent if he is: (1) [l]ess than 16 years old [see note 5, supra]; or (2) [m]entally defective [see note 10, infra]; or (3) [m]entally incapacitated [see note 9, infra]; or (4) [p]hysically helpless [see note 8 infra]."*
7. *If he is 16 years or older and she is less than 12*

RAPE.—Cont'd.

years old, Code of Ala. 1975, § 13A-6-61(a)(3) or, if she is more than 12 years old but less than 16 years old and she is at least 2 years younger than the actor. Code of Ala. 1975, § 13A-6-62(a)(1).

8. *According to Code of Ala. 1975, § 13A-6-60(7), "[s]uch term means that a person is unconscious or for any other reason is physically unable to communicate unwillingness to an act."*
9. *According to Code of Ala. 1975, § 13A-6-60(6), "[s]uch term means that a person is rendered temporarily incapable of appraising or controlling his conduct owing to the influence of a narcotic or intoxicating substance administered to him without his consent, or to any other incapacitating act committed upon him without his consent."*
10. *According to Code of Ala. 1975, § 13A-6-60(5), "[s]uch term means that a person suffers from a mental disease or defect which renders him incapable of appraising the nature of his conduct."*
11. *Emphasis added.*
12. *Owens v. State, 29 Ala. App. 53, 191 So. 899 (1939).*
13. *Emphasis added.*
14. *Emphasis added.*

REAL ESTATE, TAKING OR RETAKING POSSESSION OF. Code of Ala. 1975, § 13A-7-60.

Charged as: Taking or retaking possession of real estate.

It is a crime for: "any person having no title or bona fide claim of title thereto or right of possession, who enters upon any land, and on demand of the owner or person entitled to the possession thereof, refuses to surrender such possession, or any person or his privy, who, having been dispossessed of any real estate by an officer under legal process from any court having jurisdiction of the subject matter; or any person or his privy, who voluntarily surrenders possession of the lands as a result of a judgment of a court of competent jurisdiction and goes back into the possession of such real estate by force or otherwise; or who, having regained possession of such real estate, holds the same by force or threats without having been restored to the possession of such real estate by an order of a court of competent jurisdiction."

REAL ESTATE, TAKING OR RETAKING POSSESSION OF. —Cont'd.

Classification.

Statutory punishment: fine of $200.00 to $1000.00 and not less than 6 months in county jail.

Cross references.

See TRESPASS, CRIMINAL.

RECEIVING STOLEN PROPERTY.

Code of Ala. 1975, §§ 13A-8-16 through 13A-8-19.

"(a) A person commits the crime of receiving[1] stolen[2] property[3] if he intentionally receives, retains or disposes of stolen property knowing that it has been stolen or having reasonable grounds to believe it has been stolen, unless the property is received, retained or disposed of with intent to restore it to the owner.[4]

"(b) If a person:

"(1) On two separate occasions within a year prior to the commission of the instant offense of receiving stolen property is found in possession or control of stolen property; or

"(2) Possesses goods or property which have been recently stolen; or

"(3) Regularly buys, sells, uses or handles in the course of business property of the sort received, and acquired the property without making reasonable inquiry[5] whether the person selling or delivering the property to him had a legal right to do so, this shall be prima facie evidence that he has the requisite knowledge or belief.

"(c) The fact that the person who stole the property has not been convicted, apprehended or identified is not a defense to a charge of receiving stolen property." § 13A-8-16 of the Alabama Code.

Degrees of receiving stolen property:

"Receiving stolen property which exceeds $1,000.00 in value constitutes receiving stolen property in the first degree." § 13A-8-17(a) of the Alabama Code.

"Receiving stolen property:

"(1) Which exceeds $100 in value but does not exceed $1,000 in value; or

"(2) Of any value under the circumstances described in subdivision (b)(3) of section

RECEIVING STOLEN PROPERTY.
—Cont'd.

13A-8-16; constitutes receiving stolen property in the second degree." § 13A-8-18(a) of the Alabama Code.

"Receiving stolen property which does not exceed $100.00 in value constitutes receiving stolen property in the third degree." § 13A-8-19(a) of the Alabama Code.

Classification.

Class B felony, receiving stolen property in the first degree.

Class C felony, receiving stolen property in the second degree.

Class A misdemeanor, receiving stolen property in the third degree.

Comments.

These sections make punishable, to the same extent as in the theft sections (§§ 13A-8-2 through 13A-8-9 of the Alabama Code), the buying, receiving, concealing or aiding in concealing property with the knowledge it has been stolen, or having reasonable grounds to believe it has been stolen. The degree of the crimes is generally dependent upon value, although heavier penalties are available against dealers in stolen property or pawn brokers. Ultimate restoration is no defense.[6] The mere possession of recently stolen goods gives rise to a factual inference of the scienter required to convict,[7] but not to a presumption of guilty as a matter of law.[8] Under this statute the receiver may be convicted before the thief himself.

Defenses.

(1) Lack of intent.

(2) Lack of knowledge property is stolen.

(3) Intent to restore to the owner upon acquisition of the property.

(4) Claim of right.[9]

Cross references.

See THEFT OF LOST PROPERTY; THEFT OF PROPERTY.

---

1. *"RECEIVING. Such term includes, but is not limited to, acquiring possession, control or title and taking a security interest in the property." Code of Ala. 1975, § 13A-8-1(11).*
2. *"STOLEN. Obtained by theft, theft by appropriating lost property, robbery or extortion." Code of Ala. 1975, § 13A-8-1(12).*

RECEIVING STOLEN PROPERTY.
—Cont'd.

3. *"PROPERTY. Any money, tangible or intangible personal property, property (whether real or personal) the location of which can be changed (including things growing on, affixed to or found in land and documents, although the rights represented hereby have no physical location), contract right, chose-in-action, interest in a claim to wealth, credit or any other article or thing of value of any kind.*

   "Commodities of a public utility nature, such as gas, electricity, steam and water, constitute property, but the supplying of such a commodity to premises from an outside source by means of wires, pipes, conduits or other equipment shall be deemed a rendition of a service rather than a sale or delivery of property." Code of Ala. 1975, § 13A-8-1(10). See Theft of Services, Code of Ala. 1975, § 13A-8-10.
4. *"OWNER. A person, other than the defendant, who has possession of or any other interest in the property involved, even though that interest or possession is unlawful, and without whose consent the defendant has no authority to exert control over the property.*

   "A secured party, as defined in section 7-9-105(i), is not an owner in relation to a defendant who is a debtor, as defined in section 7-9-105(d), in respect of property in which the secured party has a security interest, as defined in section 7-1-201(37)."
5. *Reasonable inquiry is a question of fact and a burden which the dealer is in a better position to bear.*
6. *Johnson v. State, 41 Ala. App. 351, 132 So. 2d 485 (1961).*
7. *Stanley v. State, 46 Ala. App. 543, 245 So. 2d 827 (1970).*
8. *Milligan v. State, 45 Ala. App. 113, 226 So. 2d 172 (1969).*
9. *"(a) It is a defense to a prosecution under sections 13A-8-2 through 13A-8-11 (theft of property, theft of lost property, theft of services and unauthorized use of vehicle) that the actor honestly believed that he had a claim to the property for services involved which he was entitled to assert in the manner which forms the basis for the charge against him.*

   "(b) The burden of injecting the issue of claim of right is on the defendant, but this does not shift the burden of proof." Code of Ala. 1975, § 13A-8-12.

RECIDIVIST. See HABITUAL FELONY OFFENDER.

RECKLESS DRIVING. See MOTOR VEHICLE CRIMES.

RECKLESS ENDANGERMENT. Code of Ala. 1975, § 13A-6-24.

"A person commits the crime of reckless endangerment if he recklessly engages in conduct which creates a substantial risk of serious physical injury[1] to another person."

Classification.

Class A misdemeanor.

Comments.

This statute defines a new crime covering reckless conduct that creates a substantial risk of, but does not result in, serious physical injury. It is intended to supplement the revised assault offenses covered in this article. The statute does not require any particular person to be actually placed in danger, but rather deals with potential risks, as well as cases where a specific person actually is within the area of danger. The range of conduct proscribed is not limited; application of this statute will be defined only by cases tried under it.

Defenses.

(1) Failure to prove conduct was "reckless" in nature.

(2) Failure to prove risk created was substantial.

(3) Failure to prove risk of injury sustained would be serious and/or physical.

(4) Consent.

Query.

What is the standard to be employed in determining if the risk created is substantial? Would mere inaction ever constitute "engages in conduct?"

Cross references.

See "Recklessly," defined in § 13A-2-2(3) of the Alabama Code. See MOTOR VEHICLE CRIMES.

1. *Serious physical injury is defined in Code of Ala. 1975, § 13A-1-2(9) as "[p]hysical injury which creates a substantial risk of death, or which causes serious and protracted disfigurement, protracted impairment of health or protracted loss or impairment of the function of any bodily organ."*

RECKLESS OPERATION OF AIRCRAFT. See AVIATION.

RECORDING OR RECORDING DEVICE. See COPYING, SALE, OR POSSESSION OF RECORD[ING] DEVICE.

REFUSAL TO PERMIT AN INSPECTION. See INSPECTION, REFUSAL TO PERMIT.

REFUSING TO AID A PEACE OFFICER. See PEACE OFFICER, REFUSING TO AID.

REFUSING TO ASSIST IN FIRE CONTROL. Code of Ala. 1975, § 13A-10-6.

"A person commits the crime of refusing to assist in fire control if, upon command by a fireman[1] or peace officer identified to him as such, he intentionally disobeys a reasonable order or regulation made in relation to the conduct of persons in the vicinity of a fire."

Classification.

Class C misdemeanor.

Comments.

Section 13A-10-5 of the Alabama Code applies only to commands for assistance in making a lawful arrest or preventing a crime. Section 13A-10-6 of the Alabama Code affects the conduct of persons in the vicinity of a fire. Both sections require that the person requesting assistance identify himself and that the request be reasonable. The commentary indicates that there is not an affirmative duty to assist in the "complicated and hazardous" work of modern fire fighting. Whether the complexity or hazards of aiding a peace officer in a lawful arrest or prevention of crime might be considered as to the reasonableness of the request is not known at this time. Prior law had no element of reasonableness. It was no excuse that a citizen thought his assistance would be futile or dangerous.[2]

REFUSING TO ASSIST IN FIRE CONTROL.—Cont'd.

Defenses.

(1) Lack of identification.
(2) Unreasonable request.
(3) Lack of intent to disobey.

Cross references.

See ARSON; FORCE IN MAKING AN ARREST OR PREVENTING AN ESCAPE; OBSTRUCTING GOVERNMENTAL OPERATIONS.

---

1. *"Any officer of a fire department or any other person vested by law with the duty to extinguish fires." Code of Ala. 1975, § 13A-10-1(1).*
2. *Doughterty v. State, 106 Ala. 63, 17 So. 393 (1895).*

REGISTRATION OF FELONS. See FELONS, REGISTRATION OF.

REGISTRATION OF SEX OFFENDERS. See SEX OFFENDERS, REGISTRATION OF.

REMOVAL, CONCEALMENT OF DELINQUENT CHILD. See CUSTODY, INTERFERENCE WITH; JUVENILE PROCEEDINGS; KIDNAPPING; UNLAWFUL IMPRISONMENT.

REPEAT OFFENDER. See HABITUAL FELONY OFFENDER.

REPORT, REQUIRED, FAILURE TO FILE. Code of Ala. 1975, § 13A-10-4.

Charged as: Failing to file required report.

"(a) A person commits the crime of failing to file a required report if, knowing the he is required by law to submit a written report to a designated public servant,[1] he intentionally fails to submit the report within the time provided by law.

"(b) Failure to submit a report within 10 days after receipt of proper notification that the report legally is due shall constitute prima facie evidence of:

"(1) Knowledge of a legal duty to submit the report; and

"(2) Intentional failure to submit the report.

"(c) This section applies to the failure to submit a specific report only when a separate statutory provision makes such failure subject to the operation of this section."

Classification.

Violation.

Comments.

This section does not in itself make any act a crime. The purpose of this section is to prevent duplication of various punishments for failure to file various reports (i.e., filing accident report governed by Title 32 of the Alabama Code.) Liability exists only if the defendant knows that he is required by law to submit a written report and intentionally fails to do so.

Defenses.

(1) Lack of intent.
(2) Lack of knowledge written report is required.
(3) Omission in separate statute(s) of provision requiring a report as per this section.

---

1. *"Any officer or employee of government, including legislators, judges and any person or agency participating as an adviser, consultant or otherwise in performing a governmental function." Code of Ala. 1975, § 13A-10-1(7).*

REPRESENTATION BY LEGISLATOR FOR COMPENSATION PROHIBITED; DISCLOSURE REQUIRED OF OTHER PUBLIC OFFICIALS UNDERTAKING SUCH REPRESENTATION. Code of Ala. 1975, § 36-25-10.

"If a public official or employee, or member of his family, or a business with which any of them is associated, shall for a fee represent a client or constituent before any quasi-judicial board or commission, governmental regulatory agency or executive department or agency, notice of such representation must be given within five days after the first day of such appearance to the state ethics commission in the manner prescribed by the commission. No member of the legislature shall for a fee, reward or other

REPRESENTATION BY LEGISLATOR FOR COMPENSATION PROHIBITED, ETC.—Cont'd.
compensation represent any person, firm or corporation before the public service commission or the state board of adjustment."

Comments.
Apparently pro bono public representation would be permissible.

Defenses.
(1) Not a public official or employee, nor a member of a public official's (or employee's) family nor associated in business with a public official or employee or their family.
(2) No fee was charged.
(3) Did not represent the client in question.
(4) Did not represent the client before one of the agencies in question.
(5) Gave timely notice.

Cross references.
See CONFIDENTIAL INFORMATION, MISUSE OF; CONFLICT OF INTEREST, FAILURE TO DISCLOSE; ETHICS VIOLATIONS; TRADING IN PUBLIC OFFICE.

RESISTING ARREST. Code of Ala. 1975, § 13A-10-41.
"A person commits the crime of resisting arrest if he intentionally prevents or attempts to prevent a peace officer[1] from effecting a lawful arrest of himself or of another person."

Classification.
Class B misdemeanor.

Comments.
This section does not distinguish violent and nonviolent methods of resistance. The arrest being made must be a lawful arrest or the resistance is not covered by this section.

Defenses.
(1) Lack of intent.
(2) Person effecting arrest was not a peace officer.

Cross references.
See FORCE IN DEFENSE OF A PERSON; FORCE IN MAKING AN ARREST OR PREVENTING AN ESCAPE; FORCE IN

RESISTING ARREST.—Cont'd.
RESISTING ARREST (PROHIBITED); OBSTRUCTING GOVERNMENTAL OPERATIONS; PEACE OFFICER, REFUSING TO AID; PUBLIC DUTY.

---

1. *"Any public servant vested by law with a duty to maintain public order or to make arrests for crime, whether that duty extends to all crimes or is limited to specific crimes." Code of Ala. 1975, § 13A-10-1(5).*

RETAKING OR TAKING POSSESSION OF REAL ESTATE. See REAL ESTATE, TAKING OR RETAKING POSSESSION OF.

RETARDED. See INSANITY.

RIFLE, SHOTGUN WALKING CANE, CARRYING. Code of Ala. 1975, § 13A-11-54.
Charged as: Carrying rifle or shotgun walking cane.
"Any person who carries a rifle or shotgun walking cane shall, on conviction be fined not less than $1,000.00 and be imprisoned in the penitentiary not less than two years."

Classification.
Although there is no designated classification, considering the imposition of a sentence, classification would be most consistent with a Class B felony.

Comments.
Although broad in its applications, the statute ought to be read subject to the defenses cited in chapter 13A-3 of the Alabama Code (especially the section on execution of public duty).[1] Even so construed, the statute may be subject to constitutional attack.[2]

Defenses.
(1) Void for vagueness.
(2) Weapon not rifle or shotgun walking cane.
(3) Execution of public duty.
(4) License or privilege.
(5) Exempt military officer.

---

1. *Code of Ala. 1975, § 13A-5-6.*
2. *Code of Ala. 1975, § 13A-3-22. See also Code of Ala. 1975, § 13A-11-105 (exemption from this article); Papachristou v. City of Jacksonville, 405 U. S. 156, 92 S. Ct. 839, 31 L. Ed. 2d 110 (1972).*

RIOT. Code of Ala. 1975, § 13A-11-3.

"A person commits the crime of riot if, with five or more other persons, he wrongfully engages in tumultuous and violent conduct[1] and thereby intentionally[2] or recklessly[3] causes or creates a grave risk of public terror or alarm."

Classification.

Class A misdemeanor.

Comments.

Riot is the culmination and function of the crimes of unlawful assembly and rout, resulting in force and violence that threatens someone publicly. The purpose of the statute is to define the boundary past which dissent and protest become an intolerable burden on the minimum need for order. Violence, real or threatened, and unreasonable interference, real or threatened, with lawful public or private activity is conduct sufficient to support a prosecution for "riot." The statute requires conduct by a total of at least six persons. Yet only one person is required to act with force and violence supported by the mere physical presence of the others.

Defenses.

(1) Failure to prove five or more other persons involved.

(2) Failure to prove conduct was violent.

(3) The risk of public terror or alarm was not "grave."

Query.

At what point does a lawful assembly become an unlawful assembly? May a corporate entity be prosecuted under the statute? Would an argument based on the "locality rule" be proper in regard to the standard to be used in determining what constitutes "public terror or alarm?"

Cross references.

See DISORDERLY CONDUCT; DISORDERLY PERSONS, FAILURE TO DISPERSE; LOITERING; RIOT, INCITING TO; UNLAWFUL ASSEMBLY.

---

1. Code of Ala. 1975, § 13A-2-1(4) defines conduct as "[a]n act or omission and its accompanying mental state."

RIOT.—Cont'd.

2. "A person acts intentionally with respect to a result or to conduct described by a statute defining an offense, when his purpose is to cause that result or to engage in that conduct." Code of Ala. 1975, § 13A-2-2(1).

3. "A person acts recklessly with respect to a result or to a circumstance described by a statute defining an offense when he is aware of and consciously disregards a substantial and unjustifiable risk that the result will occur or that the circumstance exists. The risk must be of such nature and degree that disregard thereof constitutes a gross deviation from the standard of conduct that a reasonable person would observe in the situation. A person who creates a risk but is unaware thereof solely by reason of voluntary intoxication, as defined in subdivision (e)(2) of section 13A-3-2, acts recklessly with respect thereto." Code of Ala. 1975, § 13A-2-2(3).

RIOT, INCITING TO. Code of Ala. 1975, § 13A-11-4.

Charged as: Inciting to riot.

"A person commits the crime of inciting to riot[1] if he commands, solicits, incites or urges another person to engage in tumultuous and violent conduct[2] of a kind likely to cause or create a grave risk of public terror or alarm."[3]

Classification.

Class A misdemeanor.

Comments.

This statute covers conduct that does not reach the level of either the crime of "riot" or the crime of "unlawful assembly." The same conduct, however, might be punished under the "criminal solicitation" statute. The justification for providing a separate statute may rest on the premise that a general call to "go out and revolt" does not amount to criminal solicitation since a specific crime must have been "solicited;" yet, under certain circumstances the same call would constitute an incitement to riot. This statute differs from the offenses of "riot" and "unlawful assembly" in that it does not require the participation of six or more persons; the solicitation of only one other person is sufficient. Approval or

RIOT, INCITING TO.—Cont'd.

cooperation by the person solicited is not a prerequisite for prosecution under the statute.[4]

Defenses.

(1) Conduct not of both a tumultuous and violent nature.

(2) Risk created is not "grave."

(3) Risk created is not of nature to evoke "public terror or alarm."

(4) First Amendment to United States Constitution.

(5) Failure to prove conduct amounted to "solicitation."

Query.

Under the proper circumstances, could inaction or nonspeech constitute the conduct proscribed by this statute? Is it possible that the advocacy of exercising a legal right in a nonspecific manner could be prohibited by this statute?

Cross references.

See DISORDERLY CONDUCT; DISORDERLY PERSONS, FAILURE TO DISPERSE; HARASSMENT OR HARASSING COMMUNICATIONS; LOITERING; RIOT; SOLICITATION; UNLAWFUL ASSEMBLY.

---

1. *"A person commits the crime of riot if, with five or more other persons, he wrongfully engages in tumultuous and violent conduct and thereby intentionally or recklessly causes or creates a grave risk of public terror or alarm." Code of Ala. 1975, § 13A-11-3(a).*
2. *"CONDUCT. An act or omission and its accompanying mental state." Code of Ala. 1975, § 13A-2-1(4).*
3. *"A person is criminally liable for an offense if it is committed by his own behavior or by the behavior of another person for which he is legally accountable as provided for in sections 13A-11-1 through 13A-11-14, or both." Code of Ala. 1975, § 13A-2-20.*
4. *"A person is legally accountable for the behavior of another person if he is made accountable for the behavior of such person by the statute defining the offense or by specific provision of this title." Code of Ala. 1975, § 13A-2-21.*

ROBBERY. Code of Ala. 1975, §§ 13A-8-40 through 13A-8-44.

"A person commits the crime of robbery in the first degree if he violates section 13A-8-43 and he:

"(1) Is armed with a deadly weapon[1] or dangerous instrument;[2] or

"(2) Causes serious physical injury[3] to another." § 13A-8-41(a) of the Alabama Code.

"A person commits the crime of robbery in the second degree if he violates section 13A-8-43 and he is aided by another person actually present." § 13A-8-42(a) of the Alabama Code.

"A person commits the crime of robbery in the third degree if in the course of committing a theft[4] he:

"(1) Uses force against the person of the owner or any person present with intent to overcome his physical resistance or physical power of resistance; or

"(2) Threatens the imminent use of force against the person of the owner or any person present with intent to compel acquiescence to the taking of or escaping with the property." § 13A-8-43(a) of the Alabama Code.

Classification.

Class A felony, robbery in the first degree.
Class B felony, robbery in the second degree.
Class C felony, robbery in the third degree.

Comments.

The objective of this law is to protect the potential victim from harm, or from being placed in fear of harm, as well as to protect that person's property rights. The basic elements of robbery are contained in the third degree classification. They are (1) the use or threat of imminent[5] use of force against (2) the owner or another person present with (3) the intent to overcome physical resistance in (4) the course of committing a theft or escaping with the property. This last element includes attempted thefts or flight.[6] The classification of second degree robbery requires additionally the presence of an accomplice. The offense in the first degree requires the elements of the offense in the third degree and that the offender be armed with a deadly weapon or dangerous instrument, or cause serious physical injury to another. The injury caused to another

ROBBERY.—Cont'd.

need not be intended. Possession of an article used to lead a person to believe it is a deadly weapon or dangerous instrument, or the assertion that one is so armed constitutes prima facie evidence that the offender is so armed. This evidence can be refuted by the defendant, which in turn, may reduce a Class A felony charge to a Class C felony charge. Except for those instances that constitute prima facie evidence that the offender is armed, what distinguishes the first degree classification is whether the offender is in fact armed, or causes injury; not the state of mind of the victim. § 13A-8-44 of the Alabama Code specifically disallows claim of right as a defense to this crime.

Cross references.

See ASSAULT; EXTORTION; THEFT OF PROPERTY.

---

1. *"DEADLY WEAPON. A firearm or anything manifestly designed, made or adapted for the purposes of inflicting death or serious physical injury, and such term includes, but is not limited to, a pistol, rifle or shotgun; or a switch-blade knife, gravity knife, stiletto, sword or dagger; or any billy, blackjack, bludgeon or metal knuckles." Code of Ala. 1975, § 13A-1-2(11).*
2. *"DANGEROUS INSTRUMENT. Any instrument, article or substance which, under the circumstances in which it is used, attempted to be used or threatened to be used, is highly capable of causing death or serious physical injury, and such term includes a 'vehicle' [any propelled device by which any person or property is transported on land, water or in the air, and includes motor vehicles, motorcycles, motorboats, and aircraft, and any vessel, whether propelled by machinery or not]." See Code of Ala. 1975, §§ 13A-1-2(12), 13A-1-2(13), and 13A-8-1(9).*
3. *"SERIOUS PHYSICAL INJURY. Physical injury which creates a substantial risk of death, or which causes serious and protracted disfigurement, protracted impairment of health or protracted loss or impairment of the function of any bodily organ." Code of Ala. 1975, § 13A-1-2(9).*
4. *" 'IN THE COURSE OF COMMITTING A THEFT' embraces acts which occur in an attempt to commit or the commission of theft, or in immediate flight after the attempt or commission." Code of Ala. 1975, § 13A-8-40(b).*
5. *Threat of force must be present or "imminent"; it cannot be in the future. See Extortion, Code of Ala. 1975, §§ 13A-8-13 through 13A-8-15.*
6. *Robbery, is broader in scope than common law robbery. It includes instances where violence is used or threatened "in the course of committing a theft," which includes an attempted theft, or flight, as well as a completed theft. See Code of Ala. 1975, §§ 13A-8-40 through 13A-8-44.*

SALE OF. See specific title (e.g. COAL; RECORDING DEVICE, etc.).

SENTENCING. Code of Ala. 1975, §§ 13A-5-6 and 13A-5-7.

The defendant has a right to be present at the time he is sentenced,[1] and he has the right to be represented by counsel unless this right is waived.[2]

Apparently, defense counsel has the right to address the trial judge and to call the court's attention to any factor he believes will be helpful to the client.[3] The court in Green v. United States[4] said that the defendant has the right of common law allocution before he is sentenced, at least if this right is not waived. Before a defendant is sentenced, he has a right (1) to personally address the judge in his own behalf and (2) to present any information in mitigation of punishment.[5]

In addition to the right of the defendant and his counsel to address the court, the judge may be willing to hear from other interested persons on matters relating to the sentence to be imposed, particularly if there has not just been a pre-sentence hearing. If there is any doubt about whether a particular judge will hear from other witnesses at the sentencing, defense counsel should be doubly sure to have such persons present for the pre-sentence hearing.

At the time of sentencing, defense counsel may summarize the favorable comments which have been made about the defendant and urge the judge to consider some rehabilitative program or other alternative to confinement. Hence, it has been said that an accused "cannot be punished by a more severe punishment because he unsuccessfully exercised his constitutional right to stand trial rather than plead guilty."[6]

SENTENCING.—Cont'd.

After the trial judge has orally informed the defendant of his sentence, he normally should advise him of the following: (1) his right to appeal; (2) his right to appeal without cost if he is unable to pay the cost of appeal; (3) his right to appointment of counsel for the appeal if he is unable to employ counsel; (4) his right to have the sentence reviewed by a panel of superior court judges if the sentence is for five years or more; (5) the length of time within which an appeal must be filed; and (6) the length of time in which he may petition to have his sentence reviewed by a panel of superior court judges.

It should be noted that Rule 26.11 of Alabama's Proposed Rules of Criminal Procedure provides for the following:

(a) Consecutive Sentences. Separate sentences of imprisonment imposed on a defendant for two or more offenses, whether they are charged in the same charging instrument or by separate charging instruments joined for trial, shall run consecutively unless the judge at the time of sentencing directs otherwise.

(b) Concurrent Sentences. The court, at the time of sentencing, in its discretion may direct that the sentence being imposed will be served concurrently with any other sentence which has previously been imposed on the defendant, either by sentencing court or by any other court.

(c) Reconsideration. If service of a sentence or sentences shall begin after service of one or more intervening sentences has been completed, the court on its own motion, or on motion of either party, within the period provided for correction or reduction of sentence under Rule 24.3 of Alabama's Proposed Rules of Criminal Procedure, may in its discretion reconsider the court's prior ruling and order nunc pro tunc that the sentence or sentences be served concurrently.

In addition, Rule 24.3 of Alabama's Proposed Rules of Criminal Procedure provides as follows:

(a) Correction. The court may correct an illegal sentence at any time and may correct a sentence imposed in an illegal manner within the time provided herein for reduction of sentence.

(b) Reduction. The court may reduce a sentence within 120 days after the sentence is imposed, unless a notice of appeal has been filed, or within 120 days after receipt by the court of a mandate issued upon affirmance of the judgment or dismissal of the appeal, or within 120 days after entry of any order or judgment of Supreme Court of Alabama denying review of, or having the effect of upholding, a judgment of conviction. The court may also reduce a sentence upon revocation of probation.

The Comment following Rule 24.3 of Alabama's Proposed Rules of Criminal Procedure states that the rule was taken from Rule 35 of the Federal Rules of Criminal Procedure. In 1979, the following was added to Rule 35: "Changing a sentence from a sentence of incarceration to a grant of probation shall constitute a permissible reduction of sentence under this subdivision." This amendment was made so as to make it clear that a judge has the discretion to reduce a sentence from incarceration to probation. However, as indicated by the rulings in United States v. Murray[7] and Affronti v. United States,[8] and Rule 35 itself, if the defendant is already incarcerated, the provision for reduction of the sentence from incarceration to probation is not applicable, since subsection (b) of both the Federal and Alabama rules restrict the court's discretion to a 120 day time limit.[9] In light of the fact that the Alabama rule was drafted in 1977 and taken from the Federal rule, will Alabama also follow the 1979 amendment to the Federal Rule? This author believes that we should and will.

Class A felony (maximum): 10 yrs.—99 yrs.

Class B felony (maximum): 2 yrs.—20 yrs.

Class C felony (maximum): 1 yr. & 1 day—10 yrs.

Class A misdemeanor (maximum): Not more than 1 yr.

Class B misdemeanor (maximum): Not more than 6 mos.

SENTENCING.—Cont'd.

Class C misdemeanor (maximum): Not more than 3 mos.

Section 13A-5-7(b) of the Alabama Code states that "[s]entences for violations shall be for a definite term of imprisonment in the county jail, not to exceed 30 days."

Under § 13A-5-6(a)(4) and (5) of the Alabama Code, as amended by Act 81-940 (effective as of May 27, 1981), where a deadly weapon (or firearm) is used or attempted to be used, the following sentences are applicable:

Class A felony: Minimum of 20 yrs.

Class B felony: Minimum of 10 yrs.

Class C felony: Minimum of 10 yrs.

Sections 13A-5-11 and 13A-5-12 of the Code of Alabama provide:

Class A felony (maximum): $20,000

Class B felony (maximum): 10,000

Class C felony (maximum): 5,000

Class A misdemeanor (maximum): 2,000

Class B misdemeanor (maximum): 1,000

Class C misdemeanor (maximum): 500

Section 13A-5-12(b) of the Alabama Code provides "a fine for a violation shall be for a definite amount, fixed by the court, not to exceed $200.00, or any amount not exceeding double the pecuniary gain to the defendant or loss to the victim caused by the commission of the offense."

Section 13A-5-9 of the Alabama Code provides additional penalties for "habitual felony offenders":

(1) Current class A felony conviction and 1 prior felony conviction: Life, or 15 yrs.—99 yrs.

(2) Current class A felony conviction and 2 prior felony convictions: Life.

(3) Current class A felony conviction and 3 prior felony convictions: Life without parole.

(4) Current class B felony conviction and 1 prior felony conviction: Equal to that of a class A felony.

(5) Current class B felony conviction and 2 prior felony convictions: Life, or 15 yrs.—99 yrs.

(6) Current class B felony conviction and 3 prior felony convictions: Life.

(7) Current class C felony conviction and 1 prior felony conviction: Equal to that of a class B felony.

(8) Current class C felony conviction and 2 prior felony convictions: Equal to that of a class A felony.

(9) Current class C felony conviction and 3 prior felony convictions: Life, or 15 years.—99 yrs.

Section 13A-4-1(f) of the Alabama Code provides as follows:

"Criminal solicitation is a:

"(1) Class A felony if the offense solicited is murder.

"(2) Class B felony if the offense solicited is a Class A felony.

"(3) Class C felony if the offense solicited is a Class B felony.

"(4) Class A misdemeanor if the offense solicited is a Class C felony.

"(5) Class B misdemeanor if the offense solicited is a Class A misdemeanor.

"(6) Class C misdemeanor if the offense solicited is a Class B misdemeanor.

"(7) Violation[10] if the offense solicited is a Class C misdemeanor."

Section 13A-4-2(d) of the Alabama Code provides as follows:

"An attempt is a:

"(1) Class A felony if the offense attempted is murder.

"(2) Class B felony if the offense is a Class A felony.

"(3) Class C felony if the offense attempted is a Class B felony.

"(4) Class A misdemeanor if the offense attempted is a Class C felony.

"(5) Class B misdemeanor if the offense attempted is a Class A misdemeanor.

"(6) Class C misdemeanor if the offense attempted is a Class B misdemeanor.

"(7) Violation if the offense attempted is a Class C misdemeanor."

Article 2, § 13A-5-30 through § 13A-5-38 of the Alabama Code, and Act 81-178, approved on March 31, 1981 and effective as of 12:01 a.m. on July 1, 1981, provide the parameters within which the death sentence (or life without parole) may be invoked.

Finally, while neither the double jeopardy

SENTENCING.—Cont'd.

nor equal protection clause prevents a state from imposing a more severe second sentence, due process requires that there be a finding of facts justifying a greater sentence if a defendant is resentenced for the crime for which he has previously been sentenced.[11] From a constitutional standpoint, where vindictiveness is not present and a defendant is retried before a jury, the jurors may impose a greater sentence.[12]

Where a judge imposes a more severe sentence upon a defendant after a new trial, North Carolina v. Pearce[13] states that "the reasons for his doing so must be based upon objective information concerning identifiable conduct on the part of the defendant occurring after the time of the original sentencing proceeding."[14] Even when a defendant obtains a new trial which is conducted before another judge who has no knowledge of the first sentence, a sentence greater than that of the first judge cannot be imposed in the absence of the requirements of North Carolina v. Pearce.

Rule 26.12 of the Proposed Alabama Rules of Criminal Procedure provides that where a judgment has been set aside on appeal, by collateral attack or on a post-trial motion, the court may not impose a sentence for the same offense, or for a different offense based on the same conduct, which is more severe than the prior sentence unless new facts are introduced in evidence showing more aggravated circumstances than appeared at the original trial. Upon any resentencing the defendant shall be given credit for any time already served on the prior sentence.

Cross references.

See N. Chiarkas, Alabama Criminal Trial Practice, §§ 26-4 through 26-8.

---

1. *Ball v. United States, 140 U. S. 118, 11 S. Ct. 761, 35 L. Ed. 377 (1890). But see Smith v. Henderson, 190 Ga. 886, 10 S. E. 2d 921 (1940). However, the voluntary absence of the accused amounts to a waiver of his right to be present. Byrd v. Ricketts, 233 Ga. 779, 780, 213 S. E. 2d 610 (1975). Under Georgia law, a defendant does not have a right to be present when he is resentenced if the new sentence cannot be greater than the former sentence. See N. Chiarkas, Alabama Criminal Trial Practice, § 26-6.*
2. *See Tully v. Scheu, 607 F. 2d 31 (3rd Cir. 1979), holding that "the constitutional right to counsel at the hearing during which sentence is pronounced applies with equal force and effect to the sentence reduction hearing."*
3. *See Townsend v. Burke, 334 U. S. 736, 68 S. Ct. 1252, 92 L. Ed. 1690 (1948).*
4. *Green v. United States, 365 U. S. 301, 81 S. Ct. 653, 5 L. Ed. 2d 670 (1961).*
5. *Green v. United States, 365 U. S. 301, 304, 81 S. Ct. 653, 5 L. Ed. 2d 670 (1961).*
6. *Baker v. United States, 412 F. 2d 1069 (5th Cir. 1969).*
7. *United States v. Murray, 275 U. S. 347, 48 S. Ct. 146, 72 L. Ed. 309 (1928).*
8. *Affronti v. United States, 350 U. S. 79, 76 S. Ct. 171, 100 L. Ed. 62 (1955).*
9. *8A Moore's Federal Practice, ¶ 35.02 (2nd ed. 1976).*
10. *See Acts 1977, No. 607, § 210, page 812.*
11. *North Carolina v. Pearce, 395 U. S. 711, 723, 89 S. Ct. 2072, 23 L. Ed 2d 656 (1969).*
12. *Michigan v. Payne, 412 U. S. 47, 93 S. Ct. 1966, 36 L. Ed. 2d 736 (1973); Chaffin v. Stynchcombe, 412 U. S. 17, 93 S. Ct. 1977, 36 L. Ed. 2d 714 (1973). Of course where the jury fixes the second sentence, no finding of facts is necessary.*
13. *North Carolina v. Pearce, 395 U. S. 711, 89 S. Ct. 2072, 23 L. Ed. 2d 656 (1969).*
14. *North Carolina v. Pearce, 395 U. S. 711, 726, 89 S. Ct. 2072, 23 L. Ed. 2d 656, 670 (1969).*

SERVICE ON REGULATORY BOARDS AND COMMISSIONS REGULATING BUSINESS WITH WHICH PERSON ASSOCIATED IS PROHIBITED. Code of Ala. 1975, § 36-25-9.

"Unless expressly provided otherwise by law, no person shall serve as a member or employee of a state, county or municipal regulatory board or commission or other body that regulates any business with which he is associated."

Comments.

As this is a blanket prohibition, violations of this section would likely occur only in circumstances where such member or employee failed to disclose his association with a regulated business. According to § 36-25-1(2) of the Alabama Code, the

SERVICE ON REGULATORY BOARDS AND COMMISSIONS, ETC.—Cont'd.

association requires that such person be an officer, owner, partner, employee or holder of more than 10% of the fair market value of such business. It is unclear what the term holder was intended to represent. (i.e. a term of art under U. C. C., etc?).

Defenses.

(1) Is not a member of a board that regulates his business.

(2) Is not a holder of more than 10% of the fair market value of the business in question.

Cross references.

See CONFIDENTIAL INFORMATION, MISUSE OF; CONFLICT OF INTEREST, FAILURE TO DISCLOSE; TRADING IN PUBLIC OFFICE.

SEX OFFENDERS, REGISTRATION OF. Code of Ala. 1975, §§ 13A-11-200 through 13A-11-203.

Charged as: § 13A-11-200: Persons convicted of certain offenses to register with sheriff in county of residence; registration on moving from one county to another; § 13A-11-201: Sheriff to maintain register and supply information to department of public safety; § 13A-11-202: Department of public safety to maintain register; register to be open only to law enforcement officers and agencies.

"If any person, except a delinquent child, as defined in section 12-15-1, residing in Alabama, has heretofore been convicted, or shall be convicted in any state or municipal court in Alabama or so convicted in another state in any court having jurisdiction similar to the jurisdiction of state and municipal courts in Alabama for any of the offenses hereinafter enumerated, such person shall, upon his or her release from legal custody, register with the sheriff of the county of his or her legal residence within 30 days following such release or within 30 days after September 7, 1967, in case such person was released prior to such date. The offenses above referred to are generally any act of sexual perversion involving a member of the same or the opposite sex, or any sexual abuse of any member of the same or

SEX OFFENDERS, REGISTRATION OF.—Cont'd.

the opposite sex or any attempt to commit any of these acts . . .

"Any person having been so convicted shall upon moving his legal residence from one county to another register with the sheriff of the county to which he has moved within 30 days after such removal. It shall be unlawful for a convicted sex offender as described in this article to fail or refuse to register as herein required."

Classification.

Statutory penalty: imprisonment for not less than one year and not more than five years and a possible fine of not more than $1,000.00.

Comments.

These provisions affect persons who have been convicted of committing or attempting to commit various sex acts. Violation must be knowing and willful.[2] Unlike the provisions on the registration of felons, these provisions apply even if the sex offender's civil rights have been restored by competent legal authority.[3] The sheriff in each Alabama county is required to maintain a register of all the names of persons registered by him and notify the state department of public safety of the name of the person registered and nature of the crime for which the offender was convicted.[4] The state department of public safety is also required to maintain this roster of convicted sex offenders. The roster is open to inspection only by law enforcement officers or agencies.[5]

Defenses.

(1) Lack of knowledge.[6]

(2) Not a willful[7] violation.

(3) Not convicted of one of the offenses cited in § 13A-11-200 of the Alabama Code.

Cross references.

See FELONS, REGISTRATION OF; INCEST; INDECENT EXPOSURE; OBSCENE MATTER, IMPORTATION, DISPLAY, DISTRIBUTION, ETC.; PROSTITUTION; RAPE; SEXUAL MISCONDUCT; SODOMY.

---

1. *Without limiting the generality of this statement, specifically included are: rape, as proscribed by Code of Ala. 1975, §§ 13A-6-1 and 13A-6-62;*

SEX OFFENDERS, REGISTRATION OF.—Cont'd.

sodomy, as proscribed by Code of Ala. 1975, §§ 13A-6-63 and 13A-6-64; sexual misconduct, as proscribed by Code of Ala. 1975, § 13A-6-65; indecent exposure, as proscribed by Code of Ala. 1975, § 13A-6-68; promoting prostitution in the first or second degree, as proscribed by Code of Ala. 1975, §§ 13A-12-111 and 13A-12-112; obscenity, as proscribed by Code of Ala. 1975, § 13A-12-131; incest, as proscribed by Code of Ala. 1975, § 13A-13-3.

2. *Code of Ala. 1975, § 13A-11-203.*
3. *Compare with Code of Ala. 1975, § 13A-11-181.*
4. *Code of Ala. 1975, § 13A-11-201.*
5. *Code of Ala. 1975, § 13A-11-202.*
6. *"A person acts knowingly with respect to conduct or to a circumstance described by a statute defining an offense when he is aware that his conduct is of that nature or that the circumstance exists." Code of Ala. 1975, § 13A-2-2(2).*
7. *"A willful act is one done intentionally, knowingly, and purposely, without justifiable excuse, as distinguished from an act done carelessly, thoughtlessly, needlessly or inadvertently." Padget v. State, 36 Ala. App. 355, 56 So. 2d 116 (1952).*

SEXUAL ABUSE. Code of Ala. 1975, §§ 13A-6-66 and 13A-6-67.

A person[1] commits sexual abuse when he subjects another person[2] to sexual conduct[3] by forcible compulsion[4] or when that other person is incapable[5] of giving consent.[6] There is sexual abuse in the first degree (§ 13A-6-66 of the Alabama Code) and sexual abuse in the second degree (§ 13A-6-67, of the Alabama Code). Sexual abuse by forcible compulsion is always sexual abuse in the first degree. Without forcible compulsion there remains only two distinctions: (1) whether the other person was incapable of consent; and (2) ages of the parties. First, a person can be incapable of giving consent because he was (at the time) physically helpless,[7] mentally incapacitated[8] or by some other factor.[9] If he was physically helpless or mentally incapacitated, the sexual abuse was in the first degree. If he was incapable of consent because of some other factor, the sexual abuse was in the second degree. Second, if the actor was at least 16 years of age and the "victim"[10] was less than 16 years of age, there are two issues: (1) if the "victim" was under 12 years old, it is sexual abuse in the first degree; (2) if the "victim" is more than 12 years old but less than 16 years old and the actor is 19 years old or older, the sexual abuse is in the second degree. If neither age categories are met, there is no sexual abuse based on the age of the parties.

Classification.

Sexual abuse in the first degree is a Class C felony.

Sexual abuse in the second degree is a Class A misdemeanor.

Comments.

As in rape and sodomy, we are excluding from the protection of this statute any person married[11] to or living with[12] the actor. More importantly, a strict reading of the drafters' definition of sexual abuse[13] is limited to touching by the actor and those persons (regardless of age) that are forced or otherwise enticed without their consent to touch the sexual or other intimate parts of the actor.[14] As in rape or sodomy, be aware of the possible equal protection issues involved where an offense excludes groups based on a condition of marriage, living in cohabitation, etc. See Query, infra.

Defenses.

(1) Consent.

(2) Married to the person claiming sexual abuse.

(3) Living with the person claiming sexual abuse (see Query, infra.)

(4) Actor is less than 16 years old. Also, if he is over 16 years old but less than 19 years old, he may defend against sexual abuse in the second degree.

(5) The "contact" was for a purpose other than that of "gratifying the sexual desire of either party" (e.g., to embarrass, annoy, show off, etc.)

(6) Additional defenses might include attacks on the statute as being vague or violative of equal protection (see Query, infra.)

Query.

Under § 13A-6-66(a)(3) of the Alabama Code a person who is "**less**[15] than 12 years old" is

SEXUAL ABUSE.—Cont'd.

protected; and, in § 13A-6-67(a)(2) of the Alabama Code, a person who is "**more**[16] than 12 years old (but less than 16 years old) is protected"; however there is no mention of the person who **is** 12 years old. Of course, there is the argument that "more than 12 years old" includes the "12 year old." This might be convincing if the drafters did not go to such pains in defining the age of the suspect. Note, in the same code sections (§§ 13A-6-66(a)(3) and 13A-6-67(a)(2) of the Alabama Code) the accused's age is defined as "being 16 years old, or older"[17] or "being 19 years old or older." I could assume that if the drafters (in § 13A-6-67(a)(2) of the Alabama Code) intended that he be 12 years or older, they would have stated that he be "12 years or older" and not, as they did, state that he be "more than 12 years old." This could raise a question of vagueness, assuming the drafters did not intend to exclude 12 year olds from the protection of the statute (which otherwise would raise an even more important defense).

The possible victims of sexual abuse (see § 13A-6-60(3) of the Alabama Code) are limited to "any person who is not married to the actor." Additionally, "[p]ersons living together in cohabitation are married for purposes of [sexual offenses]." It would appear that it is not required that the husband and wife be living together for the husband to defend on this ground to the charge of sexual abuse. What of the "living in cohabitation" situation? Under adultery, "living in cohabitation" would exist if there was a weekly interaction; that is, he visits her once a week on a regular basis (or intending to visit on a regular basis). Can he raise this defense? Would it matter if he was "living in cohabitation" with several persons (although separately)? If he were married and "living in cohabitation" with one or more other persons, can he make use of this defense? Can he (like his married counterpart) after an absence of a week (month, year) still claim that they are "living in cohabitation" and, thereby, defend against the charge of sexual abuse?

SEXUAL ABUSE.—Cont'd.

It would appear that no matter how one answers the question presented above, the issue of vagueness is apparent.

Cross references.

See RAPE; SEXUAL MISCONDUCT; SODOMY.

---

1. *Although the definition of sexual abuse specifically excludes persons married to each other or living together, if a spouse aids a third person in the sexual abuse of his mate, both the acting spouse and the third party could be charged with sexual abuse.*
2. *As defined and restricted by Code of Ala. 1975, § 13A-6-60(4), "Persons living together in cohabitation are married for purposes of this article, regardless of the legal status of their relationship otherwise."*
3. *Sexual contact is defined by Code of Ala. 1975, § 13A-6-60(3) as "[a]ny touching of the sexual or other intimate parts of a person not married to the actor, done for the purpose of gratifying the sexual desire of either party."*
4. *Forcible compulsion is defined by Code of Ala. 1975, § 13A-6-60(8), as "[p]hysical force that overcomes earnest resistance or a threat, express or implied, that places a person in fear of immediate death or serious physical injury to [herself] or another person."*
5. *He is incapable of giving consent if he is less than 12 years old (Code of Ala. 1975, § 13A-6-66(a)(3)); or being more than 12 years old but less than 16 years old, he has sexual contact with an actor who is 19 years old or older (Code of Ala. 1975, § 13A-6-67(a)(2)); or he was, at the time, mentally defective (Code of Ala. 1975, § 13A-6-60(5), see also note 9, infra); or he was at the time, mentally incapacitated (Code of Ala. 1975, § 13A-6-60(6), see also note 8, infra); or he was at the time physically helpless (Code of Ala. 1975, § 13A-6-60(7), see also note 7, infra).*
6. *Consent or, rather, the lack of consent is defined by Code of Ala. 1975, § 13A-6-70. Code of Ala. 1975, § 13A-6-70(a) states that "[w]hether or not specifically stated, it is an element of every offense defined in this article, with the exception of subdivision (a)(3) of section 13A-6-65, that the sexual act was committed without consent of the victim." Code of Ala. 1975, § 13A-6-70(b) establishes that the lack of consent results from either forcible compulsion; or incapacity to consent. Note that "[i]f the offense charged is sexual abuse, any circumstances, in addition to forcible compulsion or incapacity to consent, in which the victim does not expressly or impliedly*

SEXUAL ABUSE.—Cont'd.

acquiesce in the actor's conduct" constitutes lack of consent. And, Code of Ala. 1975, § 13A-6-70(c) establishes that "[a] person is deemed incapable of consent if he is: (1) [l]ess than 16 years old [see note 4, supra]; or (2) [m]entally defective [see note 9, infra]; or (3) [m]entally incapacitated [see note 8, infra]; or (4) [p]hysically helpless [see note 7, infra]."

7. *According to Code of Ala. 1975, § 13A-6-60(7), "[s]uch term means that a person is unconscious or for any other reason is physically unable to communicate unwillingness to an act."*
8. *According to Code of Ala. 1975, § 13A-6-60(6), "[s]uch term means that a person is rendered temporarily incapable of appraising or controlling his conduct owing to the influence of a narcotic or intoxicating substance administered to him without his consent, or to any other incapacitating act committed upon him without his consent."*
9. *It would appear that not only would this include the issue of "mentally defective" (see RAPE, note 9, supra) but* **any** *other factor that could act upon his ability to appraise the nature of his conduct.*
10. *I recognize that in criminal law (unlike tort law) the State is the real victim. However, its use here is merely to distinguish from, and establish the relationship to, the actor.*
11. *Code of Ala. 1975, § 13A-6-60(3).*
12. *Code of Ala. 1975, §§ 13A-6-60(3) and 13A-6-60(4).*
13. *Code of Ala. 1975, § 13A-6-60(3); see also note 3, supra.*
14. *A strict reading of Code of Ala. 1975, § 13A-6-60(3) could cause one to view the person being charged as the actor. If this was the intention, we would fail to protect even those "forced" to touch the sexual parts of the actor. However, a broad reading might allow us to assume that the "toucher" is the actor regardless of relative position or who is to be ultimately charged. Under this reading the protection would be greater.*
15. *See Query following RAPE, supra.*
16. *See Query following RAPE, supra.*
17. *See Query following RAPE, supra.*

SEXUAL ASSAULT. See CHILD, ENTICING FOR IMMORAL PURPOSES; RAPE; SEXUAL ABUSE; SEXUAL MISCONDUCT; SODOMY.

SEXUAL MISCONDUCT. Code of Ala. 1975, § 13A-6-65.

"A person commits the crime of sexual misconduct if:

"(1) Being a male, he engages in sexual intercourse with a female without her consent, under circumstances other than those covered by sections 13A-6-61 and 13A-6-62, or with her consent where consent was obtained by the use of any fraud or artifice; or

"(2) Being a female, she engages in sexual intercourse with a male without his consent; or

"(2) He or she engages in deviate sexual intercourse with another person under circumstances other than those covered by sections 13A-6-63 and 13A-6-64 . . ."

Classification.

Class A misdemeanor.

Comments.

There are four issues that should be considered. First, § 13A-6-65(1) of the Alabama Code specifically includes cases in which a male obtained the consent of a female "by the use of any fraud or artifice." However, this is not the case under § 13A-6-65(2) of the Alabama Code, thus raising a possible equal protection argument. Second, although female is clearly defined and uncommonly limited by § 13A-6-60(4) of the Alabama Code,[1] "male" is not defined by the Alabama Code. Thus, we are left to either assume its ordinary meaning (i.e., any male person) and thus raise an equal protection question relative to who may bring an action under § 13A-6-65(1) of the Alabama Code, as opposed to § 13A-6-65(2) of the Alabama Code.[2] Or, we must be willing to accept an equally uncommon definition of male (as we are asked to for female under § 13A-6-60(4) of the Alabama Code) without statute, commentary or expressed intention. Third, it might be argued that § 13A-6-65(3) of the Alabama Code is overly broad and lacks proper notice. It is not clear what kind of behavior it is aimed at preventing. Deviate sexual intercourse, for example, can only (by definition)[3] be committed by persons not married[4] to each

SEXUAL MISCONDUCT.—Cont'd.

other. Thus, "deviate sexual intercourse" differs from "sexual intercourse" both in condition[5] and method.[6] Be alerted to the vast case law prohibiting the punishing of a condition. Finally, § 13A-6-65(3) of the Alabama Code is so vague that it is not capable of interpretation as was originally intended by the drafters or as finally changed by the legislature.[7] Too much discretionary prosecutorial power was left in the hands of law enforcement.

Defenses.

(1) Consent (except under § 13A-6-65(3) of the Alabama Code).

(2) Actor married to the female claiming the sexual misconduct under § 13A-6-65(1) of the Alabama Code (there is some question[8] as to whether this defense is open to a female being accused by her husband of sexual misconduct under § 13A-6-65(2) of the Alabama Code).

(3) Living in cohabitation is viewed in the same way as being married is for purposes of this charge.[9]

(4) Consider attacks on the statute under both due process and equal protection (see Comments, supra).

Query.

Does § 13A-6-65 of the Alabama Code prohibit a female from obtaining the consent of a male by fraud or artifice? In addition, § 13A-6-65 of the Alabama Code encourages cohabitation as a form of protection from a vengeful partner.

Cross references.

See RAPE; SEXUAL ABUSE; SODOMY.

---

1. *According to Code of Ala. 1975, § 13A-6-60(4), a female is "[a]ny female person who is not married to the actor. Persons living together in cohabitation are married for purposes of this article, regardless of the legal status of their relationship otherwise."*
2. *That is, if we assume a "male" is "any male person," it would appear that Code of Ala. 1975, § 13A-6-65 prevents a wife from charging her husband with sexual misconduct (based on their relationship) but does not prevent a husband from charging his wife with sexual misconduct.*
3. *According to Code of Ala. 1975, § 13A-6-60(2), deviate sexual intercourse includes "[a]ny act of sexual gratification between persons not married to each other, involving the sex organs of one person and the mouth or anus of another."*
4. *According to Code of Ala. 1975, § 13A-6-60(4), "[p]ersons living together in cohabitation are married for purposes of this [offense], regardless of the legal status of their relationship otherwise."*
5. *Limited to that group of persons that are not married or living with each other.*
6. *Must involve the mouth or anus of one person and the sex organs of the other.*
7. *According to the comments following Code of Ala. 1975, § 13A-6-65, "[i]n the original draft, § 13A-6-65(a)(3) covered deviate sexual intercourse without lawful consent under the same terms and circumstances as subdivision (a)(1) covers vaginal intercourse. If both actors were adult and both consented, there was no offense; but this subdivision was changed by the legislature to make all homosexual conduct criminal, and consent is no defense. However, § 13A-6-65(a)(3) does not apply to married persons, as this not within the basic definition of 'deviate sexual intercourse.'" § 13A-6-60(2). See also § 13A-6-70(b)(3).*
8. *The question is solely one of interpretation and intention.*
9. *Code of Ala. 1975, § 13A-6-60(4).*

SHOPPING CARTS, ABANDONMENT OR REMOVAL.

Code of Ala. 1975, §§ 13A-8-61 and 13A-8-62.

Charged as: Abandonment on public streets, sidewalks, parking lots, etc.; Removal from premises without consent of owner.

"It shall be unlawful for any person to abandon a shopping cart[1] upon any public street, sidewalk, way or parking lot, other than a parking lot on the premises[2] of the owner." § 13A-8-62 of the Alabama Code.

"It shall be unlawful for any person to remove a shopping cart from the premises, posted[3] as provided in section 13A-8-63, of the owner of such shopping cart without the consent, given at the time of such removal, of the owner or of his agent, servant or employee." § 13A-8-61 of the Alabama Code.

Classification.

Class C misdemeanor.

SHOPPING CARTS, ABANDONMENT OR REMOVAL. —Cont'd.

Comments.

Two offenses are established: (1) abandonment and (2) removal. A copy of the statute must be posted in three prominent places as well as at all exits.

Defenses.

(1) No intent to abandon.

(2) Consent to removal.

(3) Lack of or inadequate notice.

Query.

This offense could provide a lesser offense to plead to instead of theft.

---

1. *"The term 'shopping cart,' when used in this article, shall mean those pushcarts of the type or types which are commonly provided by grocery stores, drugstores or other merchant stores or markets for the use of the public in transporting commodities in stores and markets and incidentally from the store to a place outside the store." Code of Ala. 1975, § 13A-8-60.*
2. *"It shall be unlawful for any person to remove a shopping cart from the premises, posted as provided in section 13A-8-63, of the owner of such shopping cart without the consent, given at the time of such removal, of the owner or of his agent, servant or employee. For the purpose of this section, the 'premises' shall include all the parking area set aside by the owner, or on behalf of the owner, for the parking of cars for the convenience of the patrons of the owner." Code of Ala. 1975, § 13A-8-61.*
3. *"The owner of the store in which the shopping cart is used shall post in at least three prominent places in his store, and at each exit therefrom, a printed copy of this article, which copy shall be printed in type no smaller than 12 points." Code of Ala. 1975, § 13A-8-63.*

SIGNATURE OBTAINED BY DECEPTION. Code of Ala. 1975, § 13A-9-11.

Charged as: Obtaining signature by deception.

"A person commits the crime of obtaining a signature by deception[1] if with intent to defraud[2] or to acquire a substantial benefit[3] for himself or another, he causes another by deception to sign or execute a written instrument."[4]

SIGNATURE OBTAINED BY DECEPTION.—Cont'd.

Classification.

Class A misdemeanor.

Comments.

The purpose of this statute is to punish one who fraudulently induces another to sign a writing which disadvantages the signer. Such conduct was not strictly within the purview of the former provisions and may or may not amount to forgery under present statutes.

Defenses.

(1) Lack of requisite knowledge for deception.

(2) Lack of intent to injure another person's interest that has value.

(3) The writing signed is incapable of being used to the advantage or disadvantage of some person.

(4) Lack of intent to acquire a substantial benefit.

Cross references.

See FORGERY; THEFT OF PROPERTY.

---

1. *Code of Ala. 1975, § 13A-8-1(1).*
2. *Code of Ala. 1975, § 13A-9-2(8).*
3. *"Substantial benefit" according to the commentary following Code of Ala. 1975, § 13A-9-11 is "a benefit having pecuniary significance."*
4. *Code of Ala. 1975, § 13A-9-1.*

SIMULATION, CRIMINAL. Code of Ala. 1975, § 13A-9-10.

Charged as: Criminal simulation.

"A person commits the crime of criminal simulation if:

"(1) He makes or alters any object, with intent to defraud,[1] so that it appears to have an antiquity, value, rarity, source or authorship that it does not in fact possess; or

"(2) He possesses or utters[2] an object so simulated with knowledge of its true character and with intent to defraud."

Classification.

Class A misdemeanor.

Comments.

The section is not concerned with written

SIMULATION, CRIMINAL.—Cont'd.

materials. It is concerned with objects, such as paintings, having value because of their rarity, antiquity, authorship or source. The offense is deception.[3] Each subdivision contains two separate offenses. Under (1), if the offender, with intent to defraud, either makes or alters an object, he is culpable. Under (2), if the offender, with intent to defraud, either knowingly possesses or utters a simulated object, he is culpable.

Defenses.

(1) Lack of intent to defraud.

(2) Lack of knowledge of the object's true character.

(3) Lack of possession, as defined in § 13A-1-2(7) of the Alabama Code, i.e., defendant may not have had physical possession or may not have been exercising dominion or control over the property.

(4) To subsection (2): a lack of knowledge of the object's true character or a lack of intent to defraud.

(5) The falsity has no pecuniary significance, or is "puffing" by statements unlikely to deceive ordinary persons, and is not, therefore, deception.[4]

Cross references.

See FORGERY; THEFT OF PROPERTY.

---

1. *An intent to defraud is "[a] purpose to use deception, as defined in section 13A-8-1(1) [see note 3, infra], or to injure another person's interest which has value." Code of Ala. 1975, § 13A-9-1(8). Value is "[t]he market value of the property at the time and place of the criminal act."*

"Whether or not they have been issued or delivered, certain written instruments, not including those having a readily ascertainable market value such as some public and corporate bonds and securities shall be evaluated as follows:

"a. The value of an instrument constituting an evidence of debt, such as a check, draft or promissory note, shall be deemed the amount due or collectible thereon or thereby, that figure ordinarily being the face amount of the indebtedness less any portion thereof which has been satisfied.

"b. The value of any other instrument that creates, releases, discharges or otherwise affects

SIMULATION, CRIMINAL.—Cont'd.

any valuable legal right, privilege or obligation shall be deemed the greatest amount of economic loss which the owner of the instrument might reasonably suffer by virtue of the loss of the instrument.

"When the value of property cannot be ascertained pursuant to the standards set forth above, its value shall be deemed to be an amount not exceeding $100.00.

"Amounts involved in thefts committed pursuant to one scheme or course of conduct, whether from the same person or several persons, may be aggregated in determining the grade of the offense; provided, that only one conviction may be had and only one sentence enforced for all thefts included in such aggregate." Code of Ala. 1975, § 13A-8-1(14). See Code of Ala. 1975, § 13A-9-1(8).

2. *"To 'utter' means to directly or indirectly offer, assert, declare or put forth a forged instrument as genuine." Code of Ala. 1975, § 13A-9-1(12).*

3. *"Deception occurs when a person knowingly:*

"a. Creates or confirms another's impression which is false and which the defendant does not believe to be true; or

"b. Fails to correct a false impression which the defendant previously has created or confirmed; or

"c. Fails to correct a false impression when the defendant is under a duty to do so; or

"d. Prevents another from acquiring information pertinent to the disposition of the property involved; or

"e. Sells or otherwise transfers or encumbers property, failing to disclose a lien, adverse claim or other legal impediment to the enjoyment of the property when the defendant is under a duty to do so, whether that impediment is or is not valid, or is not a matter of official record; or

"f. Promises performance which the defendant does not intend to perform or knows will not be performed. Failure to perform, standing alone, however, is not proof that the defendant did not intend to perform.

"The term 'deception' does not, however, include falsity as to matters having no pecuniary significance, or puffing by statements unlikely to deceive ordinary persons. 'Puffing' means an exaggerated commendation of wares or services." Code of Ala. 1975, § 13A-8-1(1).

4. *Code of Ala. 1975, § 13A-8-1(1).*

SLANDER. See LIBEL AND DEFAMATION.

SLUGS, UNLAWFULLY USING. Code of Ala. 1975, § 13-9-17.

Charged as: Unlawfully using slugs.

"A person commits the crime of unlawfully using slugs[1] if:

"(1) With intent to defraud[2] the supplier, or another person, of property[3] or a service[4] sold or offered by means of a coin machine,[5] he inserts, deposits or uses a slug in that machine; or

"(2) He makes, possesses or disposes of a slug with intent that it be used unlawfully in a coin machine as provided in subdivision (a)(1) of this section."

Classification.

Class B misdemeanor.

Comments.

A person is guilty of unlawfully using slugs if he either makes, possesses or uses a slug in a machine. Under previous Alabama statutes, no criminal intent was required for unlawful use, but the making or possession of a slug required an intent to cheat or defraud the owner, licensee or other person entitled to the contents. A fraudulent intent is now required for either method of commission.

Defenses.

(1) Lack of intent.

Cross references.

See THEFT OF PROPERTY; THEFT OF SERVICES.

---

1. *"A metallic or other object or article which by virtue of its size, shape or any other quality is capable of being inserted, deposited or otherwise used in a coin machine as an improper but effective substitute for a genuine coin, bill or token." Code of Ala. 1975, § 13A-9-16(2).*
2. *"A purpose to use deception, as defined in section 13A-8-1(1), or to injure another person's interest which has value, as defined in section 13A-8-1(14)." Code of Ala. 1975, § 13A-9-1(8).*
3. *"Any money, tangible or intangible personal property (whether real or personal) the location of which can be changed (including things growing on, affixed to or found in land and documents, although the rights represented hereby have no physical location), contract right, chose-in-action, interest in or claim to wealth,*

SLUGS, UNLAWFULLY USING. —Cont'd.

credit or any other article or thing of value of any kind.

"Commodities of a public utility nature, such as gas, electricity, steam and water, constitute property, but the supplying of such a commodity to premises from an outside source by means of wires, pipes, conduits or other equipment shall be deemed a rendition of a service rather than a sale or delivery of property." Code of Ala. 1975, § 13A-8-1(10). See Theft of services, Code of Ala. 1975, § 13A-8-10.

4. *" 'Services' includes but is not necessarily limited to, labor, professional services, transportation, telephone or other public services, accommodation in motels, hotels, restaurants or elsewhere, admission to exhibitions, computer services and the supplying of equipment for use." Code of Ala. 1975, § 13A-8-10.*
5. *"A coin box, turnstile, vending machine or other mechanical or electronic device or receptacle designed:*

   "a. To receive a coin or bill of a certain denomination or a token made for the purpose; and

   "b. In return for the insertion or deposit thereof, automatically to offer, provide, assist in providing or permit the acquisition of property or a public or private service." Code of Ala. 1975, § 13A-9-16(1).

SODOMY. Code of Ala. 1975, §§ 13A-6-63 and 13A-6-64.

A person[1] commits sodomy when he engages in deviate sexual intercourse[2] with another person[3] by forcible compulsion[4] or when that other person is incapable[5] of giving consent[6] or under the age of consent. There is sodomy in the first degree (§ 13A-6-63 of the Alabama Code) and sodomy in the second degree (§ 13A-6-64 of the Alabama Code). Sodomy by forcible compulsion is always sodomy in the first degree. Without forcible compulsion there are two distinctions: (1) whether the other person was incapable of consent; and (2) ages of the parties. First, a person can be incapable of giving consent because he was (at the time) physically helpless,[7] mentally incapacitated[8] or mentally defective.[9] If he was physically helpless or mentally

SODOMY.—Cont'd.

incapacitated, the sodomy was in the first degree. If he was mentally defective, the sodomy was in the second degree. Second, if the actor was at least 16 years of age and the "victim"[10] was less than 16 years of age, there are two issues: (1) if the victim was under 12 years old, it was sodomy of the first degree; (2) if the victim is more than twelve years old (but less than sixteen) and the actor at least 2 years older than the "victim," the sodomy is of the second degree. If neither age categories are matched, there is no sodomy based on the ages of the parties.

Classification.

Sodomy in the first degree is a Class A felony.

Sodomy in the second degree is a Class C felony.

Comments.

It would appear that the only differences in the wording of law, between rape and sodomy, is that, in sodomy, the actor can be male or female and the "victim" can be male or female. Since "deviate sexual intercourse" excludes persons married to each other (see note 2, infra) and § 13A-6-60(4) of the Alabama Code clearly establishes that "[p]ersons living together in cohabitation are married for purposes of this [offense], regardless of the legal status of their relationship otherwise," it would also appear that if two males (or two females) were living under these conditions[11] one could not bring a charge of sodomy against the other. It might be argued that including the marital exception in § 13A-6-60(1) of the Alabama Code, combined with the incorporating of the "living together in cohabitation" clause of § 13A-6-60(4) of the Alabama Code, evidences the drafters' recognition of homosexual relationships under certain circumstances notwithstanding the "catch-all" intention of § 13A-6-65(3) of the Alabama Code.

If the drafters intended to parallel rape, it should follow (as in rape) that he ("victim") must demonstrate that he was legally incapable of giving consent; **or** that he refused consent **and** "earnestly resisted."

SODOMY.—Cont'd.

Of course, fear of (immediate) death or (serious) physical injury will excuse the failure to "earnestly resist." Unlike rape, the possible victims of sodomy are not limited to women. However, limiting the group, as in rape, to "victims" not married to, or "living in cohabitation" with, the actor, could raise some solid equal protection arguments (depending on the nature of the case), as well as some notice or vagueness problems. See Query, infra.

Defenses.

(1) Consent.

(2) Married to the person claiming the sodomy.

(3) Living with the "person" claiming sodomy (see Query, infra).

(4) The actor is less than 16 years old. (Also, look at the relative ages of both under sodomy in the second degree.)

(5) It would also seem possible to defend by showing that, although he did not explicitly give consent, he was capable of consenting and did not "resist in earnest." The comments indicate that that may be a successful defense even if he said "no."

(6) Additional defenses might include attacks on the statute as being vague or violative of equal protection (see Query, infra.)

Query.

In § 13A-6-63(a)(3) of the Alabama Code, a person who is "**less**[12] than 12 years old" is protected; and, in § 13A-6-64(a)(1) of the Alabama Code, a person who is "**more**[13] than 12 years old is protected"; however there is no mention of the person who **is** 12 years old. Of course, there is the argument that "more than 12 year old" includes the "12 year old." This might be convincing if the drafters did not go to such pains in defining the age of the suspect. Note, in the same code sections (§§ 13A-6-63(a)(3) and 13A-6-64(a)(1) of the Alabama Code) the accused's age is defined as "being 16 years or older." Thus one could assume that if the drafters (in § 13A-6-63(a)(1) of the Alabama Code) intended that he be 12 years or older, they would have stated that he be "12 years or older" and not, as they

SODOMY.—Cont'd.

did, state that he be "more than 12 years old." This could raise a question of vagueness assuming the drafters did not intend to exclude 12 year olds from the protection of the statute (which otherwise would raise an even more important defense).

The possible victims of sodomy (see § 13A-6-60(1) and (4) of the Alabama Code) are limited to "any person who is not married to the actor." Additionally, "[p]ersons living together in cohabitation are married for purposes of [sexual offenses]." It would appear that it is not required that the husband and wife be living together for the husband to defend on this ground to the charge of sodomy. What of the "living in cohabitation" situation? Under adultery, "living in cohabitation" would exist if there was a weekly interaction; that is, he visits her once a week on a regular basis (or intending it to be on a regular basis.) Can he raise this defense? Would it matter if he was "living in cohabitation" with several persons (although separately)? If he were married and "living in cohabitation" with one or more other persons can he make use of this defense? Can he (like his married counterpart) after an absence of a week (month, year) still claim that they are "living in cohabitation" and, thereby, defend against the charge of sodomy? It would appear that no matter how one answers the questions presented above, the issue of vagueness is apparent.

Another group that, it would appear, is not protected (see §§ 13A-6-60(6) and 13A-6-63(a) (2) of the Alabama Code) would be any person who is temporarily incapable of appraising or controlling his conduct owing to the influence of a narcotic or intoxicating substance, or to any other incapacitating act committed upon him, as long as it was **not** without his consent (this could be less than "with his consent"). This would appear to be the case even if the person administering the narcotic, intoxicant, etc., did so with the intent of rendering him incapable of appraising or

SODOMY.—Cont'd.

controlling his conduct so that, in the words of the drafters, "he may gain access to [him]."

Cross references.

See RAPE; SEXUAL ABUSE; SEXUAL MISCONDUCT.

---

1. *Although the charge of sodomy specifically excludes married couples, it would seem clear that if a person aids a third party in "sodomizing" his spouse, both the married actor and the third party could be charged with sodomy.*
2. *According to Code of Ala. 1975, § 13A-6-60(2), deviate sexual intercourse includes "[a]ny act of sexual gratification between persons not married to each other, involving the sex organs of one person and the mouth or anus of another."*
3. *According to Code of Ala. 1975, § 13A-6-60(4), "[p]ersons living together in cohabitation are married for purposes of this article, regardless of the legal status of their relationship otherwise."*
4. *Forcible compulsion is defined by Code of Ala. 1975, § 13A-6-60(8), as "[p]hysical force that overcomes earnest resistance or a threat, express or implied, that places a person in fear of immediate death or serious physical injury to [himself] or another person."*
5. *He is incapable of giving consent if he is less than 12 years old (Code of Ala. 1975, § 13A-6-63(a)(3); or, being more than 12 years old but less than 16 years old, he is at least 2 years younger than the actor (Code of Ala. 1975, § 13A-6-64(a)(1); or he was, at the time, mentally defective (Code of Ala. 1975, § 13A-6-60(5); see note 9, infra); or he was at the time, mentally incapacitated (Code of Ala. 1975, § 13A-6-60(6), see also note 8, infra); or he was, at the time, physically helpless (Code of Ala. 1975, § 13A-6-60(7); see note 7, infra).*
6. *Consent or rather the lack of consent is defined by Code of Ala. 1975, § 13A-6-70. Code of Ala. 1975, § 13A-6-70(a), states that "[w]hether or not specifically stated, it is an element of every offense defined in this article, with the exception of subdivision (a)(3) of section 13A-6-65 that the sexual act was committed without consent of the victim." Code of Ala. 1975, § 13A-6-70(b), establishes that the "[l]ack of consent results from (1) [f]orcible compulsion; or (2) [i]ncapacity to consent." Note also that "[i]f the offense charged is [not sodomy but rather] sexual abuse, any circumstances, in addition to forcible compulsion or incapacity to consent, in which the victim does not expressly or impliedly acquiesce in the actor's conduct," constitutes lack of consent, and Code of Ala. 1975, §*

SODOMY.—Cont'd.

13A-6-70(c), establishes that "[a] person is deemed incapable of consent if he is: (1) [l]ess than 16 years old [see note 5, supra]; or (2) [m]entally defective [see note 9, infra]; or (3) [m]entally incapacitated [see note 8, infra]; or (4) [p]hysically helpless [see note 7, infra]."

7. *According to Code of Ala. 1975, § 13A-6-60(7), "[s]uch term means that a person is unconscious or for any other reason is physically unable to communicate unwillingness to an act."*
8. *According to Code of Ala. 1975, § 13A-6-60(6), "[s]uch term means that a person is rendered temporarily incapable of appraising or controlling his conduct owing to the influence of a narcotic or intoxicating substance administered to him without his consent, or to any other incapacitating act committed upon him without his consent."*
9. *According to Code of Ala. 1975, § 13A-6-60(5), "[s]uch term means that a person suffers from a mental disease or defect which renders him incapable of appraising the nature of his conduct."*
10. *I recognize, of course, that in criminal law (unlike tort law) the State is the real victim. However, its use here is merely to distinguish from and establish the relationship to the actor.*
11. *It should be noted that Black's Law Dictionary 236 (5th ed. 1979), defines cohabitation as the living "together as husband and wife." The mutual assumption of those marital rights, duties and obligations which are usually manifested by married people, including but not necessarily dependent on sexual relations."*
12. *Emphasis added.*
13. *Emphasis added.*

SOLICITATION. Code of Ala. 1975, § 13A-4-1.

Charged as: Criminal solicitation.

"A person is guilty of criminal solicitation if, with the intent[1] that another person engage in conduct constituting a crime, he solicits, requests, commands or importunes such other person to engage in such conduct."[2]

Classification.

Section 13A-4-1(f) of the Alabama Code provides that "[c]riminal solicitation is a:

"(1) Class A felony if the offense solicited is murder.

"(2) Class B felony if the offense solicited is a Class A felony.

"(3) Class C felony if the offense solicited is a Class B felony.

"(4) Class A misdemeanor if the offense solicited is a Class C felony.

"(5) Class B misdemeanor if the offense solicited is a Class A misdemeanor.

"(6) Class C misdemeanor if the offense solicited is a Class B misdemeanor.

"(7) Violation if the offense solicited is a Class C misdemeanor."

Comments.

As is pointed out in the comments following § 13A-4-1 of the Alabama Code, it should be noted that where "the solicitation is successful, the solicitor is criminally liable for the substantive crime solicited as an accomplice. If the solicitation does not result in commission of the crime, but the person solicited agrees, the solicitor and the solicitee are liable for conspiracy." Solicitation is relatively new[3] to Alabama law, although in accord with the basic principles covered in the statutes discussed above. The proposal is patterned primarily after the new New York and Michigan formulations, New York Penal Law §§ 100.00—100.20, Michigan Revised Criminal Code § 1010. The need for such anticipatory offense is obvious. There is a need to distinguish solicitation cases from "attempts," especially where the type of "overt" conduct required by the defendant in order to equate an attempt is sometimes unclear or uncertain. And, it would appear that the intention "is to create a general solicitation crime punishable on a par with the crime solicited and independently of the crime of attempt. Model Penal Code § 5.02; New York Penal Law §§ 100.00—100.20; Michigan Revised Criminal Code § 1010; Proposed Revision Texas Penal Code § 15.03; Proposed New Federal Criminal Code § 1003; Colorado Criminal Code § 40-2-301."

Defenses.

Section 13A-4-1 of the Alabama Code demands that a person not "be convicted of criminal solicitation upon the uncorroborated testimony of the person allegedly solicited, and there must be proof of circumstances corroborating both the

SOLICITATION.—Cont'd.

solicitation and the defendant's intent."

Section 13A-4-1 of the Alabama Code provides two major defenses to the charge of solicitation. Section 13A-4-1(b) provides that "[a] person is not liable under this section if, under circumstances manifesting a voluntary and complete renunciation of his criminal intent, he (1) notified the person solicited of his renunciation and (2) gave timely and adequate warning to the law enforcement authorities or otherwise made a substantial effort to prevent the commission of the criminal conduct solicited. The burden of injecting this issue is on the defendant, but this does not shift the burden of proof."

And, § 13A-4-1(c) of the Alabama Code provides that "[a] person is not liable under this section when his solicitation constitutes conduct of a kind that is necessarily incidental to the commission of the offense solicited. When the solicitation constitutes an offense other than criminal solicitation which is related to but separate from the offense solicited, defendant is guilty of such related offense only and not of criminal solicitation."

However "[i]t is no defense . . . that the person solicited could not be guilty of the offense solicited because of:

"(1) Criminal irresponsibility or other legal incapacity or exemption; or

"(2) Unawareness of the criminal nature of the conduct solicited or of the defendant's criminal purpose; or

"(3) Any other factor precluding the mental state required for the commission of the offense in question."[4]

And "[i]t is no defense . . . that [the] defendant belongs to a class of persons who by definition are legally incapable in an individual capacity of committing the offense that he solicited another to commit."[5]

Cross references.

See ATTEMPT; CONSPIRACY.

---

1. *The comments following this section point out that "[t]he mens rea . . . is essentially the same as that required for attempts. Liability requires that the defendant solicited specific conduct, a limitation that avoids vagueness and the potential for prosecution in cases of general political agitation. Present Alabama law similarly requires that the endeavor be to commit a 'specific' felony or misdemeanor and to move to 'concrete action.'"*
2. *The comments following this section point out that "[s]ince solicitation makes criminal a communication that is likely to be within the peculiar knowledge of only several persons, more evidence is required than just the testimony of the person allegedly solicited, and there must be circumstances corroborative of both the making of the solicitation and that its making was in earnest." Of course, it is not essential to liability under this section that the person solicited commit or attempt to commit the crime advocated, or that he even agreed to do so. § 13A-4-5. People v. Quentin, 296 N. Y. S. 2d 443 (1968)." See also Foster v. State, 332 So. 2d 399 (Ala. Cr. App. 1976).*
3. *The comments following this section point out that "[i]n Alabama, until 1967, there was doubt as to whether the crime of solicitation even existed, as there was no statute nor case law on the subject, although the concept of advising, inciting, etc., was an element of a few other crimes, e.g., bribery, subornation of perjury, inciting to riot, overthrow of government. But solicitation as a crime, per se, was uncertain."*
4. *Code of Ala. 1975, § 13A-4-1(d).*
5. *Code of Ala. 1975, § 13A-4-1(e).*

SOLICITATION OR RECEIPT OF FEES BY PUBLIC OFFICIAL, EMPLOYEE, OR FAMILY MEMBER THEREOF. Code of Ala. 1975, § 36-25-7.

Charged as: Solicitation or receipt of money for advice or assistance; failure to disclose fees received for services.

"(a) No public official or employee or his family shall solicit or receive any money in addition to that received by the official or employee in his official capacity for advice or assistance on matters concerning the legislature, an executive department or any public regulatory board, commission or other body.

"(b) No public official or employee or business with which he is associated shall receive any fee, salary, wages or other

SOLICITATION OR RECEIPT OF FEES BY PUBLIC OFFICIAL, EMPLOYEE, OR FAMILY MEMBER THEREOF.—Cont'd.

compensation for services provided to the state or any of its agencies or to any county, or municipality or instrumentalities thereof unless a disclosure statement provided for in this section shall be filed with the commission by the person rendering the services."

Comments.

The basic elements of § 36-25-7(a) of the Alabama Code are: (1) a public official, employee or family member thereof; (2) solicit or receive; (3) money, separate and apart from compensation received in his official capacity; (4) that in return for such money; (5) he gave advice or assistance; (6) on matters concerning the legislature, an executive department, or any public regulatory board, commission or other body. Considering the language of other provisions of this chapter, the fact that this section prohibits only monetary compensation may be significant. In some instances other sections are directed at "anything of value." Therefore it is arguable that this section was not intended to prohibit compensation in forms other than money. However, it is difficult to imagine this was the actual intent of the drafters. Section 36-25-7(b) of the Alabama Code requires: (1) a public official, employee or business with which he is associated (§ 36-25-1(2)); (2) receive a fee, salary, wage or other compensation; (3) for services; (4) provided to the state (including agencies, counties or municipalities); and (5) failure to disclose same as provided in this section. The required disclosure statement must include the name of the employer, the amount of compensation and date of employment. There is no express requirement that the nature of the employment or services provided be disclosed. It should be noted that the section fails to provide any standard by which to distinguish advice or assistance

SOLICITATION OR RECEIPT OF FEES BY PUBLIC OFFICIAL, EMPLOYEE, OR FAMILY MEMBER THEREOF.—Cont'd.

(for which receipt of money is prohibited) from services (for which receipt of fees is permitted, although disclosure is required). The offer of payment or actual payment for advice, assistance or services is itself not an offense under this section. Both offenses under this section are strict liability offenses, (i.e. no intent to defraud, conceal, etc., is required).

Defenses.

(1) Payment was for services not prohibited.

(2) Payment for services was to a family member not required to be disclosed.

Cross references.

See BRIBERY OF PUBLIC SERVANTS; ETHICS VIOLATIONS; TRADING IN PUBLIC OFFICE.

SPEED. See CONTROLLED SUBSTANCES.

SPORTS, OFFENSES RELATING TO.

Code of Ala. 1975, §§ 13A-11-141 through 13A-11-143.

"A person commits the crime of sports bribery if he:

"(1) Confers, or offers or agrees to confer any benefit upon a sports participant[1] with intent to influence him not to give his best efforts in a sports contest;[2] or

"(2) Confers, or offers or agrees to confer any benefit upon a sports official[3] in return for an agreement from him to perform his duties improperly." § 13A-11-141(a) of the Alabama Code.

"A person commits the crime of receiving a sports bribe if:

"(1) Being a sports participant, he solicits,[4] accepts or agrees to accept any benefit from another person upon an agreement or understanding that he will thereby be influenced not to give his best efforts in a sports contest; or

"(2) Being a sports official, he solicits, accepts or agrees to accept any benefit from another person upon an agreement or

SPORTS, OFFENSES RELATING TO. —Cont'd.

understanding that he will perform his duties improperly." § 13A-11-142(a) of the Alabama Code.

"A person commits the crime of tampering with a sports contest if, with intent to influence the outcome of a sports contest, he:

"(1) Tampers[5] with any sports participant or sports official, or with any animal, equipment or other thing involved in the conduct or operation of a sports contest, in a manner contrary to the rules and usages purporting to govern the sports contest in question; or

"(2) Substitutes a sports participant, animal, equipment or other thing involved in the conduct or operation of a sports contest, for the genuine person, animal or thing." § 13A-11-143(a) of the Alabama Code.

Classification.

Class A misdemeanor.

Comments.

These statutes are designed to prohibit interference with the course of sports events. The statutes apply to amateur and professional sports activities in proscribing conduct that constitutes bribing, receiving a bribe, or tampering with a sports event. No benefit need actually be conferred on a participant or official to create culpability under the statutes prohibiting bribery or receipt of a bribe. The State must prove specific intent to convict a person of sports bribery.

Conduct that constitutes tampering with a sports contest is not clearly defined. The statute provides that substitution of a participant, animal, equipment or other thing used in a sports contest constitutes criminal tampering. The commentary following the statute makes a vague reference to the "ordinary rules and usages of sports events" by which tampering should be measured. It may be possible that one who bribes a participant or official in a sports contest may also be charged with "tampering" with a sports contest.

Defenses.

(1) Sports bribery — giving or receiving:

SPORTS, OFFENSES RELATING TO. —Cont'd.

(a) No discussion, offer, or agreement to confer or accept a benefit.

(b) Person conferred with not a sports participant or sports official.

(c) Event not a sports contest.

(d) No discussion or agreement that sports participant would not give his best efforts or a sports official would not perform his duties properly.

(2) Tampering with a sports contest:

(a) Lack of intent to influence outcome.

(b) All interaction with persons or things involved in sports contest was in accord with rules and usages involving the sports contest.

(c) Event not a sports contest.

---

1. *"Any person who participates or expects to participate in a sports contest as a player, contestant or member of a team, or as a coach, manager, trainer or other person directly associated with a player, contestant or team." Code of Ala. 1975, § 13A-11-140(2).*
2. *"Any professional or amateur sport, athletic game or contest, or race or contest involving machines, persons or animals, viewed by the public, and for which admission is charged." Code of Ala. 1975, § 13A-11-140(1).*
3. *"Any person who acts or expects to act in a sports contest as an umpire, referee or judge, or otherwise to officiate at a sports contest." Code of Ala. 1975, § 13A-11-140(3).*
4. *Solicitation as used in criminal law means to command, authorize, urge, incite, request, or advise another to commit a crime. Black's Law Dictionary 1249 (5th ed. 1979), citing Model Penal Code, § 5.02.*
5. *To meddle so as to alter a thing, especially to make illegal, corrupting or perverting changes. Black's Law Dictionary 1305 (5th ed. 1979), citing United States v. Tomicich, 41 F. Supp. 33, 35 (E. D. Pa. 1941).*

STATUTE OF LIMITATIONS.

Statutes of limitations are founded on the premise that, even if one has a just cause, it is unjust not to put the adversary on notice to defend within a period of limitation and that the right to be free of stale claims in time comes to prevail over the right to prosecute them.[1] However, limitations vary

STATUTE OF LIMITATIONS.—Cont'd.

both in degree and specificity. For example:

There is no statute of limitations in Alabama for murder,[2] manslaughter in the first degree, arson, forgery or counterfeiting.[3] On the other hand, a prosecution for conversion of state or county revenue must commence within six years after the conversion.[4] In all other felonies, prosecution must commence within three years after the commission of the offense.[5] The prosecution of a misdemeanor must generally be commenced within twelve months after the commission of the offense.[6] Note, a prosecution for unlawfully taking or using (temporarily) the property of another must be commenced within thirty days after the commission of the offense.[7]

A prosecution may be commenced by indictment, warrant or by binding over the offender.[8]

Any act declared criminal and punishable in different ways by different provisions of law shall be punished only under one of such provision.[9]

Cross references.

See N. Chiarkas, Alabama Criminal Trial Practice, § 14-23 (Limitations of prosecution); N. Chiarkas, Alabama Criminal Trial Practice Forms, § 14-80 (Motion to disqualify district attorney and assistant district attorney; rule nisi).

---

1. *Twitchco, Inc. v. U. S., 348 F. Supp. 330 (M. D. Ala. 1972).*
2. *Code of Ala. 1975, § 15-3-5; Chambliss v. State, 373 So. 2d 1185 (1979), cert. denied, 373 So. 2d 1211.*
3. *Code of Ala. 1975, § 15-3-5.*
4. *Code of Ala. 1975, § 15-3-3; see also, Holcombe v. Pierce, 253 Ala. 173, 43 So. 2d 640 (1949).*
5. *Code of Ala. 1975, § 15-3-1.*
6. *Code of Ala. 1975, § 15-3-2; see also, Scott v. State, 45 Ala. App. 49, 227 So. 2d 436 (1969).*
7. *Code of Ala. 1975, § 15-3-4.*
8. *Code of Ala. 1975, § 15-3-7; Scott v. State, 45 Ala. App. 49, 227 So. 2d 436 (1969).*
9. *Code of Ala. 1975, § 15-3-8; Yelton v. State, 56 Ala. App. 272, 321 So. 2d 234 (1975), cert. denied, 294 Ala. 745, 321 So. 2d 237.*

STOCK AT LARGE UNDER COMMON FENCE. Code of Ala. 1975, § 13A-7-61.

Charged as: Allowing stock to run at large under common fence.

It is a crime for "[a]ny one of several persons occupying or cultivating lands under a common fence [to] . . . turn stock of any kind into such inclosure, or knowingly suffers such stock to go at large therein without the consent of all the persons owning or cultivating such lands. . . ."

Classification.

Statutory punishment: fine of $5.00 to $50.00 in addition to amount of actual damages inflicted, which are held as part of the penalty and go to the injured party.

STORING GUNPOWDER. See GUNPOWDER, STORING.

STRICT LIABILITY. Code of Ala. 1975, § 13A-2-3.

This section[1] states that "[the] minimum requirement for criminal liability is the performance by a person of conduct which includes a voluntary act or the omission to perform an act which he is physically capable of performing. If that conduct is all that is required for commission of a particular offense, or if an offense or some material element thereof does not require a culpable mental state on the part of the actor, the offense is one of 'strict liability.' If a culpable mental state on the part of the actor is required with respect to any material element of an offense, the offense is one of 'mental culpability.' "

Comments.

The drafters justify the existence of strict liability offenses, not only on public necessity, but "on the ground that it would be difficult or impossible of proof and conviction if the prosecution had to adduce an element of 'intentional', 'knowingly' and the like. Sometimes the ends accomplished, the evil or harm sought to be regulated or prohibited, are deemed to justify the means."[2]

Cross references.

See LIABILITY.

STRICT LIABILITY.—Cont'd.

---

1. *The comments following Code of Ala. 1975, § 13A-2-3, present these examples of strict liability crimes: "Haywood v. State, 280 Ala. 171, 190 So. 2d 728 (1966) (on public road under influence of liquor malum prohibitum offense; the legislature may make the doing of an act criminal without regard to the intent or knowledge of the doer). Leonard v. State, 38 Ala. App. 138, 79 So. 2d 803, cert. denied, 262 Ala. 702, 79 So. 2d 808 (1955) (operating truck of excessive axle rate; guilty knowledge immaterial). Smith v. State, 223 Ala. 346, 136 So. 270 (1931) (statute respecting weights and measures makes seller guarantor of quantity or weight of commodities he sells regardless of his intent or knowledge). Dixon v. State, 40 Ala. App. 465, 115 So. 2d 262 (1959) (dicta: violation of the speed limit occurs when the rate prescribed is passed, regardless of the state of mind of the operator. Likewise, in statutory rape, belief that the female is of the age of consent is immaterial)."*
2. *See the comments following Code of Ala. 1975, § 13A-2-3. The comments also give the following examples: "U. S. v. Balint, 258 U. S. 250 (1922) (selling drugs violated federal Narcotics Act even though defendant did not know they contained opium). U. S. v. Parfait Power Puff Co., 163 F. 2d 1008 (7th Cir. 1947), cert. denied, 332 U. S. 851 (conviction under Pure Food, Drug and Cosmetic Act affirmed even though defendant company unaware of substituted deleterious substance by manufacturer)."*

SUNDAY, CERTAIN ACTS PROHIBITED. Code of Ala. 1975, § 13A-12-1.

Charged as: Certain acts prohibited on Sunday.

"Any person who compels his child, apprentice or servant to perform any labor on Sunday, except the customary domestic duties of daily necessity or comfort, or works of charity or who engages in shooting, hunting, gaming, card playing or racing on that day, or who, being a merchant or shopkeeper, druggist excepted, keeps open store on Sunday, shall be fined not less than $10.00 nor more than $100.00, and may also be imprisoned in the county jail, or sentenced to hard labor for the county, for not more than three months. However, the provisions of this section shall not apply to the operation of railroads, airlines, bus lines, communications, public utilities or steamboats or other vessels navigating the waters of this state, or to any manufacturing establishment which is required to be kept in constant operation, or to the sale of gasoline or other motor fuels or motor oils. Nor shall this section prohibit the sale of newspapers, or the operation of newsstands, or automobile repair shops, florist shops, fruit stands, ice cream shops or parlors, lunch stands or restaurants, delicatessens or plants engaged in the manufacture or sale of ice; provided, that such business establishments are not operated in conjunction with some other kind or type of business which is prohibited by this section. It shall also be lawful to engage in motorcycle and automobile racing on Sunday, whether admission is charged or not; except, that this proviso shall not be construed to prevent any municipality from passing ordinances prohibiting such racing on Sunday."

Classification.

A violation.

Comments.

Since there is no accompanying commentary to this section, which largely consists of exceptions to the general rule, enforcement would appear to be limited. In addition, it should be noted that the "child, apprentice or servant" who performs the labor cannot be charged under this statute, only the person who "compelled" them to work.

Defenses.

(1) Failure to prove defendant "compelled" another to perform labor on Sunday.

(2) Failure to prove the person compelled is within the scope of this statute (child, apprentice, or servant).

(3) The challenged conduct falls within the "customary domestic duties of daily necessity or comfort, or works of charity."

(4) The challenged conduct falls within one of the exceptions.

(5) The possibility of an "equal protection" challenge.

Query.

What is the definition of merchant and

SUNDAY, CERTAIN ACTS PROHIBITED.—Cont'd.

shopkeeper? Would a "child, apprentice or servant" also qualify as the shopkeeper if they are sales personnel?

Cross references.

See Punishment and sentences generally, § 13A-5-1 of the Alabama Code; Punishment of offenses, § 13A-1-7 of the Alabama Code. See SUNDAY, HOLDING PUBLIC MARKETS AND TRADING.

SUNDAY, HOLDING PUBLIC MARKETS AND TRADING. Code of Ala. 1975, § 13A-12-2.

Charged as: Holding public markets and trading therein on Sunday.

"Any person who opens, or causes to be opened, for the purpose of selling or trading, any public market[1] or place on Sunday, or opens, or causes to be opened, any stall or shop therein, or connected therewith, or brings anything for sale or barter to such market or place, or offers the same for sale therein on that day, or buys or sells therein on that day, including livestock or cattle; shall, on conviction, be punished as prescribed in section 13A-12-1."

Classification.

A violation.

Comments.

This statute supplements certain acts prohibited on Sunday, § 13A-12-1 of the Alabama Code. It prohibits sales and trading by the public on Sunday (i.e., "flea markets"). The enforceability of this statute is questionable.

Defenses.

(1) Lack of intent to enter into proscribed conduct.

(2) The possibility of an "equal protection" challenge.

Cross references.

See Punishment and sentences generally, § 13A-5-1 of the Alabama Code; Punishment of offenses, § 13A-1-7 of the Alabama Code. See SUNDAY, CERTAIN ACTS PROHIBITED.

SUNDAY, HOLDING PUBLIC MARKETS AND TRADING.
—Cont'd.

---

1. *"Any place where people assemble for the purchase and sale of goods, wares and merchandise, provisions, cattle or other articles is a market house or place within the meaning of this section." Code of Ala. 1975, § 13A-12-2.*

SURVEILLANCE. Code of Ala. 1975, § 13A-11-32.

"A person commits the crime of criminal surveillance if he intentionally engages in surveillance[1] while trespassing in a private place."[2]

Classification. Class B misdemeanor.

Comments.

This law is intended to protect the right of privacy derived from § 5 of the Constitution of Alabama of 1901. Specifically it criminalizes visual or photographic surveillance accomplished while trespassing. The statute is unclear as to whether any trespass will suffice or whether the trespass must be upon property owned or controlled by the subject of the surveillance. The later interpretation would seem too narrow to accomplish the goal of the statute. If a trespass were not committed, the party under surveillance should not be heard to complain (within the meaning of § 13A-11-32 of the Alabama Code). Obviously a nontrespasser could as easily have made the observation, which in turn quashes any reasonable expectation of privacy the party under surveillance might assert. Thus, making trespass an element of the crime begs a constitutional challenge unless a narrow interpretation of trespass (i.e., to mean only trespass of the property of the party under surveillance) is established. The definition of the term surveillance as "secret observation" may well provide an unintended defense. It might be argued that a photographer who boldly invaded one's privacy did not commit criminal surveillance because he did not try to conceal or conduct his activities in secret. In accordance with § 13A-11-37 of the Alabama Code, upon conviction for this offense the state may

SURVEILLANCE.—Cont'd.
obtain forfeiture of the device or equipment by court order.

Query.
This statute does not track the language of federal legislation[3] or decisions[4] and in specific instances may be in conflict with the established body of law regarding privacy, newsman's privilege and the like.

Defenses.
(1) Observation not secret.
(2) Lack of requisite trespass.
(3) No reasonable expectation of privacy.
(4) Public access to point of observation.
(5) Accused is a peace offficer engaged in the lawful performance of his duties.[5]
(6) Accused was "an officer, employee or agent of a communication common carrier who, while acting in the normal course of his employment, and while engaged in any activity which was a necessary incident to the rendition of his service or to the protection of the rights or property of the carrier of such communication, intercepted, disclosed or used a communication transmitted through the facilities of that carrier."[6]
(7) Accused relied in good faith on a lawful court order or legislative authorization.[7]

Cross references.
See Forfeiture of Eavesdropping Device, § 13A-11-37 of the Alabama Code. See DIVULGING ILLEGALLY OBTAINED INFORMATION; EAVESDROPPING; TRESPASS, CRIMINAL.

---

1. *"SURVEILLANCE. Secret observation of the activities of another person for the purpose of spying upon and invading the privacy of the person observed." Code of Ala. 1975, § 13A-11-30(3).*
2. *"PRIVATE PLACE. A place where one may reasonably expect to be safe from casual or hostile intrusion or surveillance, but such term does not include a place to which the public or a substantial group of the public has access." Code of Ala. 1975, § 13A-11-30(2).*
3. *Code of Ala. 1975, § 13A-11-36.*
4. *Code of Ala. 1975, § 13A-11-36.*
5. *Code of Ala. 1975, § 13A-11-36.*
6. *Code of Ala. 1975, § 13A-11-36(a)(2).*
7. *Code of Ala. 1975, § 13A-11-36(a)(3).*

TAKING OR RETAKING POSSESSION OF REAL ESTATE. See REAL ESTATE, TAKING OR RETAKING POSSESSION OF.

TAMPERING. Code of Ala. 1975, §§ 13A-7-25, 13A-7-26.
"A person commits the crime of criminal tampering[1] in the first degree if: having no right to do so or any reasonable ground to believe that he has such a right, he intentionally causes substantial interruption or impairment of a service rendered to the public by a utility."[2] § 13A-7-25(a) of the Alabama Code.
"A person commits the crime of criminal tampering in the second degree if: having no right to do so or any reasonable ground to believe that he has such a right, he:
"(1) Intentionally tampers with property[3] of another for the purpose of causing substantial inconvenience to that person or to another; or
"(2) Intentionally tampers or makes connection with property of a utility." § 13A-7-26(a) of the Alabama Code.

Classification.
Class C felony — first degree.
Class B misdemeanor — second degree.

Comments.
This offense in the first degree is designed to criminalize any interference of a substantial nature with service rendered to the public by a utility. It is intended to protect the public safety. The defense attorney's argument ought to link the lack of injury or damage with the claimed lack of "substantial interruption or impairment." The emphasis of the statute is on the interference with property or service. Subsection (1) of the offense in the second degree is directed at the protection of the individual from "substantial inconvenience." The right of the utility to be free from tampering is protected by subsection (2), which does not require any larcenous intent that would be necessary to charge one with theft of services. Absent the right to do so, or absent reasonable grounds to believe that a person had such a right, this subsection imposes strict liability on one who tampers.

TAMPERING.—Cont'd.

Defenses.

(1) Right, or reasonable belief of right.

(2) Lack of substantial interruption or impairment (first degree).

(3) Lack of substantial inconvenience (second degree).

Cross references.

See GOVERNMENTAL RECORDS, TAMPERING WITH; JURY TAMPERING; MISCHIEF, CRIMINAL; PHYSICAL EVIDENCE, TAMPERING WITH; THEFT OF SERVICES; WITNESSES, TAMPERING WITH.

---

1. *"Tamper," according to Code of Ala. 1975, § 13A-7-24(1), is defined as follows: "To improperly interfere, meddle with or make an unwarranted alteration in the condition of the property of another."*
2. *"Utility," according to Code of Ala. 1975, § 13A-7-24(3), is defined as follows: "An enterprise which provides gas, electric, steam, water, sewage, transportation or communication services, and any institution that provides health and safety protection or other public services; it may be either publicly or privately owned."*
3. *"Property," according to Code of Ala. 1975, § 13A-7-24(2), is defined as follows: "Any tangible or intangible property, real or personal, public or private, and includes the commodities and services of a utility nature, such as gas, electricity, steam and water."*

TELEPHONE. See HARASSMENT OR HARRASSING COMMUNICATIONS; PARTY LINES.

TEMPTATION. See ENTRAPMENT.

TEMPTING. See ENTRAPMENT.

THEFT OF LOST PROPERTY. Code of Ala. 1975, §§ 13A-8-6 through 13A-8-9.

"A person commits the crime of theft of lost property if he actively obtains or exerts control[1] over the property[2] of another which he knows to have been lost or mislaid, or to have been delivered under a mistake as to the identity of the recipient or as to the nature of the amount of the property, and with intent to deprive[3] the owner[4] permanently of it, he fails to take reasonable measures[5] to discover and notify the owner." § 13A-8-6 of the Alabama Code.

Degrees of theft of lost property:

"The theft of lost property which exceeds $1,000.00 in value[6] constitutes theft of lost property in the first degree." § 13A-8-7 of the Alabama Code.

"The theft of lost property which exceeds $100.00 in value but does not exceed $1,000.00 in value constitutes theft of lost property in the second degree." § 13A-8-8 of the Alabama Code.

"The theft of lost property which does not exceed $100.00 in value constitutes theft of lost property in the third degree." § 13A-8-9 of the Alabama Code.

Classification.

Class B felony, theft of lost property in the first degree.

Class C felony, theft of lost property in the second degree.

Class A misdemeanor, theft of lost property in the third degree.

Comments.

There is no distinction between lost and mislaid property. Theft of property encompasses situations in which a thief obtains or exerts unauthorized control, while theft of **lost** property only requires a thief to obtain or exert control. There are cases[7] in which a victim voluntarily parts with possession of his property without the thief having furnished any material inducement or action to gain it, such as when the victim mistakenly believing that he is turning over or delivering one particular sum or thing when in fact he is delivering a different sum or thing. The victim may also believe the thief is one person when, in fact, he is someone else. In either situation, the potential thief is not liable until he knows of the mistaken delivery and there has elapsed a reasonable time allowing for discovery of and notice to the owner.

For classification, the theft of lost, mislaid or misdelivered property has been equated to the theft of property. The extent of criminal liability does not turn on technical differences between whether the property

THEFT OF LOST PROPERTY.
—Cont'd.

was lost, mislaid or simply placed somewhere for safekeeping.

Defenses.

(1) Lack of knowledge property is lost or mislaid.

(2) Reasonable measures having been taken to notify the owner.

(3) Claim of right.[8]

(4) Consider value, relative to a reduction in degree.

Cross references.

See SHOPPING CARTS, ABANDONMENT OR REMOVAL; THEFT OF PROPERTY.

---

1. *"OBTAINS OR EXERTS CONTROL or OBTAINS OR EXERTS UNAUTHORIZED CONTROL over property includes but is not necessarily limited to the taking, carrying away or the sale, conveyance or transfer of title to, or interest in, or possession of, property, and includes but is not necessarily limited to conduct heretofore defined or known as common law larceny by trespassory taking, common law larceny by trick, larceny by conversion, embezzlement, extortion or obtaining property by false pretenses." Code of Ala. 1975, § 13A-8-1(7).*
2. *"PROPERTY. Any money, tangible or intangible personal property, property (whether real or personal) the location of which can be changed (including things growing on, affixed to or found in land and documents, although the rights represented hereby have no physical location), contract right, chose-in-action, interest in or claim to wealth, credit or any other article or thing of value of any kind.*

   "Commodities of a public utility nature, such as gas, electricity, steam and water, constitute property, but the supplying of such a commodity to premises from an outside source by means of wires, pipes, conduits or other equipment shall be deemed a rendition of a service rather than a sale or delivery of property." Code of Ala. 1975, § 13A-8-1(10). See Theft of services, Code of Ala. 1975, § 13A-8-10.
3. *"To 'DEPRIVE . . .' means:*

   "a. To withhold property or cause it to be withheld from a person permanently or for such period or under such circumstances that all or a portion of its use or benefit would be lost to him; or

   "b. To dispose of the property so as to make it unlikely that the owner would recover it; or

THEFT OF LOST PROPERTY.
—Cont'd.

   "c. To retain the property with intent to restore it to the owner only if the owner purchases or leases it back, or pays a reward or other compensation for its return; or

   "d. To sell, give, pledge, or otherwise transfer any interest in the property; or

   "e. To subject the property to the claim of a person other than the owner." Code of Ala. 1975, § 13A-8-1(2).
4. *"OWNER. A person, other than the defendant, who has possession of or any other interest in the property involved, even though that interest or possession is unlawful, and without whose consent the defendant has no authority to exert control over the property.*

   "A secured party, as defined in section 7-9-105(i), is not an owner in relation to a defendant who is a debtor, as defined in section 7-9-105(d), in respect of property in which the secured party has a security interest, as defined in section 7-1-201(37)."
5. *What the reasonable measures were under the circumstances of the mistaken delivery are facts within the jury's capability of establishing. Code of Ala. 1975, §§ 13A-8-6 through 13A-8-9.*
6. *"VALUE. The market value of the property at the time and place of the criminal act.*

   "Whether or not they have been issued or delivered, certain written instruments, not including those having a readily ascertainable market value such as some public and corporate bonds and securities shall be evaluated as follows:

   "a. The value of an instrument constituting an evidence of debt, such as a check, draft or promissory note, shall be deemed the amount due or collectible thereon or thereby, that figure ordinarily being the face amount of the indebtedness less any portion thereof which has been satisfied.

   "b. The value of any other instrument that creates, releases, discharges or otherwise affects any valuable legal right, privilege or obligation shall be deemed the greatest amount of economic loss which the owner of the instrument might reasonably suffer by virtue of the loss of the instrument.

   "When the value of property cannot be ascertained pursuant to the standards set forth above, its value shall be deemed to be an amount not exceeding $100.00.

   "Amounts involved in thefts committed pursuant to one scheme or course of conduct, whether from

THEFT OF LOST PROPERTY. —Cont'd.

the same person or several persons, may be aggregated in determining the grade of the offense; provided, that only one conviction may be had and only one sentence enforced for all thefts included in such aggregate." Code of Ala. 1975, § 13A-8-1(14).

7. *Bailey v. State, 58 Ala. 414 (1877); see also Cooper v. Commonwealth, 110 Ky. 123, 60 S. W. 938 (1901).*
8. *"(a) It is a defense to a prosecution under sections 13A-8-2 through 13A-8-11 (theft of property, theft of lost property, theft of services and unauthorized use of vehicle) that the actor honestly believed that he had a claim to the property or services involved which he was entitled to assert in the manner which forms the basis for the charge against him.*

   "(b) The burden of injecting the issue of claim of right is on the defendant, but this does not shift the burden of proof." Code of Ala. 1975, § 13A-8-12.

THEFT OF PROPERTY. Code of Ala. 1975, §§ 13A-8-2 through 13A-8-5.

"A person commits the crime of theft of property if he:

"(1) Knowingly obtains or exerts unauthorized control[1] over the property[2] of another, with intent to deprive[3] the owner[4] of his property; or

"(2) Knowingly obtains by deception[5] control over the property of another, with intent to deprive the owner of his property." § 13A-8-2 of the Alabama Code.

Degrees of theft of property:

"(a) The theft of property which exceeds $1,000.00 in value,[6] or property of any value taken from the person of another, constitutes theft of property in the first degree.

"(b) The theft of a motor vehicle, regardless of its value, constitutes theft of property in the first degree." § 13A-8-3 of the Alabama Code,

"(a) The theft of property which exceeds $100.00 in value but does not exceed $1,000.00 in value, and which is not taken from the Person of another, constitutes theft of property in the second degree.

* * *

"(c) The theft of a credit card or a debit card, regardless of its value, constitutes theft of property in the second degree.

"(d) The theft of a firearm, rifle or shotgun, regardless of its value, constitutes theft of property in the second degree.

"(e) The theft of property which exceeds $25.00 in value, and which is taken from or in a building where said property is sold or stored, constitutes theft of property in the second degree.

"(f) The theft of any substance controlled by chapter 2 of Title 20 or any amendments thereto, regardless of value, constitutes theft of property in the second degree.

"(g) The theft of any livestock which includes cattle, swine, horses, mules, asses or sheep, regardless of their value, constitutes theft of property in the second degree." § 13A-8-4 of the Alabama Code.

"The theft of property which does not exceed $100.00 in value and which is not taken from the person of another or the theft of property which does not exceed $25.00 in value if taken from or in a building where said property sold or stored constitutes theft of property in the third degree." § 13A-8-5(a) of the Alabama Code.

Classification.

Class B felony, theft of property in the first degree.

Class C felony, theft of property in the second degree.

Class A misdemeanor, theft of property in the third degree.

Comments.

The purpose of these sections is to create a unified theft offense that eliminates the distinctions between the common law crimes of larceny, embezzlement and false pretenses. These property crimes, possessing the same general nature, are treated as not being theoretically different. This may reduce the risk of variance between pleading and proof, and, upon a charge of theft, may allow a conviction upon evidence of the commission by anyone of the traditional offenses of larceny, embezzlement or false pretenses. The basic elements of the offense are (1) the obtaining of control over property in which another

THEFT OF PROPERTY.—Cont'd.

has an interest, and (2) the deliberate diversion of it for the offender's own purposes.

This statute replaces all prior Alabama embezzlement statutes because it defines theft as knowingly obtaining or exerting unauthorized control over the property of another, with intent to deprive the owner of his property. Under this formulation, the relationship of the offender to the owner, the problems of the intent required and the way in which the property came into the control or possession of the offender, are removed.

The separate crime of false pretenses is included in theft definition by including the obtaining of another's property by deception. No longer does it matter whether title, as well as possession, has passed. Any deception that takes advantage of the confidence of the victim, including a promise the offender has no intention of performing, is included.

It does not matter whether the property is real or personal, but whether it is movable. This statute makes a chose-in-action subject to theft. It should be noted that the theft of a credit or debit card, airplane ticket, etc., which generally depend upon their face values is a different offense from the theft or services (§ 13A-8-10 of the Alabama Code), and is also different from the statutory offenses of forgery[7] or illegal use of a credit or debit card.[8]

Defenses.

(1) Lack of intent to deprive.

(2) Unknowingly obtained the property of another.

(3) Claim of right.[9]

(4) Consider value, relative to reducing the degree.

Cross references.

See COPYING, SALE, OR POSSESSION OF RECORDED DEVICE; CREDIT CARD OR DEBIT CARD, ILLEGAL POSSESSION OF OR FRAUDULENT USE; EXTORTION; FORGERY; MISAPPLICATION OF PROPERTY; RECEIVING STOLEN PROPERTY; ROBBERY; SHOPPING CARTS,

THEFT OF PROPERTY.—Cont'd.

ABANDONMENT OR REMOVAL; THEFT OF LOST PROPERTY; THEFT OF SERVICES.

---

1. *"OBTAINS OR EXERTS CONTROL or OBTAINS OR EXERTS UNAUTHORIZED CONTROL over property includes but is not necessarily limited to the taking, carrying away or the sale, conveyance or transfer of title to, or interest in, or possession of, property, and includes but is not necessarily limited to conduct heretofore defined or known as common law larceny by trespassory taking, common law larceny by trick, larceny by conversion, embezzlement, extortion or obtaining property by false pretenses." Code of Ala. 1975, § 13A-8-1(7).*
2. *"PROPERTY. Any money, tangible or intangible personal property, property (whether real or personal) the location of which can be changed (including things growing on, affixed to or found in land and documents, although the rights represented hereby have no physical location), contract right, chose-in-action, interest in or claim to wealth, credit or any other article or thing of value of any kind.*

   "Commodities of a public utility nature, such as gas, electricity, steam and water, constitute property, but the supplying of such a commodity to premises from an outside source by means of wires, pipes, conduits or other equipment shall be deemed a rendition of a service rather than a sale or delivery of property." Code of Ala. 1975, § 13A-8-1(10). See Theft of services, Code of Ala. 1975, § 13A-8-10.
3. *"To 'DEPRIVE . . .' means:*

   "a. To withhold property or cause it to be withheld from a person permanently or for such period or under such circumstances that all or a portion of its use or benefit would be lost to him; or

   "b. To dispose of the property so as to make it unlikely that the owner would recover it; or

   "c. To retain the property with intent to restore it to the owner only if the owner purchases or leases it back, or pays a reward or other compensation for its return; or

   "d. To sell, give, pledge, or otherwise transfer any interest in the property; or

   "e. To subject the property to the claim of a person other than the owner." Code of Ala. 1975, § 13A-8-1(2).
4. *"OWNER. A person, other than the defendant, who has possession of or any other interest in the property involved, even though that interest or possession is unlawful, and without whose*

THEFT OF PROPERTY.—Cont'd.

consent the defendant has no authority to exert control over the property.

"A secured party, as defined in section 7-9-105(i) is not an owner in relation to a defendant who is a debtor, as defined in section 7-9-105(d), in respect of property in which the secured party has a security interest, as defined in section 7-1-201(37)."

5. *"DECEPTION occurs when a person knowingly:*

"a. Creates or confirms another's impression which is false and which the defendant does not believe to be true; or

"b. Fails to correct a false impression which the defendant previously has created or confirmed; or

"c. Fails to correct a false impression when the defendant is under a duty to do so; or

"d. Prevents another from acquiring information pertinent to the disposition of the property involved; or

"e. Sells or otherwise transfers or encumbers property, failing to disclose a lien, adverse claim or other legal impediment to the enjoyment of the property when the defendant is under a duty to do so, whether that impediment is or is not valid, or is not a matter of official record; or

"f. Promises performance which the defendant does not intend to perform or knows will not be performed. Failure to perform, standing alone, however, is not proof that the defendant did not intend to perform.

"The term 'deception' does not, however, include falsity as to matters having no pecuniary significance, or puffing by statements unlikely to deceive ordinary persons. 'Puffing' means an exaggerated commendation of wares or services." Code of Ala. 1975, § 13A-8-1(1).

6. *"VALUE. The market value of the property at the time and place of the criminal act.*

"Whether or not they have been issued or delivered, certain written instruments, not including those having a readily ascertainable market value such as some public and corporate bonds and securities shall be evaluated as follows:

"a. The value of an instrument constituting an evidence of debt, such as a check, draft or promissory note, shall be deemed the amount due or collectible thereon or thereby, that figure ordinarily being the face amount of the indebtedness less any portion thereof which has been satisfied.

"b. The value of any other instrument that creates, releases, discharges or otherwise affects any valuable right, privilege or obligation shall be deemed the greatest amount of economic loss which the owner of the instrument might reasonably suffer by virtue of the loss of the instrument.

"When the value of property cannot be ascertained pursuant to the standards set forth above, its value shall be deemed to be an amount not exceeding $100.00.

"Amounts involved in thefts committed pursuant to one scheme or course of conduct, whether from the same person or several persons, may be aggregated in determining the grade of the offense; provided, that only one conviction may be had and only one sentence enforced for all thefts included in such aggregate." Code of Ala. 1975, § 13A-8-1(14).

7. *Code of Ala. 1975, §§ 13A-9-2 through 13A-9-4.*
8. *Code of Ala. 1975, § 13A-9-14.*
9. *"(a) It is a defense to a prosecution under sections 13A-8-2 through 13A-8-11 (theft of property, theft of lost property, theft of services and unauthorized use of vehicle) that the actor honestly believed that he had a claim to the property or services involved which he was entitled to assert in the manner which forms the basis for the charge against him.*

"(b) The burden of injecting the issue of claim of right is on the defendant, but this does not shift the burden of proof." Code of Ala. 1975, § 13A-8-12.

THEFT OF SERVICES. Code of Ala. 1975, §§ 13A-8-10 through 13A-8-10.3.

"(a) A person commits the crime of theft of services if:

"(1) He intentionally obtains[1] services known by him to be available only for compensation by deception,[2] threat,[3] false token or other means to avoid payment for the services; or

"(2) Having control over the disposition of services of others to which he is not entitled, he knowingly diverts those services to his own benefit or to the benefit of another not entitled thereto.

"(b) 'Services' includes but is not necessarily limited to labor, professional services, transportation, telephone or other public services, accommodation in motels, hotels, restaurants or elsewhere, admission to exhibitions, computer services and the supplying of equipment for use.

THEFT OF SERVICES.—Cont'd.

"(c) Where compensation for services is ordinarily paid immediately upon the rendering of them, as in the case of motels, hotels, restaurants and the like, absconding without payment or bona fide offer to pay is prima facie evidence under subsection (a) that the services were obtained by deception.

"(d) If services are obtained under subdivision (a)(1) from a hotel, motel, inn, restaurant or cafe, no prosecution can be commenced after 120 days from the time of the offense." § 13A-8-10 of the Alabama Code.

Degrees of theft of services:

"The theft of services which exceeds $2,000.00 in value[4] constitutes theft of services in the first degree." § 13A-8-10.1 of the Alabama Code.

"The theft of services which exceeds $100.00 in value but does not exceed $2,000.00 in value constitutes theft of services in the second degree." § 13A-8-10.2 of the Alabama Code.

"The theft of services which does not exceed $100.00 in value constitutes theft of services in the third degree." § 13A-8-10.3 of the Alabama Code.

Classification.

Class B felony, theft of services in the first degree.

Class C felony, theft of services in the second degree.

Class A misdemeanor, theft of services in the third degree.

Comments.

Services are not included in the general definition of property.[5] No conflict, therefore, exists between these sections and the sections concerning theft of property (§§ 13A-8-2 through 13A-8-5 of the Alabama Code). In addition to obtaining services by deception, which normally involves some misrepresentation relied upon by the supplier, these sections include other means to avoid payment. An unknown or unauthorized tampering, or making connection, with the equipment of a public utility or other supplier of services are included in this crime.

THEFT OF SERVICES.—Cont'd.

Defenses.

(1) Lack of intent.

(2) Fact that service obtained is sometimes available without compensation.

(3) Claim of right.[6]

(4) The alleged theft of services was obtained from a hotel, motel, inn, restaurant or cafe more than 120 days prior to the commencement of the prosecution.[7]

Cross references.

See TAMPERING; THEFT OF LOST PROPERTY; THEFT OF PROPERTY.

---

1. *"OBTAINS. Such term means:*
"a. In relation to property, to bring about a transfer or purported transfer of a legally recognized interest in the property, whether to the obtainer or another; or
"b. In relation to labor or service, to secure performance thereof." Code of Ala. 1975, § 13A-8-1(6).

2. *"DECEPTION occurs when a person knowingly:*
"a. Creates or confirms another's impression which is false and which the defendant does not believe to be true; or
"b. Fails to correct a false impression which the defendant previously has created or confirmed; or
"c. Fails to correct a false impression when the defendant is under a duty to do so; or
"d. Prevents another from acquiring information pertinent to the disposition of the property involved; or
"e. Sells or otherwise transfers or encumbers property, failing to disclose a lien, adverse claim or other legal impediment to the enjoyment of the property when the defendant is under a duty to do so, whether that impediment is or is not valid, or is not a matter of official record; or
"f. Promises performance which the defendant does not intend to perform or knows will not be performed. Failure to perform, standing alone, however, is not proof that the defendant did not intend to perform.
"The term 'deception' does not, however, include falsity as to matters having no pecuniary significance, or puffing by statements unlikely to deceive ordinary persons. 'Puffing' means an exaggerated commendation of wares or services." Code of Ala. 1975, § 13A-8-1(1).

3. *"THREAT. A menace, however communicated, to:*
"a. Cause physical harm to the person threatened or to any other person; or

THEFT OF SERVICES.—Cont'd.

"b. Cause damage to property; or

"c. Subject the person threatened or any other person to physical confinement or restraint; or

"d. Engage in other conduct constituting a crime; or

"e. Accuse any person of a crime or cause criminal charges to be instituted against any person; or

"f. Expose a secret or publicize an asserted fact, whether true or false, tending to subject any person to hatred, contempt or ridicule; or

"g. Reveal any information sought to be concealed by the person threatened; or

"h. Testify or provide information or withhold testimony or information with respect to another's legal claim or defense; or

"i. Take action as an official against anyone or anything, or withhold official action, or cause such action or withholding; or

"j. Bring about or continue a strike, boycott or other similar collective action to obtain property which is not demanded or received for the benefit of the group which the actor purports to represent; or

"k. Do any other act which would not in itself substantially benefit the actor but which is calculated to harm substantially another person with respect to his health, safety, business, calling, career, financial condition, reputation or personal relationships." Code of Ala. 1975, § 13A-8-1(13).

4. "VALUE. The market value of the property at the time and place of the criminal act.

"Whether or not they have been issued or delivered, certain written instruments, not including those having a readily ascertainable market value such as some public and corporate bonds and securities shall be evaluated as follows:

"a. The value of an instrument constituting an evidence of debt, such as a check, draft or promissory note, shall be deemed the amount due or collectible thereon or thereby, that figure ordinarily being the face amount of the indebtedness less any portion thereof which has been satisfied.

"b. The value of any other instrument that creates, releases, discharges or otherwise affects any valuable right, privilege or obligation shall be deemed the greatest amount of economic loss which the owner of the instrument might reasonably suffer by virtue of the loss of the instrument.

"When the value of property cannot be ascertained pursuant to the standards set forth above, its value shall be deemed to be an amount not exceeding $100.00.

"Amounts involved in thefts committed pursuant to one scheme or course of conduct, whether from the same person or several persons, may be aggregated in determining the grade of the offense; provided, that only one conviction may be had and only one sentence enforced for all thefts included in such aggregate." Code of Ala. 1975, § 13A-8-1(14).

5. "PROPERTY. Any money, tangible or intangible personal property, property (whether real or personal) the location of which can be changed (including things growing on, affixed to or found in land and documents, although the rights represented hereby have no physical location), contract right, chose-in-action, interest in or claim to wealth, credit or any other article or thing of value of any kind.

"Commodities of a public utility nature, such as gas, electricity, steam and water, constitute property, but the supplying of such a commodity to premises from an outside source by means of wires, pipes, conduits or other equipment shall be deemed a rendition of a service rather than a sale or delivery of property." Code of Ala. 1975, § 13A-8-1(10). See Theft of services, Code of Ala. 1975, § 13A-8-10.

6. "(a) It is a defense to a prosecution under Code of Ala. 1975, sections 13A-8-2 through 13A-8-11 (theft of property, theft of lost property, theft of services and unauthorized use of vehicle) that the actor honestly believed that he had a claim to the property or services involved which he was entitled to assert in the manner which forms the basis for the charge against him.

"(b) The burden of injecting the issue of claim of right is on the defendant, but this does not shift the burden of proof." Code of Ala. 1975, § 13A-8-12.

7. Code of Ala. 1975, § 13A-8-10(d).

TOMBSTONE. See DESECRATION OF TOMBSTONES.

TRADING IN PUBLIC OFFICE. Code of Ala. 1975, § 13A-10-63.

"A person is guilty of trading in public office if:

"(1) He offers, confers or agrees to confer any pecuniary benefit[1] upon a public servant[2] or party officer[3] upon an agreement or understanding that he himself will or may be appointed to a public office or public employment or designated

TRADING IN PUBLIC OFFICE.
—Cont'd.

or nominated as a candidate for public office; or

"(2) While a public servant or party officer, he solicits, accepts or agrees to accept any pecuniary benefit from another upon an agreement or understanding that that person will or may be appointed to a public office or public employment or designated or nominated as a candidate for public office."

Classification.

Class A misdemeanor.

Comments.

The purpose of this section is to prohibit the sale or purchase of a public office. Payment is limited to pecuniary benefits; therefore, working in a campaign in return for an appointment to office in the event that the candidate is elected is not a criminal activity. Contributions to a political campaign fund are specifically exempted.[4]

Defenses.

(1) No agreement between the parties.

(2) Pecuniary benefit was not to obtain public office for the person making the offer but for a third party.

(3) Political contribution (campaign funds, etc.).

Cross references.

See Corrupt Practices, § 17-22-1 et seq. of the Alabama Code; Giving aid or contribution to political party or candidate, § 10-2A-70 of the Alabama Code. See BRIBERY OF PUBLIC SERVANTS.

---

1. *"PECUNIARY BENEFIT. Benefit in the form of money, property, commercial interests or anything else the primary significance of which is economic gain. Expenses associated with social occasions afforded public servants and party officers shall not be deemed a pecuniary benefit within the meaning of this article." Code of Ala. 1975, § 13A-10-60(b)(2).*
2. *"PUBLIC SERVANT . . . includes persons who presently occupy the position of a public servant, as defined in section 13A-10-1(7), or have been elected, appointed or designated to become a public servant although not yet occupying that position." Code of Ala. 1975, § 13A-10-60(b)(3).*
3. *"PARTY OFFICER. A person who holds any position or office in a political party, whether by election, appointment or otherwise." Code of Ala. 1975, § 13A-10-60(b)(4).*
4. *"This section does not apply to contributions to political campaign funds or other political contributions." Code of Ala. 1975, § 13A-10-63(b).*

TRAFFIC ACCIDENTS. See MOTOR VEHICLE CRIMES.

TRAFFICKING IN CANNABIS, COCAINE, ETC. See CONTROLLED SUBSTANCES.

TRAITOR. See TREASON.

TRANSPORTATION OF. See specific title (e.g. COMMODITIES, etc.).

TREASON. Code of Ala. 1975, § 13A-11-2.

"(a) A person[1] commits the crime of treason if he levies war[2] against the State of Alabama or adheres to its enemies,[3] giving them aid and comfort.[4]

"(b) No person shall be convicted of treason unless upon the testimony of two witnesses to the same overt act[5] or upon confession in open court."

Classification.

Class A felony.

Comments.

There are two ways to commit treason: (1) levy war against the State; or (2) adhere to its enemies, giving them aid and comfort. This law is designed to punish conduct or acts rather than mental processes. In support of this objective approach it retains the "two-witness rule," which regulates the amount of evidence necessary to convict. State statutes purporting to penalize subversion against the United States are unconstitutional. Congress has preempted the field through the Smith Act and other federal legislation. Pennsylvania v. Nelson, 350 U. S. 497, 76 S. Ct. 477, 100 L. Ed. 640 (1956).

Defenses.

(1) Adherence to the enemy without giving aid and comfort is not treason. U. S. v. Cullen, 454 F. 2d 391 (1971).

TREASON.—Cont'd.

(2) Giving aid and comfort to the enemy without adherence is not treason.

(3) There must be a assembly of persons in force to overthrow the government or to coerce its conduct in order to constitute "levying of war." U. S. v. Greathouse, C. C. Cal., 26 F. Cas. No. 15, 254; 4 Sawy. U. S. 457 (1863).

(4) Failure to produce at least two witnesses to testify to the same overt act.

Query.

Can a corporate entity be "a person" within the meaning of this statute?

Cross references.

See RIOT; RIOT, INCITING TO; UNLAWFUL ASSEMBLY.

---

1. *"PERSON. A human being, and where appropriate, a public or private corporation, an unincorporated association, a partnership, a government or a governmental instrumentality." Code of Ala. 1975, § 13A-1-2(6).*
2. *"Levies war" means assembling persons in force, to overthrow the government or to coerce its conduct. U. S. v. Greathouse, C. C. Cal., 26 F. Cas. No. 15, 254; 4 Sawy. U. S. 457 (1863).*
3. *The Alabama Code does not define the concept of "adhering to its enemies," but according to commentary following the treason statute, the United States Constitution and federal court decisions are the sources of many terms found in the Alabama statute. Any intentional act which furthers or tends to strengthen hostile designs of enemies constitutes adhering. Agee v. Muskee, 629 F. 2d 114 (1980).*
4. *"Aid and comfort" is not defined in the Alabama Code, but as an element of the crime of treason against the United States, it may consist of a mere attempt. Culpability may be found even if the hostile enterprise is unsuccessful and the defendant's conduct is of no assistance. Agee v. Muskee, 629 F. 2d 114 (1980).*
5. *An "overt act," though not defined in the Code, is found in the United States Constitution and means a step, motion, or action really taken in the execution of a treasonable purpose, as distinguished from mere words, and also from a treasonable sentiment, design, or purpose not issuing in action. United States v. Fricke, 259 F. 673, 676 (D. C. N. Y. 1919).*

TRESPASS AND OPERATION OF VEHICLES ON AIRPORTS, LANDING FIELDS, OR OTHER AERONAUTICAL FACILITIES. See AVIATION.

TRESPASS, CRIMINAL. Code of Ala. 1975, §§ 13A-7-2 through 13A-7-4.

Charged as: Criminal trespass.

"A person is guilty of criminal trespass in the first degree if he knowingly[1] enters or remains unlawfully[2] in a dwelling."[3] § 13A-7-2(a) of the Alabama Code.

"A person is guilty of criminal trespass in the second degree if he knowingly enters or remains unlawfully in a building[4] or upon real property which is fenced or enclosed in a manner designed to exclude intruders."[5] § 13A-7-3(a) of the Alabama Code.

"A person is guilty of criminal trespass in the third degree when he knowingly enters or remains unlawfully in or upon premises."[6] § 13A-7-4(a) of the Alabama Code.

Classification.

Class A misdemeanor, criminal trespass in the first degree.

Class C misdemeanor, criminal trespass in the second degree.

Violation, criminal trespass in the third degree.

Comments.

The type of property trespassed determines the degree of the offense since all other elements of the crime are identical among the divisions. The elements of criminal trespass in the first degree are: (1) knowingly entering or remaining, (2) unlawfully, (3) in a dwelling. The offense in the second degree requires only that the unlawful presence be "in a building or upon real property which is fenced or enclosed in a manner designed to exclude intruders." Finally, the offense in the third degree requires only that the offender be "in or upon premises." If the property is "unimproved and apparently unused," there can be no trespass unless there is a "no trespassing" notice, either by conspicuous posting or by direct communication. Note,

TRESPASS, CRIMINAL.—Cont'd.
it is well settled that license, or privilege to enter or remain, does not automatically open the whole property for unlimited duration.

Defenses.

(1) Honest belief of license or privilege.
(2) Did not knowingly enter or remain.
(3) Was not a dwelling (first degree).
(4) Was not in a building or upon enclosed real property (second degree).
(5) The fence or enclosure was not designed to exclude intruders (i.e., decorative; to keep animals in) (second degree).
(6) Was not upon premises (third degree).

Cross references.

See Civil trespass, §§ 3-1-11; 3-4-6; 4-2-7; 6-2-34; 6-3-2; 6-6-316; 6-5-90; 6-5-214; 6-5-216; 6-5-217; 6-5-262; 6-5-263; 9-5-34; 9-5-35; 23-1-59; and 33-7-9 of the Alabama Code; Immunity from arrest for trespass, § 35-2-32 of the Alabama Code. See BURGLARY; MISCHIEF, CRIMINAL; REAL ESTATE, TAKING OR RETAKING POSSESSION OF.

---

1. *Must know that his entry or continued presence is unlawful.*
2. *Code of Ala. 1975, § 13A-7-1(4), "not licensed, invited or privileged to do so."*
3. *Code of Ala. 1975, § 13A-7-1(3), "used or normally used . . . for sleeping, living or lodging therein."*
4. *Code of Ala. 1975, § 13A-7-1(2) ". . . . includes any vehicle, or watercraft used for the lodging of persons or carrying on business therein."*
5. *The commentary admits this "may present occasional difficulty." This presents a problem of vagueness and intent of the statute.*
6. *Code of Ala. 1975, § 13A-7-1(1) "any building or real property."*

UNAUTHORIZED USE, POSSESSION, ETC. OF AIRCRAFT. See AVIATION.

UNAUTHORIZED USE OF VEHICLE/UNLAWFUL BREAKING AND ENTERING A VEHICLE. Code of Ala. 1975, § 13A-8-11.

"(a) A person commits the crime of unauthorized use of a vehicle if:

"(1) Knowing that he does not have the consent of the owner,[1] he takes, operates, exercises control over or otherwise uses a propelled vehicle,[2] or

"(2) Having custody of a propelled vehicle pursuant to an agreement between himself or another and the owner thereof whereby the actor or another is to perform for compensation a specific service for the owner involving the maintenance, repair or use of the vehicle, he intentionally uses or operates it, without the consent of the owner, for his own purpose in a manner constituting a gross deviation from the agreed purpose; or

"(3) Having custody of a propelled vehicle pursuant to an agreement with the owner thereof whereby it is to be returned to the owner at a specified time, he knowingly retains or withholds possession thereof, without the consent of the owner, for so lengthy a period beyond the specified time as to render the retention or possession a gross deviation from the agreement.

* * *

"(b) A person commits the crime of unlawful breaking and entering a vehicle if, without the consent of the owner, he breaks into and enters a vehicle or any part of a vehicle with the intent to commit any felony or theft. For the purposes of this section, 'enters' means to intrude:

"(1) Any part of the body; or

"(2) Any physical object connected with the body."

Classification.

Class A misdemeanor, unauthorized use of a vehicle, generally.

Class B felony, unauthorized use of a vehicle where a person by force or threat of force takes, operates, usurps or exercises control over a propelled vehicle with an operator or one or more passengers aboard.

Class C felony, unlawful breaking and entering a vehicle.

Comments.

This section provides for a lesser punishment for the crime commonly known as joy riding

UNAUTHORIZED USE OF VEHICLE/UNLAWFUL BREAKING AND ENTERING A VEHICLE.—Cont'd.

than would a charge of theft of property (see § 13A-8-3 of the Alabama Code). Both the ordinary wrongful "borrowing" or taking situation and the excessive misuse or wrongful withholding of a vehicle by a bailee who originally obtained possession or custody legally are covered.

This section includes the offense of burglary of a motor vehicle. Burglary is technically concerned with the unlawful entering or remaining in buildings and dwellings. None of the degrees of burglary cover the illegal entry of vehicles. Additionally, burglary requires proof of only an entry, while breaking and entering are required for this section.

Defenses.

(1) Claim of right.[3]

Cross references.

See MISCHIEF, CRIMINAL; MOTOR VEHICLE CRIMES; OBSCURING IDENTITY OF VEHICLE; THEFT OF PROPERTY.

---

1. *"OWNER. A person, other than the defendant, who has possession of or any other interest in the property involved, even though that interest or possession is unlawful, and without whose consent the defendant has no authority to exert control over the property.*

   "A secured party, as defined in section 7-9-105(i), is not an owner in relation to a defendant who is a debtor, as defined in section 7-9-105(d), in respect of property in which the secured party has a security interest, as defined in section 7-1-201(37)." Code of Ala. 1975, § 13A-8-1(8).

2. *"PROPELLED VEHICLE. Any propelled device in, upon or by which any person or property is transported on land, water or in the air, and such term includes motor vehicles, motorcycles, motorboats, aircraft and any vessel propelled by machinery, whether or not that machinery is the principal source of propulsion." Code of Ala. 1975, § 13A-8-1(9).*

UNAUTHORIZED USE OF VEHICLE/UNLAWFUL BREAKING AND ENTERING A VEHICLE.—Cont'd.

3. *"(a) It is a defense to a prosecution under sections 13A-8-2 through 13A-8-11 (theft of property, theft of lost property, theft of services and unauthorized use of vehicle) that the actor honestly believed that he had a claim to the property or services involved which he was entitled to assert in the manner which forms the basis for the charge against him.*

   "(b) The burden of injecting the issue of claim of right is on the defendant, but this does not shift the burden of proof." Code of Ala. 1975, § 13A-8-12.

UNLAWFUL ASSEMBLY. Code of Ala. 1975, § 13A-11-5.

"A person commits the crime of unlawful assembly if he assembles[1] with five or more other persons for the purpose[2] of engaging in conduct constituting the crime of riot or if, being present at an assembly that either has or develops such a purpose, he remains there with intent[3] to advance that purpose."

Classification.

Class B misdemeanor.

Comments.

This statute is intended to cover those who have assembled for the purpose of rioting or who are on their way to a riot. It constitutes an expanded concept of attempted riot. This statute requires that at least six persons be involved. The superceded provision required that only two persons be involved. Peaceable assemblies are not within the scope of the statute. However, violence or threatened violence transforms the peaceable assembly into an "unlawful assembly," and "the state has an obvious interest in the preservation and protection of peace and good order within her border." Devine v. Wood.[4] It should be noted that those who are present at the assembly are not within the scope of this statute unless they have the requisite knowledge and intent. The apparent purpose behind requiring requisite knowledge and intent coupled with mere presence at an unlawful assembly is to recognize that otherwise the

UNLAWFUL ASSEMBLY.—Cont'd.

statute might be found to be constitutionally invalid for suppressing the rights of free speech and assembly.

Defenses.

(1) Failure to prove six persons assembled.

(2) Failure to prove the purpose of the assembly was to engage in conduct constituting the crime of riot.

(3) Lack of knowledge of the purpose of the assembly.

(4) Failure to prove that the act of remaining present was with the intent to advance "rioting."

Query.

There is some question as to whether the element of intent can be proven objectively where a person is merely present at an unlawful assembly.

Cross references.

See DISORDERLY CONDUCT; DISORDERLY PERSONS, FAILURE TO DISPERSE; HARASSMENT OR HARASSING COMMUNICATIONS; LOITERING; RIOT; RIOT, INCITING TO; SOLICITATION.

---

1. *Physical presence is required in order for one to "assemble" within the meaning of this statute.*
2. *Knowledge of the unlawful purpose is a prerequisite to prosecution.*
3. *Specific intent must be proven as one of the elements of the offense.*
4. *Devine v. Wood, 286 F. Supp. 102 (M. D. Ala. 1968).*

UNLAWFUL IMPRISONMENT. Code of Ala. 1975, §§ 13A-6-41 and 13A-6-42.

"A person commits the crime of unlawful imprisonment in the first degree if he restrains[1] another person under circumstances which expose the latter to a risk of serious physical injury."[2] § 13A-6-41(a) of the Alabama Code.

"A person commits the crime of unlawful imprisonment in the second degree if he restrains another person." § 13A-6-42(a) of the Alabama Code.

Classification.

Class A misdemeanor, first degree.

Class C misdemeanor, second degree.

Comments.

The key word in defining false imprisonment is "restraint." To restrain a person, the actor must do so knowingly, intentionally, unlawfully, and without consent. This lack of consent includes physical force or acquiescence by an incompetent or child under 16 if done without the consent of the person or agent having custody.

The offense is raised from second degree to first degree when the imprisoned person is exposed to serious physical injury (e.g., locking a person in small closet risking suffocation).

Under § 13A-7-42(b) of the Alabama Code, a person does not commit a crime if the person restrained is less than 18 years old, the actor is a relative[3] of the child, and the actor's sole purpose is to assume lawful control of the child. The only acceptable motive for this restraint is to gain legal custody. The purpose of this section is to keep custody battles out of criminal courts. However, this defense does not apply to unlawful imprisonment in the first degree. While the burden of raising this issue is on the defendant, this should not be interpreted as shifting the burden of proof.

Defenses.

First degree:

(1) Restraint was not done knowingly or intentionally.

(2) No physical force used.

(3) Victim acquiesced and was over 16 and competent.

(4) No risk of serious physical injury.

Second degree:

(1) Restraint was not done knowingly or intentionally.

(2) Person restrained was a child less than 18, the actor was a relative and the sole purpose was for lawful control.

Query.

It appears that a person could still be convicted of unlawful imprisonment in the second degree if the child was less than 18, and the actor is a relative, and if the actor didn't initiate legal action for custody within a reasonable period of time.

Cross references.

See CUSTODY, INTERFERENCE WITH; KIDNAPPING.

UNLAWFUL IMPRISONMENT.
—Cont'd.

---

1. *"RESTRAIN. To intentionally or knowingly restrict a person's movements unlawfully and without consent, so as to interfere substantially with his liberty by moving him from one place to another, or by confining him either in the place where the restriction commences or in a place to which he has been moved. Restraint is 'without consent' if it is accomplished by:*
 "(a) Physical force, intimidation or deception, or
 "(b) Any means, including acquiescence of the victim, if he is a child less than 16 years old or an incompetent person and the parent, guardian or other person or institution having lawful control or custody of him has not acquiesced in the movement or confinement." Code of Ala. 1975, § 13A-6-40(1).
2. *"SERIOUS PHYSICAL INJURY. Physical injury which creates a substantial risk of death, or which causes serious and protracted disfigurement, protracted impairment of health or protracted loss or impairment of the function of any bodily organ." Code of Ala. 1975, § 13A-1-2(9).*
3. *"RELATIVE. A parent or stepparent, ancestor, sibling, uncle or aunt or other lawful custodian, including an adoptive relative of the same degree through marriage or adoption." Code of Ala. 1975, § 13A-6-40(3).*

UNSWORN FALSIFICATION TO AUTHORITIES. Code of Ala. 1975, § 13A-10-109.

"A person commits the crime of unsworn falsification to authorities if, with an intent to mislead a public servant[1] in the performance of his duty, he makes or submits any written statement, which he does not believe to be true, in an application for pecuniary[2] or other benefit, or a record or report required by law to be submitted to any governmental agency."

Classification.

Class C misdemeanor.

Comments.

This section establishes a crime of unsworn falsification to authorities even where the form does not bear notice. The falsification must have been in an application for pecuniary or other benefit, or in a record or report required by law to be submitted to the government. The attorney should consult the provisions of §§ 13A-10-104[3] ("Perjury prosecution for inconsistent statements; highest degree of perjury for which conviction may be had") and 13A-10-107[4] ("When retraction of false statement bar to perjury conviction") of the Alabama Code, since they are applicable to all prosecutions under this section.

Defenses.

(1) Lack of intent.
(2) Public servant not performing his duty when falsification was made to him.
(3) Belief statement is true.
(4) No benefit derived.

Cross references.

See FALSE ALARM; FALSELY REPORTING AN INCIDENT; PERJURY.

---

1. *"PUBLIC SERVANT. Any officer or employee of government, including legislators and judges and any person or agency participating as an adviser, consultant or otherwise in performing a governmental function." Code of Ala. 1975, § 13A-10-1(7).*
2. *"PECUNIARY BENEFIT. Benefit in the form of money, property, commercial interests or anything else the primary significance of which is economic gain. Expenses associated with social occasions afforded public servants and party officers shall not be deemed a pecuniary benefit within the meaning of this article." Code of Ala. 1975, § 13A-10-60(b)(2).*
3. *Code of Ala. 1975, § 13A-10-104. Perjury prosecution for inconsistent statements; highest degree of perjury for which conviction may be had:*
 "(a) Where a person has made statements under oath which are inconsistent to the degree that one of them is necessarily false, each having been made within the jurisdiction of this state and within the period of the statute of limitations, the prosecution may proceed by setting forth the inconsistent statements in a single count alleging in the alternative that one or the other was false and not believed by the defendant to have been true when made. In such case, it shall not be necessary for the prosecution to prove which statement was false, but only that one or the other was false and not believed by the defendant

UNSWORN FALSIFICATION TO AUTHORITIES.—Cont'd.

to be true.

"(b) The highest degree of perjury of which the defendant may be convicted shall be determined by hypothetically assuming each statement to be false and perjurious. If perjury of the same degree would be established by the making of each statement, the accused may be convicted of that degree at most. If perjury of different degrees would be established by the making of the two statements, the accused may be convicted of the lesser degree at most."

4. Code of Ala. 1975, § 13A-10-107. When retraction of false statement bar to perjury conviction:

"No person shall be convicted of perjury if he retracted his false statement in the course of the same proceeding in which it was made before it became manifest that the falsification was or would be exposed. Statements made in separate hearings at separate stages of the same trial or administrative proceeding shall be deemed to have been made in the course of the same proceeding. The burden of injecting the issue of retraction is on the defendant, but this does not shift the burden of proof."

USE OF AIRCRAFT FOR HUNTING, ETC., PROHIBITED. See AVIATION.

USE OF NOXIOUS SUBSTANCE OR POISON. See NOXIOUS SUBSTANCE, USE OR POSSESSION OF.

USE OF OFFICIAL POSITION OR OFFICE FOR PERSONAL GAIN. Code of Ala. 1975, § 36-25-5.

"No public official or employee shall use an official position or office to obtain direct personal financial gain for himself, or his family, or any business with which he or a member of his family is associated unless such use and gain are specifically authorized by law."

Comments.

Only the public official or employee can commit this offense. The other requisite elements are: (1) direct personal financial gain to self, family or business; (2) through use of the official position or office; and (3) such use or gain is unauthorized by law. This section specifically provides that it shall not be construed to prohibit a legislator from exercising his legislative duties unless in a manner prohibited by the Alabama Constitution.

Defenses.

(1) The accused is neither a public official or employee.
(2) There was no gain.
(3) The gain was not direct, personal and/or financial.
(4) Any gain was not a result of use of official position or title.
(5) The gain was specifically authorized by law.

Cross references.

See Counties and municipal corporations, §§ 11-43-54, 11-43-161, 11-44-46, 11-44-47, 11-44-48, 11-44-94. See ETHICS VIOLATIONS.

VANDALISM. See MISCHIEF, CRIMINAL.

VEHICLE, UNAUTHORIZED USE. See AVIATION; MOTOR VEHICLE CRIMES; OBSCURING IDENTITY OF VEHICLE; UNAUTHORIZED USE OF VEHICLE/UNLAWFUL BREAKING AND ENTERING A VEHICLE.

VEHICULAR HOMICIDE. See MOTOR VEHICLE CRIMES.

WEAPONS. See FIREARMS, POSSESSION BY PERSONS PARTICIPATING IN, ATTENDING, ETC., DEMONSTRATIONS AT PUBLIC PLACES; FIREARMS, USE WHILE FIGHTING IN PUBLIC PLACE; PISTOL, BOWIE KNIFE, SELLING TO MINORS; PISTOLS, LICENSE TO CARRY; PISTOLS, POSSESSION AND DELIVERY; RIFLE, SHOTGUN WALKING CANE, CARRYING; WEAPONS, CARRYING CONCEALED.

WEAPONS, CARRYING CONCEALED. Code of Ala. 1975, §§ 13A-11-50 and 13A-11-53.

A person commits the crime of carrying concealed weapons when he carries

WEAPONS, CARRYING CONCEALED.
—Cont'd.

concealed about his person, a bowie knife, or knife or instrument of like kind or description; or a pistol,[1] or firearm of any kind or an air gun; or carries concealed about his person brass knuckles, slingshots or other weapon of like kind or description.

Classification.

Statutory penalty: $50.00 to $500.00 fine, and/or up to six months hárd labor in the county jail.

Comments.

The statute is one of strict liability. If a weapon is concealed, it is a violation of the law. Thus, even a child who carries a slingshot inside his pocket while playing in the neighorhood might be in violation of the statute.

Defenses.

(1) Person had good reason to fear an attack — this may justify concealment or mitigate punishment.

(2) Person was on his own property or property under his control. This includes a private dwelling.

(3) Person is:

a) Licensed to carry such weapon;

b) A sheriff, deputy, police officer of an incorporated town or city acting in lawful discharge of the duties of his office;

c) A United States marshall or deputy;

d) A United States postal carrier in a rural area in discharge of his duties;

e) A bonded constable, such as a conductor, railway mail clerk, and an express manager, in discharge of his duties; or

f) A park ranger in the discharge of his duties.

Cross references.

See FIREARMS, POSSESSION BY PERSONS PARTICIPATING IN, ATTENDING, ETC., DEMONSTRATIONS AT PUBLIC PLACES; PISTOL, BOWIE KNIFE, SELLING TO MINORS; PISTOLS, LICENSE TO CARRY; PISTOLS, POSSESSION AND DELIVERY; RIFLE, SHOTGUN WALKING CANE, CARRYING.

WEAPONS, CARRYING CONCEALED.
—Cont'd.

---

1. A pistol is "any firearm with a barrel less than 12 inches in length." Code of Ala. 1975, § 13A-11-70(1).

WIRETAP OR WIRETAPPING. See DIVULGING ILLEGALLY OBTAINED INFORMATION; EAVESDROPPING; EAVESDROPPING DEVICE, POSSESSION OF; SURVEILLANCE.

WITNESSES, TAMPERING WITH.

Code of Ala. 1975, § 13A-10-124.

Charged as: Tampering with a witness.

"A person commits the crime of tampering with a witness if he attempts to induce a witness or a person he believes will be called as a witness in any official proceeding,[1] to:

"(1) Testify falsely or unlawfully withhold testimony;[2] or

"(2) Absent himself from any official proceeding to which he has been legally summoned."

Classification.

Class B misdemeanor.

Comments.

Tampering with a witness applies when persuasion, fraud, or advice are used to induce a prospective witness to disobey a summons, to testify falsely, or to withhold testimony. Note that where §§ 13A-10-121 to 13A-10-123 of the Alabama Code were aimed at attempts to influence the testimony generally, this offense is narrowed to inducement of a witness to testify falsely or to withhold testimony unlawfully.

This section does not apply when a witness absents himself so as to avoid a summons but does apply to any attempt to persuade a witness to absent himself from an official proceeding once he has received a summons.

Defenses.

(1) No persuasion, advice or fraud was used.

(2) The attempt to influence did not fall into the area of testifying falsely or of withholding testimony but rather a more

WITNESSES, TAMPERING WITH.
—Cont'd.

general area.

(3) The inducement was only to evade a possible summons.

(4) The inducement was not based on a belief the person would be called as a witness (i.e., advice to neighbor).

Cross references.

See ATTEMPT; BRIBERY OF PUBLIC SERVANTS; COERCION; EXTORTION; SOLICITATION.

WITNESSES, TAMPERING WITH.
—Cont'd.

---

1. *Official proceedings as defined in Code of Ala. 1975, § 13A-10-100(b)(5) includes those witnesses before "any legislative, judicial, administrative, or other government agency or official authorized to hear evidence under oath."*
2. *"[O]ral or written statements, documents or any other material that may be offered as evidence in an official proceeding." Code of Ala. 1975, § 13A-10-120(2).*